WALSINGHAM:
PILGRIMS AND PILGRIMAGE

To Frances, Andrew and David

WALSINGHAM:
Pilgrims and Pilgrimage

ST PAULS

Cover images: Panels of engraved glass, designed by Sally Scott, in the Chapel of Reconciliation.
Cover design and reprographics: DX Imaging, Watford.

ST PAULS Publishing
187 Battersea Bridge Road, London SW11 3AS, UK
www.stpaulspublishing.com

ISBN 978-0-85439-811-9

A catalogue record is available for this book from the British Library.

Set by Tukan DTP, Stubbington, Fareham, UK
Printed by Gutenberg Press, Malta

ST PAULS is an activity of the priests and brothers of the Society of St Paul who proclaim the Gospel through the media of social communication.

Contents

Omnibz eccie sce *Carta Gaufridi de Tauarches de Wudicok eccie.* fidelibz Gaulfr de tauarches que est in xpo salute. Notum sit uobis me dedisse et concessisse deo et sce marie et Edw[i]o clico meo ad ordinem religionis quem ipe prudent instituendu pro salute anime mee et parentu et amicor meor in ppetuam elemosinam capellam quam mater mea fundauit in Wallinghm in honore gloriose uiginis marie una cu possessione eccie oium scor eiusdem uille et omnibz ptinentiis suis tam in tris quam in decimis et redditibz et humagus et omnibz rebz quas pfatus Edwinus possedit die qua ego iter ierosolimitanu suscepi et nominatim xx solidos annuatim de meo dominio reddendos p duabz pbz denariarum dni mei. necnon et trium de snaringel qua Basilis dedit deo et piedce capelle scz dimidiam agram in uilla de snaringes que iacet iuxta truum et domu elmoi et uin acs in campis eidem uille ... Hanc itaqz donacionem meam et concessionem ut pdcs Edwinus et ei successores regularem uitam pfessi meor tulle iure ppetuo in ecclesiastica teneant possessione carte mee et sigilli mei attestacce ad honore dei et beate marie petue uiginis corroboro atqz confirmo. Hui vero dona cois et concessionis testes sunt. Alanus pbr de Turkoldia et c *Confirmacio Robi de Wicur*

Willo dei gra Norwicensi epo et omnibz sce eccie fidelibz tam psentibz qm futuris Robert de Wicur salm. Notu sit uob me dedisse et concessisse deo et sce marie et canonicis de Wallinghm oms possessiones qs ipa eccia possedit die qua Gaufrid de tauarches iter ierosolimitanu suscepit p salute aie mee et parentu meor in petuam elemosinam cu omnibz suis ptin in tris in decimis et redditibz. Et noiatim truum qua pfatus .G. dederut Robto de Sprotel sicut ipe Robs ei concessit. Et truum de snaringes qua Basilis dedit deo et eccie beate marie annuente dno .G. Concedo etiam eis xx solid de molendino meo in Walsingh usqz illis de alias pudeam. Hanc itaqz donacoim carte mee et sigilli mei attestacce confirmo quin ipi canonici iure petuo in ecclesiastica teneant possessione. Huius conces sionis sunt testes. Petrus decanus et c *Carta Rogi comitis de Clare de eccia oim* *scor de parua Wallinghm*

Willo dei gra Norwicensi epo et omnibz sce eccie fidelibz tam psentibz qm futuris. Roger comes Clar salm. Notu sit uobis me dedisse et concessisse deo et sce marie et clicis meis de Wallinghm Rado atqz Gaufrido ad ordinem canonicale regularem instituendu p salute aie mee et paren tu meor in petua elemosinam capellam qua Richeldis mat Balfr de tauarches fundauit in Wallinghm cu omnibz ptinenciis in tris in decimis et redditibz et cu oibz possessionibz qual ipa capella possedit die qua pdcs .G. de tau iter ierosolimitanu suscepit una cu possessione eccie oim scor eiusde uille. Et quicq in futuru ptinuerit dno uille et canonice potuit adipisci. Concedo etiam eis molendinu unde .G. de tau duas garbas decime sue adquietare solebat. uno quoqz anno monachis de Clar xx solidos reddendo. Et qd homines de eade uilla et quicq nolumus ad pdcm molendinu libe et sine om pbibicce molant. sicut solebunt in tpe .G. Hanc itaqz donacoim

FOREWORD

The Blessed Virgin Mary has been claimed by almost every Christian state or region as its own special protectress. Very frequently, Mary is designated as a nation's 'queen', as with Poland or Ireland. England, however, has a more unusual tradition, which holds that the country is Our Lady's Dowry. English Catholics like to claim that this tradition has its origins in the very great devotion which the English had for Our Lady before the Reformation, and a certain amount of historical research supports the belief that England did indeed have a particularly marked Marian piety during the Middle Ages. The re-establishment of the greatest of England's Marian shrines has therefore been a source of delight to Catholics and Anglicans for many decades now, and Walsingham finds a worthy historian in Michael Rear, whose own experiences of the Shrine and whose scholarly abilities make him ideally suited to the task that he set himself in writing this book.

A visitor to Walsingham once said that the present-day shrine was 'a bit like the nineteenth-century invention of Scotland and Wales' – that is, the enactment of a romantic fantasy of the Middle Ages – and the visitor in question did not regard this as being in any way a bad thing. In so far as her comment is accurate, it pinpoints something that is probably an important element in the visit of many Walsingham pilgrims: it is a place that gives one a sense of being removed from the hustle and bustle of modern life, and taken into a world where things are more beautiful and peaceful. Yet this experience is surely not just the entry into a romantic fantasy: it has the capacity to take us into the heart of what Christian pilgrimage is about. The romantic's world of beauty and peace can become the threshold of that more profound realm of beauty and peace which are discovered when the soul is embraced by God. And it is Mary, the Mother of God and the abiding spirit of Walsingham, whose soul and body have been embraced by God more closely than those of anyone else who has ever lived, and who opens to the pilgrim the possibility of a glimpse of Heaven in the land that is her dowry.

Christian authors from early centuries onwards compare Christ's mother to Paradise. Thus, Robert Southwell says of her conception, 'Earth breeds a heaven for God's new dwelling-place'. This Marian spirit – the spirit which, as Louis de Montfort would say, attracts Christ to itself – pervades Little Walsingham. Yet even – or especially – the holiest of places has to be managed by fallible human beings, whose pettiness and meanness can sometimes predominate over the pilgrim's spiritual quest. Yet I have seen men who were engaged in longstanding hostilities being moved to embrace one another in forgiveness on pilgrimage to Walsingham, and I have received profound Christian teaching there, from pilgrims and staff alike.

The conflicts which take place at sacred sites are now well documented in the academic studies of pilgrimage, and Michael Rear's account of Walsingham shows how a place that has truly been chosen by the Lord can weather such storms and continue to be a place of inspiration, joy and reconciliation. A young man who was sceptical about Catholicism in general once joined a pilgrimage to Walsingham, 'to see what it's like', and returned saying, in awed tones, 'It's such a *holy* place'. Michael's book shows us both the humanity and the holiness of this pearl in Our Lady's Dowry.

Dr Sarah Jane Boss
Senior Lecturer in Theology and Religious Studies
Roehampton University

PREFACE

Walsingham, England's Nazareth, has long been a place of pilgrimage. The year 2011 marks 950 years since the foundation of Our Lady's Shrine in East Anglia.

During the Middle Ages the Chapel built by Richeldis became the most renowned of all Our Lady's Shrines in England, and Michael Rear explains why it was that pilgrims sought her prayers. He traces the events which led to the Shrine's destruction in the reign of Henry VIII, the conspiracy to save it, and details the remarkable story of its restoration by Catholics and Anglicans. Finally, he explores its meaning, spirituality and potential, for the crowds of pilgrims who flock there once more.

Pilgrimage, of course, has always had about it an element of protest. In the Middle Ages, when life was short and brutish for the majority who had little control over their comings and goings, a pilgrimage set them free if only for a season. It gave a strong sense that life is an intentional journey. They were going to places, and ultimately to the heavenly Jerusalem. The constant stream of royal pilgrims was something of a leveller. They were privileged, yet also in need of Our Lady's prayers and God's blessing. One Holy House found room for all.

The protest continues even in our own day for different reasons. Today's culture is at once both rationalist and highly emotional, secular in outlook yet discovering that such a world view brings only temporary satisfactions. Pilgrimage to holy places like Walsingham or Compostella, or the Holy Land itself, has a surprisingly irresistible attraction, as people with or without faith, or those who are just unsure, search for meaning and significance. Some come intentionally; some are simply passing by and collide with the truths of which Walsingham speaks, and so find themselves to be pilgrims.

Michael Rear loves this place, and is uniquely equipped to tell its story. We thank him and have much pleasure in commending *Walsingham: Pilgrims and Pilgrimage.*

+ Lindsay Urwin O.G.S.   Alan Williams S.M.
Administrator, Anglican Shrine   Director, National Catholic Shrine

INTRODUCTION
AND ACKNOWLEDGEMENTS

Ever since my parents took me on pilgrimage to Walsingham when I was seven years old I have been drawn back there, as many others are, again and again. Mary, under her title, Our Lady of Walsingham, has always been there in my life. Far from being an unnecessary distraction as some have suggested, still less a detraction from the honour we pay to her Son, I have always thought of the Mother and Son together, as they were in their home at Nazareth, and at the foot of the cross, and as they are in the statue that is revered in Walsingham.

Little did I imagine that one day I might have the privilege of living and working in Walsingham, yet this is what I did for nearly twenty years. During that time my interest in the spirituality and history of the Shrine, from its origins until its destruction at the Reformation, grew. I learned a good deal about its restoration by Roman Catholics at the Pontifical Shrine in King's Lynn and in the Slipper Chapel, and by Anglicans at the Shrine and Holy House in the village, and the reason why thousands upon thousands of pilgrims and visitors consequently come to this beautiful small Norfolk village. The medieval village was built for pilgrims, and its history has come full circle. In its literature each Shrine naturally focuses on its own history, while invariably mentioning the other, but in lesser detail, yet the restoration of them both actually has a common source and a history that is entwined. In earlier days there was great rivalry and misunderstanding, which has given way to a deepening unity and cooperation, which, as everyone says, is how it should be. There is only one Holy Mother of God, even though there are two centres of devotion to her at Walsingham. As I realised how much they have in common, and in the light of this growing unity, it seemed to me there was room for a new book which describes the restoration of both Shrines, including some details that have not been written up before, as well as including what is known of the religious history of Walsingham before and after Richeldis built the Holy House in 1061. Few Roman Catholics know much about the restoration of the Anglican Shrine, and many Anglicans know little about the restoration of the Catholic Shrine, and I hope this book will contribute to a fuller understanding. It is not a history book only, but one which I hope conveys something of the spirituality and prayer of the place, which is what brings pilgrims to Walsingham, and takes us back there time and time again.

The decision to write the book was actually made on a retreat at Loreto. For in Loreto is said to be the actual House of Mary that once stood in Nazareth and which was copied by Richeldis when she built its replica in Walsingham. I found it a deeply moving and prayerful experience to reflect in silence and celebrate Mass in that Holy Shrine. But could it be true that this House really was once occupied by Mary and her family? The legend is that angels carried it over the Adriatic Sea from Nazareth to Loreto, but I quickly discovered that there is more history behind the story than meets the sceptical eye. This led me to study the excavations in Nazareth beneath the Basilica of the Annunciation, which is where the House of Mary is said to have once stood, in front of the cave that pilgrims visit today. All of this enabled me to set the foundation of the Shrine in Walsingham within the historical context of the rise of Islam and the crusades, and the Great Reform in the Medieval Church. The date of its foundation, 1061, has been disputed, and I hope to have shown that it is at least defensible.

Anyone setting out to write about Walsingam today should be aware of the immense contribution made by Howard Fears, a local historian, who has gathered together in a number of privately-printed volumes a comprehensive collection of sources relating to the history of the village from its beginnings until now. He has been exceptionally helpful. We are all indebted to John Dickinson, Colin Stephenson, Leonard Whatmore, Donald Hole, Claude Fisher, Martin Gillett, Arthur Bond, Sister Elizabeth Obbard ODC, Peter Rollings, Michael Yelton, and others who have researched the story of Walsingham and made it well known over the years.

In particular I must thank the archivists, Anne Milton of the Catholic Shrine and Isabel Syed, the honorary archivist of the Anglican. Not only did they both throw open their archives, but they read my drafts, made suggestions, answered questions, and corrected errors, for which I am extremely grateful. I might add that mistakes there still must be, but they are mine entirely. Keith Syed, Fr Russell Frost, and Jan and Luigia Paulusz have assisted me with their translations from Arabic, abbreviated Latin and Italian. It is rather invidious to try name all those who have generously helped, and there are many Anglicans and Roman Catholics whose conversations over the years have given me information and ideas, particularly for the last Chapter. But, as well as the above, I must mention Dr David Roffe, Mgr Anthony Stark, Fr Peter Rollings, Fr Alan Williams S.M., Fr Noel Wynn S.M., Bishop Lindsay Urwin, and David Rear, who assisted in various ways, Cathy Rear and Keith Syed who read and improved the text, and Dr Sarah Jane Boss, Director of the Centre for Marian Studies at Roehampton University, whose teaching deepened my under-standing of the devotion I have always had for Mary, the Mother of God. What has been a joy to write I entrust to Our Lady of Walsingham, a small return for the blessings, answered prayer and guidance she has given me over the years.

Michael Rear

CHAPTER 1

FROM MERCURY TO MARY

Centuries before the first pilgrims found their way to the little Holy House that Richeldis built in Walsingham, other pilgrims had been travelling those same roads to Walsingham.

Artefacts from what was almost certainly an ancient Shrine of Mercury have been discovered at the southern end of the important Roman settlement of Walsingham and Wighton. Three very different figures of Mercury, two goats, three cocks and three silver rings, all testify to a Roman cult of Mercury, while a collection of brooches, enamelled seal-boxes of different shapes, some round, others square, others leaf- and lozenge-shaped, and over 4,659 Temple coins, indicate it was a place of pilgrimage. Some of the brooches and seal-boxes appear to be of second century AD, while coins prove there were still pilgrimages at the end of the fourth century. A three-horned deity and a silver ring inscribed TOT (for the Celtic deity Toutanes) and some Iron Age coins possibly suggest an even older Celtic shrine on which the Romans built. Belief in the power of other gods is indicated by little masks of Cupid and satyrs relating to Bacchus, Silvanus and Faunus; a figurine and a mount of Minerva, and finger-rings with images of Ceres, Neptune and Mars. So significant are these discoveries that rather than being merely a temple within a small town, it has been suggested that the Mercury Temple itself may be the very reason for Walsingham's existence.[1]

We know a good deal about devotion to the Roman god, Mercury. Taken over from the Greeks, who knew him as Hermes, the Saxons venerated him as Woden. He gave his name to one of the planets, and to Wednesday (in Latin, *dies Mercurii*). He was the chief messenger of Jupiter, king of the gods, and like the messenger Archangel Gabriel, he was depicted with wings, though his were on his feet or helmet. He was known as the guide of souls, the giver of good fortune and riches, the patron of merchants and traders.

His name survives in *mercantile*. Mercury's festival was celebrated on 15 May. Guilds of merchants met on that day, and because he was also the god of pilgrims and travellers his Temple in Walsingham would have been thronged. It would have been like the National Pilgrimage.

Why did the crowds flock to Mercury's Shrine at Walsingham and what did they do there? Much the same as medieval Catholic pilgrims to Our Lady's Shrine, and pilgrims today. They went in search of spiritual refreshment, physical healing, and answers to prayer. Often they wrote their prayer requests on a scroll, together with a promise or vow they would fulfil if their prayer was heard. These they sealed in boxes like those found at Walsingham. The promise might be to sacrifice a small animal such as a ram or goat or cockerel. Or like medieval pilgrims to make a gift, a votive offering, perhaps a piece of jewellery such as the brooches that have been unearthed. Poorer people might offer Temple coins. That Christians did the same and at the same period we know from the third-century leaf-shaped Christian votive offering of silver that was buried at Water Newton, (the largest and finest collection of early Christian gold and silver found anywhere in the Roman Empire, now in the British Museum).[2] This is just like the pagan plaques found, for example, at Barking, Stony Stratford and Ashwell, except that it is marked with the Chi-Rho.

Standing 15.7 cm. high this figure of Mercury, the Messenger of the Gods, was found in the Temple area of the Roman settlement of Great Walsingham. He wears his petasos, a winged hat, and there are tiny wings on his ankles. His right hand holds a purse, for he was a patron of merchants. His left hand would have held a caduceus, a staff.

It is quite unlike classical figures of Mercury. The patterned treatment of his hair is typical Romano-British work, and although the proportions have not been fully understood, it is a fine example of native craftsmanship.

18

Evidence has been found at the Temple site in Walsingham of metalworking where cult objects like brooches and pilgrim souvenirs were made, though some of the more elaborate brooches seem to have been imported from the continent. Other trinkets may have been manufactured at nearby Snettisham.[3] And we know that at the medieval Shrine there was such an industry too.

Further investigation of the Walsingham site may well turn up tablets inscribed with prayers like those found in many Roman Shrines in Britain, including the Mercury Shrine at Uley in Gloucestershire. Here Coracus begs Mercury that neither Vitalinus nor Natalinus, who had stolen an animal, may have health *unless* they repay the stolen animal, and give the god 'the devotion which he himself has demanded of them.' The sentiments may not be the same as a Christian would pray, but at least he is praying for the good of the thief. A tablet from a Temple at Old Harlow was written by a distressed lover, entrusting to Mercury his love for Eterna, adding 'and if Timotheus does not desist in his pursuit of Eterna he will risk angering the god for his presumption.'[4] Others prayed for healing, especially in connection with holy wells.

It is clear that there are striking similarities between pagan pilgrims and their later Christian counterparts, but Jean Bagnall Smith, who has described the Walsingham finds in detail, has made a more startling suggestion. Noting some Saxon finds on the site indicating that the Shrine may have survived after the Roman occupation, she has raised the intriguing question of whether there could be any sort of continuity between the pagan Roman Temple and the famous medieval Christian shrine.[5]

A Tradition of Sanctity

The Romans invaded Britain in AD 43, rapidly occupying the southeast, and bringing their own religions to supplement the pagan religions of the native Celts. Indeed, the Romans had a profound effect upon Celtic religion, banning human sacrifice, which they thought abhorrent. They also introduced to these people, whose gods were associated with war, nature, fertility, the earth, trees, streams and wells, the idea of making personal prayers to a deity, and of taking vows in the presence of a priest in a sacred place. That this happened at Walsingham seems evident. Woodland groves and timber constructions were often replaced by stone buildings.[6] In Lydney Park, in the Forest of Dean, have been found the remains of a Roman temple with four side-chapels, a hostel and dining room for pilgrims, together with a large and well-appointed bathhouse. It was clearly designed for great crowds.[7] It was built on the edge of an Iron Age fort and an earlier Celtic shrine. The facilities provided for pilgrims, whether pagan or Christian, medieval or modern, have hardly changed.

A *tradition of sanctity*[8], as it has been called, extends not only from Celtic Temples to Roman Temples but on to Romano-British Christian sites as well. Martin Henig concludes that 'the use of pagan sanctuaries may, on occasion, have provided a spur to future development in the Middle Ages.'[9] So Jean Bagnall Smith's suggestion of continuity is not so startling as at first it may seem.

Indeed it is fully in line with the earliest Christian practice. When pagans were first being converted to Christianity some Jewish Christians insisted they be circumcised and made to keep the rigours of the Jewish law. But the apostles' ruling was to lay on them 'no greater burden' than was necessary.[10] St Paul was revolted by the idolatry he found in Athens, but this did not stop him admiring their 'sacred monuments', and using the altar to an Unknown God, to proclaim the 'God whom you already worship without knowing it.'[11] It was absolutely essential to make a clean break from idolatry, holding Christ in the Blessed Trinity to be the one true God. But in other respects the Church proved very flexible. The earliest Christian art is preserved in the catacombs where Christians were buried in Rome. They continued to adorn their tombs and mausolea with the usual pagan decorations of flowers and trees, grazing sheep and stags, and peacocks, but alongside them are scenes from the Bible, and representations of Baptism and the Eucharist. You find many paintings of Orpheus (who in Roman mythology journeyed to the underworld and back) cheek by jowl with the raising of Lazarus, Jonah, and Daniel in the lion's den, as resurrection motifs. An Orpheus mosaic has been found in England in a Christian Roman villa at Woodchester.

Even the Good Shepherd surrounded by sheep, seen everywhere on walls and ceilings in the catacombs, and in the earliest statue of Jesus ever found (now in the Vatican Museum) of him carrying home a lost sheep on his shoulders, was a pagan figure which Christians eagerly adopted as a perfect image of the Saviour. The Chi-Rho, which became a distinctive Christian symbol, and remains so, was originally pagan, and ironically is found stamped on the coins of Emperor Decius, one of the worst persecutors of the Church!

In the Vatican necropolis, beneath the basilica, not 15 metres from St Peter's tomb, is a mausoleum containing a stunning mosaic of Jesus in the guise of Apollo, the sun-god, his chariot rising in the sky. In the late third century it was thought completely appropriate for the Christian parents of Julius Tarpeianus to decorate his tomb in this way. The sun's daily journey in the darkness, and his victory over it at the dawn of a new day was a fitting symbol of Christ's resurrection. Sunday, the day of the sun, was the day Jesus rose from the dead, and the day in consequence when Christians met to celebrate the Eucharist.[12] Christians made pilgrimages to the tombs of martyrs, and they celebrated a *Refrigerium*, a sacred meal, beside them, just as they did when they visited the tombs of their loved ones, and as they had when they were pagans.

Professor Luke Timothy Johnson observes that Christianity reached the Greco-Roman world very quickly, and it should occasion no surprise that Gentile Christians carried over into the worship of the Lord some of the assumptions, religious experiences, and practices of Greco-Roman religiousness.[13]

The earliest Romans brought their pagan religions to Britain, but it was not long before they began to bring Christianity too. Just when it arrived is uncertain. The principal source is Bede's Ecclesiastical History. Based on the best sources available to him it was completed in 731, and cannot be wholly reliable. But he does record that a King of Britain, Lucius, wrote to the Pope in the year 156 asking to become a Christian. 'His pious request was quickly granted and the Britons preserved the faith which they had received, inviolate and entire, in peace and quiet, until the time of the Emperor Diocletian.'[14] It was during Diocletian's persecution (304) that St Alban, a Roman soldier, was martyred. When Emperor Constantine passed his Edict of Toleration (Milan) in 313, the future of the Church in the Roman Empire was assured. By then Christianity was well established in Britain. In 314 there were several bishops in Britain, three of whom, believed to be Eborius of York, Restitutus of London and Adolphus, possibly of Caerleon, attended the Council of Arles.

The British Museum contains a wonderful display of fourth-century

Christian artefacts including wall paintings from a Roman villa in Lullingstone, whose owner had been pagan and then after his conversion set apart rooms for Christian worship. There are spoons with Christian inscriptions from Mildenhall in Suffolk, mosaics, including the head of Christ, from Hinton St Mary, as well as the fine Water Newton collection of early Christian silver and gold.

We also know that as paganism declined, Christians took over its Temples all over the Roman Empire, and re-dedicated the sites. This happened in Britain. Many holy wells were Christianised. Some were re-dedicated to Our Lady or other saints, or turned into baptisteries. James Rattue identifies thirteen that certainly were, but warns against assuming all pagan wells were Christianised.[15] Chedworth Water-shrine was Christianised as early as the fourth century. St Samson of Dol, in about 560, caught a group of pagans venerating a sacred stone near Rigg, North Cornwall, so he christened it by carving a Chi-Rho upon it with his pocket-knife. The great prehistoric monolith at Rudston, Yorkshire, stands next to the church built there to divert religious veneration from paganism to Christ.[16]

Christianity spread so rapidly that few pagan sites in England seem to have survived beyond 450. K.R. Dark strongly refutes the idea that there was a pagan revival in the late fourth century.[17] The Thetford Treasure, not far from Walsingham, deposited in the final two decades of the fourth century, is the last more or less dated group of pagan material in Britain. Henig considers that as early as 429 a large proportion of British society was Christian.[18] But it was not to last long.

The Anglo-Saxon Invasions of East Anglia

Roman rule in Britain ended in 410 when the last of the legions departed. The long borders of the Empire could no longer be defended from barbarian tribes, and the fall of the Western Roman Empire was imminent. Britain was plunged into what Gildas, the early fifth-century writer, called *bella civilia*, civil wars. Within fifty years pagan Germanic tribes of Saxons, Angles and Jutes invaded eastern and central Britain. Jutes settled in Kent, Saxons in middle Britain and the Angles, from whom we get the name England, settled in East Anglia. The commonly accepted view, from Bede,[19] has been that eastern and central Britain was completely overwhelmed by these Anglo-Saxon invaders, who massacred the population, destroyed their religions, both pagan and Christian, driving the Britons in front of them, 'like land crabs before an incoming tide,'[20] into the western reaches of Wales and Cornwall and the north-west. Higham is among those who have challenged this view as a result of archaeology, aerial photography, and by new studies of Anglo-Saxon charters, and literature. The theory of a virtual replacement of the British people by the Saxons, Jutes and Angles seems no longer credible.

Bede cites Gildas lamenting that the Britons had done nothing to convert the invaders[21] and that England was a 'barbarous, fierce and un-believing nation.'[22] The Anglo-Saxons may well have both disrupted religious practice and obliterated evidence. The jury is still out, but the prevailing view is that the immigration from Germany may not have been vast, consisting mainly of aristocrats and warriors who settled down as landowners. They may even have been welcomed by the peasantry for bringing social order out of the *bella civilia*. The fact that English completely replaced the native British and Latin languages (though of course some words found their way into English) does not necessarily prove, as had been assumed, that the British were driven out. Whole communities of Britons may have adopted Anglo-Saxon language and culture because it was in their interests to do so.

Dorothy Watts offers evidence that Christianity survived in some areas occupied by Angles, Saxons, and Jutes.[23] Dark has similarly argued that the decline of British political control did not occur until the later sixth and seventh centuries because this control by local leaders was assisted by the Church, bishops in particular, who kept alive the Roman modes of life, including the faith.[24] Christianity has often proved to be astonishingly tenacious in the memories and handed-down traditions of families and communities. It is not impossible that Christianity reached Walsingham in Roman times, but there is no evidence of it. An early Christian finger-ring engraved *vivas in Deo* (may you live in God) was found at Brancaster, but of course a visitor may simply have dropped it.[25]

The Mercury Shrine, assuming it was not Christianised, may have been respected by the Saxons. The Saxon god, Woden, most important of all their gods, from whom their kings claimed descent, was Mercury under a different name. If they recognised him they would be unlikely to destroy his Temple.

But they were brutal. Gildas records the shock of the British when Saxons killed prisoners, including those who had surrendered themselves into slavery. Tacitus mentions that Germanic tribes offered human sacrifices to Mercury in the first century. It was still going on in the eighth century, for when St Boniface went from England to spread the Gospel in Germany he told the Pope he found them selling slaves for human sacrifices,[26] though there is no incontrovertible evidence that they brought the practice over to Britain.

Whether Walsingham became Christian in Roman times or whether it remained pagan it is certainly possible that a *tradition of sanctity* continued at least until the re-conversion of East Anglia to Christianity.

The Re-conversion of England

Appeals from England for Christian teachers were reaching Rome. Gregory, the founder and Abbot of a monastery on the Coelian Hill in Rome, was shocked and deeply concerned by what he had heard about the barbarian invasions and set out with some monks on a mission to England. But after three days the Pope recalled him, and within a year or two he was himself reluctantly elected Pope. Wasting no time he dispatched his Prior, Augustine, with forty of his monks to re-evangelise the country, and with instructions to work with the British bishops and not usurp them. They landed in Kent in 597, and after the conversion of King Ethelbert, whose wife, Bertha, was already a Christian and had a chaplain and little church, St Martin's in Canterbury, their mission was almost immediately successful.

Pope Gregory kept in close touch with Augustine, constantly answering his questions. One of these concerned pagan temples. Should they be demolished, or should the older policy of re-consecrating them be followed? These are his instructions, conveyed by St Mellitus, after his visit to Rome.

> I have decided after long deliberation about the English people, namely that the idol temples of that race should by no means be destroyed, but only the idols in them. Take holy water and sprinkle it in these shrines, build altars and place relics in them. For if the shrines are well-built, it is essential that they should be changed from the worship of devils to the service of the true God.[27]

There is more to it than saving the cost of building churches. He goes on,

> When the people see that their shrines are not destroyed they will be
> able to banish error from their hearts and be more ready to come to
> places they are familiar with, but now recognising and worshipping the
> true God.

Not only will the people appreciate being able to continuing worshipping in
a familiar place, but they should also maintain their religious festivals, and turn
their shrines into centres of Christian pilgrimage and celebration:

> And because they are in the habit of slaughtering much cattle as
> sacrifice to devils, some solemnity ought to be given them in exchange
> for this. So on the day of dedication or the festivals of the holy martyrs,
> whose relics are deposited there, let them make themselves huts from
> the branches of trees around the churches which have been converted
> out of shrines, and let them celebrate the solemnity with religious
> feasts.

There is abundant evidence that some Roman temples in England were
consecrated and put to Christian use. Churches were probably built on temple
land at Witham in Essex, Icklingham in Suffolk, and Uley in Gloucestershire,
where there was a monastery in the fifth century. Uley seems to present a
classic case of religious continuity from the Iron Age to the seventh or eighth
century.[28] Like Walsingham it had been dedicated to Mercury.

The finest and most prestigious shrine in England was at Bath. This is a
good example of the *tradition of sanctity*. The spring was already a major Celtic
shrine to the goddess Sulis. The Romans respected its significance and
potential and kept its dedication, adding their own additional consecration to
Minerva. Nothing remains of the original Celtic wooden structure because
the Romans overlaid it with much larger and substantial stone buildings.
As well as bathing, pilgrims drank the spring-water, perhaps pouring it over
afflicted parts of the body, and a number of pewter vessels for this purpose
have been identified there, as at other shrines.[29] Bath was destined to have a
great Abbey on the site and continued to be a healing shrine in which men
bathed 'wholly naked with every garment cast off', to the great offence of
King Henry VI among others![30]

Our main interest is with East Anglia, and begins around the year 600
with the visit of King Redwald of East Anglia to King Ethelbert of Kent, who

persuaded him to become a Christian. Bede is scathing about what happened next:

> Returning home he was seduced by his wife and certain perverse teachers; he turned away from the sincerity of faith, and his last state was worse than his first . . . in one and the same temple he had an altar for the Christian sacrifice and another small altar on which to offer victims to devils. Ealdwulf, who was ruler of the kingdom up to our time, used to declare that the temple lasted until his time and that he saw it when he was a boy.[31]

It is thought by some that Redwald, who died in 627, is buried in Sutton Hoo, and perhaps there is evidence of syncretism in the two Christian Byzantine spoons (perhaps Baptism presents) interred there alongside pagan artefacts. It also shows how difficult it was to persuade people to break away decisively from their old beliefs. It does not mean that they did not become Christians, but underlines the tenacity of pagan culture.

If King Redwald tried to have the best of both worlds, his son, Eorpwald, proved a worthier upholder of the Christian Faith, but after only four years he was killed in battle and in 631 was succeeded by King Sigbert, who may have been Redwald's stepson. Sigbert had spent his youth in Gaul where he had become a devout Christian, impressed by the effect of Christianity and its schools. Bede relates that Saint Honorius, the Archbishop of Canterbury, called St Felix, (a priest, probably from one of the monastic houses founded by the Irish missionary, St Columnbanus in Burgundy) to be a missionary bishop to assist King Sigbert.[32]

Few records survive about the progress of conversion for, not only did the Vikings destroy the monasteries but the two earliest East Anglian sees of Dommoc and Elmham ceased to exist. (It is not even certain whether Dommoc, where Sigbert established the cathedral for Felix, should be identified as Dunwich, Walton or Felixstowe). Elmham was restored, not much before 955. Henceforward only one bishop served the whole of East Anglia. The East Anglian see was transferred to Thetford in 1071-2, and eventually about 1095 to Norwich. With such breaks in continuity it is not to be wondered at that no pre-Viking age manuscripts or charters have been preserved.[33] Sigbert, with the assistance of Felix, also established a school in his kingdom for boys, on the model that he had seen in Gaul.

The Mission was strengthened in around 633 by the arrival of the Irish royal hermit and missionary St Fursey, with a number of priests and brethren. Sigbert provided a monastery site in an old Roman fort called Cnobheresburg, usually, but not conclusively identified as Burgh Castle near Yarmouth.[34] For seventeen years St Felix laboured faithfully as Bishop of East Anglia, establishing with St Fursey a Church which converted the Angles, and stood firm until the Viking invasions. Felix had founded a monastery at Soham and it was here that he died, on 8 March 647, and was buried. His relics were later translated to Ramsey Abbey. Coincidentally, St Fursey died in the same year.

Meanwhile, King Sigbert became the first of a number of Anglo-Saxon kings to abdicate and enter a monastery, which he had built with St Fursey. Bede does not say where, but later sources name it as Beodricesworth (Bury). According to Bede, Sigbert did not die peacefully there, but was killed in battle. He had been unwillingly dragged out of his monastery to face an invasion from Mercia in 647. Mindful of his vows, Sigbert refused to carry anything more than a stick and was killed, and soon venerated as a martyr.

Just when the Mission of Felix and others reached Walsingham is not known, nor whether the Mercury Temple still existed and had been converted, or whether they found any survivals of Christianity there at all. Circumstantial evidence that it may have become a Christian centre is provided by the Old English name Walsingham. Flavell Edmunds[35] considered it meant *Home of the Children of the Well*, suggestive of its pagan origin. More recently it has been assumed to mean the *ham* (settlement), of the *ingas* (people or followers) of a pagan chieftain, e.g. *Waels* (Wals) originating in the earliest phase of Anglo-Saxon settlement. But John McNeal Dodgson points out that *ingas* may also be evidence of a later stage of settlement, including a Christian one.[36] Gavin Smith makes the further suggestion that in some cases *ingas* may recall the followers not of pagan chieftains but of early missionaries, indicating religious communities at monastic sites, for example *Guthlacingas,* the followers of Guthlac, founder of Crowland Abbey in Lincolnshire at the beginning of the eighth century, and *Berclingas,* 'the monks of Berkeley' in Gloucestershire.[37] Or a church on a former pagan site.[38] He also considers that the *inga-ham* names on the continent perhaps originated with missionaries who went there from East Anglia.[39]

This could mean that the Mercury Shrine, if it had survived, became Christian in the seventh century. Soon there were certainly Saxon churches in

Great Walsingham dedicated to St Peter's and All Saints, and another All Saints, most likely on the site of St Mary's, Little Walsingham.

The Viking Invasions

The next threat to Christianity in England came from the Vikings who made a savage raid on the undefended Lindisfarne Abbey in 793, partly destroying it. Over the next years many monasteries in the north were attacked, including Iona in 802. Monks were slaughtered, libraries of priceless books destroyed, records lost. Lindisfarne was abandoned, and the monks trailed around northern England with their greatest possession, the relics of St Cuthbert, until they found a home in Durham in 995. The assessment of David Knowles was that there was a 'complete collapse of monasticism by the end of the ninth century.'[40] But, as Tim Pestell points out, not only is there a lack of documentary evidence for their pre-Viking existence in East Anglia, but it is virtually impossible to verify the destruction of monasteries archeologically.[41] The safekeeping of precious relics of saints greatly assisted the continuity of communities, and Pestell shows that this happened in East Anglia.

The Viking raids in England were sporadic at first but in the 860s larger armies were assembled bent on conquest. In 865 they forced the East Angles to help supply an army, which went north and captured York and on to the kingdom of Northumbria. Returning to East Anglia in 870 they encountered stiff opposition from King Edmund, but he was captured, refused to renounce the Christian Faith, and was martyred.

Destructive of monasteries, churches, and shrines as they were, astonishingly, only twenty-five years after Edmund's martyrdom a remarkable coin was minted known as the St Edmund Memorial Coinage. 2000 coins have been found and they bear a cross, and in Latin the inscription, *O St Edmund the King*. Not only does this prove that Edmund was revered as a saint within twenty-five years of his death by the Danish successors of his murderers, but that Christianity was strong and vigorous in Norfolk.[42] Thus, as Pestell points out, while there is no direct evidence, literary or archaeological, of the physical survival of churches, it certainly suggests the vigorous continuity of pre-Viking clergy and communities, not only in focussing defiance against the invaders, but in converting them. The Vikings even took the cult and veneration of St Edmund back to their Scandinavian homelands. Moreover, since in East Anglia most monasteries and parishes were on local estates and belonged to local aristocracy there was never going to be widespread apostasy, and this would certainly have been true of Walsingham.

The cult of St Edmund is shrouded in legend but it seems certain his body was brought to King Sigbert's monastery at Beodricesworth, soon to be replaced by a greater monastery and renamed Bury St Edmunds. A road, a pilgrim way, known as 'the King's Road' was built from the main port of East Anglia, at St Felix's Dunwich (Felixstowe), to Bury St Edmunds, the route of the modern A14. So these great saints of East Anglia were linked together. Veneration of St Edmund spread all over England. Sixty churches were dedicated to him and he was declared the first Patron Saint of England. His shrine was destined to be of major importance in medieval England, not least for kings who wished to re-connect with their Anglo-Saxon past. Edmund's symbol of three crowns, representing his kingship, his martyrdom, and his virginity can still be seen on many emblems, crests, and flags all over East Anglia to this day.

The Vikings had conquered England. The most remembered Viking King was Cnut who in 1016 became king of England, and after further campaigns in Scandinavia could claim by 1027 to be king of the whole of England and Denmark, Norway and parts of Sweden. From King Cnut's wife, Emma, was descended Edward the Confessor, in whose reign, according to the old Ballad of Walsingham, the Lady Richeldis built the Shrine.

Conclusion

So, back to Walsingham. What happened to the Mercury Shrine? Did it become a Christian centre in Roman times or remain pagan? Did it survive the Anglo-Saxon invasions and continue as a place of pagan or Christian pilgrimage? And if so what did St Felix do with it? If he found there a pagan shrine did he follow the advice of Pope Gregory and re-consecrate it? This is the question raised by the discovery of the Mercury Temple objects. It is not impossible. But, as Diana Webb has said, 'continuity of pilgrim behaviour in England as elsewhere is one thing, but to demonstrate continuity of use at particular sites, from pagan through Roman to Anglo-Saxon times, is quite another.'[43]

Obviously there is no continuity of site. The Priory in Little Walsingham, where the medieval Shrine stood, is a mile away from the pagan Temple area in Great Walsingham. It is nonetheless on the same Roman road, and there may have been any number of reasons for choosing a neighbouring site, and diverting pilgrims to it. And there is something intriguing about the site of the Holy House. Close by are the twin wells, thought to exist before Richeldis built the Holy House. Christians often re-consecrated pagan wells for Christian use, and dedicated them to the Blessed Virgin Mary.

If there was no continuity from Roman times it is a most extraordinary coincidence that such a significant centre of pagan pilgrimage should become Our Lady's greatest place of Christian pilgrimage in medieval England. But without further excavation of the site we shall never know. Even if there was no functional continuity from the Roman period, the celebrated medieval shrine at least represents the tenacity of a specifically ritual/religious tradition.[44]

There certainly is continuity in the very idea of pilgrimage itself, common to pagans, Jews, Christian, Moslems and people with all kinds of faith. Jesus went with Mary and Joseph each year to Jerusalem. Roman Christians, like Helena, the mother of Emperor Constantine, went there too, and ever since her an unending stream of pilgrims. With pilgrimage to the Holy Land, and difficulties that arose there, the history of Our Lady's Shrine in Walsingham begins.

CHAPTER 2

FROM WALSINGHAM TO NAZARETH

The Pynson Ballad

We know from the Charters in the Walsingham Cartulary that the Holy House of Walsingham was built by Richeldis de Favarches. This brief historical record was expanded in a poem of twenty-one verses, generally known as the Pynson Ballad. When the printing press was invented in Germany in 1439 the Church was swift to take advantage of the new technology. William Caxton, the first English printer, famously published Chaucer's *Canterbury Tales*. Richard Pynson became the royal printer and his most prestigious work was King Henry VIII's *Assertio Septem Sacramentorum* against Lutheranism, for which the Pope gave Henry the title Defender of the Faith. Missals, Books of Hours, Prayer Books, many in English, spiritual classics, treatises, and pamphlets on the Faith streamed from his press, an indicator of the vitality of the Church on the eve of the Reformation.

Most medieval pilgrims must have been illiterate, but for the benefit of those able to read, brass plaques or manuscripts giving the history, spirituality and an account of the miracles of the particular shrine were affixed to a wall. Glastonbury had a large fourteenth-century manuscript of six leaves in a wooden frame, now in the Bodleian Library. The printing press offered new possibilities. Richard Pynson produced parchments to be hung up at the Shrine of the Holy Blood of Hailes and the Shrine of St Walstan in Norfolk, which, like his Walsingham Ballad, is written in Rhyme Royal of seven decasyllabic lines.[1]

The Walsingham Ballad (Appendix 2), printed around 1496, is preserved in the Pepys Library of Magdalen College, Cambridge. It was originally written to be affixed to a wall near the Shrine.[2] The reader is instructed to 'beholde and se', while the 'lettred that will have more intellygence of the fundacyon

(foundation) of this chapell here' are invited to ask for books! The Anglican Pilgrim Hymn serves the same purpose, as does its Welcome Centre, and the frieze in the cloisters at the Roman Catholic Shrine, because now, as then, it cannot be assumed that all pilgrims know about the history and meaning of the Shrine, and it is important they do.

From the Ballad we learn that Rychold (Richeldis), 'a noble widow sometime lady of this towne', 'in living full virtuous', in 1061 during the reign of Edward the Confessor, 'wishing to honour Our Lady with some work bounteous', was led in spirit by Our Lady to Nazareth to see the place where Gabriel had greeted her. Our Lady asked that a replica of the house should be built in Walsingham so that 'all that seek me there shall find succour', and 'where shall be had in a memorial the great joy of my salutation' (annunciation).

She was asked to make careful note of the dimensions of the house in Nazareth, and instructed her workmen to build it near some twin wells. Things went badly in the building of it. The widow remained all night in prayer, and next morning not only had the house been completed to perfection by angels' hands, but it had been moved 'two hundred foot or more' from where they had tried to build it. Soon crowds of pilgrims were coming, sick people were cured, mariners found safety, possessed people were freed and innumerable miracles were performed. The Ballad ends rejoicing that England can be 'compared to the land of promise Sion', 'the Holy Land'; it is 'Our Lady's Dowry'.

We know that the House Richeldis built, the House destroyed at the Reformation, was rectangular, and the Ballad lays stress on its being an exact replica of Mary's House in Nazareth. But the pilgrim to Nazareth today is shown, not a rectangular house, but a cave, a Grotto, described as the House of Mary, above which stands the noble Basilica of the Annunciation. This raises the question of what exactly Richeldis copied, and why it is evidently no longer there.

More fundamentally, is it really credible that the House in which Mary lived at Nazareth was still standing there more than a thousand years later when Richeldis is said to have built its replica in 1061? And if it was, where is it now? There is a mysterious story of the House being transported in 1296 from Nazareth to Loreto, where it is venerated today. To discuss these questions we need the resources of archaeology and literary sources.

The Old City of Nazareth

Nazareth is not mentioned in the Old Testament, nor for that matter are the towns of Cana and Capernaum, for the Old Testament has little interest in Galilee. The Jewish historian, Josephus, (who was born in Jerusalem about AD 37 and died in Rome in about 97) tells us in his autobiography that there were two hundred and forty towns and villages in Galilee, but he mentions by name only about forty-five of them, not including Nazareth. This suggests that Nazareth was not very large or important.

Nathaniel implied this when John told him that they had found the Messiah, Jesus of Nazareth. 'From Nazareth?' said Nathaniel, 'Can any good come from that place?'[3] The word 'city' used of Nazareth and other small places in the Gospels evinces Greek influence in the writing of the Gospels, and is no indication of size.[4]

Nazareth was completely overshadowed by its neighbouring town, Sepphoris, less than four miles to the north, which Herod Antipas had selected in 3 BC as the site of his government. He began a vast building programme, which lasted for decades, bringing together labourers and artisans from the neighbouring villages. It has been suggested that 'carpenter' meant not simply a woodworker, but someone engaged in the building trade, and that Jesus and Joseph, the carpenters, may well have found employment there.[5]

Nazareth is built on the edge of a valley with the steep slope of a hill on one side of it down which worshippers from the local synagogue attempted to hurl Jesus to his death.[6] The grotto venerated as Mary's House is on this slope.

There is little scope for archaeology in Nazareth today with its densely-housed population of 65,000, one third Christian and two-thirds Moslem. But excavations under the auspices of the Anglo-Israel Society, which published a Report in 2007, discovered a farm, with a winepress, remains of three watchtowers, olive-crushing stones, components of an irrigation system on the terraces, and evidence of stone quarrying, in the grounds of the hospital where they were working.[7] They concluded that the farm was in use from a century or two before Christ through to the early Byzantine period,[8] so it was most likely occupied in the lifetime of Mary. More interesting has been the discovery in 2009, by archaeologist Yardena Alexandre, Excavations Director at the Israel Antiquities Authority, of what he described as the house of a 'simple Jewish family.' Alexandre's team found remains of a wall, a hideout, a courtyard and a water system that appeared to collect water from the roof and supply it to the home. The discovery was made when builders dug up the courtyard of a former convent to make room for a new Christian centre, just yards from the Basilica. Archaeologist Stephen Pfann, president of the University of The Holy Land, noted: 'It's the only witness that we have from that area that shows us what the walls and floors were like inside Nazareth in the first century.'[9]

The site beneath the present Basilica of the Annunciation around the Grotto was thoroughly investigated by the Franciscan archaeologist, Fr Bellarmino Bagatti. The Basilica took nine years to build and was completed in 1969. A church of exceptional quality, it contains magnificent stained glass, and mosaics depicting, among other things, Our Lady of Walsingham and the Holy House from the medieval Priory seal. It replaces an earlier one, built in 1730 and enlarged in 1877. After this was demolished in 1954, to make way for the present church, Fr Bagatti and his team set to work. They added substantially to what had been discovered by earlier investigations and also gathered together important literary sources to shed light on what had happened on the site of Mary's House from its earliest days.

Bagatti's excavations unearthed a number of grottos, silos for grain (one very close to the Grotto), and cisterns for water and oil, typical of an agricultural village. Twenty-thee tombs were also found, at a distance of 250–750 yards from the Grotto of the Annunciation, indicating the limits of the village, since these would have been outside the settlement. Most significantly, several grottos had been adapted for domestic purposes with walls abutting them to form a room, rather like a stone conservatory. And this, it is presumed, is what the house of Mary may have been like: a rectangular building in front of a cave. But the rectangular building is no longer there.

The building of successive churches on the site made it impossible for Fr Bagatti to see the Grotto in its original state, but it is a large cave measuring 5.5 metres by 6.14 metres, including an apse made when it was adapted into a place of worship. An archaeologist in 1730, Benedict Vlamink, noted fragments of mosaic in the apse, but none remain today.

The first reference to a church on the site comes from the 'Anonymous Pilgrim of Piacenza,' who visited the place about 570. He tells us that the House of Mary 'is now a Basilica.' Rather touchingly he adds that the Jewesses of that city 'are better looking than any other Jewesses in the whole country. They declare that this is St Mary's gift to them, for they also say that she was a relation of theirs.'[10] Is it possible that members of the family of Mary still lived in the village? Is anything known about the family after the lifetime of Mary? The surprising answer is a very great deal.

Relatives of Jesus in Nazareth

Reading the Gospels carefully you can distinguish four groups among the followers of Jesus. There was a large following, the disciples, which could on occasion number thousands. There were the twelve apostles, sometimes called simply The Twelve, or the Twelve Disciples. There was an inner group comprising Peter, James and his brother, John. And there was another group, frequently overlooked, his relatives, sometimes called his brothers, among whom is invariably his mother.

We are given the names of some relatives. Preaching in the local synagogue at Nazareth St Mark tells us the congregation was astounded when they heard him.

> Where did the man get all this? What is this wisdom that has been granted to him, and these miracles that are worked through him? This is the carpenter, surely, the son of Mary, the brother of James and Joset and Jude and Simon? His sisters, too, are they not here with us? And they would not accept him.[11]

St Matthew records the same episode with a variant spelling of one name: James, and Joseph, Simon and Jude. And he has, 'This is the carpenter's son, surely?'[12]

Three Gospels, with slight variations, record the anxiety of his relatives:

> He was still speaking to the crowds when suddenly his mother and his brothers were standing outside and were anxious to have a word with him.[13]

> His mother and brothers came looking for him, but they could not get near to him because of the crowd.[14]

A quite serious situation developed:

> (Jesus) went home again, and once more such a crowd collected that they could not even have a meal. When his relations heard of this, they set out to take charge of him; they said, 'He is out of his mind.'[15]

These passages imply that the relatives of Jesus, like the Twelve, failed to understand. The Gospel writers quite deliberately draw attention to this because they hope their readers will make the same journey into faith that the relatives and apostles eventually did. So, when St Luke wrote his account of the Day of Pentecost he wants us know that the Mother of Jesus and his brothers were there too as well as the apostles. Now they all understand.

They were all of one heart, and the Holy Spirit came upon them all. After witnessing the ascension of Jesus:

> They went back to Jerusalem … and when they reached the city they went to the upper room where they were staying; there were Peter and John, James and Andrew, Philip and Thomas, Bartholomew and Matthew, James the son of Alphaeus and Simon the Zealot, and Jude son of James. With one heart all these joined in continuous prayer, together with some women, including Mary the mother of Jesus, and with his brothers.[16]

The Holy Spirit empowered them to go out and preach the Gospel, and this the relatives did, as well as the Twelve.[17]

The relationship of Jesus and his brothers has been much discussed, and three views have been proposed, named after three fourth-century proponents of each. Helvidius suggested they were blood brothers, an idea that won little support until the nineteenth century. Epiphanius thought the brothers were sons of Joseph from an earlier marriage, a view held in the Orthodox Churches. Jerome considered they were cousins, a belief generally held in the Catholic Church. None of the sixteenth-century Reformers doubted the perpetual virginity of Mary. Luther, for example, asserted, 'A virgin before the conception and birth, she remained a virgin also at the birth and after it.'[18] Mary's virginity is understood as inherent to her dedication and her spiritual motherhood of the Church.

What more do we know about the relatives? As well as the four named brothers, James and Joseph, Simon and Jude, and the unnamed sisters in the Gospels, we do know the names of other relatives. Hegesippus, who lived in mid second century Palestine, quoted by the Church historian, Bishop Eusebius, who lived from 260-339, tells us that Joseph, the foster-father of Jesus, had a brother called Clopas, an uncommon name of which only two instances survive, both in the Gospels.[19] St John says that Mary, the wife of Clopas, stood at the foot of the cross.[20] This means that an aunt of Jesus, as well as his mother, accompanied him on his last journey to Jerusalem. St Luke tells us that Clopas, using the Greek name, Cleopas, was one of the disciples who met the Risen Lord on Easter evening on the way to Emmaus.[21]

There was, therefore, a very considerable family to keep the memory of Mary's home alive, over quite a long period of time. Professor John Meier considers that 'in a village like Nazareth, with some 1,600 people, the extended family of Jesus probably made up a sizeable proportion of a population where many people would be distantly related to one another by blood or marriage.'[22] Certainly the home of Mary would have been well known in the village and most probably still occupied by the family.

The Ministry in Palestine of the Relatives of Jesus

There is yet more to discover in just how important the relatives were. While Peter and the apostles travelled further afield, the relatives of Jesus were responsible for spreading the Gospel in the Holy Land. Eusebius tells us that they presided over every Church in Palestine.[23]

The best-known relative was James, (not to be confused with the apostle James, brother of John) who held the leadership of the Church in Jerusalem, the mother church. St Paul held him in the highest regard. Josephus records his martyrdom in the year 62 under the orders of Ananus II (son of Arenas and brother-in-law of Caiaphas) who had him stoned.[24]

According to Hegesippus, the successor of James in Jerusalem was Simon (or Simeon in the Greek version of his name).[25] He was the son of Clopas, and so the office remained in the family of Jesus. During the reign of Emperor Trajan (98-117) he too was martyred.

We also know a great deal about the family of Jude, the brother of Jesus and James, and acknowledged by almost all scholars to be the author of the epistle bearing his name. Hegesippus, quoted by Eusebius, relates a fascinating account of how two grandsons of Jude, Zocer and James, were brought before the Emperor Domitian (AD 81-96) and charged with being members of the family of Jesus.

> informed against as being of David's line, (they) were brought by the evocatus before Emperor Domitian, who was as afraid of the coming of Christ as Herod had been. Domitian asked them if they were descended from David, and they admitted it. Then he asked them what property they owned and what funds they had at their disposal. They replied that they only had 9000 denarii between them, half belonging to each; this, they said, was not available in cash but was the estimated value of only thirty-nine plethora of land from which they raised the money to pay

their taxes and the wherewithal to support themselves by their own toil … They showed him their hands putting forward as proof of their toil the hardness of their bodies and the calluses impressed on their hands by incessant labour.

When asked about Christ and his Kingdom – what it was like, and where and when it would appear – they explained that it was not of this world or anywhere on earth but angelic and in heaven, and would be established at the end of the world, when He would come in glory to judge the living and the dead, and give every man payment according to his conduct. On hearing this Domitian found no fault with them, but despising them as beneath his notice let them go free and issued orders terminating the persecution of the Church. On their release they became leaders of the Churches, both because they had borne testimony and because they were of the Lord's family; and thanks to the establishment of peace they lived on into Trajan's time.[26]

Trajan reigned from AD 98-117. Hegesippus does not say where Zocer and James lived, but the historian Julius Africanus, who lived in Emmaus in the early third century, provides the clue. From him we learn that Nazareth and Cochaba were the main bases of the relatives, as they spread the Gospel throughout Palestine. Eusebius quotes him:

From the Jewish villages of Nazareth and Cochaba, they travelled around the rest of the land, and interpreted the genealogy they had (from the family tradition) and quoting from the Book of Days (i.e. Chronicles).[27]

This suggests that Nazareth and Cochaba were the Churches over which Zocer and James presided. That they continued to earn their living as farmers is very likely, since great stress was laid upon apostles keeping themselves by the work of their own hands, so as not to be a burden on the faithful.[28]

The point Julius Africanus makes about the genealogy is that this is the way they proclaimed Jesus as the Messiah. It throws light on why St Matthew and St Luke included the genealogy of Jesus in their Gospels.[29] These are far more important than is often realised: for Palestinian Christians the genealogy of the Davidic descent of Jesus was crucial evidence of his Messiahship. Richard Bauckham argues persuasively that the genealogy used by Zocer and James and the family was the one that is preserved in St Luke's Gospel.[30]

The use of the genealogy also shows that their authority as leaders derived from belonging to the family.

Julius Africanus further reveals that the family were known as the Desposyni (from the Greek δεσπόσυνος 'of or belonging to the master or lord'). It is striking that the word δεσπότης (Master) used of Jesus is found only in the Epistle of Jude, and the closely related II Peter, so that clearly the relatives were known as the Desposyni from the earliest times. (When the word Master is found in the Gospels it translates different Greek words.) That they had this unique and collective title is extraordinarily interesting because it shows they were revered and recognised as the Lord's family and had great authority as leaders of the Palestinian Churches.

Although it is certain that the Desposyni spread the Gospel in Palestine and presided over its Churches, we have evidence that some members of the family travelled further afield. A medieval Chronicle, which Bauckham considers to be based on reliable early sources, lists the early bishops of Ctesiphon-Seleucia on the Tigris, in central Mesopotamia. Mari was the first-century founder of the Church. He was followed in turn by Abris, Abraham and Ya'qub (James). Abris is said to have been 'of the family and race of Joseph,' the husband of Mary, while Abraham was 'of the kin of James called a brother of the Lord' and James was Abraham's son.[31]

But the most astonishing proof we have that family members spread the Gospel beyond Palestine, as well as evidence that Nazareth long remained their family home, comes from the account of the martyrdom of a certain Conon, who was put to death in 250-251 in the persecution of Emperor Decius. He was a gardener on the imperial estate and was martyred in Magydos in Pamphylia in Asia Minor. When questioned in court about his place of origin and his ancestry, he replied, '*I am of the city of Nazareth in Galilee, I am of the family of Christ, whose worship I have inherited from my ancestors, and whom I recognise as God over all things.*'[32] There is absolutely no doubt about the authenticity of this, because this Conon from Nazareth, of the family of Jesus, was honoured in his homeland. In the old (pre-Byzantine) liturgical calendar his commemoration was observed as a feast proceeded by an eight-week fast.

It means that the relatives of Jesus were still living in Nazareth as late as the middle of the third century. The home of Mary would still have been known.

The Grotto of Conon

Archaeology contributes to our knowledge. Mary's Grotto beneath the basilica of the Annunciation in Nazareth has already been mentioned, but there are in fact two. The larger one is venerated as the Grotto of the Annunciation, while the smaller is known as the Grotto of Conon. Access to them both is provided beneath the high altar.

It is with the Grotto of Conon we should begin. For in front of this smaller cave is a mosaic, laid in the fourth century, bearing the inscription, *'Gift of Conon deacon of Jerusalem'*. This deacon Conon was not of course the martyr from Pamphylia, but he may have been a relative. Or he may simply have had a devotion to his martyred namesake from Nazareth whose name he bore. What is significant is that he chose to place his mosaic gift in front of this particular small Grotto, a Grotto that was venerated before he did so. For six layers of plaster have been laid on the walls of this Grotto. Within the third was found a coin of the young Emperor Constantine c.320, and so the first two coats must predate the fourth century. The earliest coat was beautifully decorated, and some of it has been uncovered and conserved. The remnant of a crown and flowering branches are to be found, together with numerous pilgrim graffiti of prayers and names, like *'O Jesus Christ, Son of God, help Genos and Elpisis the servants of Jesus and remember Achiles, Elpid(us) Paulus, Antonis.'* Some graffiti are incised, others are written in charcoal. It shows that during the third century people were going to the grotto to pray.

Most significant of all is an inscription in red, with lettering that not only indicates a third century date, but also contains words in a Greek dialect unique to Pamphylia. The inscription reads:

> The memorial I made for the light. Christ the Lord, save your servant Valeria. Here we praised the death of (the name is missing) and give to suffering the palm which (it is customary to give) to one who died for Christ. Amen.[33]

The date of this inscription, coinciding with the date of Conon's martyrdom, together with its Pamphylia dialect, makes it virtually certain that this small Grotto had been set aside c.250 by members of the family living in Nazareth, as a memorial to Conon, their relative and martyr. They chose it because of its proximity to the family home. Deacon Conon from Jerusalem offered his gift of the mosaic to embellish it a century later.

The Grotto of the Annunciation

Pilgrimages to the Holy Land have a long history. The conversion of Emperor Constantine brought persecution to an end, while his Edict of Milan of 314 which gave Christianity an established position, opened the way to pilgrimage. Devout followers of Christ wanted to pray and see where he had lived, and walk where he had walked. Constantine's mother, Helena, paved the way by her discovery of the hill of Calvary where she built the Church of the Holy Sepulchre. Egeria left an account of her pilgrimage, but most left no records of their journeys. Towards the end of the fourth century St Jerome settled in Bethlehem where he gathered a community and devoted his life to prayer and the translation of the Bible, leaving many commentaries and sermons to posterity. By the beginning of the fifth century there were said to be two hundred monasteries and hospices around Jerusalem, built to provide for pilgrims.

That early Christians were interested in keeping relics and memories we know from Eusebius. In connection with James the brother of the Lord, he happens to tell us that 'the throne of James – who was the first to receive from the Saviour and his apostles the episcopacy of the Jerusalem church … has been preserved to this day. The Christians there, who in their turn look after it with such loving care, make clear to all the veneration in which saintly men high in the favour of God were regarded in times past and are regarded today.'[34] Whether it really was the throne of James is beside the point. It just proves that in the fourth century, when Eusebius was writing, the Christians were interested in historical relics.

We have already mentioned the 'Anonymous Pilgrim of Piacenza,' who visited the place about 570 and said that the House of Mary *'is now a Basilica.'* This basilica was built by the Byzantines during the fifth century. Bagatti's painstaking work revealed a building of fine proportions, embracing an area of 48m in length and 27m wide. It contained three naves, a substantial atrium, and on the south side a convent, presumably the living quarters of the clergy. Clearly the whole church was designed to allow access to and provide protection to the sacred caves. Bagatti found extensive mosaic pavements, with iconography that suggests the Byzantine church was built prior to 427 when Emperor Theodosius II forbad putting crosses on to floors. On the left side, on a lower level, was a pavement incorporating the Grotto of Mary and the smaller grotto containing the 'Inscription of Conon.' But perhaps his most exciting discovery was the remains of an earlier synagogue on the site. Substantial pieces of carved masonry, some re-used in the Byzantine church, match the architectural remains of synagogues in other parts of Galilee that are dated between the second and fourth centuries.

What is fascinating about this synagogue is not just its situation beside the Grotto of the Annunciation, but the fact that it was a Christian synagogue. There are many signs of the cross, and numerous inscriptions and prayers. Pilgrims from at least three language groups were coming to Nazareth, Greeks, Syrians and Armenians. One partially preserved inscription reads (in Greek) *under the holy place of M … I wrote … the image I adorned of her.*[35] It is probable that the letter M was the initial letter of Mary. That name is found in its entirety at the base of a column, together with the abbreviation, XE, which in the context most likely stands for χαίρε (*Hail* Mary, the angel's greeting).

What does a 'Christian synagogue' mean? It is perhaps appropriate here to mention some of the differences between Jewish and Gentile Christianity. The very first Christians, Peter and the others, were, of course, converts from the Jewish faith. But they were not called Christians. They were known as Nazareans in New Testament times,[36] and the name stuck. It was outside Palestine, in Syria, that the word Christian was coined and came into general use.[37] Throughout the Roman Empire Christians were forbidden to build churches (as they came to call them) almost until the time of Emperor Constantine in the fourth century. They worshipped in houses, but in Palestine the Nazareans were able to build and worship in synagogues, 'Christian' (or more correctly, 'Nazarean') synagogues. This is evidently what they did in Nazareth, for remains of the Jewish synagogue have been discovered in Nazareth, the one mentioned in the Gospel[38] but the one in front of the Grotto is unmistakably Nazarean. The rectangular House of Mary became a place of worship, veneration and pilgrimage.

Although both Palestinian Nazareans and non-Palestinian Christians belonged to the one Catholic Church (as it was known from the first century) they remained very different. In the first chapter we noted how the Church did not impose the Jewish law (like circumcision) on Gentile converts. Some of St Paul's epistles are concerned with arguing that we are saved by grace and faith in Christ, not by the observance of Jewish law. Notwithstanding this, the very earliest Nazareans, as we know from the Acts of the Apostles, continued to worship in the Temple each day and remained members of the synagogue. They also observed the Laws as they had always done, including the Sabbath, while assembling for the Eucharist on Sundays.[39] Whereas the rest of the Catholic Church was led by bishops, members of Jesus' family were leaders in the Palestinian Churches. Centuries later the Nazareans were still very Jewish while the rest of the Catholic Church had long left its Jewish roots behind and was centred in Rome. Gentile Christians who settled in Palestine, like St Jerome, found it very difficult to understand the Nazareans.

According to Epiphanius, Constantine commissioned Count Joseph of Tiberias, a converted Jew, to build churches in Jerusalem and Galilee 'where nobody was ever able to build churches, since among them there were neither Hellenes, nor Samaritans, nor Christians. This then was the case especially in Tiberias, in Diocaesarea which is called Sepphoris, in Nazareth and in Capernaum.'[40] Some have mistaken this to mean that Nazareth and the other places did not have churches or Christians living in them. What Epiphanius meant was these towns did not have any who called themselves Christians. They did not have churches, as the Gentile Christians knew them, but (Christian) synagogues, and they were known as Nazareans, not Christians.

Conclusion

The insignificant village of Nazareth became a town of exceptional importance and influence because it was the home of the Blessed Virgin Mary, the place where Jesus grew up. It seems that like other houses in Nazareth, Mary's house consisted of a rectangular building attached to a cave, making, in effect, a simple two-room habitation, with the cave perhaps used for storage. A silo for grain was found adjacent to it. Nazareth became the centre from which members of the family went out to evangelise the country, and from where they became heads of the Churches in Palestine.

The family definitely lived in Nazareth well into the second century, and by the mid third century still had connections there. Conon, a member of the family, who came from Nazareth, was martyred in 250, and a memorial to him was erected in Nazareth in a cave beside the House of Mary. Around that time, if not before, it became a place of pilgrimage, and a Nazarean (Christian) synagogue was built on the site incorporating the House of Mary. Before the year 427 this synagogue was replaced by a Byzantine Basilica of great beauty and substantial size, and in the next chapter we need to discuss what happened to this Byzantine Church, and the House of Mary abutting the grotto, which Richeldis copied in Walsingham.

CHAPTER 3
THE CONQUESTS OF ISLAM

During the seventh century there arose a new religion in Arabia, founded by Mohammad, that was destined to become Christianity's deadliest foe. Mohammad did not believe Jesus to be divine, nor that he had died on the cross. These and other 'errors', he maintained, were corrected in the Koran. Nonetheless, Moslems have some devotion to Mary[1] and the Koran contains beautiful verses paraphrased from the Gospels, like this passage on the Annunciation:

> The angels said: O Mary! Lo! Allah hath chosen thee and made thee pure, and hath preferred thee above all the women of creation. O Mary! Be obedient to thy Lord, prostrate thyself and bow with those who bow ... Lo! Allah giveth thee glad tidings of a word from Him, whose name is the Messiah, Jesus, son of Mary, illustrious in the world and the Hereafter ... He will speak unto mankind in his cradle and in his manhood, and he is of the righteous.[2]

The Annunciation is thus sacred to Moslems as well as Christians, and in recognition of this the government in the Lebanon, in 2010, declared the

25 March, the Feast of the Annunciation, to be a public holiday.

Starting on the eve of Tuesday, 2 April 1968, the Blessed Virgin Mary appeared, for more than a year, over the domes of the Coptic Orthodox Church dedicated to her at Zeitoun, Cairo, in Egypt, stopping traffic and holding huge crowds spellbound. Over a quarter of a million people gathered to witness her appearances, which varied from a few minutes to nine hours, and they included Moslems and Christians, Egyptians and foreigners. Both the Coptic Church and the Catholic Church investigated the apparitions and declared them to be authentic. Rev Dr Ibrahim Said, head of all Protestant Evangelical Ministries in Egypt at the time of the apparitions, also affirmed that the apparitions were true. Evidence was taken from sick people, including blind people, who were cured.

At the end of April 1968, Fr Colin Stephenson, the Administrator of the Anglican Shrine in Walsingham, received a letter from a young Moslem in Cairo:

> I would appreciate a very frank reply from you. The fact is that last Ramadan when, for the second time only in my life, I obeyed the rules of this holy month, it came to me that I should send a gift to Our Lady. At first I ignored the whole idea because I couldn't see how one could send a gift unless one were a millionaire and regarded Our Lady to be an institution, and contributed some vast sum to Her upkeep. And since I'm not a millionaire it seemed out of the question. This idea kept cropping up however and finally it occurred to me that She might like a new collection salver. She must have a special one already, but perhaps She could do with an alternative one. Very beautiful silver salvers with those intricate Arabesque designs on them are obtainable in Khan al Khalily. But another thing I wonder about is whether it would be acceptable for Our Lady to have a salver with 'In the Name of God The Merciful The Compassionate' on it. And then, of course, will She accept a gift from a Moslem?[3]

Fr Stephenson replied that the Shrine would be honoured to have such a gift, and in due course the salver arrived, and was used for collecting alms on the altar of the Holy House. It is inscribed in Arabic with a verse from the Koran:

> In the name of God, the Merciful, the Compassionate
>
> You will find that the closest people to the (Moslem) faithful are those who say, 'We are Christians'. This is because there are priests and monks among them and they (the Christians) are not proud. God the Mighty has spoken the truth.

Sadly, relations have not been, nor are, always so cordial. After the death of Mohammad in 632, the Islamic army swept with breathtaking speed across much of western Asia and North Africa and into Europe. Making huge territorial gains from the Byzantine Empire, already weakened by Persian aggression, and not helped by divisions among Eastern Christians, it conquered Mesopotamia and parts of Persia, Egypt, Syria, Palestine, including Jerusalem, and Armenia. Constantinople was repeatedly attacked but successfully defended. Rome was attacked more than once and saved itself only by paying a huge ransom. The Arabs became a naval power and occupied part of Cyprus and the island of Rhodes. Crete was taken, then Sicily and southern Italy. By 715 Moslems occupied most of Spain and southern Gaul (France) before being driven out of Gaul at the Battle of Tours (or Poitiers) in 732. Within a few years the Islamic empire stretched from the Pyrenees to central India.

It is impossible to exaggerate the threat to Christianity. Christians were sometimes tolerated as 'People of the Book', in the hope that they would convert, but generally they endured serious hardships. They suffered severe restrictions in worship, could not ring church bells, display their faith through public processions, or make converts. Many churches were turned into mosques and they were forbidden to build new ones. Arab conquests were often followed by punitive taxation on Christians, and enslavement. Massive defections to Islam were inevitable. Military victories seemed to prove the power of Islam's God. The Monks of St Catherine's Monastery, on Mount Sinai, display a document signed by Mohammad putting the monks under his personal protection, and exempting them from paying taxes, but they too suffered under less benevolent Moslem rulers, despite allowing a mosque to be built within their compound.[4] Happily Mohammad's protection saved their library, second only to the Vatican, containing 3,000 ancient manuscripts, which includes the fifth century *Codex Syriacus* of the Gospels. By the tenth century most Christian communities had died out in Arabia. From North Africa Christians fled to Italy, Spain, Greece, Gaul, and even Germany, a fatal, but understandable exodus, from which Christianity in North Africa has never recovered. But in most countries it clung tenaciously on, proving more resistant to Islam than the faith of any other people the Arabs overran.[5]

As though this were not enough, while all this was going on floods of barbarians were pouring into regions the Arabs hadn't reached. Christian lands were under siege in all directions, battling with invaders. Vikings invaded

England, Ireland and northern France leaving their name 'Norman' (Northmen or Norsemen) still surviving as Normandy today, but they were soon converted to Christ.

Not for nothing did Jesus say the gates of Hell will not prevail against the Church. It would be Normans who would soon begin the recovery of Christian lands from Islam, for though they had become Christians they had lost none of their enthusiasm for military campaigns. The family of Richeldis was Norman.

The Conquest of the Holy Land

By 638 the Moslems had conquered Palestine, where they have remained, apart from the short period of Crusader rule, to this day, and it is with this conquest, and its effect on Nazareth, that we are most concerned. These early Moslems in the Omayyad Empire respected Christians. They were allowed to build churches and were far from unhappy under Moslem rule. In 670, thirty-two years into the occupation, a French pilgrim, Arculf, found Nazareth at peace. He describes two very large churches there, one on the site of the house of Joseph, where Jesus grew up, the other, as we have seen, over the site of the Annunciation.[6]

Forty years later the situation had deteriorated. Another pilgrim, Willibald, found only one church there, over the House of Mary, and that in the hands of the Moslems. The other church was in ruins.

In Baghdad civil wars broke out among the Moslems, the Omayyads were defeated, and were replaced in 750 by the Abbasids. Even then the Patriarch of Jerusalem could write that the Moslem authorities 'are just and do us no wrong nor show us any violence.'[7] The next two centuries witnessed an ebbing and flowing of power between the Moslems and the Christian Byzantine Empire.

The worst outrage was caused by a short period of persecution when the Fatimid Caliph al-Hakim of Cairo, the son of a Christian mother, suddenly reacted against his upbringing. Between 1004 and 1014 he confiscated church property, passed ordinances against Christians, forcing many to apostatise, burnt crosses, and ended up destroying or pillaging thirty thousand churches. In 1009 the Church of the Holy Sepulchre, the Christian holiest place, was destroyed. He also took similar action against Jews. His co-religionists were horrified and in anger against their protests he ended up attacking them too by forbidding the Ramadan fast and the pilgrimage to Mecca. His sister, Sitt al-Muluk led a conspiracy against him and he was killed.

Not until 1046 was the Church of the Holy Sepulchre fully restored. Ten years later Christian pilgrims were forbidden to enter the Church and three hundred of them were turned out of Jerusalem, but this was an isolated incident. Pilgrims came, some in parties of thousands, some in small groups, men, women and children, of every class. Nothing deterred them. The risks served to intensify their devotion and willingness to suffer with Jesus. If 1061 is accepted as the date of the building of the Holy House, then this was the period when it was 'seen' by Richeldis, and the replica built in Walsingham.

In 1067 the Turks conquered Armenia, and began their relentless conquest of the Byzantine Empire. Splendid in art and beauty, and Christian spirituality, its great empire was no match for the rising power of the Turks. Hastily the Emperor summoned an army to recapture Armenia and was routed in the infamous and fatal Battle of Manzikert in 1071. In the same year the Turks seized Jerusalem.

Emperor Alexius I appealed to Pope Urban II for help. His envoys were invited by Urban to the Council of Piacenza in 1095. The Emperor's campaign against the Turk, they reported, was going well and with more soldiers Turkish power would be broken for ever. They laid emphasis on the hardships Christians endured, and the danger to pilgrims. Pope Urban and his bishops were impressed and keen to help. Urban personally regretted the schism that had developed between the Orthodox Churches of the east and the Catholic Church of the west, and deplored the addition of the *filioque* clause in the creed that had divided them. Travelling to France in the same year, Urban, who had been subprior of Cluny, heard first hand from the monks of Cluny that not only were the roads in Asia Minor blocked to pilgrims by the Turks but that the Holy Land was now virtually closed to them.

Yet the appeal for men to take up arms could not be lightly taken. It was said of Tancred, a leading crusader who became Prince of Galilee, that he 'frequently burned with anxiety because the warfare he engaged in as a knight seemed to be contrary to the Lord's commands. The Lord, in fact, ordered him to offer the cheek that had been struck together with his other cheek to the striker.'[8] On the other hand, the Moslems in Spain had been a very real threat to Christendom a century earlier. In 997 they had captured Santiago de Compostela and destroyed the Shrine, and the struggle against them was ongoing.

At the Council of Clermont on 27 November 1095, Pope Urban II called for a Crusade. He had no doubt the war was just, and he had already supported the recovery of Spain and Sicily from the Moslems.[9] The response to his call was immediate. Cries of '*Deus vult*'! 'God wills it' are said to have interrupted him. He campaigned all over France for a year winning enthusiastic support. The Normans, aggressive adventurers from Northern France, eager for expansion, had quickly freed Sicily from the Moslems in 1060. Just as easily they conquered England in 1066. And they were keen to respond. It is very likely that Geoffrey de Favarches, the son of Richeldis, was among them.[10] The stage was set. Urban's exact words at Clermont were not recorded and five different versions are extant. The following extract from Peter the Hermit, who may have been present, gives his impression of the Pope's appeal:

> Oh, race of Franks, race from across the mountains, race chosen and beloved by God as shines forth in very many of your works set apart from all nations by the situation of your country, as well as by your Catholic faith and the honour of the holy Church! To you our discourse is addressed and for you our exhortation is intended. We wish you to know what a grievous cause has led us to your country, what peril threatening you and all the faithful has brought us.

> From the confines of Jerusalem and the city of Constantinople a horrible tale has gone forth and very frequently has been brought to our ears, namely, that a race from the kingdom of the Persians, an accursed race, a race utterly alienated from God, a generation forsooth which has not directed its heart and has not entrusted its spirit to God, has invaded the lands of those Christians and has depopulated them by the sword, pillage and fire; it has led away a part of the captives into its own country, and a part it has destroyed by cruel tortures; it has either entirely destroyed the churches of God or appropriated them for the rites of its own religion. They destroy the altars, after having defiled them with their uncleanness. They circumcise the Christians, and the

blood of the circumcision they either spread upon the altars or pour into the vases of the baptismal font.[11]

The history of the crusades is now the subject of lively debate. It was widely reported that Pope John Paul II apologised for the crusades. In fact he never used the word 'crusades', but during a visit to Rome of the Ecumenical Orthodox Patriarch Bartholomew I of Constantinople, on the Feast of Saints Peter and Paul, 2004, the Pope spoke of the Fourth Crusade:

> on this occasion we cannot forget what happened during the month of April 1204. An army that had set out to recover the Holy Land for Christendom marched on Constantinople, took it and sacked it, pouring out the blood of our own brothers and sisters in the faith. Eight centuries later, how can we fail to share the same indignation and sorrow that Pope Innocent III expressed as soon as he heard the news of what had happened? After so much time has elapsed, we can analyse the events of that time with greater objectivity, yet with an awareness of how difficult it is to investigate the whole truth of history'.[12]

Professor Jonathan Riley-Smith is one of a number of historians who are at pains to put the crusades in a balanced perspective. He writes:

> Liberals of all stripes see the crusades as examples of bigotry and fanaticism. Almost all these opinions are, however, based on fallacies. The denigrators of the crusades stress their brutality and savagery, which cannot be denied; but they offer no explanation other than the stupidity, barbarism and intolerance of the crusaders, on whom it has become conventional to lay most blame. Yet the original justification for crusading was Muslim aggression; and in terms of atrocities, the two sides' scores were about even… Some Muslims now maintain that the *jihad* should be interpreted merely as a battle against evil. But in its traditional form, it was a war for the extension of Islamic territory… fanatical Muslims, Turkish religious warriors in Asia Minor and Berber zealots in Spain were destabilising the frontiers between the religions. The development of crusading was in part a response to a huge loss of Christian territory in the East.[13]

Professor Thomas Madden writes similarly:

> The crusades were in every way a defensive war. They were the West's belated response to the Muslim conquest of fully two-thirds of the

Christian world. While the Arabs were busy in the seventh through the tenth centuries winning an opulent and sophisticated empire, Europe was defending itself against outside (barbarian) invaders and then digging out from the mess they left behind. Only in the eleventh century were Europeans able to take much notice of the East. The event that led to the crusades was the Turkish conquest of most of Christian Asia Minor (modern Turkey).[14]

The Crusaders in Nazareth

When the Crusaders reached Nazareth in 1099 they found it in ruins. The Anglo-Saxon pilgrim, Saewulf, who saw it in 1102, wrote:

> The city of Nazareth is completely devastated, and in ruins by the Saracens, but the place of the Annunciation has a very beautiful monastery.[15]

It would seem that the Crusaders lost no time in repairing the Byzantine church, and establishing a community to serve it. Its re-building is attributed to Tancred, Prince of Galilee, who made Nazareth his capital. William of Tyre wrote:

> Tancred … with extraordinary zeal built the churches of the same diocese, that is of Nazareth and Tiberias and also on Mount Tabor, and endowed them with vast lands and furnished them too with church vestments.[16]

The Grotto and House of Mary were incorporated into the northern nave reached (according to the archaeologist Bellarmino Bagatti), by two staircases. In c.1113, Abbot Daniel from Russia, described it:

> This holy place of the Annunciation has been devastated and the Franks (Normans) are the ones who have renewed the construction with the greatest care.

> A great and lofty church with three altars rises up in the middle of the village. Upon entering you can see on the left, in front of a small altar, a little but deep grotto with two small doors, one in the east and the other in the west, by which you descend into the grotto.

> Entering by the western door on your right there is a small cell, with a narrow entrance, in which the Holy virgin lived with Christ. He was raised in this tiny holy cell which contains the bed on which Jesus slept…
>
> In this same grotto, near the western door, you find the place where the Holy Virgin sat next to the door spinning the purple, that is the thread of scarlet, when the archangel Gabriel, the messenger of God, appeared to her … He presented himself before her eyes not far from the place where the holy Virgin sat. There are about six metres from the door to the spot where Gabriel stood; in that place there was erected on top of a column a small round altar of marble where the liturgy was celebrated.[17]

The charming references to the Virgin spinning purple during the Annunciation comes from the *Protevangelium of St James*, a popular second-century source of legends.

Between 1112 and 1120 Belard of Ascoli visited Nazareth and described the grotto and the room built of stones:

> The room of the Madonna, where the angel presented himself to her, was a grotto. It is situated on the side of the city. But the inside toward the east (*actually it was the north*) is not made of stones but is carved out of the rock in such a way that it is almost four paces long and just as wide.[18]

Seventy years later, Theodoric visited Nazareth in 1175 and wrote:

> there stands a venerable church resplendent with the honour of being the seat of a bishop and dedicated to Our Lady, St Mary. In this church, in the left hand apse (or aisle), are descending some fifteen steps into a certain underground cave, where towards the east a cross is impressed in the base of an altar, to show that here the (incarnation) of Christ was announced to Our Lady by the Archangel Gabriel. [19]

The Crusaders' Basilica of Nazareth was considered the greatest and most beautiful church they built in the east. Along the same axis as the Byzantine church, the Crusader Church was far larger, measuring 76m by 30m, bigger even than the present Basilica. On the south side was a series of large rooms, while on the north stood the Bishop's palace. Thanks to the work of Bagatti a great deal of the intricate relief and carved ornamentation has been unearthed and saved, including some wonderful capitals in perfect condition. Saints and other figures, floral designs and geometrical patterns adorn them.

The Destruction of the Basilica and the Holy House of Mary

The Crusader period ended all too quickly. In 1187 Nazareth fell once more to the Moslems who desecrated the church, massacred most of the inhabitants and imprisoned the rest. Nazareth became a ghost town. Permission was eventually given for pilgrims to return, and on 24 March 1251 St Louis IX, King of France, attended Mass celebrated in the grotto by his chaplain. But in 1263 the magnificent church was destroyed. In the Annals of Abu al-Fida it is written:

> During an encampment on Mt Tabor, a detachment of his army went to Nazareth on his orders and destroyed the church of that city. Nazareth for the Christians was one of their greatest places of devotion because from there the Christian religion sprang forth.[20]

Miraculously, the House of Mary beside the Grotto was spared, no doubt because although they demolished the church, the House of Mary was venerable. Similarly today, the House of Mary in Ephesus, where tradition says she lived with St John after the crucifixion, a Catholic place of pilgrimage, is venerated by Moslems as well as Christians. In 1294 a Dominican friar from Florence, Ricoldus of Monte Croce, describes a pilgrimage he made in 1288:

> Then we arrived at Nazareth. We found a great church almost completely destroyed and of the primitive buildings nothing remained except only the cell in which Our Lady had her annunciation. The Lord has preserved it to remind us of its humility and poverty. In that place there is still an altar of Our Lady where she was praying when the angel Gabriel was sent to her. There is also an altar to the archangel Michael (actually it was Gabriel) where Gabriel stood during the annunciation. In both places we celebrated Mass and preached the Word of God and then toured the city, especially those places more frequently visited by Our Lady and the child Jesus.[21]

This is the last we hear of the House of Mary in Nazareth (apart from the Grotto). For 400 years the site remained desolate, and the House of Mary had vanished. Then in 1620 the Franciscans were allowed to make their home there. Life was exceptionally harsh. They endured imprisonment and persecution, but persevered with patience and prayer. Sixty years later they were entrusted with the civil responsibility for Nazareth in exchange for an annual tribute, and in 1730 were allowed to build a new church, which they enlarged in 1877, over the sacred Grotto. Of the original stone room, the House of Mary, nothing remained, so with small, black marble slabs in front of the grotto they marked out the place which had for so long been treasured and revered as a sanctuary of prayer.

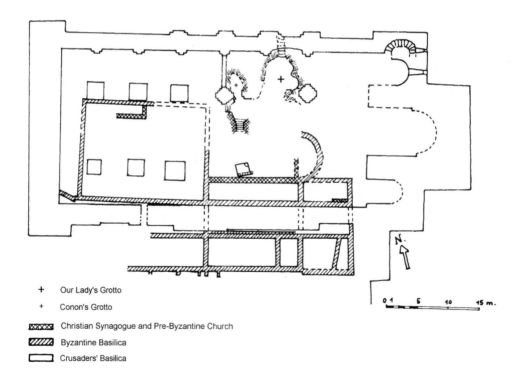

+   Our Lady's Grotto

+   Conon's Grotto

▨▨▨   Christian Synagogue and Pre-Byzantine Church

▨▨▨   Byzantine Basilica

☐   Crusaders' Basilica

0 1   5   10   15 m.

Archeological Plan of the Grottos and churches built above them.
There are no remains of Mary's House, which would have been against the grottos

From Nazareth to Loreto

On the Adriatic coast of Italy, in a region known as Marches, there is a town called Loreto, above which stands a fine Basilica, built in the fifteenth century, containing, it is said, the House of Mary, which once stood in Nazareth. The outside walls of the Holy House are decorated in marble carved over a period of seventy years by the finest craftsmen of the day, showing just how loved and venerated the House became.

Sixteenth-centry engraving of the legend that the Holy House was carried over the sea from Nazareth to Loreto by angels.

The story is that in 1291 the House of Mary was miraculously rescued from Nazareth and transported by angels. After landing at Tersatto in the Gulf of Rijeka, the House moved on to Recanati on the west coast of Italy, to its final destination, Loreto. There are beautiful paintings and sculptures recording this wonderful event, of the House, whole and entire, being carried by angels over the Adriatic Sea. It became a revered place of pilgrimage, for if faith could move mountains how much easier to move a mere house? The medieval mind saw no difficulty in this, even if modern minds are, perhaps, more sceptical.

Imagine the astonishment, therefore, of Giuseppe Lapponi, personal physician to Popes Leo XIII and St Pius X, when he discovered, in the Vatican archives, documents stating that during the Moslem invasion of the Holy Land in the thirteenth century a noble Byzantine family, surnamed *Angeli*, descended from the Emperors of Constantinople, had saved the 'materials' of Our Lady's House in Nazareth and transported them to Loreto. On 17 May 1900 Lapponi wrote in confidence to his friend, Mgr Ladrieux, future Bishop of Dijon, to inform him of his discovery and Mgr Ladrieux recorded it in his diary.[22] Later, in 1905, Lapponi also informed Henri Thédenat, a noted historian.

Guiseppe Santarelli, the historian at Loreto, thinks that maybe his delicate position as personal physician persuaded Lapponi not to tell Leo XIII, or to publicise his discovery, knowing that the Pope had a great devotion to the tradition of the Holy House. Today, however, we are more likely to recognise that far from debunking the legend, it serves rather to authenticate the very real possibility that Mary's House, the House venerated for more than a thousand years in Nazareth, the House Richeldis copied in Walsingham, does indeed stand in Loreto, where to this day it remains a pilgrimage centre of huge importance and devotion.

It is known that the Angeli family gave birth to an imperial dynasty. The first person identifiable is Costantino Angelo, husband of Theodora, the youngest daughter of Allessio I. From him descended the Angeli who reigned in Byzantium (1185–1204). Important corroboration was found by the discovery as recently as 1985, of a document in an archive at Naples, folio 181 of the *Chartularium Culisanense*, actually dated 1294. It relates how '*holy stones carried away from the house of the Blessed Virgin Mother of God*', were in the possession of Niceforo Angeli, a lord of Epirus (now Albania), descended from the Emperors of Constantinople. These 'holy stones', together with an *icon of the Blessed Virgin* and other precious objects, were given as a dowry to Philip of Anjou, the son of Charles II, King of Naples, who married Ithamar, Niceforo Angeli's daughter, in September–October 1294. The chronological coincidences are remarkable, because the Loreto history recounts that the House of the Madonna was brought to Recanati a short time later, on 9-10 December 1294.[23]

This was at a time when Christians were travelling to the Holy Land in search of precious relics and objects to bring them safely to Europe, and it is not surprising that they rescued the House of Mary, from the rubble of the basilica in Nazareth.

Certain investigations at Loreto confirm what happened. Two coins were discovered in the ground beneath the Holy House. They were minted by Guy de La Roche, who was Duke of Athens from 1285 to 1308. Guy was the son of Helen Angeli, niece of Niceforo and cousin to Ithamar. It has often been customary to deposit coins in the foundations of buildings to indicate their year of construction and at times to commemorate those directly or indirectly involved in the building, which in this case was the Byzantine family of the Angeli.

There is other evidence. In a cavity below the 'angel's window' five small crosses of red cloth were discovered, typical of crusaders. Also in the cavity were remains of an ostrich egg, a bird found in Palestine but not in Italy. It was a symbol of the Word of God, made flesh in the Virgin's womb.

Examination of the building shows that three sides of it, up to a height of three yards, are built of stone not found in the Marche region of Italy, but of a type quarried in Palestine. The upper three yards, added to give it greater height, and the fourth wall behind the altar, are made, not of stones but of local bricks. This is very significant because it suggests that the three stone walls abutted the cave in Nazareth, where a fourth would not be needed against the mouth of the cave. Another feature that makes it unique among all buildings in that part of Italy is that the Holy House stands on the ground without foundations.

Further evidence that the Holy House came from Palestine are graffiti that closely resemble some found in Nazareth, including a Greek inscription reading 'O Jesus Christ, Son of God', an inscription that is also found in the small grotto of Conon next to Our Lady's Grotto in Nazareth. There are also two Hebrew letters, *lamed* and *waw*. Moreover, the surface of the stones in Loreto appears to have been cut by a technique characteristic of the Nabataeans, whose work was widespread in Palestine in the first century and who are best known for the spectacular city of Petra. The *Chartularium Culisanense* mentions an icon was brought with the stones, and an icon in the Holy House of Loreto was replaced by a statue in 1530.

Then there is the altar. The *Chartularium Culisanense* makes no mention of any altar being brought from Nazareth, though it does mention 'other precious objects'. There was a fire in the Holy House in Loreto in 1923, which badly damaged the altar. When it was dismantled it was found to have been covering a much older altar inside it, which had been carefully preserved. This earlier altar was replaced inside the present altar after the fire. And this older altar was made of the same material as the stones of the Holy House.[24] Could this be the original altar of the Holy House, the one mentioned by Ricoldus of Monte Croce who celebrated Mass upon it? It is certainly possible, for Gregory of Nyssa (c.394) tells us that altars in those days were built with ordinary stones similar to those used to construct buildings:

> The holy altar, too, by which I stand, is stone, ordinary in its nature, nowise different from the other slabs of stone that build our houses and adorn our pavements; but seeing that it was consecrated to the service of God, and received the benediction, it is a holy table, an altar undefiled.[25]

If indeed the House in Loreto is the actual House of Mary, then it should correspond in size to the replica Richeldis built in Walsingham. It is astonishing how close they are. The width of both is the same. The interior width of Loreto is 13ft, while the width of Walsingham's measurement by William of Worcester was 12ft 10ins. There is a discrepancy in length. Loreto is 31ft long while Walsingham was only 23ft 6ins. But this difference is easily explained. The Angeli family was faced with the reconstruction of a heap of stones. It is surprising that they managed to get the width exactly right. They may simply have got the length wrong or they may have deliberately given it a little extra length in Loreto by reducing the height of original stones, which they made up for by building it higher with local bricks, and adding a barrel ceiling. If they had made the house the same length as Walsingham but four yards high instead of three, they would have used almost the same number of stones.

Conclusion

We have seen in the previous chapter strong evidence that the House of Mary in Nazareth, abutting the grotto, had a continuous history from the time of Mary, and became a place of pilgrimage, at least to the early fifth century. From then until the thirteenth century there is ample literary evidence of its continued existence. Despite the conquest of the Holy Land and centuries of

Moslem rule, and the demolition of the Basilica of the Annunciation, Moslems respected Mary's House, and against all odds it survived. Ricoldus of Monte Croce described that on his visit to Nazareth in 1288 'the great church was almost completely destroyed apart from the cell where Our Lady had her annunciation'. There is literary confirmation that in 1291 the stones of the House were removed and rebuilt in Loreto. Walsingham and Loreto together confirm it.

CHAPTER 4

THE MEDIEVAL CHURCH

The Great Reform

The building of the Holy House by Richeldis, and the foundation of Walsingham Priory, can be understood only within the historical context of the Great Reform and spiritual renewal of the Church, which began in the tenth century and was characterised by a deepening of devotion to Our Lady.

Every few centuries God raises up remarkable men and women, saints and leaders, who inspire astonishing revival and spiritual growth in the Church, and the years between about 950 and 1350 are almost unprecedented. During these centuries Christianity spread amongst all the people of Europe who had not received it before. The Slavonic nations came to Christ through the labours of Saints Methodius and Cyril (who devised their Cyrillic script), and the Czechs and Poles were converted. Pagans from Scandinavia, who had been the scourge of Christians, were converted not only where they had invaded and settled, but in their homelands of Denmark, Norway and parts of Sweden. The Gospel spread to Iceland and Greenland, to what is now Russia, and into parts of Asia, even to China and India, and possibly North America too. At the same time crusaders were recapturing some of the lands conquered by Islam.

With the dawn of the Second Millennium the winter of the Dark Ages had passed. As the Millennium unfolded existing religious orders were revitalised, new ecclesial and lay movements appeared in the Church, and great new religious orders were raised up by God. Many were French, which is interesting bearing in mind the Norman origins of Walsingham through the family of de Favarches. This era of new movements and renewal may be dated from the foundation of the Monastery of Cluny, near Lyons, in 909, by its first Abbot, St Berno. For 250 years Cluny was blessed by a succession of outstanding abbots, and its influence was immense. By the beginning of the twelfth century there were nearly twelve hundred Cluniac monasteries throughout Europe, while older Benedictine houses and others modelled themselves on Cluny spirituality, liturgy and prayer. In all houses, the almoner had to receive passers-by and needy pilgrims, travelling priests and religious, and above all the poor who came to ask for food and shelter. Cluny also promoted a Christian society through the Truce and Peace of God movements, which sought by non-violent means to pacify warring nobles and knights and uphold the rights of the defenceless and poor.

This Great Reform was strongly encouraged by Pope Gregory VII, Hildebrand, a former monk of Cluny, who was elected pope in 1073, and gave his name to the Reform. Following him came a succession of popes with a monastic formation, and it was to the monasteries that they turned to renew the Church. Gregory had written to the Abbot of Cluny asking him for 'some wise men from among his monks, suitable for him to appoint as bishops.'[1] These bishops and popes distanced themselves from political and lay control, which had caused abuse. Pope Gregory was anxious to reform and renew the parish clergy. All over Europe priests were encouraged to remain unmarried and live a life free of possessions, as exemplified by the early Christians in Jerusalem, and through celibacy and obedience have the freedom of a shared life together. Many found their vocations enriched by living in community as 'canons regular' of St Augustine, priests who lived in community, took religious vows, and sang the Divine Office together, while undertaking the pastoral care of parish churches. The Augustinian Canons were chosen to care for Our Lady's Shrine at Walsingham.

In the twelfth century the Cistercian Movement began with St Robert, a Benedictine monk seeking a stricter life of poverty, who opened a house at Cîteaux, near Dijon. Young men were attracted to its deeply challenging life, among them the great St Bernard of Clairvaux, himself influenced by the Englishman, St Stephen Harding, third Abbot of Cîteaux. In 1112 Bernard joined and brought with him about thirty of his friends and brothers. Within three years he was appointed abbot of a new foundation at Clairvaux where he remained until he died in 1153. Bernard was influential in encouraging a more profound devotion to the Blessed Virgin Mary. All those great monasteries with French names in England, like Jervaulx and Rievaulx, as well as Fountains, Byland and many others, now tragically in ruins, were Cistercian foundations, dedicated to the Blessed Virgin.

Bec, the Benedictine Monastery in northern France, also had strong influence in England. It combined deep religious devotion with scholarship. Two of its monks, Llanfranc and St Anselm, became outstanding Archbishops of Canterbury. And so the renewal went on. The list of new religious orders dating from this period seems endless. Carthusians, reflecting early monasticism in Egypt with their great austerity, Fontevrault, and Savigny, Pre-monstratensians, and many more. Then came the charismatic figure of St Francis, and his friars, who devoted themselves to living simply and preaching the Gospel all over the world. There is a lovely story of Saracen (Moslem) hordes retreating before St Clare of Assisi as she held aloft a monstrance to protect her terrified sisters in San Damiano in Assisi. Next came Dominican, Carmelite and Augustinian friars. Some communities were quite extraordinary. Our Lady appeared to St Peter Nolasco and asked him to found an order to ransom slaves, named the Mercedarians after Our Lady of Mercy. Not only did they raise vast sums of money to ransom slaves from the Moslems, but if necessary individual members offered themselves as substitutes for those whose release they sought. The Trinitarians did the same.

Most of the Religious Houses devoted themselves to caring for the poor, as well as to prayer. Hospitals were founded for the sick, and Lazar Houses for those with leprosy. One of these was opened in Walsingham. All that we think of as social work was largely carried out by the Religious Orders. They provided employment for huge numbers who worked the land. Many monasteries opened schools and were centres of education and learning.

Most of the communities had three orders for men, women (generally enclosed) and laypeople. New movements not of a monastic kind flourished as well. Parish confraternities, guilds, and associations, which developed devotion and prayer. Simplified prayer books and Books of Hours were produced. Processions, pageants in the streets, mystery plays, and pilgrimage, all helped to integrate the Faith into life, work and leisure.

1.

Pilgrims to the Mercury Shrine in Walsingham left their prayer, sealed in a beautifully enamelled box, together with a promise or vow they would fulfil when their prayer was answered. Discoveries on the site raise the question of whether there was some continuity of pilgrimage between the Mercury Shrine and the Shrine of Our Lady.

2.

3.

4.

Both pagans and Christians left votive offerings at their shrines. The gold plaque is pagan and was discovered at Ashwell, while the silver plaque found at Water Newton is Christian, marked with the Ch-Rho, part of the largest collection of 3rd century liturgical silver unearthed anywhere in the Roman Empire. In a mausoleum beneath St Peter's Basilica, Rome, is a stunning gold mosaic depicting Jesus, as Apollo the sun-god, rising, a motif of the Resurrection.

5.

6.

The Basilica of the Annunciation, in the densely populated town of Nazareth. Beneath it is the Grotto of the Annunciation,
and the Grotto of Conon, with a 4th century mosaic floor, bearing the inscription 'Gift of Conon, deacon of Jerusalem'.
In the upper part of the Basilica is the fine modern mosaic of Our Lady of Walsingham, taken from the Priory Seal.

7.

8.

9.

The deeply-venerated Holy House of Loreto, believed to be the House of Mary which once stood in Nazareth. There it would have had only three walls, because the fourth side (the wall behind the altar) abutted the Grotto. If the tradition is true, this was the House which Richeldis copied when she built its replica, made of wood, in Walsingham.

10.

11.

Documentary evidence discovered in 1985, indicates that a noble family, whose surname was Angeli, rescued the 'holy stones' of Mary's House in Nazareth from the Moslem invaders and transported them to Loreto. This seems to be the origin of the medieval legend that angels carried the House from Nazareth to Loreto. Further confirmation is provided by coins minted by Guy de la Roche, the son of Helen Angeli, found beneath the Holy House of Loreto. Crusader crosses were found in a cavity below the 'angel's window'. Part of the wall reveals Nabataean work typical of Palestine; and an inscription in syncopated Greek, 'O Jesus Christ, Son of God', is also found in the Grotto of Conon in Nazareth.

13.

12.

14. The earliest image of Our Lady discovered, dated at the end of the 2nd century, in the Catacomb of St Priscilla, Rome.
15. A large 6th century fresco of Our Lady enthroned in majesty, flanked by St Felix and St Adauctus in the Catacomb of St Commodilla, Rome. Medieval Crowned Virgin, Seat of Wisdom, statues, giving an indication of what the original Our Lady of Walsingham may have looked like: 16. The 12th century Villabuena del Bierzo image in Astorga Museum, and 17. the 13th century image in Thalbach Priory, Bregenz.

18.

19.

18. *The image of Our Lady of Walsingham set up by Fr Patten in St Mary's Church in 1922, carved from the Priory Seal. It was translated to the Holy House when the Shrine was built in 1931.*

19. *This image of Our Lady of Walsingham, replacing an earlier one, was placed in the Slipper Chapel in 1954.*

20. *Mosaic of Our Lady of Walsingham on the pulpit of Westminster Cathedral, in commemoration of Walsingham being named England's National Shrine of Our Lady, in 1934.*

20.

21.

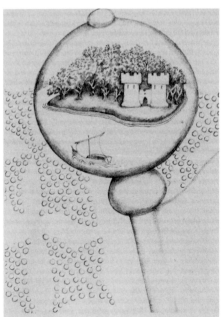

22.

Before this small portable altarpiece, known as the Wilton Diptych, the kneeling figure, the young King Richard II, who ruled England from 1377 to 1399, offered his prayers and devotions. John the Baptist rests his protective hand on the young king, while another boy-king, St Edmund (left) and his patron, St Edward the Confessor, present him to Our Lady.

This is thought to be the origin of England's title, the 'Dowry of Mary'. Christ has accepted the banner of England and handed it to an angel, and now the king, with outstretched hands, waits to receive it back in order to rule England with Our Lady's protection and as her regent.

When the painting was cleaned in 1991, the orb at the top of the banner, was found to contain a hidden painting, only half an inch in diameter, of an island set in a silver sea, on which stands a White Tower, which may represent the central White Tower of the Tower of London.

23.

24.

The arch of the east window of Walsingham Priory, built about 1385, still stands, with a plaque marking the site of the Holy House. The twin wells and the rectangular bath beside them, with an arch moved to that position from the 13th century priory. Walsingham Friary, built around 1347. Its ruins are the most substantial of any friary.

25.

Barsham Manor, the fine Tudor House from where King Henry VIII is reputed to have walked barefoot on pilgrimage to the Shrine.

26.

The Church of St Giles, Houghton. Before the Reformation this was cared for by Benedictine monks from Horsham St Faith.

27.

The screen, with its women saints on the left, where women especially poured out their hearts in prayer.

28.

30.

29.

31.

32.

29. *The Red Mount Chapel, King's Lynn, one of the few surviving wayside Chapels on the way to Walsingham. On 19 August, 1997, Mass was celebrated beside the Chapel by Bishop Peter Smith of East Anglia to mark the centenary of the restoration of the Shrine of Our Lady of Walsingham in the Church of the Annunciation, King's Lynn, and the first pilgrimage to Walsingham since the Reformation. 31. Walking the old Pilgrim Way north of Weeton, and 32. a broken Wayside Cross still marking the route. 30. A figure of Our Lord, once gleaming in gold and enamel, made in Limoges in the 13th century, was unearthed near Watlington, where it had fallen from a processional cross being carried by a group of pilgrims on the way to Walsingham.*

The Martyrs' Field at Walsingham, where Father Nicholas Mileham, the subprior, and George Guisborough, were hung, drawn and quartered, for their part in the Walsingham conspiracy to overthrow Henry VIII, and where perhaps William Allen, a Protestant, was burned at the stake in the reign of Queen Mary.

33.

34.

The Arms of Prior Vowell who surrendered the Priory, depicted in a roundel in St Mary's. It survived the fire in 1961. The most remarkable survivor is the Brass Eagle lectern from Walsingham Friary, now in the church of Wiggenhall St Mary, saved from destruction at the Reformation by the local recusant Kerville family.

35.

36.

The Shrine of Our Lady of Walsingham in the Church of the Annunciation, Kings Lynn, reconstituted in 1897 by the rescript of Pope Leo XIII. It is modelled on the Holy House of Loreto. The statue, carved in Oberammagau, was copied from an image in the church of Santa Maria Cosmedin, in Rome.

37.

37. The restored Shrines of Our Lady of Walsingham in the Anglican Holy House and 38. the Roman Catholic Slipper Chapel.

38.

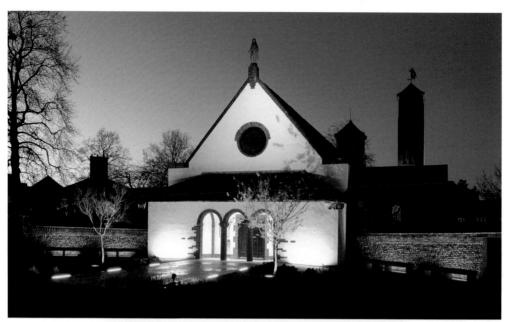

39.

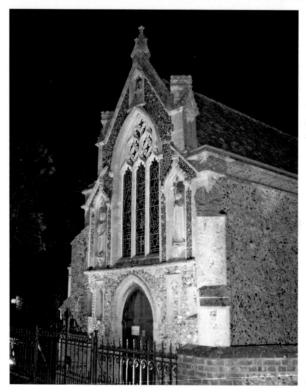

The Anglican Shrine and the Slipper Chapel at night.

40.

Cardinal Basil Hume O.S.B. was a frequent and popular pilgrim to Walsingham. On 11 May 1980, after celebrating Mass with 10,000 pilgrims in the Abbey grounds, he went to pray in the Anglican Holy House.

41.

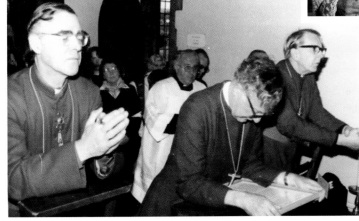

42.

Two weeks later Archbishop Robert Runcie of Canterbury led a National pilgrimage of 15,000, afterwards praying in the Slipper Chapel with Bishop Graham Leonard then Bishop of Truro (left), and Bishop Eric Kemp of Chichester (right). Deacon John Hawkes kneels behind them.

In 1982 Pope John Paul II made a Pastoral visit to England and Wales. The Holy Father asked for the statue of Our Lady of Walsingham to be placed on the altar in Wembley Stadium.

43.

44.

The Feast of Our Lady of Walsingham, 24 September, was instituted by Pope John Paul II in 2001. It is celebrated in both Shrines with ecumenical Vespers and Procession. 44. The Bishop of East Anglia presides at Mass on the Feast in the Chapel of Reconciliation.

The Feast of the Assumption is also celebrated together, with the rosary and meditations, and a Procession starting in St Mary's, stopping at the Church of the Annunciation, and culminating in the grounds of the Anglican Shrine for a firework display.

45.

46.

Devotion to the Blessed Virgin

The Great Reform was driven by deep devotion and prayer to the persons of Jesus and Mary. It is a huge mistake to infer, as some have done, that somehow Jesus and Mary are in competition, and that devotion was given to her that more properly ought to have been given to Jesus. Dr Richard Rex has shown that in the Middle Ages, far from being eclipsed by devotion to Our Lady devotion to the person of Christ was intense and passionate.[2] There is no evidence to suggest that the cult of Mary or the cult of other saints undermined belief in or devotion to Jesus Christ.

Jesus is the just judge, but he is also the Good Shepherd who cares for, seeks and saves his flock. It was his humanity to which people in the Middle Ages were drawn, and Mary, from whom he took his humanity, deepened this devotion. An example of this may be seen in the journal of a devout woman called Margery Kempe, who came from Kings Lynn, near Walsingham. Very popular in the late Middle Ages was the Pietà, the figure of Jesus taken down from the cross and placed in the arms of his mother. They were found in most parish churches and there was a revered one in the Priory Church at Walsingham. The most famous, of course, is by Michelangelo in St Peter's Rome. One day Margery was praying in St Stephen's Church in Norwich beside the Pietà, when

> she was compelled to cry full loud and to weep full sore, as if she should have died. Then came to her the priest, saying: 'Damsel, Jesus is dead long since!' When her crying ceased, she said to the priest: 'Sir, His death is as fresh to me as if he had died this same day, and so, methink, it ought to be to you and to all Christian people. We ought ever to have mind of His kindness and ever think of the doleful death He died for us.'[3]

Jacopone da Todi was a lawyer whose wife died in a tragic accident within a year of their marriage. He composed the *Stabat Mater*, which became exceptionally popular in the Middle Ages, in which we gaze on Jesus crucified through the eyes of his mother, thereby intensifying the emotion:

> For his people's sins, in anguish,
> there she saw the victim languish,
> bleed in torments, bleed and die …

> Jesu, may thy Cross befriend me,
> And thy saving death befriend me … [4]

Devotion to Christ's passion and death is deepened by sharing the grief of his Mother.

The faithful Christian, especially in sorrow, is drawn to Mary in her grief, and through her is helped to share Christ's redemptive sufferings. Like St Paul, the Christian can say, 'I rejoice in my sufferings for your sake, and in my flesh I complete what is lacking in Christ's afflictions for the sake of his body, that is, the Church.'[5] As Professor Eamon Duffy has pointed out, devotion to Our Lady of Sorrows helped people cope with the grief and suffering of successive waves of plague sweeping through Christendom in the later Middle Ages,[6] and the terribly high infant mortality rate. For distraught parents, no one understands better than Mary, whose only Son died upon the cross.

Mary also became honoured as 'Mother of Mercy' because Jesus, her Son, though he will judge, is merciful. She was painted in murals on church walls, tipping the scales of justice with her little finger, or with the weight of her rosary. Stories circulated of how Our Lady had appeared at a moment of temptation or at the hour of death, to convert and bring a sinner to seek the forgiveness of God. She points to Jesus and speaks of God's love for sinners and the whole of humanity. To the Hail Mary, composed at the start of the twelfth century, still the most popular prayer in Catholic devotion after the Lord's Prayer, were later added the words 'pray for us sinners now and at the hour of our death.'

But the Hail Mary first celebrates the joy of Mary, beginning as it does with the greetings of the angel and Elizabeth to Mary. The Angelus, marked by the ringing of a bell, emerged gradually in the thirteenth century, celebrating the joys of Mary and the incarnation. 'The angel of the Lord declared unto Mary.' The joys of Mary, an especially favourite form of piety in England, celebrating the Annunciation, Nativity, Resurrection, Ascension, and her own Coronation in Heaven were familiar to every man, woman and child from carvings, paintings, prayers, stained glass, in carols and joyful verses, as well as in Mystery Plays. Often there was a deliberate juxtaposition of Our Lady with the infant Jesus on her knee, and the Pietà of her holding the lifeless body of Jesus in her arms, as in the church at Walpole St Peter, still seen today.

The growing popularity of Our Lady in the Middle Ages, both in her joys and in her sorrows, is evident in homilies and writings, in Books of Hours, in prayers, hymns, and feasts, in art, music, drama, poetry and pilgrimage. All over Europe, the gentle sound of the *Salve Regina* was heard each day on the evening air, and the faithful in England left bequests for candles, incense and music to accompany it. Shrines distributed books of miracles granted through Mary's prayers. The use of little stones to count prayers goes back to the Desert Fathers, but as a form of meditation on the Gospel through the eyes of Mary, rosary beads became immensely popular under the influence of Carthusians and Dominicans. The Feast of the Holy Rosary was instituted after the completely unexpected and decisive victory of the Battle of Lepanto in 1571 against the Turks, for which Rosary fraternities all over Europe were praying.

Devotion to Our Lady is manifest in the dedication of churches, cathedrals and monasteries to her. Dedications to Mary and St Peter were popular in the eighth and ninth centuries, but from the tenth-century dedications to Mary markedly increase in number. Some churches were re-dedicated to her, in others her name was added before the existing patron. The Cistercians dedicated all their monasteries to her. Glastonbury (where Dunstan was Abbot before becoming Archbishop of Canterbury), Canterbury, Abingdon, Winchcombe and Winchester all offer manuscript evidence of private prayers to Mary, prayers which invariably follow prayers to the Blessed Trinity and before those to the angels and saints. Winchester, in the eleventh century, emerged as an important centre for Marian devotion.

The meaning of the name Mary has been the subject of discussion. At the end of the fourth century St Jerome thought it meant 'Star of the Sea',[7] and in the eighth century Rabanus Maurus picked this up and wrote:

> Because it is normal for a star to guide men to a safe haven, Mary, in this world into which Christ was born, is called Light-Bringer and Lady. Christ guides all to life, as long as they follow him, and Mary brought forth for us our true Light and Lord.[8]

The hymn *Ave Maris Stella* (Hail, O Star that pointest towards the port of Heaven) dates from around this time. Unsurprisingly, since Walsingham is so close to the sea, the Pynson Ballad informs pilgrims that among other miracles, Our Lady 'Maryners vexed with tempest safe to port brought.'

The twelfth century has sometimes been called a 'Marian century',[9] but its theologians were building on a long history of development from the New Testament and the Fathers. It is beyond the scope of this book to trace the whole development, other than to note the central mystery of Walsingham, the Annunciation to Our Lady. St John deliberately opens his Gospel echoing the first words of Genesis: 'In the beginning' and proclaims Jesus to be the Word of God, present at the beginning of creation, while St Luke's account of the Annunciation also draws strongly on the first three verses of Genesis, evoking the creation of the world. The Holy Spirit who hovered over creation at the beginning came upon Mary also, and this was the beginning of the new creation.[10] From the seventh century, four Feasts of the Virgin were introduced: her Purification, her Annunciation, her Assumption and her Nativity. It is not Christ's birth, but the Annunciation, nine months before Christmas, that marks the moment when the Word was made flesh, when the incarnation began. In the Middle Ages the Feast of the Annunciation was chosen to be the beginning of the civil and financial year, and because it celebrated the beginning of mankind's redemption, it was generally thought that this was also the day on which Christ died. The Annunciation is at the heart of Walsingham. In the Ballad, Our Lady asked Richeldis to model her Chapel on the House at Nazareth where the Archangel Gabriel sought her consent to be the Mother of the Lord:

> Where shall be held in memory
> The great joy of my salutation
> The first of my joys ground and original
> Cause of mankind's gracious redemption
> When Gabriel announced to me
> To be a mother through humility
> And God's son conceive in virginity.'

It was the will of God that God should be made man, but this required the will of Mary also. Her physical willingness first needed her spiritual willingness. There is a moral element in her total surrender to the will of God. Her consent to be the mother of the one the angel called 'Jesus', Saviour, was essential for the salvation of the human race. Some modern writers give the impression that Mary was simply open and docile to the will of God, but the earlier understanding is of her as a powerful woman who by her own choice and will does the will of God. This understanding of Mary's active and cooperative role in our redemption is evident in St Luke's Gospel where Mary responds to the angel with the words, 'Behold, I am the handmaid of the Lord; let it be to me according to your word.'[11] Which is why St Augustine could write, 'The angel announces; the Virgin hears, believes, conceives, faith in her mind, Christ in her womb.'[12] As Sarah Boss puts it,

> Mary is not merely the instrument of God's will in the world, nor simply the vessel through whom he realised the beginning of the world's salvation, but is also a participant who actively agreed to co-operate with God's plan.[13]

Just at the time when Walsingham was becoming known in England, St Bernard (1090-1153) was the Church's foremost preacher and theologian. Everyone from popes to princes sought his counsel, and his personal affection for and understanding of the Blessed Virgin was exceptional. In an imaginative sermon on the Annunciation he describes the whole of creation waiting and hanging on Our Lady's response to the angel:

> The whole world is waiting, prostrate at your feet. Not without reason, since upon your word depends the consolation of the wretched, the redemption of captives, the liberation of the condemned; in a word, the salvation of all the sons of Adam, of your whole race... Open, O Blessed Virgin, your heart to faith; open your lips to speak; open your bosom to your Maker. Behold! The Desired of all nations is outside, knocking at your door... Arise, then, run and open. Arise by faith, run by the devotion of your heart, open by your word. 'And Mary said: Behold the handmaid of the Lord: be it done to me according to your word.'[14]

The realisation that Mary's will was as necessary as God's will for our salvation, led to another thought, closely connected with the high respect for motherhood in the Middle Ages. No son would ever refuse a request from his mother. This is probably still true in most cultures, except the western, where Mothers wield immense influence on their children all through their lives, not merely when they are young.

In the Davidic Kingdom, and Jesus was descended from David, the King's mother ranked higher than his wife in influence and as an advocate and intercessor for the people.[15] St German of Constantinople, in the eighth century, addressed Mary with the words: 'You cannot fail to be heard, since God, as to everything, through everything, and in everything, behaves towards you as his true and unsullied mother.'[16] Since Mary is perfectly attuned to God's will, all she begs of her Son accords with his will, and she intercedes as a friend of those who ask her. St Bridget of Sweden in the fourteenth century had a vision in which Christ said to Mary: 'Ask of me whatever you please, nothing shall be refused, and all sinners who implore mercy through your intercession will surely obtain it, if they have a firm resolution to amend.'[17]

St Bernard composed the familiar and much-used prayer, the *Memorare*:

> Remember, O most gracious Virgin, that never was it known that any who fled to thy protection, implored thy help and sought thy intercession, was left unaided. Inspired with this confidence, we fly to thee, O Virgin of virgins, our Mother! To thee we come, before thee we stand, sinful and sorrowful. O Mother of the Incarnate Word, despise not our petitions, but in thy mercy, hear and answer us.

The image of Our Lady of Walsingham, as we shall see, follows early tradition in depicting Mary as an Empress, which is how she is described in the Pynson Ballad, a mother of gracious and powerful influence. No longer the simple girl from Nazareth, she is enthroned and glorified, Mother of the Incarnate Word, for He that is mighty has magnified her. The Ballad reminds us that the Holy House in Walsingham was built

> To the honour of the heavenly empress
> And of her most glorious salutation.
> When Gabriel said at old Nazareth 'Ave'
> This joy here daily remembered for to be.[18]

It is then within the context of the renewal of the Great Reform, and a deepening devotion to Our Lady, with a deep trust in her powerful intercession, that the foundation of Our Lady's Shrine in Walsingham is set. As though to announce a new springtime for the Church, a new evangelisation, a tremendous spiritual renewal of faith, Our Lady called for a Shrine to be built by Richeldis of Walsingham in England. Destined to become the most important Marian Shrine in the country, it became famous in Europe too, and English people were encouraged to think of England as belonging to Mary in a unique way, as her Dowry. This title was promoted in Walsingham, for in the Ballad we read:

> O England great cause hast thou to be glad to be
> Compared to the land of promise, Sion.
> Thou attainest by grace to stand in that degree
> Through this glorious Lady's support
> To be called in every realm and region
> The Holy Land, Our Lady's Dowry
> Thus art thou named in old antiquity.

The Dowry of Mary

Although there is a tradition that the title 'Dowry of Mary' can be traced back to Edward the Confessor, all the evidence points to an origin in the fourteenth century. In 1399 Archbishop Arundel of Canterbury wrote:

> The contemplation of the great mystery of the Incarnation has drawn all Christian nations to venerate her from whom came the first beginnings of our redemption. But we English, being the servants of her special inheritance and her own Dowry, as we are commonly called, ought to surpass others in the fervour of our praises and devotions.[19]

At the Battle of Agincourt it is said the cry went up, 'Our Lady for her Dowry!' The word dowry in this title is nothing to do with the dowry given by a bride's father to her new husband. It translates the Latin *dos*, meaning a gift or donation. It was in fact a husband's gift to his wife, part of his estate, to maintain her in the event of his death. The first clue to the meaning of Mary's Dowry comes in a manuscript in the British Museum, dated 1638, written by Silvestro Petrasancta, lamenting the Reformation:

> In the Church of St Thomas' Hospital in Rome there is a very fair painted and gilded table of Imagerie work standing before the Altar of St Edmund the martyr, once a king of England: which by the view of the wood and workmanship, seems to have been painted above a hundred years past. It is in length about five foot, and about three foot high. It is divided into five panes. In the middle pane there is a

71

picture of our Blessed Lady. In the next pane upon her left hand, kneels a young king, Saint Edmund, as it is thought, in a side robe of scarlet, who lifting up his eyes and hands towards our Blessed Lady, and holding between his hands the globe or pattern of England: presents the same to our Lady saying thus,

Dos tua Virgo pia
Haec est, quare rege, Maria

(This is your dowry, O holy Virgin,
wherefore, O Mary, may you rule over it)

His sceptre and his crown lying before him on a cushion, and St George in armour standing behind him in the same pane, somewhat leaning forward and laying his right hand in such manner upon the King's back: that he seems to present the King and his presents to our Blessed Lady. This may induce a man to think that it is no new devised speech to call England our Lady's Dowry.

The manuscript then has a Latin prayer and its English translation:

O Blessed Virgin Saint Mary, our Blessed Lady, the Mother of God, who with all other saints dost not cease to pray unto Almighty God in general, for succour in all distresses of the whole Catholic Church: I beseech thee most humbly, that as it hath pleased thee of special favour, to take upon thee the special protection of this Realm of England thy Dower: so thou wilt vouchsafe by thy special prayers to thy sweet Son Jesus Christ; to preserve the same continually, and at this present most instantly to deliver it from schism and heresy, and to restore it again to the unity of the holy Catholic Church. That all English people, above all other nations may worthily from henceforth call thee Blessed, and honour thy name for ever, saying thus:

O Blessed Virgin, praise to thee, England thy Dowry
Was lost, is turned by thee again from schism and heresy.[20]

The Hospital of Saint Thomas of Canterbury, referred to by Petrasancta, was established in 1362, to minister to English pilgrims in Rome, making it the oldest English institution outside England. Earlier on the site was a seventh-century hostel for Anglo-Saxon pilgrims. The Hospital became the English College seminary in 1579. The Imagerie work (or painting) mentioned by Petrasancta was given to the English College from where it disappeared, perhaps during the sack of Rome by French troops in 1798. However, Fr Griffiths S.J. had seen it when he was a student at the College, and described it rather differently as a king and queen kneeling, accompanied by St John the Baptist, making an offering of England to Our Lady.

This painting immediately brings to mind the Wilton Diptych in the National Gallery, one of the most beautiful and outstanding works of European art of the Middle Ages. Before this small portable altarpiece King Richard II, who ruled England from 1377 to 1399, offered his prayers and devotions. The outside is emblazoned with his badge and arms. It is called the Wilton Diptych merely because from 1705 to 1929 it remained in Wilton House in Wiltshire, the seat of the Earls of Pembroke. The Rome picture may have been somewhat modelled on it.

The kneeling king is not Edmund (as Petrasancta thought), but is identified as Richard II himself by the badge of a white hart with pearls, which the angels wear as well, though without the pearls because in heaven the adornment is heaven itself. The angels are the escorts for the King, as well as for Our Lady and her Son. Richard was only ten when he succeeded to the throne of England, and he chose King Edmund the martyr of East Anglia, another boy king, and Edward the Confessor, whose reputed coat and crown he wore at his coronation, to present him to Our Lady. Like other medieval monarchs he wished to be connected to pre-Conquest kings. John the Baptist is the one with his right hand resting on the king, because it was on the eve of St John the Baptist's day, 22 June, that he succeeded his grandfather as king.

The meaning of the scene has been much disputed, but significant new insights were afforded in 1991, when it was cleaned and conserved. In the orb at the top of the flag of St George, the patron saint of England, is a tiny painting, only half an inch in diameter, of an island with a white tower on it, and a boat on the once silver-leaf sea. In Shakespeare's Richard II, John of Gaunt speaks of England as 'this precious stone set in a silver sea', suggesting a reference to the Wilton Diptych. Richard has given his Kingdom as a *dos*, a dowry, to the Virgin. Christ has accepted the banner of England and handed it to an angel, and now the king, with outstretched hands, waits to receive it back in order to rule it with Our Lady's protection and as regent on her behalf.[21]

It is thought that the young Richard made this offering and consecration of England to Our Lady when, at the age of fourteen, he was faced with the Peasants' Revolt in 1381. Serfdom was modified slavery, which tied a man to work for his lord for life, under intolerable conditions. The Black Death in 1348 and 1350 had decimated half the population of England, and left an acute shortage of labour. The peasants seized the opportunity to demand wages and the freedom to find work; their rebellion, triggered by a new poll tax, was instigated by John Ball, an itinerant priest, and led by Wat Tyler and Jack Straw. A mob of up to 100,000 peasants descended on London on a rampage of destruction, murdering the Archbishop of Canterbury, whom they held responsible for the poll tax, and burning John of Gaunt's Savoy Palace. Richard II went to pray at the Shrine of Edward the Confessor and, according to Froissart,[22] heard Mass, and dedicated himself before the Shrine of Our Lady of Pew in Westminster Abbey, vowing, it is thought, that if the insurrection were quelled he would consecrate England as Mary's dowry. With astounding courage the young king led his barons, without telling them where he was going, to meet the rebels at Mile End, calmed them, and allowed them to disperse with promises of reforms which his regents immediately revoked. The leaders were beheaded and the revolt was crushed. This event, when he could so easily have been killed, gave Richard a deep, personal and immense devotion to Our Lady, and probably lies behind the story of the Wilton Diptych, and of England being Our Lady's Dowry.

Richard failed to be a good regent for Our Lady. He misruled, became deeply unpopular, was deposed, imprisoned and murdered in Pontefract Castle. Yet the Peasants' Revolt proved a turning point in England's history, signalling eventually the end of serfdom, leading to wages and the movement of labour, and the rise of an increasingly literate middle class in the fifteenth century, with checks on the absolute power of the king. Perhaps this was the unexpected fruit of the King's consecration of England to the one who had herself carried from the Old Testament into the New the prophets' calls for social justice, as she foretold:

> He has put down the mighty from their thrones
> and exalted those of low degree.
> He has filled the hungry with good things
> and the rich he has sent empty away.[23]

CHAPTER 5

THE GROWTH OF THE SHRINE

The Holy House

There are no surviving records about the early years of the Holy House which Richeldis built, but John Dickinson suggests 'there can be no doubt that the Shrine of Walsingham began as nothing more than a place of private devotion erected by the great lady of the parish'.[1]

The site of the Holy House was revealed during excavations in the Abbey (Priory) grounds in 1961, confirming the conclusion of James Lee-Warner in 1854. Standing on the left, that is on the north side, of the Priory church, the place is marked today by a small notice. The Holy House was evidently a substantial structure, made of wood, standing on a timber platform about six inches deep, which measured 29ft 3in x 21ft 3in. The Holy House itself measured 23ft 6in x 12ft 10in, according to William of Worcester, who recorded it in 1479. Extending thus several feet around the Holy House the platform was embedded on a thick layer of stone rubble, to provide a level surface.[2] Sadly, the excavators noted the remains of the holy and venerated Holy House that had been destroyed by fire.

This was not its first location. The Ballad relates the curious story that two sites of equal size for the Holy House were shown to Richeldis by a miracle like Gideon's fleece. Both sites were dry when the rest of the ground was heavy with dew. Unfortunately, Richeldis chose the wrong one, and her workmen started to erect it beside twin wells, which are still there today. The Ballad also tells us that 'a Chapel of St Laurence stands there now,' beside the twin wells. The construction went badly. Richeldis spent the night in prayer, and behold next morning the Holy House had been completed by angels on the other site more than two hundred feet away from the wells.

There is often some history behind a legend, and this is the case with the Ballad. The archaeologists did indeed find the site of the Holy House about two hundred feet away from the twin wells. There was a Chapel of St Laurence beside the wells, as we know from Erasmus, and many relics were kept in it. He also tells us that the twin wells were covered by a shed. Pilgrims in the later Middle Ages would need no encouragement to believe angels moved the Holy House, especially in the light of the well-known story of Loreto. And, indeed, Loreto may hold the clue. The Ballad stresses that what Richeldis built was of identical size to Mary's House in Nazareth. Richeldis had to take careful note of its dimensions. The point of this being, that to medieval thinking parallelism meant that a replica took on the holiness of the original; to all intents it was the same.[3] If angels had moved the House from Nazareth, it is only to be expected that they moved its replica also.

There may have been another explanation, as there was at Loreto (chapter 3). Was there a practical reason to relocate it? It is possible the ground may have proved too wet, and so it was moved soon after it was built. Or at a later date it may have been thought better to move the Holy House away from the holy wells when these became a focus for prayer and healing. Again, it is not impossible that what became the Chapel of St Laurence had originally been a covering for the wooden Holy House.

At any rate, the Holy House was undoubtedly in this second position, two hundred feet from the wells, when the Priory was built alongside it in 1153. The axis of the church differed by some four degrees of arc from the axis of the Holy House. This strongly suggests the position of the Holy House was sacrosanct and predated the church, and could not be moved. Not only that, but the builders had an overriding desire to build the Priory on the south side of the Holy House. In Nazareth the House of Mary, as we have seen, was positioned on that side of the church, and that is where the Augustinians wanted it to be in Walsingham because it was a replica.

In a similar way in Jerusalem there was a reputed House of Mary aligned on an axis with the Church of the Holy Sepulchre. This was emulated at Glastonbury, where a very ancient wooden chapel, dedicated to Our Lady, was carefully positioned on an axis with the Benedictine monastery, immediately to the east of it. Hearn and Willis argue that prior to the middle of the thirteenth century 'axial' chapels, following Glastonbury, appeared only in Benedictine monasteries and cathedrals, while 'shoulder' chapels, on the north side in or around the transept, following Walsingham, were generally built only in Augustinian houses.[4] Interestingly, in East Anglia, no doubt due to the influence of Walsingham, shoulder chapels were added to the Cluniac monastery at Thetford and the Benedictine monasteries of Bury St Edmunds (which was on the site of a pre-existing Anglo-Saxon Marian church), Peterborough and Ely, as well as in numerous parish churches.

Erasmus followed the traditional devotional theory about the position of the Holy House, for he mentions that the Virgin 'has her own church that she may be on her Son's right hand' (i.e. of the Priory Church).[5] This is the customary position of Our Lady beside the Cross, and aisle-end Lady Chapels up and down the country emulate it vis à vis the high altar.

We do not know when the wooden Holy House at Walsingham was first protected by a covering Chapel; it may have been before or when the 1153 priory was built, but what is certain is that after the Priory was re-built in the fourteenth century a beautiful Chapel was erected over the Holy House between 1450 and 1470, which William of Worcester described as *novum opus*, 'a new work', in 1479. It was still unfinished when Erasmus described it in 1511. 'The building is unfinished, and it is a place draughty on all sides, with open doors and open windows, and near at hand is the ocean, the father of the winds.'[6] Erasmus was not the only one to shiver. Earlier in the same year, in the middle of winter, in January, Henry VIII had been on pilgrimage, and on his return commissioned his royal glazier, Barnard Flower, famed for his work in King's College Chapel, Cambridge, to put glass in the windows at the king's expense, £43.11s.4d., in two instalments.[7] The archaeologists found shards of this stained glass. Fragments of beautiful carving which once graced this noble Chapel were also found, and a careful examination of some crockets (curved leaves) shows they were made by the same stonemason who worked on Our Lady's shrine at Woolpit.

The internal measurement of this covering Chapel, according to William of Worcester, was 48ft x 30ft, and the archaeologists confirmed this.[8] This allowed a passageway between its walls and the platform of the Holy House of about 19ft at the ends, and 9ft at the sides. Fragments of Purbeck marble tiles, which paved it, were found. Streams of pilgrims entered the Chapel through a door from the Priory, went up a few steps, and and walked around and into the Holy House, leaving by steps down to a door on the opposite side or at the front where, around the time the windows were glazed, a small porch was added. But most intriguing of all, the archaeologists found a spiral staircase in the south-west corner leading to a wall-passage on the level of the window sills, so that pilgrims could circulate and also view the Holy House from a higher level, coming down on the other side (though no trace remains of the second stair case). That the Chapel had two storeys is born out by the discovery of some pilgrim badges of the Holy House, which show this clearly. Similar complex routes around Marian buildings are found in the outer North Porch at St Mary Redcliffe, Bristol, and the Booth Porch at Hereford Cathedral.

During the excavations of 1961 several stone coffins and burial remains were found beneath and around the Holy House Chapel. One of these was identified as Sir Bartholomew Burghersh, who died in 1369. His tomb extended beneath the wooden platform on which the Holy House was built and was found covered with the grey ash of the burnt Holy House. Why he merited such an honour is not clear, but he willed this and bequeathed a silver statue of himself on horseback. He was indeed a powerful man, both in build and reputation. He accompanied the Black Prince on all his expeditions, fought in the Battle of Crécy in 1346 and was numbered among the original twenty-six Knights of the Right Honourable Order of the Garter, when it was instituted in the eighteenth year of King Edward III in 1345.

Of the beautiful interior of the Holy House, we only have the description of Erasmus, who tells us:

> within the church which I have called unfinished is a small chapel, made of wainscot, and admitting the devotees on each side by a narrow little door. The light is small, indeed scarcely any but from the wax-lights. A most grateful fragrance fills the nostyrils. When you look in… you may say it was the mansion of the saints, so much does it glitter on all sides with jewels, gold and silver.[9]

The statue of Our Lady of Walsingham stood, he tells us, 'on the right side of the altar', which from his remark that the 'Virgin has her own chapel on the right side of her Son' (the Priory), must mean on the left if you look towards the altar. The statue was small, he says, 'neither excelling in material nor workmanship, but in virtue most efficacious.'[10] There was also a statue of the Archangel Gabriel in the Chapel.[11]

The Priory

Precisely when the first community was formed to look after the Shrine we are not sure. In an undated charter we know that Geoffrey de Favarches, the son of Richeldis, gave endowments and instructions for his chaplain, Edwy, to form a religious community to care for the Holy House. There is a discussion of this in Appendix 1. What is certain is that Ralph became the first prior of the Augustinian Priory in 1153.

Augustinian houses were usually small, and Walsingham is unlikely to have ever had more than two dozen or so canons. But often they comprised only three or four, and this must have been the case in Walsingham at its foundation. Professor Christopher Harper-Bill points out that early foundations often had very informal beginnings. Soon after 1102, for example, there was a little community at West Acre consisting of a priest, his son, and two others, living practically in their lord's back garden.[12] Some Augustinian communities were formed when an already existing community of priests adopted the Rule of St Augustine. This may have been the case at Walsingham.

The Augustinian Priory church was built adjacent to the Holy House, and the excavators found remains of this Norman Church and evidence that it had a central tower. We have a good idea what it looked like. Travellers to Walsingham along the road from Swaffham Road to Fakenham may have noticed on the left a typical eleventh-twelfth century church

at Newton by Castle Acre, which looks almost identical to the church depicted on a Walsingham seal in the British Museum. The seal dates from the end of the twelfth century, and apparently depicts the 1153 priory. The seal is relatively small and insignificant, reflecting the humble beginnings of the Priory. Although too much should not be made of the details on seals, it does appear to indicate an unusually prominent transept, which on the north side may well represent the Holy House.[13]

Work on the Priory was still being undertaken in the 1190, and into the next century.[14] The reputation of the Shrine was growing, enough to attract the attention of King Henry III, who made the first recorded pilgrimage in 1226, when he was nineteen years old. He came to Walsingham before visiting the new Shrine of the Holy Cross at Bromholm, twenty-six miles away. Relics and devotion to the Holy Cross became very popular in the wake of the crusades and the sack of Jerusalem in 1204. Our Lady of Walsingham obviously made a great impression on the King, and he granted the canons an annual fair for the Feast of the Holy Cross, and a weekly market to provide a regular income.[15] More than that he must have encouraged the canons with their building. Three years later he returned, and was pleased by what they were doing, for in 1232 he gave forty oaks to make tie-beams for the roof of the church, which indicates large-scale enlargement, most likely to the chancel. Or, as the excavator suggests, only then was a permanent roof being constructed. Two years later came another gift of twenty oaks for the Prior's Chamber and Guest hall along the west side of the cloister.[16] The best surviving part of this building is an arch, moved in later times to the entrance of the garden containing the twin wells and bath.

Through all this period it was far from wealthy. The assessment of Walsingham for the feudal aid of 1235-6 was only £3.6s.8d., compared with Butley Augustinian House, for example, that was assessed at £13.6s.8d.[17] In 1250 Prior William detailed the Priory's sources of income, All Saints Great Walsingham (now in ruins), and All Saints (later St Mary's) Little Walsingham, 20 shillings income from a mill in the village, and income from eight and a half acres of land in nearby Snoring, as well as 40d worth in Walsingham and various small rents. Howard Fears thinks it may have included a field for growing saffron, for which Walsingham became famous.[18] This was not a great income.

The King was quite obviously encouraging the Shrine's development, but we have no records at all of the numbers of pilgrims it was attracting. In 1255 he confirmed further benefactions to the Priory, including three-quarters of the advowson of St Andrew's, Burnham. By 1280 the Priory Church beside the Holy House, together with the cloister, infirmary, refectory and accommodation for the prior, brethren and guests, was probably completed. A second seal of the Priory, dated probably around 1280, depicts a fine church with a great central tower. But by then the Priory had been plunged into debt.

Not for long. Like his father, Edward I proved a generous benefactor, making, during a pilgrimage to Walsingham in 1281, grants of St Peter's Great Walsingham, St Clement of Burnham (re-affirming St Andrew's) St Andrew's Bedingham, Tymelthorp and Owelton.[19] The *Taxatio* of Pope Nicholas shows that in 1291 the Priory had possessions in no fewer than eighty-six Norfolk parishes and an annual income of £79.2s.6¾d. Offerings in the Holy House were rated at £20. Such an annual income was substantial, but at the lower end for a monastic community. The offerings, however, are exceptionally high, indicating that the Shrine was now attracting pilgrims in great numbers.

The Shrine went from strength to strength. The patronage of the de Clare family guaranteed it. In 1306 Pope Clement V sanctioned the appropriation by the Priory of the church of St Peter, Great Walsingham, worth £10, which was to be served by one of the canons, and King Edward II confirmed this in 1314. Edward II, at the instigation of his Queen, Isabella, also granted the Priory a licence to acquire mortmain (permanently acquired) lands and rents worth £40 annually. Between 1300 and 1320 with the growth of the community a new refectory was built, and from the 1340s a new Prior's House with a chamber over it, private latrines and drains.[20]

In 1385, the Priory paid King Richard II £100 for the mortmain of considerable lands and manors in Norfolk, including the manors of Great and Little Ryburgh, worth £40 a year, in return for four chaplains, canons or seculars, to celebrate Mass daily in the newly-built chapel of St Anne within the Priory for the good estate of Joan, widow of Thomas de Felton, knight, and for her soul after death, and for the souls of the said Thomas, his son, and others, and to fund a light to burn daily therein at high mass. A Chapel of St Anne would be a centre of devotion for women praying for a child or with problems in pregnancy. We do not know where this chapel was, unless it was the small chapel found by the excavators on the north side of the Priory Church near the Holy House and the lay cemetery, which they thought was considerably later.

Unsurprisingly, with such wealth the archaeologists found evidence of more work on the Priory after 1300, leading to what was in effect a complete rebuilding. A great aisled church and central tower was built. In 1360 Lady Clare gave a grant for the magnificent church. The new priory, like the earlier, was aligned at an angle of four degrees to the Holy House, indicating once again that the Holy House was too sacred to move. The choir was completed by a grant from Sir Thomas Uvedale in 1367. The great knapped flint arch of the East Window was built in 1385, still standing now as Walsingham's symbol. The cloisters, the chapter house, the refectory, the infirmary, the Prior's rooms, and guest rooms were built, and the impressive gatehouse, which was completed in the fifteenth century, with the face of Christ (or is it a porter?), still looking down and welcoming pilgrims today. There is also a little monkey watching you from the left hand corner. The prior who oversaw most of this majestic new building from 1374 was John Snoring, but it soon became clear he had his own agenda.

A letter dated 6 October 1382 from King Richard II reached the canons, ordering them not to attempt anything that might prejudice his rights or those of Roger, son and heir of Edmund Mortimer, earl of March, or the laws and customs of the realm or the foundation of the house, because it had been reported to the King that Prior Snoring, 'fearing not the pain of perjury, has without craving or obtaining licence of the king or earl procured letters of the Pope to be made abbot and to rule the same (house)…in the name of abbot ... contrary to the founder's will, which would tend not only to the contempt of the king and to the prejudice of the said earl but to overset the rules and constitutions of the Priory and to impoverish the same.'[21] To be an abbot would have raised the status of Snoring immensely.

Notwithstanding this serious charge, Prior Snoring continued with his building, and with his ambitions, evidently regarding himself as abbot by Papal appointment. The canons were up in arms. So, on 1 March 1384 the King appointed the subprior as custodian of the Priory, 'divers contentions having arisen between the subprior and prior who is desirous to obtain the position of abbot therein and to that end expends its revenues and possessions wastefully'. The King further set up an inquiry led by his chancellor and keeper of the rolls, and three others, to investigate 'trespass and other offences in the Priory of St Mary, Walsingham', where 'divers quarrels had arisen between the brethren to the dissipation of its revenues, the diminution of its worship and the prejudice of Roger de Mortimer'.

Prior Snoring acted swiftly to secure his position. Within eight days he had assured the King with two sureties of 1000 marks each, that until the next Parliament he would keep the Priory and its possessions as they were, and make no appeal to Rome. The King then withdrew the inquiry, and restored Snoring as prior. On 1 April, Prior Snoring swore an affidavit to the Bishop of Norwich that he did not intend to use abbatial rights, including the ring and staff, nor appeal to Rome. But the peace did not last. It is not clear what happened, but five years later, on 21 May 1389, the Bishop of Norwich removed him and put the custody of the Priory into the hands of the priors of Coxford and Wymondham. Snoring appealed to Rome. Divisions among the canons must have been grave, because on 25 June fresh custodians were appointed and it was enjoined that no canon of the house must be appointed to administer it or dispose of its rents. Later in the year the Bishop of Norwich nonetheless appointed John of Hereford, one of the canons, as prior, on the grounds of the long absence of John Snoring.

Snoring was evidently in Rome pursuing his case to be abbot. However, after the action of the Bishop of Norwich, in November 1389, with the permission of the King, and three sureties this time of 1000 marks, he was appealing to the Pope to remain as prior, and one way or another he was restored to office. If King Richard had in the end proved to be his ally against the Bishop it was all over for him when the king was deposed in 1399, and secretly murdered in 1400. In 1399 Prior Snoring was again appealing to Rome, this time against an official of the Church Court of Canterbury who had ordered him to pay five marks to the Bishop of Norwich, which he did only when threatened with excommunication. His priorate ended abruptly. In 1400 Archbishop Arundel of Canterbury made a metropolitical visitation to Walsingham, found the prior 'deeply ensnared in a great variety of defects' and ordered his removal from office. He was granted a good pension and exempt for life from any proceedings of the Bishop of Norwich and the new prior. His legacy was one of England's finest monastic buildings, which, but for the actions of Henry VIII, would still be there, but which in the event only stood for another one hundred and thirty-eight years. Ironically, after the Reformation, when all was destroyed, the new owners designated it 'the Abbey', as it is still known today.

Impression of what the Priory was like.
The Holy House is on the left, the north side of the church. Beyond the Priory are the twin wells
covered by a wooden shed, and to the right the Chapel of St Laurence.

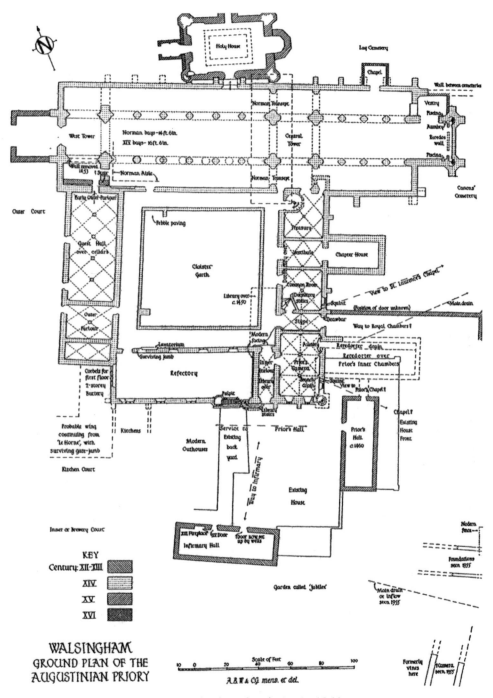

Drawn by the archaeologists in 1961

All of this building required timber and stone, and the Clipsham stone was transported from a Northamptonshire quarry owned by the Abbey of Peterborough. Timber and stone were brought along the seacoast and towed on flat-bottomed barges up the River Stiffkey, which although now constricted on the coast by a sand bank, had been navigable since Saxon times. The area between the river and Knight Street, opposite the Anglican Shrine, is known as Brooker's Dock, formerly Bruecurt's Dock, named after the prominent Norman de Brucourt family, who became lord of the manor of Walsingham.[22] Weekly fairs on Tuesdays and Fridays in Friday Market Place and annual three-day fairs transformed the village.[23] Not only was the Priory being built, but a small town also, the town we are familiar with today, laid out in a grid formation. Most of it was built to provide accommodation for pilgrims and to provide for their needs with bakers, butchers, fishmongers, brewers, grocers and shops of all kinds. A fine sixteenth-century wall painting of a hunting scene survives in a shop, 38b High Street. The old Saxon village was beyond the parish church of St Mary's.

Surviving are the twin wells, close to where Richeldis first attempted to build the Holy House. These may well have had a pagan origin since it would be unusual to have two domestic wells together, and many such wells were Christianised, and associated with healing. The first documentary reference to the wells comes from a report in the Cartulary that Thomas Gatele, the sub-prior at the beginning of the fifteenth century, had as a boy fallen into one of them, and after being taken out as dead, miraculously recovered. Erasmus mentions their use in healing: 'two wells, full to the brink; they say the spring is sacred to the holy Virgin. The water is wonderfully cold, and efficacious in curing the pains of the head and stomach.'[24] Next to the wells is a rectangular bath, which is fed by one of the wells. The visible part of this bath is later, but it is likely that the lower masonry is medieval, and it is possible that pilgrims bathed in it. Dickinson suggests that barefoot pilgims may have used it to wash their feet.[25]

The Parish Churches

The first church in an ancient settlement was always dedicated to St Peter, and although nothing remains of the earliest churches, the present St Peter's, Great Walsingham, was built all of a piece between 1330 and 1350. All the building work going on in Walsingham and in surrounding villages must have astounded the residents, who notwithstanding the attention being paid to pilgrims and the Priory, were not being neglected. Despite the loss of the chancel, St Peter's is a lovely church with a square embattled tower at the west end containing the oldest set of three bells still in use in England, an interesting arch braced roof, and most wonderful of all the rarity of a complete set of fifteenth-century pews, with carved figures of saints and strange creatures. The sharp-eyed may be able to spot what seems to be a carving of Our Lady of Walsingham on one poppy-head. Fragments of fourteenth-century glass survive in the tracery lights, and some faded wall painting including consecration crosses and lettering.

Following St Peter's, the second church in a settlement was generally dedicated to All Saints. There was once an All Saints in Great Walsingham, but it is All Saints Little Walsingham that visitors and pilgrims know well. The Priory had been dedicated to St Mary, and in the nineteenth century the parish church became known as St Mary and All Saints, but Fr Patten dropped All Saints, so that everyone now calls it St Mary's. It stands, it may be assumed, on the site of the Saxon church known by Richeldis, which was no doubt replaced by a Norman Church, before the present church was built. Not so grand as some of the magnificent churches in East Anglia, for it was never going to rival the Priory Church, it is nonetheless a fine example of Perpendicular architecture. The tower is the oldest part, dating back to the Decorated period of the fourteenth century, and it contains six exceptionally heavy bells, one of which originally hung in the Friary, while the rest of the church is later. The north aisle was the last part to be built, perhaps around 1510, along with the very fine west porch. The south porch has a lovely vaulted ceiling supporting the upper chapel of St Hugh. The greatest treasure in the church is the fifteenth-century seven sacrament font regarded as perhaps the best example in England, so noted that a replica of it was displayed at the Great Exhibition in 1851.

The font and the tower were the only parts of the building, other than the outside walls, which were saved in a disastrous fire that broke out on the night of 14–15 July 1961. It was not the first disaster in St Mary's. On the night of 5 November 1866, soon after 8.00 p.m., the church was rocked by a violent explosion of gunpowder from a bomb in the south transept placed under the newly-installed organ, which was completely wrecked. The Vicar, the Revd Septimus Lee-Warner, and his brother, the squire, were unpopular, and the vicar, as well as restoring the interior of the church had installed the organ. No villains were apprehended, no one knew anything, no one talked; but suspicion fell on the village band, whose services were no longer required to accompany services in church. Damage was limited to the organ and a roof beam, which nearly fell on the Sexton. The fire of 1961 in contrast was totally destructive.

The rebuilding of St Mary's was entrusted to Laurence King, and his light and airy interior is rightly admired. John Hayward designed the east window, depicting the history of Walsingham from the vision of Richeldis and the building of the Priory, and the portly and destructive Henry VIII, to Fr Hope Patten and the restoration of the Shrine. The organ, safely installed in a loft away from any Gunpowder Plotters, was built by Arnold, Williamson & Hyatt, an instrument with immense power and a magnificent voice.

The Friary

After this diversion into later times we go back in time along the road into Walsingham, where stands the largest surviving ruin of any friary in England, easily visible from the road that leads from St Mary's. The Augustinian canons do not come out very well in its story, for they strongly opposed its foundation by Lady Elizabeth de Burgh, Countess of Clare. The friars were such great preachers and popular confessors that the monastic orders and secular clergy, with their quieter vocations, often felt themselves eclipsed by them. Friars drew large congregations and people were generous in the fees and offerings they gave them. It was anxiety over potential loss of income that made the canons resist them. This in itself may indicate, not avarice, but that in spite of royal and noble patronage the canons depended for their livelihood on the offerings of the pilgrims. Erasmus comments that the canons 'are highly spoken of; richer in piety than in revenue.'[26] A canon used to stand in the Holy House collecting donations and obviously keeping an eye on everything. Informing Lady Elizabeth that they had to close the Priory gate at night to safeguard the jewels she and others had presented to the Shrine, the canons feared that pilgrims arriving late would go to the Friary and part with their offerings, before the Shrine was opened up in the morning.

Lady Elizabeth prevailed. On 1 February 1347 King Edward III gave her licence to found the Friary, and it received the approval of Pope Clement VI, on a site that would accommodate twelve friars. Further land was granted in the following year. They were Greyfriars, after the colour of their habit, and their purpose in Walsingham was to look after the many thousands of desperately poor pilgrims who visited the Shrine. To this end they built a substantial guesthouse measuring inside 77ft x 24ft 3in, with two storeys and an external staircase. It contained a massive fireplace. The church had a wide nave designed for preaching and a narrower choir for the brethren. There were two cloisters, the larger perhaps used for preaching, and the usual chapter house, kitchens, dormitories and ancillery buildings. Archaeology suggests that building work and extensions continued right into the early sixteenth century.[27]

The Friary did not attract patronage and gifts like the Priory, and in any case friaries were not so grand. But less exalted folk supported it. Nicholas Esthawe of Bishop's Thornton left 20s in his will. Franciscans traditionally integrated themselves into the local community, and local people left bequests. Robert Pigott (or Pigot) who lived in Walsingham, desiring to be buried at the Friary, in 1491 gave half a mark (6s. 8d.) for prayers for his burial, and a further half mark to pray for his soul and for a breakfast. He was remembered in Walsingham as a good man because he left his house in the village to care for lepers. In his will of 1491 he wrote:

> I will and devise to Robert Godfrey and others of the same place (?) my messuages called Spytele Houses with lands, freeman and villeins partaining (in Walsingham and Houghton-in-the-Dale), on condition that they settled them on John Ederich, a leper of Norwich, and Cecil his wife, for their lives, and afterwards to admit two leprous men or one of good family (of good conversation and honest disposition) of the tenement from time to time (for ever).[28]

The last mention of the Lazar House (these homes were named after Lazarus) in Walsingham was in 1787 when the Bridewell was built on the site of the 'old leper hospital'.

Another local bequest was from Robert Gray of Walsingham in 1514, who willed two pairs of silver censers, valued at ten marks each. Three years later, Dr Edward Heyward, also of Walsingham, bequeathed a sum of money including four gold coins worth half a mark each.

The Friary land extended into Friday Market, and a gateway perhaps stood where Friday Cottage is today. The friars may well have preached beside the preaching cross in Friday Market which stood outside the present Pilgrim Bureau. At the west end inside St Mary's church is a square stone with a hole in the centre (often filled with beautiful flower arrangements), which may have been the base of the cross. The Guild of the Annunciation in Walsingham raised 40 shillings towards the great bell of the Friary.[29] This is the bell, recast, that hangs in St Mary's. The friars owned the property between the High Street and Friday Market, shaped like a wedge of cheese, and a hostelry called the 'White Horse'. They obtained permission in 1351 to close part of the road from North Barsham so that pilgrims had to pass through the Friary grounds to reach Friday Market.

The Slipper Chapel

Around the time of all this development in Walsingham, the Slipper Chapel was built along the Pilgrim Way, a mile or so from the Shrine, with architectural features of the Decorated period, which suggests a date of around the 1320s or 1330s. It is not known who built it, but since the nearby church of St Giles' Houghton was served by a Benedictine cell of Horsham St Faith, some have thought they were responsible; but equally, it may have been the Priory. The Chapel owes its survival to the fact that it was purchased intact when the Priory and Friary were destroyed. Naturally it became very dilapidated over the years, and was used at various times as a poorhouse, a forge, a barn, a byre and two cottages. But even in its poor state it was enough to attract the attention of the great Victorian architect, Pugin, who made a fine sketch of it. Its survival proved providential, for since 1934 it has been the Catholic Shrine of Our Lady of Walsingham, the Roman Catholic National Shrine.

All over England pilgrim ways were marked with crosses, and the sites of more than a hundred on the way to Walsingham have been ascertained.[30]

Wayside chapels were built along the pilgrim routes: the Slipper Chapel being the last before pilgrims reached Walsingham. Obviously it was used for prayer, and as in most wayside chapels a hermit was attached to it,[31] so Mass was celebrated there. It was, and is, dedicated to St Catherine of Alexandria, whose Shrine is on Mount Sinai, the holy ground where Moses took off his shoes before the Burning Bush. Interestingly the Chapel of the Burning Bush in the apse of the Monastery Church of the Transfiguration on Mount Sinai is dedicated to the Annunciation, and the sun is said to shine across it when it rises on 25 March, the Feast of the Annunciation. The Crusaders brought her devotion back with them to Europe, and Catherine became the patron saint of pilgrims. At Sporle, on the Pilgrim Way close to Walsingham, is a wall painting, dated about 1400, depicting the life of St Catherine.

Crusader Knights of St Catherine protected pilgrims on the road to the Holy House of Mary in Nazareth. People have noticed that the Slipper Chapel is orientated to the southeast so that on her Feast Day, 25 November, the sun rises directly behind the altar.[32] These associations can hardly be a coincidence and seem to support the idea that at the Slipper Chapel (also at times called the 'Shoe Chapel') pilgrims were encouraged to take off their shoes in devotion and walk barefoot to the Shrine. Some pilgrims walked barefoot their whole journey, adding penance and seriousness to their prayers, and Henry VIII is said to have walked barefoot from Barsham Manor in East Barsham. An alternative explanation that the word slipper derives from an old English word, 'slype', meaning 'something in between' seems to have less to commend it.

All Shrines had several locations of devotion. For example, at Canterbury pilgrims would pray where the Archbishop was martyred, then at the site of his severed head, and at his tomb, and other holy places in the city associated with St Alfege and St Mildred, as well as at a rich and beautiful Shrine of Our Lady in the undercroft. Medieval pilgrims on the way to Walsingham prayed at All Saints East Barsham, where there was a Chapel called the Chapel of St Saviour or the Greeting of Our Lady,[33] before going down the lane to the Slipper Chapel. This gradual 'unfolding' added to the epiphany and the awe they experienced in the Holy House. They prayed also at the Chapel of St Laurence and the holy wells, drinking and perhaps bathing in the waters, and in the Chapel of St Thomas, which was in the precincts of the Priory.[34]

The Pietà in the Priory, and Mary's Milk above the High Altar were revered. St Giles' Houghton attracted pilgrims too.

As in Loreto where veneration focused both on the Holy House itself and on the image of Our Lady it contained, in Walsingham too both the Holy House and statue were revered. But when people left gifts in their wills they were almost invariably left, not to 'the Shrine' or to 'the Holy House', but to 'Our Lady of Walsingham' or 'Our Lady at Walsingham'. In a very personal way it was a gift to Our Lady. We need to look more closely at the sacred and deeply loved image of Our Lady of Walsingham.

CHAPTER 6

THE IMAGE OF
OUR LADY OF WALSINGHAM

Jews were forbidden by the Ten Commandments to make 'a carved image or any likeness of anything in heaven above or on earth beneath or in the waters under the earth.'[1] Idolatry was the danger. And how could you create an image of God who was invisible and unseen? No one could look on the Lord and live.[2]

But once St Paul had written, '(Christ) is the image (*Gk. Icon*) of the unseen God,'[3] it changed everything. God had revealed his likeness. The disciples had gazed on the image of God. In the Incarnation the Word was made flesh. God had taken on himself our human nature, was born of a human mother, and a tradition grew up that St Luke had painted her portrait. It opened up the glorious history of Christian art.

Gentile Christians had no inhibitions about images, never having grown up with the Jewish Law, and they were very familiar with statues of gods and goddesses. Unsurprisingly, the earliest images they made of Our Lady bear a striking likeness to ancient statues of goddesses because that was a familiar form. The Mother Goddesses, like this Greek Goddess, dated 500 BC, were probably objects of personal devotion, used by women in propitiation for fertility and in the difficulties of pregnancy and childbirth, in the same way as images of Our Lady became.

The oldest Christian paintings to have survived are found in the dust-dry catacombs of Rome, where Christians decorated their tombs and mausolea. In the Catacomb of Priscilla was discovered the earliest known painting of Our Lady. Like many pagan statues, and Our Lady of Walsingham, she is seated and holding her Son. Also in this catacomb is a picture of Mary sitting with Jesus on her knee, receiving the Magi, the Wise Men. In the Catacomb of Commodilla is a large sixth-century fresco of Our Lady enthroned in majesty, flanked by St Felix and St Adauctus, who according to the inscription are introducing to her a lady who has died, called Turtura. On a wall in the sacristy of Santa Maria in Cosmedin, in Rome, where guidebooks are sold, is a priceless treasure that once graced Constantine's Basilica of St Peter. It is a stunning eighth-century mosaic of the Epiphany visit of the Wise Men. By then the Epiphany to the Wise Men had become a favourite scene in Christian art, for ever associating these seated images with wisdom.

Our Lady, Seat of Wisdom

Ironically the reason we know what Our Lady of Walsingham looked like is that she was depicted on the seal of the Priory appended to its Deed of surrender in the reign of Henry VIII, who destroyed it. By another coincidence the only piece of original stained glass, which survived the fire of 1961 in St Mary's, is a small roundel containing the arms of Prior Richard Vowell who signed the Deed.[4] The cinquefoils in it are for the prior and the five lilies are for the Priory.

If you go to the Bishop's Palace built by Gaudi in Astorga, in Northern Spain, now a Museum because it was so grand that no bishop ever dared live there, you will find a roomful of what look like statues of Our Lady of Walsingham, row upon row of them. It is a sad sight because you want to kneel and pray, but before which one? They come from parish churches all over Spain where they had been loved and venerated, many of them since the twelfth century, but from where they would now risk being stolen. The sheer number on display shows just how popular and common these statues, known as 'Seat of Wisdom' statues, were.

People today often interpret the New Testament literally or else as form-critics, but in New Testament days and for a long time after, they looked for allegory, glimpsing signs or 'types' of the New Testament within the Old. For example, the Letter to the Hebrews allegorises Jesus as the High Priest entering the Sanctuary of the Temple, containing the Ark of the Covenant.[5] St Paul saw the crossing of the Red Sea as 'Baptism into Moses,' and Christ as the spiritual rock in the desert from which water flowed;[6] Adam was the first man, and Christ the last or new Adam.[7] It was not long before Mary was called the new Eve. The disobedience of the first Eve was reversed by the obedience of the second Eve.

The opening words of St John in his Gospel suggest that he was thinking allegorically by linking Jesus with Wisdom in the Book of Proverbs, 'I was set up from everlasting from the beginning before ever the world was. I was with him, forming all things.'[8] Similarly for St Paul, Christ 'is the power and the wisdom of God.'[9] But Wisdom is a female figure in the Old Testament and so it was not long before Wisdom was personified by Mary as well as by Jesus, and readings from the Wisdom books were read on her feasts.

Solomon is the uniquely Wise Man of the Old Testament, and much is made of his splendid throne:

> The king also made a great ivory throne, and overlaid it with pure gold. The throne had six steps and a footstool of gold, which were attached to the throne, and on each side of the seat were arm rests and two lions standing beside the arm rests.[10]

Sarah Boss has noticed that an illumination in the 1130-1140 Eynsham manuscript of Saint Augustine's Commentary on Psalms 101-150 shows the Virgin and Child seated on a throne like Solomon's, with its lions.

96

The image of Our Lady of Walsingham, and similar statues, also show Mary seated on a throne, a Seat of Wisdom. She is the crowned Virgin-Mother. But not only is Mary enthroned; Christ is enthroned on her knee. So she herself becomes the Seat of Wisdom. Christ is the Wisdom of God, and it is Mary who bears him.

Wisdom statues soon became connected with the Wise Men who brought gifts to the infant Christ. As well as standing in churches, the statues were used in processions and pageants in which clerics would dress up as the Wise Men and go in search of the child. When they found him they would fall down and worship him. 'So when worshippers look upon an image of this kind, they are being enjoined to stand in the place occupied by the Wise Men in St Matthew's Gospel. It is now we who fall down and worship the child and offer him our gifts.'[11] And the Greek word used by St Matthew is προσήνεγκαν, which literally means the Wise Men fell prostrate before him. It is deep obeisance, adoration, homage.

The Enthroned Virgin-Mother

Christian art, as well as doctrine, received a huge boost with the definition of Mary as θεοτόκος (*Theotokos*) at the Council of Ephesus in 431. *Theotokos* is generally translated 'Mother of God', but more accurately it means, 'the one who gave birth to the one who is God'.[12] The definition was made after Nestorius, the Patriarch of Constantinople, had suggested that it was only the human nature of Jesus that had been born of Mary. He is said to have preached 'I cannot call a three month old baby God'. This heresy left open the possibility of another; that Christ's divine nature had come down upon him only at his baptism. So, *Theotokos* means that Jesus is born both truly God and truly human. The Word was made flesh within the womb of the Blessed Virgin Mary.[13] It also ensured, as St John Damascene said, that when venerating her icon 'we do not, in pagan fashion, regard her as a goddess but as the *Theotokos*.'[14]

In celebration of this definition Pope Sixtus III built the Basilica of St Mary Major in Rome with its stunning fifth-century mosaics of the Annunciation and Epiphany. Mary is no longer the lowly maid from Nazareth, 'for he that is mighty has magnified me'. 'The Almighty has done great things for me.'[15] The mosaic celebrates the dignity to which God raised her, the crowned Virgin-Mother, and she is enthroned, holding her divine and human Son. She is an Empress. The maid of Nazareth has become a powerful and majestic figure, and her power, deriving from her Motherhood, is evident in her powerful intercession with her Son, who would never refuse her requests. The mosaic clearly follows the Wisdom tradition of the early paintings associated with the Epiphany to the Wise Men. The Image of Our Lady of Walsingham is derived from these very earliest images of Our Lady and the tradition of depicting her as the Seat of Wisdom and the crowned Virgin-Mother enthroned. The Walsingham Ballad calls her the 'heavenly Empress'.

The earliest recorded free-standing statue of Our Lady was made in 946 for the cathedral of Clermont (now Clermont-Ferrand) in south-east central France. Although it has been destroyed it survives in a manuscript.[16] It is easy to see here the origin of all those Seat of Wisdom and Virgin-Mother statues in Astorga, and Our Lady of Walsingham. Jesus is not a baby but a small adult, behind his head a cruciform halo, a sign of his imperial authority as Pantocrator, Ruler of All. His right hand is raised in blessing, the other extended. Sometimes, as at Walsingham, He holds a book in his left hand to signify He is the Word of God. His bare feet signify his humanity. In some Renaissance paintings one of the Wise Men kisses the child's bare foot, so the bare feet also evoke the ancient Wisdom motif. The enthronement may also relate to Mary being of King David's House and line. For the same reason she holds in her hand the Rod of Jesse, if not a lily for her purity.

These statues were first made in southeast France in the tenth century and during the eleventh spread to Northern France. It is unsurprising that the de Favarches family, or perhaps the de Clares, should have chosen a French statue. We do not know when the statue was placed in the Holy House of Walsingham, but such statues were no longer made after the end of the thirteenth century. In the later Middle Ages a style more realistic and lifelike became popular, one of the most widespread being the Pietà, a statue of Jesus taken down from the cross reposing in the arms of his mother.

The Uniqueness of Our Lady of Walsingham

We have noted the similarity between Our Lady of Walsingham and other statues of the type. But there are three features, not found on any other statues, which make her unique.

There are seven rings on the sides of her throne, three on one and four on the other. Obviously the number is significant or they would have been balanced. The usual explanation is that they stand for the seven sacraments. If this is so the statue has to be dated post 1160, for it was only in that year that the number seven was determined.[17] It is more likely, however, that they pick up the Wisdom theme. Peter Damien, a friend of Pope Gregory VII, whom we met in the Great Reform, preached on the Nativity of Mary:

> First a house had to be built, into which the King of heaven would come down and deign to be a guest. I mean the house of which it is said through Solomon, 'Wisdom has built herself a house, she has set up her seven pillars' (Prov 9:1). For this virginal house is supported by seven pillars because the venerable Mother received the seven gifts of the Holy Spirit.[18]

The second feature of the medieval image of Our Lady of Walsingham, which makes her unique, is of great interest, and is not disconnected with Solomon's Temple (or at least the second Temple). On the Priory seal are what seem like two looped curtains around the statue, and it is a shame that these have not been reproduced around the statues in the Anglican and Catholic Shrines today. For they are not decorative drapes, as may be assumed, but represent the veil of the Temple that was torn in two from top to bottom at the moment Jesus died on the cross.[19] The writer of the Epistle to the Hebrews uses allegory to explain that 'through the blood of Jesus we have the right to enter the sanctuary, by a new and living way through the curtain, that is to say, his body.'[20] Exactly the same torn curtain in the Temple is seen in a ceiling at the Shrine in Loreto.

Hidden behind the veil of Solomon's Temple in Jerusalem, within the Holy of Holies, stood the Ark of the Covenant, which the Israelites believed dated back to the time of Moses and in which he placed the stone tablets on which God had engraved the Ten Commandments, and in a later tradition a sample of Manna also. The Ark was a chest made of acacia wood covered inside and out with purest gold. It was revered as a throne on which God was invisibly enthroned between two cherubim. Here God had chosen to dwell and the Ark was the sign of his Presence. The *Shekinah*, the bright cloud of glory, overshadowed it. No one was allowed to touch the Ark. Wherever the Israelites travelled they carried the Ark on poles until eventually King David brought it to Jerusalem, which henceforth become known as 'Zion, City of God.' But before doing so he asked, 'How can the Ark of the Lord come to me?' and it spent three months in the hill country of Judah in the house of Obed-edom, whose family were blessed by its presence.[21]

Approaching the Ark, King David leapt and danced before the Lord, and shouted in great rejoicing. David was not the man chosen to build the Temple on account of his sins, but his son, Solomon, the Wise, built the Temple and enshrined the Ark within the Holy of Holies, screened from view by the veil. Once again the *Shekinah*, the cloud and glory of the Lord, overshadowed it.[22]

It is clear that St Luke had all this in mind when he drew up his account of Mary's annunciation and her visitation to Elizabeth.[23] The Ark was overshadowed by the glory of the *Shekinah*, the bright cloud, and so was Mary overshadowed. Like the Ark, Mary spent three months in the hill country of

Judah. Like David the child in Elizabeth's womb leapt for joy. Like David asking how the Ark of the Lord could come to him, Elizabeth asked, 'Why is this granted me, that the Mother of my Lord should come to me?'

The Ark contained the Word of God in stone, but the womb of Mary contained the Word of God made flesh. Mary is the Ark of the new Covenant. She is covered with purest gold within and without because she is sinless, pure and incorruptible. No one was allowed to touch the Ark, it was sacred, consecrated, set apart for God alone, and so was she.

The identification of the Ark with Mary was fulfilled by St John. The Ark of God disappeared when the first Temple was destroyed in 587 BC. The Israelites had a tradition that it was rescued by Jeremiah and hidden in a place of safety in the desert, in a cave on Mount Nebo.[24] On the last day it will appear again. John saw its reappearance in a symbolic vision:

> The sanctuary of God in heaven opened, and the Ark of the Covenant could be seen inside it. Then came flashes of lightning, peals of thunder and an earthquake, and violent hail. Now a great sign appeared in heaven: a woman, adorned with the sun, standing on the moon, and with the twelve stars on her head for a crown. She was pregnant and in labour.

Then a huge red dragon tried to kill the child (as Herod had done), but she gave birth to a male child,

> the son who was to rule all the nations with an iron sceptre (not gold, for he came as a servant), and the child was taken straight up to God and to his throne, while the woman escaped to the desert, where God had made a place of safety ready … The dragon was enraged with the women and went away to make war on the rest of her children, that is, all who obey God's commandments and bear witness for Jesus.'[25]

First the Ark appears, the prefigurement, and then the reality in Mary. At the foot of the cross St John tells us that Mary became John's mother, but not only John's. She is the mother of all the disciples, that is 'the rest of her children who obey God's commandments and bear witness for Jesus.' At the foot of the cross she becomes the Mother of the Church. And the woman who appeared in heaven signifies both Israel and the Church. Like the Ark, Mary had escaped to a place of safety in the desert.

Early preachers and writers saw Mary as the Ark. In a homily attributed to St Athanasius of Alexandria (c.296–373):

> O noble Virgin, truly you are greater than any other greatness. For who is your equal in greatness, O dwelling place of God the Word? To whom among all creatures shall I compare you, O Virgin? You are greater than them all O Ark of the Covenant, clothed with purity instead of gold! You are the Ark in which is found the golden vessel containing the true manna, that is, the flesh in which Divinity resides.[26]

The Catholic Catechism picks up the theme:

> Mary, in whom the Lord himself has just made his dwelling, is the daughter of Zion in person, the Ark of the Covenant, the place where the glory of the Lord dwells. She is 'the dwelling of God … with men'.[27]

Archbishop Rowan Williams of Canterbury also reflected on it:

> From the sanctuary of heaven, from the terrifying emptiness between the cherubim of the ark, God enters another sanctuary, the holy place of a human body … Jesus enthroned between the cherubim; Jesus enthroned on Mary's lap: the utterly astonishing fact of God's glory fully living in a human being, with all the startling effects that has on how we see and understand what it is to be human.[28]

The veil is torn apart so we can gaze, even touch now, Mary, the Ark of the Covenant holding the Word of God for us all to see, worship and embrace. Such is the image of Our Lady of Walsingham.

The third unique feature in the statue of Our Lady of Walsingham, again not reproduced on modern statues, we learn from Erasmus, the priest, scholar, and Catholic reformer, who came on pilgrimage to Walsingham in 1512. To him we owe the only description of the Holy House and statue that we have. He tells us that beneath the feet of the Virgin is what the French called a toad-stone, a green jewel on which was imprinted a toad. On being asked in his colloquy why they attach a toad to the Virgin, Erasmus explains, 'because all filthiness, malice, pride, avarice, and whatever belongs to human passion, has been by her subdued, trodden underfoot, and extinguished.'[29] In the Book of Genesis, in the Garden of Eden, God says to the serpent, 'I will put enmity between you and the woman, and between your seed and her seed; he shall bruise your head, and you shall bruise his heel', but the iconography goes back to the Vulgate translation, which reads, not He but 'She will crush your head, and you will lie in wait for her heel', linking up in a way with the idea we have just seen in St John of the dragon being enraged with the woman.

Sarah Boss points out that 'the motif of the woman trampling the serpent underfoot was applied to Mary's immaculate conception, since her freedom from sin was a sign of the devil's total defeat.'[30] Quoting the art historian, Maurice Vloberg, Boss affirms that the earliest certain representation of the Virgin trampling on the head of a serpent is a wooden statue ordered for the church of St Mary of Cremona in 1407. It was not uncommon in France for animals to be carved on a jewel, but it is quite extraordinary to find a toad or serpent beneath the feet of Our Lady on what is most likely a twelfth-century statue. If the statue of Our Lady of Walsingham represents the Immaculate Conception it would be early indeed. From the seventeenth century images representing the Immaculate Conception depict Mary as a solitary figure, sometimes standing on a serpent, sometimes standing on the moon, yet it was from her divine motherhood that the doctrine of the Immaculate Conception derived and, as Sarah Boss has commented, 'it could be argued that any symbolic depiction of the Immaculate Conception should incorporate a representation of Christ.'[31]

Interestingly, the Feast of Our Lady's Conception is for ever associated with England. It originated in the East, but it reached England before anywhere else in the West, perhaps from the many Greek monks in Southern Italy, or through Anglo-Saxons living in Constantinople. We also know of a Greek monk, Constantine, in Malmesbury Abbey in 1030.

They began to celebrate the Feast at Winchester Abbey and Canterbury, monasteries greatly affected by the Gregorian Reform, and it spread to Ramsey Abbey, which is only sixty miles from Walsingham, through the appointment, in 1062, of Aelfige as acting-Abbot. He was also Abbot of St Augustine's, Canterbury, after having been a monk of the Old Minster, Winchester. Anselm, in his collection of Marian miracles, gives a lovely account of how Aelfige was sent to the King of Denmark by William the Conqueror, to ensure peace with the Danes:

After he had spent much time there, he asked and received permission from the king to return home, and setting out on the sea with his companions he flew swiftly over the smooth surface of the sea. And when he was sailing calmly in this way, suddenly a violent storm rose in the sea and, when hope of safety or getting away or escaping disappeared, they turned to God and thus called for help: 'O Almighty God, have pity on us in this ordeal lest, devoured by the sea, we are united in eternal punishment.' When they had finished speaking this and many similar prayers, suddenly they saw a person, decorated with episcopal insignia, near the ship. He called Abbot Aelfige to him and addressed him in these words: 'If you wish to escape from the danger of the sea, if you wish to return to your native country safely, promise me in the presence of God that you will solemnly celebrate and observe the feast-day of the conception of the mother of Christ.' Then the abbot answered: 'How can I do this or on what day?' The messenger said: 'You will celebrate it on the eighth day of December, and will preach it wherever you can, that it may be celebrated by everybody.' Aelfige said: 'And what sort of divine service do you command us to use on this feast?' He replied to him: 'Let every service, which is said at her nativity, be said also at her conception. Thus, when her birthday is mentioned at her nativity, let her conception be mentioned at the other celebration.' After the abbot agreed this, he reached the English shore with a favourable wind blowing. Soon he made known everything he had seen and heard wherever he could, and he ordered in the church at Ramsey, over which he had presided, that this feast be celebrated on 8 December.[32]

The Feast probably had the support of Archbishop Stigand, because he was a close associate of Abbot Aelfige, and held the sees of Winchester and Canterbury in plurality. Stigand, incidentally, held lands in Walsingham. But in 1070 he was deposed under the ecclesiastical changes after the Norman Conquest. Llanfranc became the new Archbishop. He reformed the calendar and abolished the Feasts of the Presentation and Conception of Our Lady.

The feast and doctrine of the Immaculate Conception were controversial. Owing to the abiding influence of St Augustine who, though he believed in the sinlessness of Mary, taught that original sin was transmitted through the procreative seed, there was huge resistance to celebrating the conception of Mary, because she must have been conceived in original sin. Even St Thomas

Aquinas, and St Bernard, for all his devotion to Our Lady, resisted the doctrine. St Anselm, however, who succeeded Llanfranc as Archbishop in 1093, opposed Augustine's view of Original Sin, and the way became clearer. His great pupil Eadmer, a monk of Canterbury, wrote a Tractate on the Conception of St Mary, and gradually the celebration of the feast gained ground, helped greatly by the teaching of Duns Scotus, but it was not until 1476 that it was formally approved.

It is not impossible that the toad beneath the feet of Our Lady of Walsingham may have been intended to be a powerful early statement of her Immaculate Conception. It would be good for it to be restored on the statues in the Shrines.

Images like Our Lady of Walsingham are stylised, iconographic, and with theological content. As with icons there is meaning in the details. They were carried in procession, and the faithful were enjoined to stand in the place occupied by the Wise Men and worship the Lord. But there is more. These medieval statues gave Mary huge and far-seeing eyes. Sarah Boss picks this up:

> As you gaze on the image, the Virgin in particular might give the impression of looking into you and through you, so that explicit tokens of lordship, such as the throne, are undergirded by the impression of some power, which is greater than the political, but less easily defined. As the viewer of such an image, you might feel to be the object of the statue's gaze, and to be in some way subject to its uncanny authority.[33]

It is thus an image intended to raise up the worshipper to the true dignity of being one of the children of God, to instil in us a sense of the sacred, and of our own worth. It is an image of the Incarnation, the central mystery of the Shrine in Walsingham, the awesome truth that

> the human woman who gives her body to divinity becomes the Mother of God, and is thereby exalted to a position which is higher even than that of the all-spiritual angels, for she is enthroned as Queen of Heaven. The willingness of the spirit to be united with matter, the potential of matter to receive the spirit, and the bonding of divinity with the physical creation: these are the truths, which the Virgin and Child embody.[34]

It acclaims the truth that we are all called, in the words of St Peter, 'to become partakers of the divine nature'[35] and in the prayer of the Liturgy, that we 'may we come to share in the divinity of Christ, who humbled himself to share in our humanity.'[36] Our destiny is to be crowned, like Mary, in the Kingdom of God.

CHAPTER 7

PILGRIMAGE AND PILGRIMS

Britain, even before the Norman Conquest, was honeycombed with local shrines. We are told in the Chronicle of Evesham Abbey, written around 1230, that 'in the olden time, before the coming of the Normans into England, the monastery was through the workings of God's mercy so often lit up by the miracles of this holy man that it was rare for the sun to go down on a Saturday without some sick person, in the grips of some infirmity or trouble, having obtained relief through St Ecgwin.'[1] By the Middle Ages pilgrimage had become a popular and distinctive feature of Christian life, with good reason. Life for the vast majority was brutal and short, disease was rampant, and a miracle often the only hope of healing and relief from pain. Eamon Duffy tells us that shrines

> opened a window of hope on a daunting world of sickness, pain and natural calamity. Men and women fled to the protection of the saints from a world in which children fall from trees or tumble down wells, crawl into fires, or jump in play onto sharpened sticks or untended metal spits. Workmen are crushed or ruptured by heavy loads or blinded by branches, women die in the agonies of prolonged childbirth. We catch a glimpse of a whole gallery of devastating diseases – bone cancer, gangrene, epilepsy, paralysis – of homes wrecked by insanity, and entire families of villages decimated by plague or famine. The sick and the halt clustered round the shrines, sleeping on or near it for days and nights at a time, touching the diseased parts of their body to sacred stone or wood.[2]

Many miracles were recorded. Bishops and shrine authorities would sometimes solicit testimonies of miracles, and these were investigated within the protocols of the time. Whenever they believed themselves cured pilgrims were expected to bring along witnesses, and if a miracle were certified a solemn *Te Deum* would be sung. Word soon got round. When a certain Withgar was cured of a crippling condition at St Etheldreda's shrine at Ely, 'the news travelled far. Flocks of invalids were attracted, and marvels of healing were performed.'[3] And according to the Pynson Ballad of Walsingham:

> Many sick have been cured here by our Lady's might
> Dead again revived, of this is no doubt
> Lame made whole, and blind restored to sight
> Mariners vexed with tempest safe to port brought
> Deaf, wounded, and lunatics that hither have sought
> And also lepers have recovered here,
> By our Lady's grace from their infirmity.[4]

Pilgrims, Relics, Images and Saints

People gathered, as we still do, to pray beside the tomb or relic of a saint. By a similar instinct people often speak to a loved one at their grave or in their home, feeling they are near. Who can gainsay them? We belong to the communion of saints. In the monastery at Worcester there is a touching description of the monks who, 'if they ailed at all in body or were troubled in mind they whispered it to the bishop (Wulfstan) just as though he were still alive.'[5]

Reports of a miracle could all too quickly establish a cult, and the Church was aware of the dangers. In 1102, Anselm, Archbishop of Canterbury, issued a warning that 'no-one should, with audacious innovation, treat springs or dead bodies or other things as holy, which we have known to happen, without episcopal authorisation'.[6] Formal canonisation procedures were tightened during the twelfth century, with increasing emphasis on verification. The record had to conform to what were currently taken to be scientific standards of truth.[7] Yet there was an ambiguity, for saints had first to prove their sanctity by performing miracles (as is still the case for canonisation today), before a cult was allowed, but it was miracles that led to the cult. Pilgrims had no compunction in abandoning an old shrine if a new shrine was reporting more powerful helpers.

Saints who had worked miracles during their lifetime would naturally continue to do so after their death, indeed more so, and the medieval mind saw nothing odd in removing a relic from the body of a saint and giving it as a gift to a monastery or to an eminent person such as a king. When relics were distributed they enabled more devout persons to come into contact with the saint, who could thereby help more people, especially in a large town, which lacked a canonised saint.

The most prized relic was the True Cross, which Helena had discovered in Jerusalem, and also the Precious Blood of Jesus, some dried blood thought to have dripped from the cross, or sometimes the Precious Blood of the Mass. The crusaders were keen to bring back relics from the Holy Land, some genuine and others of more doubtful provenance. Although the Church requires strict authenticity for relics, on another level it isn't so important. If you have ever kissed a relic of the True Cross or venerated a crucifix in the Liturgy on Good Friday you will know that it is devotion to the cross and the love of Jesus that occupies your mind, and the object itself is simply a focus for devotion. Real damage was done, however, in the sixteenth century by a scandalous trade in spurious and incredible relics, to the mockery of Catholic reformers like Erasmus, and the furious indignation of Protestants.

Images became popular after about 1200 and, as devotion to Our Lady increased, they opened up a whole new opportunity for pilgrimage and the proliferation of shrines all over Europe. Bishops during the fourteenth century were vigilant to try and ensure that the statues themselves were not credited with supernatural powers or the cause of idolatry, but certain images, like Our Lady of Walsingham, attracted exceptional devotion and established a reputation for miracles, and answers to prayer. King Richard II noted that miracles strengthened people's faith, and they undoubtedly strengthened his own faith and devotion, as when Archbishop Arundel informed him of a miracle at Canterbury, and when he himself witnessed one of his own household cured of blindness when they were on pilgrimage at Ely.[8] Testimonies of miracles were variously used in canonisation procedures, for devotional reading and, as they are today, in preaching, to inspire faith and trust in Jesus Christ, as evidence of God's activity in the world.

Grateful pilgrims who had been healed would often leave at the shrine a votive offering, perhaps a plaque of silver or wax, sometimes fashioned into the shape of a body part, perhaps a leg or arm, that had been healed. People were less inhibited than we may be, but even Thomas More was amused at the Shrine of St Valery in Picardy, specialising in genital disorders, infertility, and impotence, to see hanging on the walls 'none other thynge but mennes gere and womens gere made in waxe.'[9] Litters on which the sick had been carried, sticks, and crutches, were left behind at shrines as proof of healing, models of ships by those saved from shipwreck or drowning. People who prayed at home for healing, might promise to make a pilgrimage of thanksgiving to the particular saint or shrine, if they were cured. Much as in the old pagan pilgrimage to Mercury, they would bring a votive offering in gratitude that the prayer had been heard. Two Welsh soldiers, Thomas Basseagle of Cardiff and John Williams of Howell, vowed that if they survived the Battle of Agincourt they would make a pilgrimage to Walsingham. Sadly they got themselves into some sort of trouble in Cawston, and were whisked off to prison in Cambridge before they got there.[10]

No records survive to tell us how many pilgrims came to Walsingham, and only scanty references provide us with names, but the roads were thronged. It was one of a few that developed from a local shrine to attract pilgrims from all over England and beyond. Eamon Duffy points out that in the late Middle Ages the great majority of people frequented their local shrines in huge numbers, rarely travelling further than the nearest market town, perhaps to the cathedral.[11] And most of them, according to Susan Morrison, were women and lower class, for the men were more tied. The majority of those with the time or powerful motivation to travel to foreign shrines like Jerusalem, Rome and Compostela were male and upper class.[12]

From the pilgrim Etheria in the fourth century, to St Bridget of Sweden in the fourteenth, and Margery Kempe, the devout woman from King's Lynn who travelled to shrines all over Europe, and from the records of wills and gifts, we know just how seriously devout women took their pilgrimages. But there was understandable concern for their safety. Thomas Walsham, a former canon of Walsingham, was accused of raping a Walsingham woman, Emma, wife of William Bole, and stealing goods and chattels worth £20 from her purse, when they were on a pilgrimage to Canterbury in 1398.[13] For fear of this many women travelled disguised as men. In the *Gentle Herdsman*, a romantic ballad found in a manuscript dated about 1650 (composed, it may be assumed, either before or just after the destruction of the Shrine at Walsingham, while the memory was fresh in peoples' minds) a woman pilgrim disguised as a man, burdened with a grievous offence, asks a shepherd the way to Walsingham. After expressing his surprise that someone so young and fair of face could possibly have committed a great crime, she tells him:

> 'I am not what I seeme to be,
> My clothes and sex doe differ far:
> I am a woman, woe is me!
> Born to greefe and irksome care.'[14]

Walsingham did, however, draw women in great numbers, with its most prized relic of Our Lady's milk as well as its image of Our Lady. The needs of women are heart rending: to become pregnant, for help to stop haemorrhaging, after miscarriages, to expel a dead foetus, to have a safe delivery, postpartum problems, pain, and lack of milk, often their only hope a miracle.

There are about eighty rood screens surviving in Norfolk churches, and Susan Morrison is interested to note the significance of some of the women saints depicted in them on pilgrim routes to Walsingham.[15] In East Dereham church the pilgrim on the way to Walsingham would kneel before the painting of St Withburga and a tame deer that provided her with milk, and before St Etheldreda (or Audrey) who had two chaste marriages and is depicted as an abbess, with two does who supplied the community she founded at Ely with milk. St Dorothy is depicted on the screen at North Elmham and on many others, and she was the patron saint invoked against miscarriage. St Barbara, who was invoked in childbirth, appears in East Dereham and in other places. St Margaret of Antioch, another patron saint of childbirth, appears on many screens, including Ranworth, which has many other women saints and children as well.

Most interesting is the screen in the beautiful church of Houghton St Giles, above the Slipper Chapel, where pilgrims would pray, and still do, during their pilgrimage to Walsingham. All the women saints in the screen are on the left (the 'women's side' of a medieval church, still maintained by brides), while the men are on the right. Here childless women would pray and find solace gazing at women with their children. St Emeria (it is thought) and the young Servatius, St Mary Salome with James and John, Our Lady with her Son, Mary Cleophas and her four sons, Elizabeth who conceived in old age, with her son John, and St Anne, the mother of Our Lady, teaching her to read. Before them women would pour out their hearts for a child. St Giles, the church's patron, a saint made popular by the crusaders, is well known as the patron saint of lepers, beggars, and those who are lame, but he was also invoked by women unable to conceive and by nursing mothers. He is depicted with a deer who supplied him with milk while living as a hermit.

The need for healing was not the only motive for pilgrimage. Those who had not embraced the hardships and ascetic life of a monk might voluntarily undertake a pilgrimage, countering their relatively comfortable life. An arduous pilgrimage was a form of self-denial, and it was often linked with almsgiving to help the poor or fellow pilgrims along the way. 'Love covers a multitude of sins.'[16] There were penniless pilgrims, and for others it was part of a pilgrimage to give alms to the poor. Richard, chaplain to the sheriff of Devon, vowed to give alms to every pilgrim he met on the road who asked him in the name of St Thomas.[17]

After the Black Death, which led to a huge labour shortage and the Peasants' Revolt of 1381, with their demand for better conditions, parliament had a purge on begging pilgrims (and university students) who were deemed capable of work, requiring letters testimonial to justify their pilgrimage, otherwise they could be jailed or put in the stocks. One fear was that servants and labourers might break their manorial service by looking for better employment elsewhere on the pretext of pilgrimage. In 1399 parliament ordered that 'no pilgrim pass out of the realm except from Dover.' This port restriction was further tightened, preventing pilgrims from leaving England without special licence. There were controls on money and valuables being taken out of the country.[18]

Pilgrimage was also a sign of repentance and remorse. Fasting or abstinence might be part of it, and some might choose to walk barefoot. After the murder of Archbishop Thomas Becket of Canterbury, for which he felt responsible, King Henry II walked barefoot to Canterbury and his 'tender feet' bled copiously.[19] Many records tell of pilgrims simply wanting to go and pray or to gain an indulgence. Indulgences were no doubt as misunderstood in medieval days as they are today. They do not earn God's forgiveness, but are meant to express sorrow or make restitution for some harm that has been done, which really deserves punishment or penance. If a man steals something then he should give it back if his sorrow is real. But if you hurt someone you are never going to see again, cannot return what has been stolen, or can never make up for what you have done, a penance helps assuage guilt and takes the place of punishment. At a time when penances were sometimes arduous or very public, they might be commuted by an indulgence instead, which is why days and time were attached to them. A penitent might go on pilgrimage, or undertake some work of mercy or generosity, to obtain an indulgence. Very oddly and mistakenly in the popular mind it came to mean so many days off purgatory because pilgrimages could be made for and dedicated to someone who had died.

People left money in their wills for a relative or someone else to make a pilgrimage on their behalf and pray for their soul. Diane Webb has documented some of them.[20] Nicholas Culpeper left four marks to his wife, Elizabeth, to complete 'my promised pilgrimages to the Blessed Mary of Walsingham and to Canterbury.' In 1433 Master Henry Wells and Dom John Sutton were to be given £10 to go to Bridlington, Beverley and Walsingham on behalf of Benedict, Minister of the Church of St David's, 'so they can fulfil my purpose with all possible speed after my death.' This concern to reap the benefits of a pilgrimage as soon as possible was frequently expressed.

Edward Storey, the Bishop of Chichester, in 1502 left five marks to his chaplain, Nicholas Taverner, to go on his behalf to Our Lady at both Southwick and Walsingham, and to St Thomas of Canterbury. In 1531 John Benett of Raunds in Northamptonshire wanted an 'honest man' to go to Walsingham for him, leaving 13s.4d to cover his daily wage as well as alms and offerings to disburse to the poor on the way. Sometimes the testator might impose conditions to enhance the value of the pilgrimage. Hugh Peyntour of London in 1361 wanted pilgrimages to various places, including Canterbury and Walsingham, on naked feet. John de Holegh, a hosier and parishioner of St Mary le Bow, Cheapside, set aside a sum of money in 1348 for 'everyone going with naked feet to offer a penny at the Shrine of Our Lady of Walsingham.'[21] One John Haly wrote early in 1531 of his intention to visit Walsingham and Cambridge, and in the following year John Beyston, a servant of the Prior of Spalding made a pilgrimage 'by order of his mother.' There were 'professional' pilgrims who responded to these appeals.

Pilgrimage, which normally was voluntary, might even be imposed as a penance for sins. Adultery was taken very seriously. Simon Heyroun of Woldham in 1320 had to go every year for seven years to Canterbury, and three times each to Hereford, Bury and Walsingham within the same period. Another adulterer had to visit Canterbury, Bury and Our Lady of Walsingham on foot.[22]

Justices often deemed pilgrimage preferable to fines for poachers, breachers of the peace, and other miscreants. They were normally sent to local shrines, perhaps the cathedral, where they could be kept under close supervision and out of mischief. Philip Crikyere had been sentenced to imprisonment at Hereford Jail for extortion, but persuaded his keeper to allow him to go on pilgrimage to Walsingham. Most regrettably, on the way back he was involved in a brawl in which he killed a man, and that is why we have a record of his pilgrimage.[23]

It would perhaps be misleading to assume that the great majority of pilgrims went in search of healing, or in thanksgiving for prayers granted, or for reasons of self-denial, indulgence, and penance. Parish Guilds, and groups of parishioners got together to go to a shrine, meeting new people and enjoying a change of scenery. They went not only to pray, but for the fellowship, festivities, and fairs, for Holy Days could be holidays from the routines of everyday life. Pilgrims circulated news and gossip all around the country. The Pastons of Norfolk first heard about the plague from pilgrims coming to Walsingham from the south.[24] From the fourteenth century we begin to hear criticism in the Church that some pilgrims seemed to have little or no religious motive at all, and that some had quite unworthy motives for going, leaving the restraints of home behind to enjoy illicit liaisons and excitement. Chaucer had great fun with his tales of lecherous pilgrims. But for most it was the journey of a lifetime to go to a famous shrine. Erasmus tells us that it was the ambition of everyone in England to go to Walsingham once during their life.

They came not only from England. As we may surmise from its huge and ornamented medieval churches, Norfolk was not the quiet corner of England we know today, but the most densely populated and richest county of England, with Norwich second only to London. Diane Webb affirms, 'the national appeal of Walsingham, aided by a position which was accessible both from the north and south, is beyond doubt.'[25] In medieval England the north coast of Norfolk was the entrance of the wider world. Its ports, cities, monasteries and shrines were popular destinations for merchants and pilgrims from northern Europe. King's Lynn was the major gateway from the continent. It was full of Religious Houses providing accommodation, and like Norwich had settled communities of 'strangers.'[26] Howard Fears offers a list of foreign pilgrims given King's licence to visit Walsingham in the 1360s, who include

John, Duke of Brittany, his nephew, the Duke of Anjou, a French hostage, Gerard de Boucher, another hostage, Amanda de Landa of Douai, Guy, Count of St Pol, and safe conduct to David Bruce, and to King David of Scotland accompanied by twenty knights.[27] One of the last to see Walsingham in all its glory was Thomas O'Reef, an Irish priest, dismissed by his bishop for 'popishness', whose visit is mentioned in 1538.[28]

It has been observed that Europe was formed by pilgrims:

> In a time when Christianity, enclosed in a world that threatened to collapse in upon itself in a systematic disintegration, was flanked one side by the pressure of Islam and blocked on the other by unknown lands and oceans, pilgrimages developed an international spirit, keeping alive the relations between different peoples, overcoming the barriers of distance and every obstacle with an incredible vitality, promoting and feeding knowledge, connections, and communion among different churches, conquering the isolation experienced by different regions.[29]

Pilgrimage in England was seasonal. There were exceptions. Henry VIII went to Walsingham in January 1511, and some pilgrims came on 7 December 1537,[30] but few travelled to English shrines between November and January. Out they came in Lent and Easter with the better weather. Unlike pilgrims today the great majority were between the ages of twenty-five and thirty-four, and the next largest group under twenty-five. Few were over forty-five, other than royalty and the wealthy who had a longer life expectancy.[31]

Some pilgrims carried a scrip and staff, as Jesus had prescribed for his seventy-two disciples on their journey, and before setting out received a blessing in a short ceremony in their parish church. On foot they might expect to travel about twenty-two miles on a good day, (as did John Paston when he walked from Norwich to Canterbury) but fewer when the roads had been churned into mud by rain and horses. Chaucer's more leisurely pilgrims made their first overnight stop at Dartford, fifteen miles from their start. The stars of the Milky Way were called the Walsingham Way, because it was said they illuminated the pilgrims' path to Walsingham. All around Walsingham there are lanes called 'Greenway', an old name for a pilgrim path.

In 2003, a figure of Our Lord was found by a labourer hoeing sugar beet in a field near Downham Market, on the pilgrim way between Ely and Walsingham. It must have fallen from a processional cross being carried by a group of pilgrims making their way to Walsingham. The figure of Christ, wearing a Colobium, fashioned in Chamleve enamel and gilt metal, stands about six inches high and was probably made in Limoges in the thirteenth century. It still retains the gentle folds of its robe with fragments of stunning colours. Few were made, but there is one in the Ashmolean Museum.[32] After it was found two men, Dave Flowers and Alan Davies, walked with it to Walsingham to complete its journey, and short services of welcome were held in the Slipper Chapel and Anglican Holy House, remembering the pilgrims who first carried it.

Roads, Bridges, Chapels and Inns

All these travellers required hostels, hospitals and inns along the routes. Archbishop Stratford in 1342 made it clear that 'poor sick pilgrims' were to be received in preference to the healthy, who could be accommodated for only one night.[33] In any case the better off would be expected to use an inn. Leonard Whatmore notes that at least a dozen Augustinian Houses in Norfolk seem to lie on the pilgrim routes to Walsingham.[34] The guesthouse of West Acre Priory was built especially large to accommodate pilgrims to Walsingham, and there was a large hospital at Castle Acre Priory that must have been used by sick pilgrims, many of whom would have died on the way. Around 1226 the Hospital at Billingford, on the pilgrim way, was founded by William de Bec, and accommodated thirteen pilgrims, but whether it originated as a pilgrim hospice is not certain. Croyland Abbey in Lincolnshire was a point of convergence for pilgrims from the north and midlands. It once had a mischievous gatekeeper who was reported to the Bishop on 30 June 1519 for laughing at pilgrims asking the way to Walsingham, and sending them off in the wrong direction.[35] People earned their living serving pilgrims. Boatmen, especially on the Thames, ferried pilgrims and horses. Traders like shoemakers and innkeepers were kept busy.

Roads and bridges had to be kept in repair and this was considered an important and charitable work, much of it undertaken by Religious Houses. Mindful, no doubt, of the many pilgrims who came by sea to Walsingham, the Prior of Walsingham built a good bridge on the road between St Andrew's Burnham and St Clement's.[36] Many bridges had a Chapel on them, and four

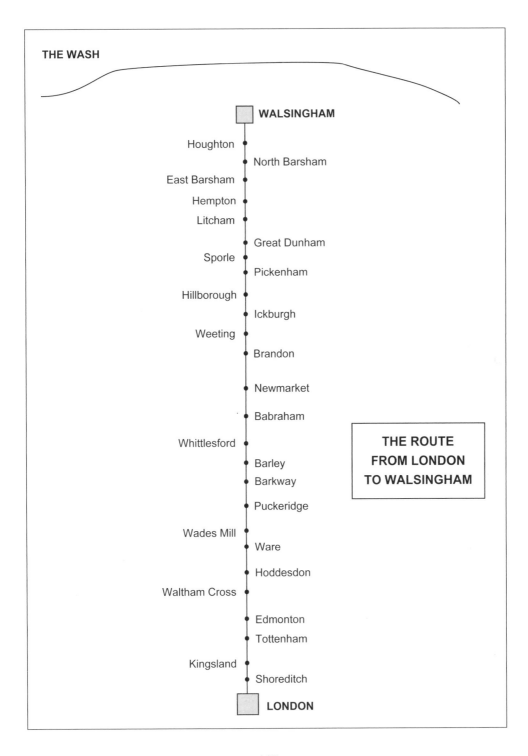

THE WASH

WALSINGHAM

Houghton
North Barsham
East Barsham
Hempton
Litcham
Great Dunham
Sporle
Pickenham
Hillborough
Ickburgh
Weeting
Brandon
Newmarket
Babraham
Whittlesford
Barley
Barkway
Puckeridge
Wades Mill
Ware
Hoddesdon
Waltham Cross
Edmonton
Tottenham
Kingsland
Shoreditch

LONDON

**THE ROUTE
FROM LONDON
TO WALSINGHAM**

of them survive. Rotherham has a particularly fine example, the Chapel of Our Lady, built in 1483. At St Ives is the Chapel of St Ledger, built in the early fifteenth century, and now used for Mass again. These bridge chapels were served by hermits who maintained the bridge.

All the pilgrim roads had chapels on them, where pilgrims stopped for Mass and prayers, but sadly few survive. There is a ruined one at Wighton, near Walsingham, and nearby ones at Hilborough, South Acre, West Acre, Priors-Thorns, Cockley Cley, Stanhoe, and Caston, where as in other places the local Guild of our Lady kept a lamp burning.[37] Along with the Slipper Chapel, the finest survivor is the Red Mount Chapel at King's Lynn, where the routes to Walsingham from the north and west converged, meeting pilgrims from the Baltic, Netherlands or Scotland, in this port, which was as important to the Middle Ages as Liverpool in the Industrial Revolution.[38] The 'Gild of Our Lady on the Mount' had a chapel there in 1329, where pilgrims would gather, and between 1483 and 1485 the soil was raised around it and the present octagon with two storeys was built above it. The upper storey is a chapel, and between it and the lower chapel the priest had his sacristy. The fan tracery resembles that of the chapel of King's College, Cambridge, which gives an idea of the quality of this perpendicular style building with its buttresses and stone windows. Prior William Spynke, of the nearby Benedictine Monastery of St Margaret's, a cell of Norwich Cathedral, was responsible for the work, and he employed Robert Currance as his architect. It was designed for a constant flow of pilgrims because two staircases run around it. Alas, it did not have a long life, for in 1536 the town's friaries and monasteries were dissolved under the orders of Henry VIII, and in 1538 the pilgrimage to Walsingham came to an end. Our Lady's Chapel eventually fell into decay and became a cistern, a stable, observatory and even a gunpowder store, but in the nineteenth century it was restored through the efforts of two Anglican priests, and has been further restored and opened to the public, and a Catholic Mass is once again celebrated there.

Once they reached journey's end pilgrims found abundant accommodation. St Alban's had 92 *hostitia* (inns). Glastonbury had 95 or more. Some of these pilgrim hostels were grand buildings still standing today, as they are in Walsingham. It is not known how many there were in Walsingham, but we know of twenty-one.[39] Opposite St Mary's, Church House probably occupies the site of The George. There was a Guild of St George in the parish church, a favourite saint brought back from the Holy Land by the crusaders. On the High Street, where Swallows restaurant stands, was probably The White Horse, and a little beyond it Dow (Dove) House, later called The Beere (Bear). Then in Friday Market Place is The Black Lion. Formerly known as The Crownyd Lion, it has always been one of the most important inns in Walsingham, once again a pilgrims' haunt. The Cock was just off Station Road in the little turning on the right beside Chantry House, and at the top of Station Road is the imposing Guisborough House, once The King's Head. Back towards the High Street, on a part of the street formerly known as Thorngate, stood The Moon and Stars, referring to Our Lady, and The Saracen's Head, a reference to the crusades or the Mercedarians who ransomed Christian slaves from the Saracens (Moslems). One of these may have been the present Oxford Stores. Turning left into the High Street is an entry beside the Guild Shop, once occupied, it is thought, by The Ram. The Falcon on the left of the High Street comprised the Old Bakehouse and Falcon House, an impressive property with Georgian facades, that conceal the older building behind, in which there was a banqueting hall beneath a fine beamed roof still to be seen. Erasmus is believed to have stayed here. Next was The Swan, occupied now by the Marist Sisters, on the corner of Swan entry, the route believed to have been taken by George Guisborough and Fr Nicholas Mileham to their execution for involvement in the Walsingham Conspiracy to save the Shrine from destruction in the reign of Henry VIII.

Not all of the inns had a good reputation, for after Easter 1431 four of them were destroyed in a fire. A chronicler wrote, 'no mortal person knows by whose agency or how this disaster occurred, unless it were vengeance because their inmates extorted such excessive and unjust charges for food from the pilgrims who came there.'[40] A little up Swan Entry, extending over the archway, was The Angel, which in 1532 was referred to as 'The Angel now wasted', meaning that it may have been one of the four inns destroyed by arson.

At the end of the High Street the road narrows into Bridewell Street, named after the prison behind the cottages on the left, standing on the site of the old leper hospital. Along Bridewell Street around Chapel Yard was The Chekker or Chequers, perhaps once used for changing money, and maybe the inn where Edward I, as a youth, was nearly killed by falling masonry, a miraculous escape he attributed to Our Lady of Walsingham. At the end of

Bridewell Street on the left was The Bolt and Toun (Tun). Opposite Bridewell Street on Egmere Road, around Robin Hood Cottage, was The White Hart, the emblem of Richard II, and a little higher up the Mayden's (Maiden's) Head. Going back down Guild Street, on the left, around the newer houses in Crown Yard, once stood The Crown, possibly the large house on the left that became a bakery. At the bottom of Guild Street, the fish and chip shop stands on the site of The Exchange Inn, a strategic location for pilgrims arriving from the coast. Finally, we know of The Bull, named not after the animal, but more likely a Papal Bull, an important document from the pope to which was attached his 'bulla' or seal. And it is as thronged with pilgrims today, as it must have been of old. These are the inns we know of, but there were, no doubt, many more.

The Priory had a guesthouse reserved for more important pilgrims, the long building incorporating the Museum today, while the Friary offered free accommodation to the poor. It is likely that private householders supplemented their incomes by providing food and lodging to pilgrims on their journey and at their destination, which they did again in Walsingham for many years after Fr Patten restored the Anglican Shrine. Doubtless pilgrims of old had stories to tell. The author recalls staying at Miss Struggles' house in the High Street, which she warned us was haunted by Bishop O'Rorke, and was littered with bewildering notices like, 'Men must not shave in the bathroom', and 'The toilet must only be flushed in the morning'.

Pilgrim Badges and Ampullae

Like holidaymakers and pilgrims today, and the old pilgrims to Mercury, the medieval pilgrim liked to bring back some souvenirs or gifts, pilgrim badges, or 'signaculae' as they were called, most often a brooch secured by pin or clasp to the hat or clothes. They were a proof that pilgrims had reached their destination, and they were treasured gifts to take home to those they had prayed for and remembered at the shrine. King Henry VII spent 65 shillings to buy badges for himself and his retinue, having prayed devoutly to be preserved from his enemies.[41] Perhaps too, they conveyed something of the blessings experienced at the shrine, and were a focus for continuing devotion. Samples of soil and scrapings from the tombs of saints were taken, and the pilfering of fragments of stone from the Holy Sepulchre and other places in the Holy Land, and the carving of graffiti, became so serious it was forbidden under pain of excommunication. Signaculae might be made of all kinds of material from glass, pottery or wood to brass or gold, but the majority were made of a tin-lead alloy.

Walsingham badges have been uncovered in London and other places, as well as in Norfolk, and Brian Spencer has made a detailed study of them.[42] Mass production of badges seems to have begun at Canterbury in the twelfth century, and quickly reached Walsingham. When Cromwell's commissioners came to Walsingham Priory in 1536 they reported finding what they called 'a secrete privye place within the house … in wiche there were instrewmentes, pottes, belowes, flyes of such strange colours as the lick none of us had scene, with poyses and other things to sorte, and dewyd gould and silver, nothing there wantinge that should belonge to the arte of multyplyeng.'[43] This was evidently the Priory workshop for making pilgrim badges, which the hostile commissioners were trying to suggest, was for forgery. A similar one existed at Canterbury.

Two fifteenth-century moulds for making Walsingham Pilgrim Badges were found near St Mary's Walsingham, and they are made of fine-grained limestone imported from Solnhofen, Bavaria, the very best for manufacturing high quality badges. These particular moulds were used to produce five-pointed star badges of the Annunciation, one of which included an arrow. Best quality eutectic pewter was often used, an alloy of three parts tin to two parts lead, which shone brightly. Badges with a higher lead content were no doubt produced for the mass market, not only in the Priory but also by local shopkeepers, while others were made of silver, gold or copper alloy.[44] In the second half of the fifteenth century the technique of die-stamping was invented, and this was taken up enthusiastically in Walsingham.[45] Unsurprisingly, since it was at the heart of the Shrine's devotion, of all the surviving Walsingham badges, those depicting the Annunciation are by far the most numerous, and there is an especially beautiful golden one 1¼ins. in diameter in the Museum of London. More curious are hunting horns inscribed *Ave Maria*,

found in London, which Spencer suggests may represent 'the hunting horn on which Gabriel sometimes blows his Ave to the Virgin.'[46]

You find, as you would expect, badges of Our Lady of Walsingham. Other Marian shrines contained statues of the crowned virgin, but it may be assumed that badges found around King's Lynn are from Walsingham. One type depicts pilgrims kneeling before her. The large far-seeing eyes, typical of the medieval statue are clearly visible.

Badges of the Holy House have also been found in huge numbers, indicating that although the statue was an object of great devotion, the Holy House remained one too. They depict a two-storey building, which archaeology confirms was the case, and may be a

good representation of what it actually looked like. Spencer describes them: 'Varying considerably in size and date, they invariably show a roof with three crosses on the ridge and a 'clerestory' of three windows beneath it, perched on the gable-ends of an upper story.

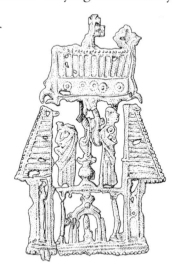

In the middle of this floor stands either the statue of Our Lady or a scene of the Annunciation. Under the eaves, a lower story has a central doorway flanked by windows.'[47]

Badges of the Shrine's famous miracle of the Knight's Gate have been found in Norfolk and London. It happened in 1314. The miracle is still recalled in Walsingham today by the Knight's Gate, a doorway, opposite Knight Street and the Anglican Shrine. Dickinson notes that it has been radically restored, but that on the inner face are the remains of a pointed arch, which may be of thirteenth century date.[48] Erasmus describes what happened:

> a knight (*identified as Sir Raaf Boutetourt by the eighteenth-century historian and topographer, Francis Blomefield, who had access to a different source*), seated on his horse, escaped by this door from the hands of his enemy, who was at the time closely pressing upon him. The wretched man, thinking himself lost, by a sudden aspiration commended his safety to the Virgin, who was so near: for he had determined to fly to her altar, if the gate had been open. And lo! The unheard-of occurrence! On a sudden the man and horse were together within the precincts of the church, and the pursuer fruitlessly storming without…(Our guide) pointed out a brass plate near to the gate representing the knight who was saved, attired in the fashion then usual in England, and which we now see in old pictures.[49]

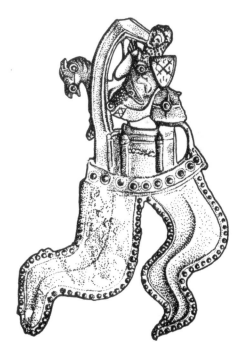

In the badge the knight's hands are joined in prayer; he and his horse are already half through the little doorway, above a star of wavy rays.

The relic of Mary's Milk, kept on the Priory's high altar, was commemorated by a badge in the shape of a monstrance containing a little white phial. Walsingham's Pietà was obviously very popular because it too features on badges found in several places in England, including the Beauchamp Chapel in St Mary's, Warwick.[50] Spencer points out that the remarkably large number of Walsingham badges dating from the turn of the fifteenth century shows how immensely popular Walsingham was right up to its destruction.

Pilgrims not only returned home with badges, but like Walsingham pilgrims today they took back water from the holy wells in containers, *ampullae*, as they were called, though they were very small and the water was sealed within them. Dating from the second quarter of the thirteenth century they came in different shapes and sizes, with handles so they could be worn around the neck. Wooden boxes were used before this date. Some *ampullae* incorporating a scallop shell have been found in King's Lynn and are assumed to be from Walsingham, for although the scallop shell is especially associated with Santiago de Compostela, it became an emblem of pilgrimage generally. Some of these shell *ampullae* include the Annunciation lily-pot on the floor between Gabriel and Our Lady, and one was found buried in a grave at Thetford with a man whose skeleton revealed a diseased hip bone.[51] He must have carried it in the hope of being cured, and his relatives buried it with him. Others are known to have done the same. His particular *ampulla* had an R engraved in a circle beneath the lily-pot, and it has been suggested that it may refer to Richeldis.[52]

Some *ampullae* were in the shape of a church, within which is Our Lady or the Annunciation, and one in beautiful condition shows the Coronation of Our Lady by her Son. It is, of course, difficult to identify which shrine all these *ampullae* came from, though some of them have a crowned W engraved upon them, which may well locate them to Walsingham where King Henry III had Our Lady crowned in gold.

How devoted people were to shrines and pilgrimages is very evident in their generosity when they got there, and in their bequests. In her study of wills, Diana Webb concluded that a testator wealthy enough to think of several shrines, would be most likely to include Walsingham or Canterbury or both. The wealthy might leave precious statues, jewellery and expensive gifts. There are many records of gifts and these are but a few examples. Archbishop Walter Reynolds of Canterbury, who died in 1327, left altar ornaments and fittings to Our Lady of Walsingham.[53] Henry, Earl of Lancaster, who died in 1345, gave a picture of the Annunciation, valued at 400 marks. His son, Duke Henry left valuable vessels.[54] John, Earl of Warenne bequeathed jewels and plate to Our Lady of Walsingham and to several other shrines. Lady Elizabeth de Burgh, Countess of Clare, who founded the Friary in Walsingham, bequeathed £4, two cloths of gold, and a silver enamel cup to the Priory in 1360. A few years later Sir Thomas Uvedale gave a silver tablet gilt of the Annunciation, a painted image of Our Lady, and 10 marks towards the building of the choir. In 1380 Edmund, Earl of March, devised to the Holy House forty marks and an elaborate set of white vestments and altar furnishings.[55] 1381 the Earl of Suffolk bequeathed a silver statue of a mounted knight bearing his arms. In 1433 the Bishop of Worcester left his collection of relics that he had acquired in Rome. Sir William Estfeld, mercer, and twice Lord Mayor of London in the fifteenth century, bequeathed a gold collar set with precious stones and pearls to Our Lady of Walsingham. The earl of Warwick's wife, Isabella, in 1439 willed several bequests of images to Our Lady of Walsingham and to other shrines near Warwick. Lady Anne Scrope of Harling left 'beads of gold laced with crimson silk and gold' to Walsingham and three other shrines. William Mauleverer in 1498 left a diamond ring 'that King Richard gave me' to Our Lady of Walsingham. Dame Catherine Hastings, in 1507, left to Our Lady of Walsingham her 'velvet gown'.

Wills provide evidence of others not so notable but equally generous and devout. The Lincoln wills for the years 1516–32 contain fourteen bequests to Our Lady of Walsingham from people of no great social importance, mostly small sums of money from 4d to 1s. Richard Smyth left offerings for three masses in successive years, and Catherine Barton a girdle with a silver buckle. Anne Barett of Bury bequeathed her coral beads, wedding ring and things hanging on it.[56]

This evidence of pilgrimage and pilgrims is necessarily fragmentary, all the registers of the Priory and Friary having been destroyed. We do, however, have a good deal of information about the pilgrimages of England's kings and queens, whose public duty it was to uphold the Christian Faith in their realm, support its major shrines and churches, and set an example of personal piety to their people.

CHAPTER 8

ROYAL PATRONAGE

No one in eleventh-century Europe would have understood the distinction we make between Church and State, between the religious and the secular. At their coronation kings became God's chosen and anointed representatives on earth, as did bishops and priests at their ordination. Christendom was a single entity in which the Pope and his bishops, monarchs and their princes, shared their God-given responsibilities. Jesus had sent out the apostles to teach and baptise whole nations, not just individuals, and St Paul understood the responsibility of the Church to encourage good government.[1] Both Jewish and Pagan converts were familiar with the interconnections between religion and politics in their former religions, and these were naturally carried over into Christianity.

Emperor Constantine quickly grasped Christianity's potential for constructing social cohesion and stability, and conversely the danger for society when the Church was divided. Eusebius said Constantine thought of himself as a 'bishop of external affairs'. He convened General Councils of the Church. He appointed and deposed bishops, and so did Medieval kings. Responsibility for the spiritual welfare of the people was shared, but the boundaries were blurred. Many early bishops had been distinguished public officials in the Roman Empire. St Ambrose, Bishop of Milan, had been governor of Northern Italy. Pope Gregory the Great, a former Prefect of Rome, was unwillingly pulled out of his monastery to rebuild the city and protect the Empire against barbarian invasions. He did it but lamented it.

> At one moment I am forced to take part in certain civil affairs, next I must worry over the incursions of barbarians ... now I must accept political responsibility in order to give support to those who uphold the rule of law ... when I try to concentrate and gather all my intellectual resources for preaching, how can I do justice to the sacred ministry

of the Word? I am often compelled by the nature of my position to associate with men of the world and sometimes I relax the discipline of my speech.[2]

In the Middle Ages royal power within the Church increased to such an extent that politics more than spirituality could often determine the election of a pope or choice of a bishop. Scholarly bishops in the tradition of St Anselm and Robert Grosseteste were replaced by administrators and noblemen. Yet some became great and holy men. The ambiguity of the relationships of popes, bishops, kings and nobles not infrequently gave rise to abuses and bitter conflicts of interest. The quarrel between King Henry II and his great friend Thomas Becket resulted in the Archbishop's death. When Henry appointed him as Archbishop, Thomas began to live a converted life, so that instead of being the puppet Henry expected, Thomas upheld the rights of the Church against him. Absolute kings could be checked by the power of popes and bishops.

Kings as much as anyone were conscious of their need to seek strength from God and the assistance of saints. They were impelled too, some of them, by personal piety, penitence, or the hope of healing. The Royal Court was more than the seat of government or a venue for entertainment; it was a centre of worship with Mass and devotions each day.[3] Christian faith and practice, prayer and piety, were integral to the understanding of kingship. Kings were aware of their public duty to support major churches in their kingdom, and may have had reason to promote particular cults in connection with the monarchy itself, as, for example, St Edmund and St Edward the Confessor. King Cnut, whose Viking ancestors had martyred the young Edmund, naturally sought the help of his prayers at Bury. He set the pattern for royal pilgrimage, often spending the Feast of the Purification of Our Lady at St Ethelburga's in Ely, and going to many other shrines, including Rome, a sign, according to Hermann the Archdeacon, of his transformation from 'wild beast' to exemplary king.[4] After St Edmund was established, around 1020, as a national English saint, the age of 'mass' pilgrimage began.[5] St Edmund drew almost all the monarchs of England, many of whom were keen to connect with the Anglo-Saxon kings, especially after the Conquest, which had led to resentment and rebellion.

The Angevins

Henry II had an evident devotion to Our Lady. Mid-winter was a dangerous time for those who had to cross the English Channel, so he chose 8 December 1154, the Feast of the Immaculate Conception, a distinctively English feast, for his arrival from France for his coronation. He crossed the Channel again on the Feast of the Purification in 1156, and in 1158 on the Feast of the Assumption.[6] Our Lady was already being invoked as the principal protector of those at sea: *Stella Maris*, Star of the Sea, derived from the great sixth-century hymn of Venantius Fortunatus, *Ave Maris Stella*. Born in France, Henry had been the earliest known pilgrim to the new Shrine of Our Lady of Rocamadour in 1166. The martyrdom of Thomas Becket in 1170 by four knights plunged Henry II into sorrow and penitence, even though he was absolved of the murder. Shortly after it he walked barefoot with bleeding feet from the leper hospital at Harbledown to Canterbury in reparation, spending the whole night fasting and in prayer. He went back to Rocamadour in 1170, as well as to Bury and to Ely, Geddington, and Winchester where the relics of St Petroc were brought to him for veneration. 1170 was a year of deep remorse and penitence; responsibility for the death of Becket weighed heavily upon him. There is no record of him ever coming to Walsingham, suggesting that the shrine was not yet of great repute.

After 1173, Henry II was plagued by his rebellious and ambitious sons. Richard, who succeeded him, spent little time in England, and hardly spoke English. Then came King John, an excommunicated monarch, who brought down the Pope's interdict on England and the rebellion of his barons, which led to the Magna Carta. Pilgrimage played no part in their lives.

The Plantagenets

Henry III was only nine when King John died in 1216, and he made the first recorded pilgrimage to Our Lady of Walsingham in 1226. He became devoted to her, in his early years especially, sometimes staying several days. His last pilgrimage was less than two months before his death in September 1272; at least eleven pilgrimages in all. His gifts were generous, the oaks for building we have mentioned, various rents and gifts of land, but more devotional presents too, an embroidered chasuble, as well as substantial quantities of wax and tapers, including three thousand tapers for the Feast of the Assumption in 1241. In addition to the Holy Cross fair he granted a whole week's fair from the Annunciation in return for a candle to be kept burning for him before the altar. Most beautiful of all he gave twenty marks for a gold crown in 1246 to be placed on the image of Our Lady.[7]

Saints did not merely receive honour; it was thought they honoured the nation. Our Lady of Walsingham honoured England. So did relic acquisitions such as that of the Holy Blood, which Henry III received as a gift and in 1247 installed with tremendous solemnity in Westminster Abbey. The Bishop of Norwich who preached, said, 'the King of England, who was known to be the most Christian of all Christian princes' had received this gift 'in order that it might be reverenced more in England than in Syria, which was now nearly desolate; for in England, as the world knew, faith and holiness flourished more than in any other country throughout the world.'[8]

From the lists of kings, and sometimes queens, who made the pilgrimage to Walsingham, the impression may be given that they favoured Our Lady of Walsingham above all other shrines. Some of them, like Henry III and his son, Edward I, perhaps did, but they too visited many other shrines as well, integrating them into travels around the realm. Henry rarely went to Walsingham without calling at Bromholm Priory to venerate the relic of the True Cross. St Edmund in Bury was naturally part of his East Anglian tours. Wherever kings travelled around their realm they invariably paid their respects to saints en route, and sometimes arranged their travels around the shrines to honour feast days.[9]

Wherever they travelled the court went with them. The logistics of accommodating everyone, perhaps six hundred and more, and feeding them all was immense. In his 1256 East Anglian tour in Lent, a modest time when no meat was eaten, Henry nonetheless ordered twenty-five gallons of nut oil, 2000 chestnuts, and a daily supply of mackerel, some salted, some packed in bread. Outside Lent wine was ordered by the tun.[10] Nobles, bishops, abbots, and priors were expected to entertain the king lavishly.

All kings revered St Edward the Confessor in Westminster Abbey. In 1269 the new Abbey was consecrated, and Henry III himself helped carry the Confessor's coffin to its new resting place, in a rich and worthy shrine. He named his eldest son Edward and his youngest Edmund. Of his personal devotion there is no doubt. He was awed by the holiness of Anglo-Saxon kings who had abdicated and become monks, and loved the early English saints, especially Edmund. His saintly cousin, Louis IX of France, once urged him to hear more sermons and fewer masses. Henry replied with a smile that if one had a beloved friend, one would surely prefer to see him rather than just hear him talked about![11]

Edward I followed in his father's footsteps, and with good cause. When he was a youth he was playing chess in a vaulted room. Moments after he left the table a large stone from the ceiling fell on the place where he had been sitting. His chronicler wrote, 'because of which miracle he ever afterwards most ardently honoured Our Lady of Walsingham.'[12] One account tells us that the incident actually happened in Walsingham at the Chekkers (Chequers) Inn. Nonetheless it was to Bury, the Shrine of the young King Edmund, he went, straight after his father's death in 1272, and not to Walsingham until nearly five years later. Four more years passed before another visit, and then a further three. His Welsh campaigns frequently took him to St Wulfstan at Worcester. In 1289 he went to Walsingham with his Queen Eleanor, 'to fulfil his vows.' For the same reason he went again in 1292, after which his visits became almost annual and often lengthy. In 1294 he spent two weeks of Lent there. Similarly, he spent much of November 1296 in Bury with his nobles before proceeding to Ipswich for the wedding of his daughter, and eventually on to Walsingham for the Feast of the Purification of Our Lady. Here in the Holy House he concluded a treaty of reconciliation with the Earl of Flanders.[13] Many kings liked to be there for the Purification, suggesting that it may have been Walsingham's principal feast. A generous benefactor, as we have seen, his more personal offerings including several valuable gold brooches for the statues of Our Lady and St Gabriel in the Holy House, and before Our Lady's milk above the high altar of the Priory.[14] He sent a gilded kneeling image of himself to the Shrine, as his father had done at Bromholm, to be placed before Our Lady, in the manner of patrons who commissioned sacred paintings, and were included in the picture.

His son, Edward II, cared little for his duties as a king, disappointed his subjects and has been judged incompetent and deceitful. He made sixteen pilgrimages to Canterbury, and some to St Alban's. At the instigation of Queen Isabella he granted Walsingham Priory rights to acquire lands, going there with her in 1315, the first year of the great famine. He returned in 1326, the last full year of his reign, for the Purification, by then badly needing her help and compassion. Lacking the capacity to rule well, and a homosexual, his aggrieved wife conspired to force his abdication in favour of their fourteen year-old son. Imprisoned and starved, his tragic life came to a terrible end, murdered, the story goes, with a red-hot spit thrust into his bowels. Strangely, he was later popularly regarded as a saint, his grave became a place of pilgrimage and his great-grandson, Richard II, unsuccessfully petitioned Rome for his canonisation. After the murder of her lover, the pitiable Isabella spent much of her thirty years of widowhood at Castle Rising, from where she made frequent pilgrimages to find solace in nearby Walsingham.[15]

Young Edward III fulfilled all expectations of a medieval monarch, turning out to be a great soldier and leader, gaining the respect of his nobles and restoring the dignity of the throne. In his early years he frequented Bury, St Alban's, and Walsingham, and later when he was unable to come as often as he liked because of his war with France he regularly sent offerings to Walsingham and other Marian shrines. And, of course, he never forgot St Edward at Westminster and St Edmund at Bury. Most memorably he went to Walsingham with his new bride, Queen Philippa, having first sent ahead a carpenter from Windsor to build them a home in part of what is now the Black Lion. We know this because the roof structures are not of a Norfolk type, but are only found around Windsor. During a turbulent sea crossing from France in 1343 Edward made many vows and promises of works of piety. And as soon as he landed safely at Weymouth he went to London to greet his queen and set off on foot for Canterbury, and then to his father's grave at Gloucester, to Walsingham, and 'other holy places' on horseback, modestly escorted.

His eldest son, Edward, the Black Prince, who died a year before his father and never reigned as king, went to Bury and Walsingham in 1346 to pray before the Crécy campaign, joining his father at Canterbury. And they made other pilgrimages together. French hostages in England were allowed to go on pilgrimage to Walsingham and Canterbury, and the Black Prince accompanied King John II of France to Canterbury to make offerings to St Thomas and Our Lady in the crypt.[16]

It was therefore the Black Prince's son who succeeded to the throne in 1377 as Richard II, at the age of ten, the first coronation in England for fifty years. He was fifteen when he began his pilgrimages to Canterbury, offering devotions at its various shrines, and in the following spring he went on pilgrimage with his queen, to Walsingham, Norwich, Bury and Ely, where one of his courtiers was cured of blindness through the intercession of St John the Baptist and St Etheldreda.[17] He is not recorded at Walsingham again, but patronised some lesser known or newer shrines, including York, Tewkesbury, Evesham, St Chad at Lichfield and St Winifred's Well at Holywell. He was always keen to hear about miracles, and when Archbishop Arundel sent news of a miracle that Becket had wrought he wrote back effusively, saying 'we are strictly bound to thank the High Sovereign Worker of Miracles and to offer gratitude and thanks, which we desire to do unfeignedly and with all our power.'[18] He had a particular devotion to pre-conquest saints like St Winifred, St Etheldreda and St Ethelburga, and a deep desire for the intercession of St Edward the Confessor and St Edmund. Nigel Saul suggests that as the years went by he developed a more personal piety than his predecessors and that his devotion to the pre-conquest kings was to draw down the blessings of holiness on the royal line,[19] and because, in the late Middle Ages, the reign of Edward the Confessor, in particular, was revered as a golden age of peace. Both Edward and Edmund are portrayed on the Wilton Diptych, as we have noted in connection with the title 'Dowry of Mary,' which was used for the first time during his reign. Deeply unpopular at the end of his reign he was on the point of crossing to Ireland in 1399 when he told his council he wanted first to go on pilgrimage to Canterbury, but was afraid of passing through London and Kent. The Archbishop personally guaranteed his safety and he was escorted from Chester and back under heavy guard. His fears were justified. Next year he was imprisoned in the Tower, then moved to Pontefract Castle and, like his great-grandfather, murdered.

The House of Lancaster

His usurper, Henry IV, was haunted by guilt for the rest of his life for the murder of an anointed king, and all his misfortunes seemed to him like divine retribution. Inevitably his reign was blighted because he had no real claim to the throne. He had earned a reputation as a pilgrim and crusader in the Holy Land in the early 1390s, and he was crowned on the Feast of the Translation of St Edward the Confessor. No one doubted his piety and deep interest in the Church (he intervened with the Archbishop of Canterbury to help heal the Great Schism in the papacy). Records of pilgrimages are scanty in the fifteenth century, though we do know that the King went to Canterbury several times, and in 1406 he was very ill and wrote to his bishops to ask them to pray for his health. In the summer he travelled north to Lynn to see off his daughter, Princess Philippa, for her marriage in Denmark, calling on the way to pray at St Alban's, Bury, Thetford, Wymondham and Walsingham, all of which had reputations for healing.[20] By 1413 he had died, and in his will he wrote, 'I, Henry, sinful wretch…ask my lords and true people forgiveness if I have mistreated them in any wise.'[21]

His son, Henry V, in his short life and reign, went on pilgrimage to Canterbury, of course, and broke new ground in going to Bridlington to venerate St John, who was said to have prophesied that the throne would come to the House of Lancaster. And in the glory of the victory of Agincourt in 1415 he was quick to give thanks at Canterbury as soon as he landed at Dover. Reaching London he processed to St Paul's and venerated the Holy Cross, and thence to Westminster. France occupied the rest of his reign, and his pilgrimage to Walsingham came in 1421 when he brought his new French Queen, Catherine, whom he had married in Troyes Cathedral, on a royal progress to Beverley and Bridlington, and down through Lincoln, to Walsingham and Norwich. Henry's death at the age of 35 or 36 in 1422 left him with a glittering reputation, but with a son who inherited the throne of England and of France when not one year old.

Little Henry VI was frequently paraded on public occasions with his mother, while a Regency Council governed England, until he assumed the duties of kingship in 1437, the year his mother died. From Christmas 1433 until St George's Day in April 1434 he was 'dumped' on the Abbey of St Edmund's, Bury, and went back there on pilgrimage each year from 1446 to 1449. 1448 was a fervent pilgrimage year. He went to Canterbury, and later on a journey, which took him to Westminster, Waltham Abbey, Walsingham, Norwich and Bury, from where he also went to the Shrine of Our Lady at Woolpit. Returning to Westminster, he took off again to Shaftsbury, Glastonbury, Bristol and Malmesbury. Not content with that, later in the year he went up to York for a few days and then to St Cuthbert in Durham for several more, staying with the bishop and attending First Vespers, the Procession, Mass and Second Vespers on St Michael's Day. Then down to Beverley and York once more, and Lincoln. In 1449 we see him on the old East Anglian tour to Ely and Walsingham, Norwich, Bury, and to Woolpit again as well.[22]

We have mentioned the requirement of nobles, bishops and abbots to entertain the king lavishly. The Prior of Walsingham entertained Henry VI regally with venison, viand Royale, stewed capon, crane and bittern, boarshead in castell of pastry, custard with a leoparde therein sitting, basted pig, curlews and young rabbits, peacock in shining feathers, great brun, powdered ham, leach of three colours, and as a spectacle a Pelican sitting on her nest with her byrds and an image of Mr Kat holding a book.[23]

Pilgrims came to Walsingham in all kind of need, and Henry VI's wife, Queen Margaret, was no exception after eight years of a childless marriage. She came on pilgrimage and gave sumptuous oblations, including a jewel-encrusted tablet of gold, having at the centre an angel with a cameo head, bearing a ruby and pearl cross, a symbol of the Annunciation and precursor of the passion. It was valued at £29 and was one of the queen's most expensive purchases.[24] And her prayer was answered by the birth of Prince Edward in 1453.

Completely ill-equipped for kingship, Henry VI's reign was engulfed by the loss of France and the Wars of the Roses, until like others before him he was deposed and murdered in prison. More suited in some ways, perhaps, to the Religious Life, he is remembered for the foundations of Eton and King's College, Cambridge. His confessor, John Blacman, related how he said of the boys, 'I would rather have them somewhat weak in music than defective in knowledge of the scriptures.'[25] He abhorred bloodshed, pardoned criminals, and even stopped the execution of a traitor saying, 'I will not have any Christian man so cruelly handled for my sake.' The library of St Cuthbert's College, Ushaw, has a Primer of 1408 in which on the flyleaf is printed a Prayer to Henry VI, part of which reads:

> O blyssed king so full of vertue
> The flowr of all knyghthood that never was fyled
> Thou pray for us to Christe Jhesu
> And to hys modyr Mary myld.[26]

The House of York

Edward IV, his son, was everything that the people seemed to expect of their monarch, exceptionally good looking, a great warrior, an insatiable womaniser, lavish in hospitality, interested in cultural pursuits and fascinated by the printing press, whose inventor, William Caxton, was a friend and beneficiary. But he was not greatly interested in pilgrimage, though he was supposed to have a devotion to St Anne, Our Lady's mother, which was confirmed by a miracle. He was at Mass one day at Daventry in 1471 when St Anne suddenly opened the doors which concealed her image, and closed them again as though to remind the monarch that he had promised to pray and make an offering at the first image of her that he saw.[27] The Paston family heard rumours from time to time that he was going to Walsingham, including once with his wife. And he certainly was there in June 1466 after going to Bury, the year after he granted Prior Thomas and Walsingham Priory a licence to acquire more land, in return for praying for the good estate of the king and queen and for their souls after their death.[28] In 1468 he went to Walsingham with a large retinue that included his brother, Richard, Duke of Gloucester, where he was joined by the Duke of Norfolk and some two hundred men.[29]

The brief reign of Richard III left little time for pilgrimage, and ended with the Battle of Bosworth, which gave the Tudors the crown.

The Tudors

Henry VII sought Our Lady's help frequently. Two years into his reign, in 1487, with his throne in peril from the rebellion of Lambert Simnel, we are told he 'came to the place called Walsingham where he prayed devoutly before the image of the Blessed Virgin Mary (who is worshipped there with special devotion), that he might be preserved from the wiles of his enemie.' And after the battle of Stoke he sent Christopher Urswick 'to offer thanks for the victory in the Shrine of the Blessed Virgin and to place the standard there as a memorial of the favour he had received from God.'[30] He may also have come in 1489 and 1498. His will refers to a silver-gilt image of himself which he had previously given to be placed before Our Lady, and asking for another to be set before the Shrine of Thomas Becket in Canterbury. In 1505 he brought his four-year-old son, Henry.[31]

This little pilgrim was eighteen when he ascended the throne as Henry VIII on the death of his father in 1509. Sir Henry Spelman, the English Antiquarian, went to school in Walsingham in the 1570s and affirmed that people still talked about Henry VIII walking barefoot from Barsham Manor on pilgrimage to Walsingham, and that he gave her a necklace of great value.[32] This may have been at the beginning of his reign when he was praying that his wife, Katherine of Aragon, whom he married in 1509, would produce a male heir. She gave birth to Prince Henry on New Year's Day, 1511; in the depths of winter he set off to give thanks to Our Lady of Walsingham even before Katherine had been churched, and spent a week there, such was his delight and devotion. Tragically, Prince Henry died within two months, and this was the start of Henry's anguish. The fact that his wife had given him a son and heir must have seemed an answer to prayer, but to have the child so cruelly snatched away must go some way to account for the ferocity of his anger later in life. Yet he continued to seek Our Lady's help and, as we have seen, he paid for the windows of the Holy House Chapel to be glazed.

Queen Katherine came to Walsingham too. In September 1513 she wrote to Henry, who was in France, to congratulate him on taking Torney and to tell him of the great victory over the Scots at Flodden Field, concluding, 'And with this I make an ende, praying God to sende you home shortly, for without this noo joye here can be accomplished; and for the same I pray and now goo to Our Lady at Walsyngham that I promised soo long agoo to see.'[33] In March 1517 she went again, doubtless to thank God that after seven years she had at last given birth to a daughter, Mary, and to pray with raised hopes that she would soon produce a son, the male heir that she and Henry desperately wanted. Cardinal Wolsey, Henry's great friend and adviser, the Chancellor of England, and Cardinal Archbishop of York, also came to Walsingham in the same year praying to be healed of a stomach problem.

By then Henry was tiring of pilgrimages, and travelling around his realm staying with his nobles and bishops, preferring to live in the magnificent palaces he built around London. He chose to occupy his time making war, or failing that with jousting, hunting, tennis and other sports, while leaving administration to his loyal Cardinal of York. Nonetheless he maintained some devotion to Our Lady of Walsingham and kept a candle burning before her shrine, sent other gifts, and paid for a priest 'singing before Our Lady at Walsingham.'[34] But one last sombre entry in the Letters and Papers of the Reign of Henry VIII, dated September 29 1538, hints at the catastrophe then unfolding:

> For the King's Candle before Our Lady of Walsingham, and to the Prior there for his salary, NIL.[35]

CHAPTER 9

DESTRUCTION

Intimations of Reform

There is an ancient and respectable tradition of criticism of pilgrimage, which in any case has never been a requirement of the Christian Faith. Many Religious superiors, for example, were unhappy about monks, and especially nuns, travelling around. Their spiritual quest for the heavenly Jerusalem was preferable to a mere physical journey to Jerusalem.[1] From the fourteenth century criticism became more vocal. Thomas à Kempis, in that most popular Catholic classic, *The Imitation of Christ*, expressed his concern.

> When men go to see such things (holy bones in their setting of silk and gold) it is often out of curiosity and a wish for change of scenery; they come back little inclined to amend their lives, especially when their pilgrimage has been a mere light-hearted dashing hither and thither, without any real touching of the heart.[2]

The behaviour of some pilgrims was giving the rest a bad name in the later Middle Ages, not helped by the policy of sending miscreants on pilgrimage as a punishment, preferable to fines and other penalties. Secular courts, not only in England, but also even in Flanders, sent villains on pilgrimage to Canterbury, Walsingham and other shrines.[3] Rowdy behaviour, drunkenness and worse were all but inevitable. One way to address the problem was with satire and biting humour. William Langland, in *The Vision of Piers Plowman*, a masterpiece of satirical Catholic medieval literature, written around 1370, had a dream of pilgrims,

> with crooked staves who set out for Walsingham, with their whores behind them, dressed up in copes to look different from the rest, and, hey presto! They've become hermits – gentlemen of leisure.'[4]

Repentance asked a pilgrim (Greed) whether he had ever repented or made restitution. Greed replied that he had indeed rifled some merchants' bags at the inn. Repentance exploded 'That wasn't restitution, it was downright robbery. You deserve to be hanged for that.' 'But I thought rifling was restitution' protested Greed. 'I've never learned to read, and I assure you I don't know a word of French. Nobody does who comes from the far end of Norfolk.'[5]

Similarly, Chaucer, at the end of the fourteenth century, satirised pilgrims going to Canterbury for less than worthy motives, with their drinking and carousing in taverns. The pompous knight, the lecherous wife of Bath, the rowdy miller, make hilarious tales, the only priest coming out of the story untarnished being the parish priest, perhaps indicating the respect in which they were generally held. For the most part priests were, in fact, devout and reasonably educated men, with increasing numbers of them graduates. The ones with a poor reputation were the ill-educated local 'massing' priests, ordained only to celebrate Mass. But satire was a serious warning that all was not well.

Susan Morrison warns against taking the criticism of women pilgrims in literature at its face value. It says more about the perceptions of a woman's place being in the hearth and home. A woman in public was an unchaste woman. 'The sexual female pilgrim is a figure of disruption and danger, evoked by artists who then carefully control her through irony or satire.'[6]

There was at Walsingham, in a reliquary above the high altar of the Priory, a much prized relic of Mary's Milk, thought to have originated from scrapings from the chalky 'Grotto of Our Lady's Milk' in Bethlehem. A Franciscan pilgrim went to Bethlehem in 1553 and 'saw the cave where the Virgin remained for some time, giving suck to the infant Jesus. This place is an underground cavern and contains an altar. Mothers who have no milk are in the habit of using fragments and earth from this grotto … pilgrims take pieces of the earth of this grotto for the use of women who have no milk.'[7] The same grotto is today full of framed letters, testimonials and photographs of babies from women whose prayers have been answered.

Drinking this chalky mixture is driven by faith and by the same hope that people today have in alternative remedies, when medicine fails. But it was derided. St Bernardino of Siena, who lived from 1380-1444, was scathing:

> And, oh, oh, by the way, the milk of the Virgin Mary! Ladies, where are your heads? And you, fine sirs, have you seen any of it? You know, they're passing it off as a relic. It's all over the place. Don't you believe in it for a moment. It's not real. Don't you believe in it! Do you think that the Virgin Mary was a cow, that she would give away her milk in this way – just like an animal that lets itself be milked?[8]

He was right, of course, yet he probably had no comprehension of the distress of a woman who would try anything rather than see her baby die because she had no milk to give it. Nor had Erasmus much sympathy when he turned his satirical pen against it after his pilgrimage to Walsingham in 1512:

> He has left us so much of his Blood upon earth; she so much Milk, as it is scarcely credible should have belonged to a single mother with one child, even if the infant had taken none of it! They make the same remarks of Our Lord's cross, which is shown privately and publicly in so many places, that, if the fragments were brought together, they would suffice to freight a merchantship.[9]

When Erasmus asked a canon if he could prove it was Our Lady's milk the canon became really upset by the question. As Eamon Duffy says, Erasmus detested violence and had no desire to stoke the fires of revolution, but 'he did want to use laughter to expose absurdity and corruption … to tickle the Church into reforming itself.'[10] A former Augustinian canon himself, he belonged to an influential group of Christian humanists, along with Thomas More, who was a particular friend, and John Colet, all eager for the renewal of the Church.

More strident than satire were the vociferous attacks on pilgrims by the Lollards, a reforming movement in fourteenth-century England begun by the cleric John Wyclif who, with a group of Oxford scholars, made the first translation of the whole Bible into English (though translations of parts of it were already being made to meet the need of increasing literacy). Wyclif concluded that the true Church on earth is not a Catholic community of saints and sinners but is comprised only of those destined for salvation. He challenged the Church's authority to teach and preach, identified the papacy with anti-Christ, and condemned its Eucharistic teachings. His Bible was welcomed in the Church, beyond the Lollard circle, but regrettably he prefaced it with a 'general prologue', containing his teachings. This inevitably led Archbishop Arundel of Canterbury in 1408 to prohibit further translations without episcopal authority, engendering, as Richard Rex has pointed out 'a culture of suspicion about vernacular scripture which endured until the sixteenth century.'[11] In any case, of course, the circulation of the Bible was limited until the invention of the printing press in the later fifteenth century.

The Lollards took hold of the concern about the behaviour of pilgrims already being widely expressed, but went much further, attacking pilgrimage itself as idolatrous and a waste of money, which they thought would be better given to the poor. William Thorpe, for example, criticised the motives of pilgrims, accusing them of neglecting needy neighbours at home and spending money

> 'on vitious (vicious) hostelers, which are oft unclean women of their bodies. (They) have with them both men and women that can well sing wanton songes, and some pilgrimes will have with them bagge-pipers … they make more noice (noise) than if the King came their way, with all his clarions and many other minstrels.[12]

To which Archbishop Arundel retorted,

> I say to thee, that it is right well done, that pilgrims have with them both singers and also pipers, that when one of them that goeth barefoot, stricketh his toe upon a stone, and hurteth him sore, and maketh him to bleed, it is well done that he or his fellows begin then a song, or else take out of his bosom a bagpipe, for to drive away with such mirth, the hurt of his fellow: for with such solace, the travail and weariness of pilgrimage, is lightly and merely borne out.[13]

Another priest of Lollard sympathy, John Younge, asserted that 'every step of the pilgrim turns them to sin.' Lollards used offensive language, and Our Lady of Walsingham was a favourite target. John Skylan of Norwich said, 'no pilgrimage should be done to the Lefdy (Lady) of Falsingham (Walsingham), the Lefdy of Foulpette (Woolpit) and to Thomme of Canterbury'.[14] She was called 'the wyche of Walsingham'[15] and they objected to localised titles, like Our Lady *of* Walsingham, as evidence of idolatry.[16]

Bishops were no strangers to the danger of idolatry, and did their best to guard the faithful against it. The Fourth Lateran Council in 1215 prohibited the unlicensed veneration of relics and the English bishops enforced it. They were only too aware that the line between superstition and good practice was a thin one, that paganism could lurk under a thin veneer of Christianity, and often warned of it. In 1258 the Diocese of Bath and Wells enacted that 'stones, wood, trees or springs are not to be venerated as holy on the pretext of any dream or illusion, since by this means we believe great perils have arisen to the souls of the faithful.'[17]

The influence of Lollardy has been exaggerated, for they were never more than a small and scattered minority, and the notion that they paved the way for the English Reformation has little to be said for it.[18] In some ways they hindered reform, for their vitriolic criticism of the conduct of pilgrims, spurious relics, and fabricated miracles (on which any Catholic bishop would have agreed with them), and their vehement critique of pilgrimage and images, threw the Church on to the defensive, since any good Catholics who criticised any aspect of pilgrimage were suspected of Lollardy. In 1313 Archbishop Greenfield of York had warned against thinking that Our Lady venerated at Foston was holier than any other,[19] but some years later such views would be considered evidence of Lollardy. Chaucer was claimed as a Lollard until the late seventeenth century, though he certainly was not one. Nor were John Collet, Erasmus or Thomas More. Thomas More argued defensively that people could both assist the poor and go on pilgrimage. Even if some people did hold mistaken ideas about images and miracles, and misbehaviour sometimes occurred, this was no reason to abrogate pilgrimage itself.[20]

When confronted with the objection that some 'silly women' professed a preference for Our Lady of Walsingham or Our Lady of Ipswich, Thomas More argued that they were sensible enough to know neither was actually Our Lady who stood by the Cross after the Passion.[21] The Church was vigilant against fraud, and More records the deception in the reign of Henry VII of a young girl from Leominster who claimed to eat nothing more than daily communion, but under investigation it was found that the local curate, in collusion with her, was providing several square meals a day. The point is that the Church stopped it.[22]

Criticism of pilgrimage may have had an effect, for the offerings at many shrines, including Canterbury, did decline during the fifteenth century, though Diana Webb admits it is difficult to prove any connection. Eamon Duffy finds plenty of evidence that regional and local shrines, as well as the classic pilgrimages to Rome, Jerusalem and Compostela retained their popularity to the very moment they were outlawed, [23] and concludes that drops of income are accounted for by the fact that some shrines often did decline in popularity as newer ones gained favour. Walsingham was certainly unaffected. The *Valor Ecclesiasticus* for 1535 shows that offerings totalled £260, more than the total income of many a medium-sized monastery, with a gross income of £707. 7s. 10d.[24]

Criticism of pilgrimage was, of course, but one aspect of a growing movement for reform in the Church. Frustration was building up all over Europe as successive popes ignored the requests of many bishops for a reforming council. The Fifth Lateran Council ended in failure, when eventually it was convened in 1512, and in 1517 the German Augustinian priest, Martin Luther, burst onto the stage by publishing his 95 Theses to initiate a debate, particularly on indulgences, and call for reform. Soon he went much further than demanding a reform of abuses, by opposing the very authority and teachings of the Catholic Church itself, which he declared to be a betrayal of the Gospel. Penance, pilgrimage, fidelity to the sacraments, self-denial, even good works, he considered to contribute nothing to salvation. In recent years a number of Catholic scholars have re-examined Luther's teachings, among them Pope Benedict XVI, who considers 'Martin Luther's doctrine on justification is correct, if faith is not opposed to charity.'[25] Luther's wider interpretation of St Paul's teaching on Works, Law, and Faith, which became the bedrock of Protestantism, has been questioned by the *New Perspective on Paul* movement, a group of Protestant Biblical scholars who consider that Luther distorted Paul's teaching by setting it against the background of medieval Catholicism rather than in the context of first-century Judaism.[26] Whatever verdicts there are now on Luther, he succeeded in alarming the Catholic Church and throwing Germany into turmoil and bitter division.

Henry VIII and his Divorce

In England, King Henry VIII, a loyal and faithful Catholic, looked askance at what was stirring in Germany, and when in 1520 Luther published *The Babylonian Captivity of the Church* in which he denied Seven Sacraments and used the words anti-Christ and Babylon of the Pope and Catholic Church, the King of England grabbed his pen, assisted, perhaps, by Bishop John Fisher and Edward Lee. Thomas More recommended Henry tone down his enthusiasm for the papal primacy and ironically Henry declined to do so.[27] His rejoinder was entitled *Defence of the Seven Sacraments,* for which Pope Leo X awarded 'this great prince', the title *Fidei Defensor* (Defender of the Faith) in 1521. Henry wanted, as he wrote, 'to defend and uphold the Holy Roman Church not only by force of arms but by the resources of our intelligence and our services as a Christian.'[28] Luther was furious, wrote a diatribe against Henry, and described him as a pig, dolt, and liar who deserved to be covered in shit.[29]

It was the responsibility of a medieval monarch, both to protect his country against sedition and to defend the Church against division. Heresy, the medieval monarch feared, could bring down his kingdom. Richard II had urged the Bishop of Chichester to arrest all Lollards whose damnable errors 'would bring ruin to the diocese if not resisted by the king's majesty ... lest the wickedness of the lurking enemy thereby infect the people of the whole realm, the ruling of whom, is committed to the king from on high.'[30] Religious dissent often went along with political rebellion, as evidenced by the Peasants' Revolt and the Oldcastle Rising, and the penalties were the same, death by being burnt alive, or to be hung, drawn, quartered, and left to die. When considering the bloodshed and horror of *both* sides in the Reformation period it is important not to judge it through the anachronistic eyes of our modern democracy and sense of toleration.

Henry's defence of the Church, however, concealed deep unhappiness and turmoil in his personal life. He had been married twelve years to Katherine of Aragon, (the widow of his late brother Arthur, who died after they had been married for less than five months), but after the death of fifty-two-day old Prince Henry, (whose birth had taken Henry to Walsingham in mid-winter on a week-long pilgrimage of thanksgiving), five more pregnancies, some of which were stillborn boys, Katherine had given him one daughter, Mary. He was desperate for a male heir, mindful of the need to secure the throne. Marrying Katherine had required a dispensation from the pope, for although one biblical text seems to command a man to marry his brother's childless widow another appears to forbid it. 'If a man takes his brother's wife, it is impurity ... they shall be childless.'[31] In his predicament Henry read this text and wondered whether the pope had been right to grant the dispensation. He began to think that his marriage to Katherine was invalid and that he stood under the judgement of God.

It would be simplistic to say that the King's divorce caused the English Reformation but it certainly changed the history of England. The case was not straightforward, and dragged on, but some brief account is necessary to explain the cataclysmic events it unleashed. What initially made a quick resolution impossible was the *Sack of Rome* in 1527 by the largely Lutheran troops of Emperor Charles V, unpaid and out of control. For eight days they rampaged around the city, dressed up as popes and cardinals, turned rabid by Luther's invective against Rome and the pope, looting, burning, raping and killing. Old men were disembowelled, young men castrated, and children bounced on the points of swords. They stabled their horses in St Peter's and in the Sistine Chapel, and scribbled Luther's name on Raphael's priceless paintings. After stealing all they could carry away they left more than four thousand citizens massacred. The whole of Europe was shocked and the event was talked about for another hundred years. The terrified Pope Clement VII fled down the corridor to Castel San'Angelo, which the troops surrounded, baying for his blood. The Emperor now held the Pope a virtual prisoner.

Emperor Charles V was the nephew of Queen Katherine and no way would he allow the Pope to end the marriage of his aunt and inflict on her the distress and dishonour of divorce. Nonetheless at some stage a decree of nullity was drawn up and remains today in the Vatican archives, unsigned.[32] Henry's Chancellor, the ever-faithful Cardinal Wolsey, persuaded the Pope to allow the case to be heard in England, but Katherine wrecked the plan by appealing to Rome on the grounds that in England she could not expect a fair hearing.

Henry rested his case on conscientious scruples that his marriage to his brother's widow was offensive to God, but a love letter, in which Henry not only professed his undying love for Anne Boleyn, but actually promised to marry her, seriously undermined his plea. Somehow this letter was stolen (for there was huge support and sympathy in England for Katherine), and reached the Vatican, where it remains today in the archives. This painted a very different picture of why he wanted a divorce. Then Katherine dropped a bombshell. She signed a solemn affidavit that her marriage to Arthur had not been consummated. The King's case had fallen apart.

In 1530 eighty-three nobles (about 70% of the House of Lords of that time), including numerous abbots and bishops signed and sealed a massive petition known as the *Causa Anglica* urging the pope to annul the marriage to help give the kingdom an heir and prevent a bloody fight between successors. It also hinted at the coming schism by threatening that should the pope neglect the needs of the English, they would feel authorised to solve the issue on their own and find remedies elsewhere.

The Pope was playing for time, hoping the King might tire of Anne, and there is evidence that Henry too was in no hurry for a decision, lest it go against him. Another idea was slowly forming in his mind. In searching for a solution the name of a Cambridge theologian, Thomas Cranmer, reached Henry's ears, for suggesting an appeal to the universities of Europe on the validity of the marriage to Katherine. Although this appeal drew a predictably ambiguous response, in 1530 Cranmer and some others assembled a dossier, the *Collectanea Satis Copiosa*, which became a kind of charter of Anglicanism and the basis of the argument for a national church in which the king, not the pope, had supreme jurisdiction. Gradually, the idea of Royal Supremacy over

The Meaning of the Royal Supremacy. The frontispiece of Henry's Bible illustrates the flow of authority from God (above him) to Henry, descending from him to the clergy and to the local parish congregation via Thomas Cranmer Archbishop of Canterbury, on the left, and to the nobility through Thomas Cromwell on the right.

the Church was formed. Thomas Cromwell, the King's First Minister, pushed successive Acts through Parliament putting pressure on the clergy to recognise the King as the supreme religious authority in England. The 84 year-old Archbishop of Canterbury, William Wareham, protested strongly and told Henry that he considered all the legislation null and void, but as Henry prepared to punish him, in August 1532, he died. Thomas More, the Chancellor of England, resigned.

Suddenly there could be no more delay. Anne Boleyn was pregnant. In January 1533 Henry secretly married her, for the child had to be legitimate. Henry appointed Cranmer as Archbishop of Canterbury, while the Pope, anxious to placate Henry as long as possible, confirmed his appointment, warning though of his known Lutheran sympathies. No sooner was Cranmer consecrated than he ruled the marriage to Katherine invalid and pronounced the King legally married to Anne Boleyn. The Pope now had no choice. He announced the King's excommunication in July 1533, and his marriage to Anne null and void.

More legislation passed swiftly through parliament in 1534, and Henry was declared Supreme Head of the Anglican Church. Bishops, religious, clergy and others were required to subscribe to it on oath. Even Henry's old enemy Luther was appalled, and Calvin would later declare the title blasphemous. Henry had become the most powerful monarch ever to sit upon the throne of any European country. A reign of terror began.

Martyrdoms and Compliance

The first to die was a young Benedictine Nun, Elizabeth Barton, popularly known as The Holy Maid of Kent, an influential visionary who predicted calamity if the King did not return to his true wife. She and five priests with her were beheaded or hanged at Tyburn on 20 April 1534.

For refusing to take the oath of Supremacy three Carthusian priors, John Houghton, prior of London Charterhouse, Robert Lawrence of Beauville, and Augustine Webster of Axholme, were taken in chains to be hung, drawn and quartered at Tyburn in May 1535. The sight of them caused such anguish and commotion on the streets of London, Henry ordered that monks were to be stripped of their habits before being taken out. Three more London monks followed. One of them, Fr Sebastian Newdigate, was a personal friend of Henry VIII, who twice visited him in prison to persuade him with riches and honours to give in. Cardinal Bishop John Fisher of Rochester was beheaded, and the trial of Thomas More began. He spoke fearlessly against the new Supremacy, declaring that he 'died the King's good servant but God's first', and this boyhood friend of the King was beheaded.

Not only Catholics were put to death. Henry was Supreme Head of the Church, his word was the Word of God, and he ordered the expulsion of Dutch Anabaptists, a Protestant sect, who denied it. Fourteen who remained were burnt at the stake in 1535.

Two years later the campaign resumed. Four more Carthusian monks were martyred in York, and then thirty-eight monks and lay brothers from London Charterhouse were taken to Newgate Prison, standing chained to posts, with their hands tied behind them, and left to die of starvation. And so the bloodshed went on. More than 160 Catholics, most of them religious and priests, were martyred for refusing to accept that the King could be head of the Church.

These were the minority. Almost all the bishops, religious and clergy signed the oath accepting Henry as Head of the English Church, and repudiated the authority of the pope. Why did they capitulate so easily? Kings had quarrelled with popes before, and maybe most assumed this new argument would blow over. Signing under duress is one thing; giving mental consent is another. Kings were all-powerful and were defenders of the Church; many clergy would not grasp the doctrinal implications of the oath, and if the bishop signed so would his clergy. If the superior of the monastery signed the rest of the community would do so. This happened at Walsingham.

On 18 September 1534 Prior Richard Vowell and all twenty-one canons of Walsingham Priory, 'each in his own hand signed with the unanimous consent and assent of all, by this deed, given under our common seal in our chapter-house', affirmed 'by the pledge of our conscience and our oath' that the King is the Supreme Head of the Anglican Church and that they would never, in private or public discourse, call the Bishop of Rome by the name of Pope or Chief Bishop. Among the signatories was Canon Nicholas Mileham who within three years would be put to death.

The Dissolution of the Monasteries

Monasteries all over Europe were being reformed, and in 1524 Pope Clement VII had approved Cardinal Wolsey's request to dissolve twenty-nine small monasteries with few monks, and for their revenues to be reappropriated for charitable and educational purposes. St John's College and Jesus College, Cambridge, occupied the sites of former convents, and took over their endowments. Pope Paul III, who succeeded Pope Clement VII, established a Commission to report on the ills of the Church and to recommend reforms, and it produced the *Consilium de Emendenda Ecclesia*, (A Plan for Reforming the Church) in 1537.[33] The ills of the Church were listed in detail and lamented. The blame for the state of the Church, including the outbreak of Luther's reformation, was laid squarely on the papacy, cardinals and bishops. Among reforms it proposed the suppression of all but the most strictly observant monasteries. The Report was dynamite and was leaked; Luther obtained a copy and published it in a German translation with his own notes, which guaranteed it was shelved. But the reforming movement within the Church was unstoppable, and in 1545 the long-awaited reforming Council of Trent began.

There were 800 monasteries, priories, and convents in England and Wales, and over eight thousand monks, canons and nuns. Generally well respected in the locality, most of them provided education, hospitality, help for the poor, care for the sick, and employment on their farms. Some of them had not recovered from the Black Death, which reached England in 1348, returned in 1361, and kept recurring over the next decades, along with dysentery, smallpox and 'sweating sickness' (probably influenza). Estimates of how many of the population died varies enormously, but what is certain is that in East Anglia, which was severely affected through its frequent contact with the continent, half the parish priests died and the monasteries were decimated. Walsingham was inevitably affected and Prior Thomas was compelled to obtain a dispensation from the Pope in 1364 to ordain four canons under the canonical age, providing they had completed their twenty-second year. The Priory soon got up to strength, however, for in 1377 there were twenty canons, seventeen in 1494, twenty-five in 1514, twenty-three in 1532 and twenty-two in 1534[34] In North Creake Priory, near Walsingham, all the monks died and the monastery closed in 1506.

The King's supremacy of the Church opened up a brilliant possibility to the inventive brain of Thomas Cromwell. Princes in Luther's Germany were availing themselves of church property. The same was happening in Scandinavia and Switzerland. Supremacy meant Henry now had his hands, not only on the Church, but on all its assets and revenue, just at the time he needed money. Wars with France had drained the coffers and bills were mounting. Taxes were imposed on the clergy, and commissioners appointed to make an assessment, the *Valor Ecclesiasticus,* of the wealth and assets of the Church in 1535. In the same year a Visitation of all the Religious Houses began. Often visitors spent less than a day in a house, for they knew the agenda. Their thinly veiled brief was simply to provide Cromwell with fabricated evidence to close the smaller houses down. One of the commissioners, Dr Richard Layton, was of a particularly salacious mind with regard to the sexual appetites of monks and nuns, and his reports bore no comparison with genuine and earlier strict diocesan visitations. A hint of what was to come was that pilgrimages, relics and superstition came under fire.

The Visitation was decisive in persuading parliament to close 318 smaller monasteries, of which 100 were convents of women. The dissolution began in 1536. The motive was transparent, for the smaller houses were cynically contrasted with 'divers great and solemn monasteries of this realm, wherein (thanks be to God) religion is right well kept and observed.'[35] Yet all of these great monasteries would be destroyed between 1537 and 1540. As Richard Rex points out, 'the rhetoric of reformation soon became little more than a cloak for naked expropriation.'[36]

The commissioners appointed to Walsingham were Richard Southwell and Sir John Haydon. Even while they were there Walsingham was full of pilgrims. Predictably the Commissioners found that Canons John Lamprey, William Mileham, Richard Garret, Robert Sall, John Clenchwarton and John Watthy were guilty of 'notorious incontinency' and that 'grave superstition and much forgery was found in their feigned, pretended miracles and relics.' No surprise there because this is what they found in all monasteries. And it contrasted with the much more detailed visitation of 1526 which found no irregularity in the House and twenty-three canons *omnia bene*, other than slackness at mattins reported of two canons, and a shortage of food. The real intent of the commissioners was revealed in a letter from Richard Southwell to Cromwell, dated 25 July 1536, informing him that Sir Thomas Lestrange and Mr Hoges had sequestered 'all such money, plate, jewels and stuff as there was invented and found.'[37]

The Pilgrimage of Grace and the Walsingham Conspiracy

The loss of the smaller monasteries was disastrous, and provoked huge unrest, for many peasants depended on them for work and livelihood. In Yorkshire and Lincolnshire rebellious movements began which almost cast the despoiling king from his throne. Starting in Louth in Lincolnshire, after the closure of the abbey, and rapidly gathering support, an estimated ten thousand men held Lincoln for a week from 6-13 October 1536, demanding freedom to worship as Catholics and an end to the dissolution of the monasteries. They dispersed on the approach of the forces of the 1st Duke of Suffolk. Thomas Kendall, the vicar of Louth and its spiritual leader, was captured and executed and other local ringleaders met the same fate.

Encouraged by that uprising, a more formidable rebellion began in Beverley, East Yorkshire. Then in York twenty thousand were led by Robert Aske, a county gentleman and London barrister, who named it the Pilgrimage of Grace. Monks and nuns were restored to their houses, and the new tenants cast out. Risings followed in Durham with the great lords of the North, the Percies and Nevilles, under the banner of the Five Wounds of Christ, until by 23 October, a formidable force of thirty to forty thousand well armed men mostly on horseback, disciplined and orderly, were marching south through Doncaster. Here they met the army of the Duke of Norfolk, not one-tenth their number. With so many Norfolk noblemen away in his army the heads of three Norfolk monasteries, Walsingham, West Acre and Castle Acre, were among landowners appointed to stay at home and maintain order in the county,[38] and the suppression of monastic houses in Norfolk was temporarily halted. The rebels demanded of the King that all the monasteries be preserved both as centres of religious life and for their social value. They made further ultimatums, economic and religious, including the recognition of the headship of the pope and punishment for heretical bishops. Duped by the Duke of Norfolk that the King would hear their grievances at a parliament to be specially convened in York, the rebels dispersed, Aske persuading his followers that the King would act in good faith.

Nothing was further from the truth. The King had no intention of keeping his promise, and in January 1537 when a new uprising took place in Cumberland and Westmoreland (which Aske attempted to prevent) the Duke of Norfolk crushed the rebels. Two hundred and sixteen were put to death; nobles and knights, half a dozen abbots, thirty-eight monks, and sixteen parish priests perished under the King's order 'without pity or respect.' They were strung up in every town and village implicated in the Pilgrimage of Grace. Aske hung in chains from York Castle. The gravest threat Henry had faced, and it was a most serious threat, was over. He had reduced the Church to subservience. But England was under a reign of terror.

Some of the Norfolk men in the Duke's army returned with a 'rebel bill' that Robert Aske had produced with his demands. This dangerous document was copied and shown around in Norwich and King's Lynn, and a copy was given to some Cornish soldiers making their way to Walsingham on pilgrimage. The next thing we know is that Henry Manser, the canon in charge of the Shrine, was accused of telling some pilgrims from Lincolnshire that 'if Norfolk and Suffolk had risen when Lincolnshire and Yorkshire did they would have been able to have gone through the realm.'[39] Charges were dropped because his accuser was a 'soore and diseased beggar' who had 'cauysed an incident' at the Shrine for which the constable put him in the stocks.[40]

Meanwhile, an uprising was being planned in Walsingham, the 'most serious plot hatched anywhere south of the Trent.'[41] Early in November 1536, Ralph Rogerson, a yeoman farmer employed in the choir of Walsingham Priory, met another yeoman, John Smyth of Wighton, on the road from London. Having heard of the success of the Pilgrimage of Grace, as he thought, Smyth declared, 'it shall never be well until such time as we make an insurrection against great men', proposing himself to be leader of a hundred rebels, a conversation he was later to deny.[42] The following April, 1537, Rogerson allegedly told a fellow yeoman and chorister, George Guisborough, who belonged to the Guild of the Annunciation of St Mary the Virgin, 'You see how these abbeys go down and our living goeth away with them; for within a while Binham shall be put down and also Walsingham and all other abbeys in that country.'[43] Guisborough was said to have replied that he thought 'it very evil done for the suppressing of so many religious houses, where God was well served and many other good deeds of charity done.'[44] Soon they were recruiting men for a rebellion. A preliminary meeting took place in Binham, under cover of a game of archery. There was a further meeting in St Mary's Churchyard at Walsingham, and three or four more in various places.[45]

Within a fortnight there were two or three dozen conspirators including Guisborough and his son William (a Franciscan priest from Lynn), Canon Nicholas Mileham the sub-prior of Walsingham Priory, John Grigby the vicar of Langham, John Pecock and William Gibson, two Carmelites from Burnham, John Punt the rector of Waterden, Thomas Howse of Walsingham, John Semble a mason, Thomas Manne a carpenter, Richard Henley a plumber, Thomas Penne a husbandman from Houghton, John Sellers a tailor, Robert Hawker a butcher, Richard Malyot a yeoman and former sailor of Wells, Henry Capon, James Henley, John Malput, John Man, J. Tytyng, William Smyth, Thomas Arter, Richard Page, and Andrew Pax, the parish clerk. Others thought to be associates were William Betts a priest of Great Walsingham and former canon of the Priory, William Younger another Walsingham priest, William Parker a glover, and Robert Griggis a sheep farmer, John Smyth, William Hall, and Thomas Kyrton all from Wighton.

The involvement of so many priests proves how willing they were to defend their faith, while the presence of so many local tradesmen shows how anxious they were about their livelihood when pilgrimages ceased. Also expressed was the fear that when local gentry got hold of the monastic lands they would treat the tenants far more oppressively than the religious did. It is noteworthy that powerful noblemen were in the Pilgrimage of Grace but the gentry of Norfolk, who had much to gain from the sale of monastic lands, were willing to betray the conspirators of Walsingham.

The plan was to light the coastal beacons in Norfolk and use local musters to raise a rebellion. They were to meet on 21 May at Shepcotes Heath, seize control of important bridges on the London road, and in Lynn, the gateway to the north and west, before marching into Suffolk to augment their number, then joining up, as was thought, with the rebels from the North on the way to London, with the object (like the equally gullible Pilgrims of Grace), of telling the King their grievances. But the greater the number who were told, the greater the risk of betrayal, and when they tried to recruit John Galant of Letheringsett, a servant of Sir John Heydon, he informed his master, naming seven of the conspirators and details of the plan. Heydon dispatched him at once to tell Richard Gresham, a Norfolk man in London, who informed Cromwell. The same day he contacted Sir Roger Townshend of East Raynham, who drove to Walsingham, interrogated Robert Hawker, John Semble and Thomas Howes, and arrested the two Guisboroughs. Rogerson escaped. George Guisborough admitted his remark about the suppression of so many religious houses where God is well served, and that he had suggested 'an insurrection of the commons who were oppressed by the gentlemen.'[46] Three days later, Cromwell was interrogating the Guisboroughs in London. The speed with which he acted proves not only the effectiveness of Tudor 'justice' but the seriousness with which the threat was taken.

In a matter of days twenty-five conspirators were arrested and brought to trial in Norwich on 24 May. Henry VIII and Cromwell ordered that all conspirators were to be executed 'without sparing.' On the following day, twelve were found guilty of treason and sentenced to death, three to life imprisonment, two were remanded and eight pardoned. The two remanded were later pardoned, one of them being William Younger, the Walsingham priest, whose involvement was uncertain. Five of the conspirators, including Rogerson and Howes from Walsingham, were executed at Norwich on 26 May. For Rogerson and Howes, the most appalling and agonising death, to be hung, drawn and quartered, the others were hanged. Rogerson tried to address the watching crowd but was prevented by the executioner. On 28 May John Semble was hung, drawn and quartered, and John Sellers was hanged in Yarmouth. Canon Nicholas Mileham, the subprior, and George Guisborough were brought back to Walsingham, held and shackled overnight, it is believed, in a cellar across the road from the Priory. On Wednesday 30 April they too were hung, drawn and quartered on the field still known as the Martyrs' Field in Walsingham. On Friday, 1 June, in Lynn, Fr William Guisborough was hung, drawn and quartered, and Fr John Pecock was hanged.

Walsingham and the principal towns in the county were chosen for the brutal executions to impress upon the people of North Norfolk, who inevitably talked about what they witnessed, that the power of the King was unassailable. At Aylsham on 12 May Elizabeth Worde told two others that it was a pity the Walsingham men were discovered for 'with clubs and clouted s(h)oon shall the deed be done, for we had never good world since the King reigned.'[47]

They had to be so careful. When Thomas Westwood told Thomas Wright, a carpenter, that the wife of one of those who died in Norwich swooned for more than an hour, but that her husband got what he deserved, Wright ventured to disagree with him. For this he was arrested, but denied having disagreed.[48] It became dangerous to speak your mind. The vicar of St Clement's, Cambridge, after a beer or two in the Pump tavern, called the King a despoiler of the Church. Sensing his companion's unease, the priest said, 'Neighbour Richardson, there be no one here but you and I'. But neighbour Richardson denounced him to the mayor and his words were duly reported to Cromwell.[49]

Who betrayed Canon Mileham? In a letter to Cromwell on 3 May 1537 Townsend wrote: 'It appears by the confession of one Wattson that the sub-prior of Walsingham was infected, whom also they have taken and examined.' In a later letter to Cromwell Townsend commended Prior Vowell to his favour, for he had been the 'taker of one of the most rank traitors privy to the Walsingham Conspiracy.'[50]

On 24 May, the day of the Walsingham Conspiracy trial in Norwich, safe for the present in his monastery, Prior Vowell of Walsingham wrote to Cromwell thanking him for favours granted to himself, a kinsman in Cromwell's service, and enclosing a 'poor remembrance' which he begged the great man to accept.[51] The remembrance was a handsome one hundred pounds. It was to stand him in good stead.

The Attack on Images and Pilgrimage

The Pope had warned Henry VIII that Thomas Cranmer was a man of Lutheran sympathies. He was, in fact, one of a group of clerics who reputedly met at the *White Horse* in Cambridge, to discuss over pints of ale the reforming ideas of Martin Luther. With the sudden elevation of Thomas Cranmer, their hour had come. Among them were Hugh Latimer, Nicholas Ridley, Matthew Parker, Miles Coverdale (who translated the Psalms), and William Tyndale (soon to translate the New Testament), all of whom found themselves made Anglican bishops. On top of that Anne Boleyn was a Lutheran sympathiser with every reason for hating the papacy.

The Lutheran campaign against the Catholic Faith could now get underway in England. The King appointed Hugh Latimer Bishop of Worcester. For several years he had preached against pilgrimages, with particular venom against the Holy Blood of Hailes, not just as a spurious relic but because (he alleged) people imagined that merely to look at the blood 'put them in a state of salvation without spot of sin.'[52] Using a Convocation Sermon in the summer of 1536, he launched a blistering attack on pilgrimage as a waste of time and money, even if the images and relics they visited were not fraudulent. There was a very popular Shrine of Our Lady in Bishop Latimer's own cathedral at Worcester. In 1537 he stripped her of her finery and in June 1538 he expressed the hope that Cromwell

> will bestow our great Sibyll to some good purpose *ut pereat memoria cum sonitu (that [her] memory may perish with a bang)*. She hath been the devil's instrument to bring many, I fear, to eternal fire; now she herself, with her old sister of Walsingham, her young sister of Ipswich, with their other two sisters of Doncaster and Penrysse (Penrhys), would make a jolly muster in Smithfield. They would not be all day in burning.[53]

Latimer evidently thought this was very amusing, and it certainly reveals something of his character, for the point of his remark is that on 22 May, two weeks earlier, Father John Forest, Queen Katherine's confessor, was burned at the stake at Smithfield along with a large wooden cross. Instead of burning well the wood smouldered and Fr Forest was so long in dying and in such agony, that the crowd became enraged. Cromwell and Latimer enjoyed the spectacle, and far from being distressed were annoyed with the crowd.[54]

The critique against images gained momentum among Protestant preachers and writers. William Marshall issued an English Primer, heavily dependant on Luther, omitting the usual *Litany of the Saints* and the *Salve Regina*. Fear of reprisals meant the opposition was muted. A Treasons Act saw to that. When a preacher in Folkestone told the parishioners that the Virgin Mary 'could do no more for us than another woman' the town bailiff wanted to pull him out of the pulpit, but the vicar was afraid to do so, because he had heard that the preacher 'had a licence from the king to preach in all places.'[55]

Clergy argued against Lutheranism in Convocation, and in 1536 the *Ten Articles* were issued under the authority of the King, stating that images are useful as remembrancers, but are not objects of worship; that saints are to be honoured as examples of life, and as furthering our prayer; and that saints may be invoked as intercessors, and their holydays observed. The campaign against them nonetheless went on with increasing confusion. Even in the early 1530s many images, rood screens, and wayside crosses were being destroyed, yet some were restored, and very many remained to the end of Henry's reign. Moderate *Injunctions against Images* were issued in 1536, and more Lutheran ones in 1538 against 'wandering to pilgrimages, offering of money, candles or tapers to images or relics, or kissing or licking the same.' The seventh injunction demanded that 'such feigned images as ye know of in any of your cures to be so abused with pilgrimages or offerings of anything made thereunto, ye shall forthwith take down and delay.' The lighting of candles, a popular accompaniment of prayer, and lamps maintained by parish guilds, was forbidden, apart from the light before the Sacrament of the Altar.[56] The ringing of the Angelus was forbidden. Devotion was being gradually taken away from the lives of the faithful. William Gray of Reading composed a ballad, *The Fantassie of Idolatrie*, to celebrate the stripping of the Shrines:

> To Walsyngham a gaddyng,
> To Canterbury a maddyng,
> As men distraught of myned;
> With fewe clothes on our backes,
> But an image of waxe,
> For the lame and for the blynde.
> Thus were we poore soules
> Begyled with idolles,
> With fayned myracles and lyes,
> By the devyll and his docters,
> The pope and his proctors:
> That with such, have blerid our eyes.[57]

158

The seventh Injunction of 1538 sealed the fate of the major Shrines, and Walsingham was no exception. On 14 July 1538 Prior Vowell reported to Cromwell that the royal commissioners had taken the image of Our Lady from the chapel, 'allso all suche golde and syllver with such other thynges as weare theare' leaving in his keeping some silver. He expressed concern that the Priory would be unable to meet certain financial obligations (when pilgrimages ceased) and continued to urge, as he evidently had done before, that the Priory might be turned into a college.[58] On 18 July the image that had for centuries been loved and venerated in its Holy House, and where so much prayer and pleading had poured forth, reached London, along with statues of Our Lady of Basingstoke, Caversham, Ipswich, Penrhys, Willesden, and Worcester and others. They were taken to the residence of the Lord Privy Seal, Thomas Cromwell, Chelsea Manor, where they were burnt in the presence of the Lord Privy Seal himself.

The Shrine of St Thomas Becket was destroyed in September 1538, and its riches, including the great ruby given by Louis VIII of France, were presented to the King, and Becket declared a traitor not a saint. The Shrine of St Edmund's at Bury, equally revered by medieval kings, was burnt down. One by one all the shrines were razed.

Hopes have been entertained that the statue of Our Lady of Walsingham escaped the burning, that a copy was substituted in its place, and that one day the original may be found. More credible is the possibility that Our Lady of Ipswich was saved. There is in Nettuno, Italy, an image venerated as 'The English Lady' or 'Our Lady of Grace', the title by which Our Lady of Ipswich was known. It is a medieval statue of English provenance, and the story is that a group of English sailors rescued it, and took refuge from a storm in Nettuno, where it remained, and is greatly venerated. In Lady Lane, Ipswich, on a building where the Shrine once stood, a small statue was put up in the early 1990s replacing a 1960s plaque. A statue modelled from the original was set up in St Mary-at-the-Elms, nearby, and in September 2002 leaders of the local Anglican, Catholic, Orthodox and Methodist communities, as well as representatives of other churches and of Ipswich's Muslims, gathered to bless it. Since then, Catholics, Anglicans, and civic representatives, make an annual pilgrimage to Nettuno, which is reciprocated.

An image that was certainly saved is Our Lady of Boulogne, which was dismantled at the Reformation when Boulogne was under English rule. But in 1550 The Peace of Boulogne ended the war with France, and the French bought back Boulogne for 400,000 crowns. The English had not dared burn the image and it was returned, only to be sadly destroyed in the end by Napoleon. Pilgrimages of Anglicans and Catholics visit the restored shrine in Boulogne and there is a replica image of Our Lady of Boulogne in St Felix, Felixstowe.

Henry VIII sought to justify his destruction of the shrines, picking up on the familiar theme:

> This man loketh for a new worlde. That man compasseth some depe drifte in his head. Some one hath an especiall devocion to goe to Jerusalem, to Rome, or to sainte Iames in Galicia, leuyng his wife and children succourlesse in the meane while at home.[59]

One might wonder about the 'drifte' in Henry's head in his touching concern for other people's wives and children.

Within a month of the dismantling of the Shrine, on 4 August 1538, Sir William Petre, entered through the gatehouse of Walsingham Priory, which still remains with its welcoming figure above the gates, and in the Chapter House received the Deed of Surrender, already prepared, signed and sealed. On 25 July Sir Richard Gresham had acknowledged the instructions of Cromwell 'that the king's pleasure is that the Priory of Walsingham shall be dissolved.'[60]

By 1540 all the monasteries and convents of England had been destroyed, and the eight thousand religious evicted. Monks received pensions until they died or (in the case of priests) secured some benefice. These pensions, mostly £5 a year or more, were arguably adequate, but their real value declined in the mid-Tudor inflation. The heads of houses received more compensation, often including a former manor of the abbey, sufficient to set them up as substantial gentry. Nuns for the most part were less generously treated and had fewer opportunities to better their lot. They had to live with their families, but some tried to stay together in unofficial communal life. The friars probably did worst of all: no endowments, no pensions. All they received with their marching orders was a small cash sum.[61]

Prior Vowell, writing on 12 August 1538, had asked Cromwell for the benefice of Walsingham, and his plea was supported by Sir Richard Gresham, who wrote to Cromwell four days later to say the prior was 'both impotent and lame', urging him to be given the parsonage of Walsingham because he was 'very discreet, learned, of good name and can set forth the Word of God very well, whereof the town has great need'. In the event St Mary's (as it now is) was made subject to Houghton, and Vowell was given the parish of North Creake, described as a 'very rich living', with an exceptionally generous pension of £100 per year, but this he most probably forfeited when he married.[62] He remained at North Creake until he died in November 1550, and he was buried there. Six other canons were given parishes in Norwich diocese, remained unmarried, and received pensions varying from £4-6.

Local communities up and down the country, dependant on monasteries, were given a few sweeteners in the shape of former monastic buildings for use as parish churches, grammar schools, or town halls. Although it had been promised that the King's enhanced wealth would enable the founding or endowment of religious, charitable and educational institutions, in practice only about 15% of the total monastic wealth was reused for these purposes. A third of the monastic income was used to provide pensions for the dispossessed monks and nuns, while all the rest went into the coffers of the king. The removal of over eight hundred such institutions, including hospitals, virtually overnight, tore great gaps in the social fabric especially for the old and infirm, and in the provision of education and hospitality, with a consequent increase of 'sturdy beggars' in late Tudor England, leading to Poor Laws in the reigns of Edward and Elizabeth.

Apart from the loss of some of the finest examples of English architecture and art, the related destruction of monastic libraries was perhaps the greatest cultural loss caused by the English Reformation. Worcester Priory (now the Cathedral) had six hundred books at the time of the dissolution. Walsingham would have had far fewer, but it did have a library established by Brother William Lynn, during the time of Prior Thomas Hunt (1437-1474). Only four books are known to have survived: a handwritten and attractively illustrated twelfth-century Bible containing the books from Genesis to Ruth and a richly illuminated fifteenth-century half Breviary, which belonged to Prior Vowell, in which on the flyleaf, is written part of the Rule of St Augustine, arranged for daily reading. The third item is a collection of thirteenth and fourteenth century medical treatises, and the fourth a small collection of prayers which also once belonged to Prior Vowell.[63]

Former monastic lands were sold or leased to tenants. Henry now had grateful minor gentry and landowners to support him, and his power increased. The building and site of Walsingham Priory, together with two parcels of land belonging to it, were bought by Thomas Sydney for £90. Sydney was the Master of the Lazar House in Walsingham (though he would not have had personal care of the leprosy sufferers). According to the antiquarian, Sir Henry Spelman, who lived in Walsingham as a boy, and died in 1641 aged eighty, people thought he had purchased it for the use of the town 'but kept it to himself.'[64] The timber and stone of the Priory was sold, and a sharp-eyed visitor today may spot huge slabs of stone that were used to repair various buildings, notably Angel Cottage in Great Walsingham, which has a beautifully carved angel. The Guest House of the Priory still stands, and is the long building which incorporates the Museum and former courthouse. The Undercroft too remains, and other masonry including, of course, the glorious arch of the East Window standing as a perpetual reminder of one of England's finest buildings.

The Legacy of Henry VIII

Before the end of his life Henry knew he had started a movement rapidly racing beyond his control, and desperately he tried to rein it in. He had never embraced the Lutheran Reform, and in his mind remained Defender of the Faith, as Cromwell, Cranmer, Latimer and their friends were soon to discover. He thought of himself as a Catholic, as did Cromwell, yet they had constructed a National Church, which was the very antithesis of the universalism inherent in the name Catholic. What was his Church to believe? There was now no Pope to tell him. The Word of God came from the King, and he demanded total obedience. He was on his own with Catholics and Lutherans assaulting his ears with their conflicting views. Desperately, from 1539 to 1543, he pushed through parliamentary legislation that included the *Act Concerning True Opinions,* which gave the King the power to define doctrine. The *Act for the Advancement of True Religion* established a system of censorship, and since the reading of the Bible, which he had encouraged, had been the cause of disarray and divisions, the right to read it was now restricted to gentry, clergy and merchants.

In 1539 the *Six Articles* passed through parliament. Transubstantiation in the Eucharist was upheld in all but name, communion under one kind defended, as well as private Masses and confession. Priests were forbidden to marry and the vows of chastity made by Religious were declared binding under divine law, though the King had turned them out of their monasteries and many had already married. Latimer and another bishop, Shaxton, resigned. Cranmer, it is thought, quickly dispatched his wife to Germany for safety. In July 1540 six victims were dragged to Smithfield; three were Protestants burnt for heretical doctrine, and the other three Catholics, hanged, drawn and quartered for denying the king's supremacy. In the same year, Thomas Cromwell, who had been responsible for sending so many to their deaths, fell from favour, and met the same fate.

Henry's attack on the popular religion of his subjects remains one of the hardest aspects of his Reformation to explain. This is not to say that there were no defects in peoples' grasp of Christian doctrine, nor that they were notably successful in upholding Christian moral standards. But Henry had inherited a Church with 'a vigorous popular piety directed to the worship of God … It is arguable that the ideal of a Christian community united in belief and worship before God has never been so closely approximated as in the late medieval parish.[65] How then could he have destroyed it? Anger with Rome over the divorce, greed and syphilis explain part, but not all of it. His destruction of images makes no sense in terms of Lutheranism, for although Luther was glad to see cult images removed from churches, others he wished retained for witness and memorial. Luther was appalled by their destruction in England. In 1525 he said, 'No-one who sees the iconoclasts raging thus against wood and stone should doubt that there is a spirit hidden in them that is death-dealing, not life-giving.' Breaking images could easily lead to the killing of Christians.[66]

Richard Rex and others consider Henry cast himself in the role of an Old Testament King.[67] His policy against priests, monasteries, relics and shrines, resembles the action of King Josiah against idolatry.[68] It defined Old Testament kingship. Henry's decision to promulgate the English Bible and thoroughly inculcate the Ten Commandments is reminiscent of Josiah. King Jehosaphat purged the land of Sodomites,[69] and Henry bizarrely made homosexuality punishable by death. King Jehoash had taken from the priests all the hallowed things and gold found in the treasures of the house of the

Lord.[70] For Richard Morison, the protégé of Thomas Cromwell, and official apologist for Henry VIII, he was David, Jehosaphat, Amaziah, Josiah and Hezekiah rolled into one.[71] Perhaps the most ludicrous evidence of this is the illumination of Henry VIII in his own Psalter, as King David playing the harp.[72]

Henry VIII's legacy was religious conflict. This was not his intention. Far from it; he was head of the Church and determined what everyone believed on penalty of death. But the inevitable consequence of him breaking communion with the Pope, and his idea of a National Church, was disintegration, division, and bloodshed that in Ireland persisted beyond the end of the twentieth century. As the British Empire spread so did the religious divisions, all over the world, including to America, which has spawned an unimaginable number of denominations and sects. No one any longer believes the monarch of England to be the fount of religious truth, and so Christian doctrine has come to mean, in the minds of many, anything taught by the liveliest reformer, most erudite theologian, earnest reader of the Bible, ecclesiastical synod, or charismatic preacher.

One of the loveliest men to come through these turbulent years during and after the reign of Henry VIII was Nicholas Heath, a prophetic figure, who in 1539, the year of the *Six Articles*, Henry made bishop of Rochester and later Worcester. When Edward VI succeeded his father and the country swung in a determinedly Protestant direction Heath began to think that Thomas More, not Henry, had been right about the papacy, and in 1551 he was deprived of his bishopric and imprisoned. On Mary's accession and the country's return to Roman Catholicism he was released and restored, and in 1555 became Archbishop of York and Lord Chancellor. He was deprived of his bishopric by Queen Elizabeth, whom he had declined to crown, after making a courageous speech in the House of Lords:

> By relinquishing and forsaking the Church or See of Rome, we must forsake and fly from all General Councils: secondly from all canonical and ecclesiastical laws of the Church of Christ: thirdly from the judgments of other Christian princes: fourthly and lastly, we must forsake and fly from the holy unity of Christ's Church, and so by leaping out of Peter's ship, we hazard ourselves to be overwhelmed and drowned in the waves of schism, of sects and divisions.[73]

Yet he remained loyal to Elizabeth as his queen; and after a temporary imprisonment he passed the remaining nineteen years of his life in peace and quiet, not attending public worship but celebrating Mass in private. The queen was fond of him and visited him more than once at his house at Chobham, Surrey, where he died and was buried in 1578.

Henry VIII died on 28 January 1547 at Whitehall Palace and was buried in St George's Chapel in Windsor beside Jane Seymour, his favourite wife. Sir Henry Spelman is reported to have said that on his deathbed in all the agonies of remorse he bequeathed his soul to Our Lady of Walsingham.[74] True or not, the one who in his last will and testament, dated 30 December 1546, styled himself 'immediately under God the supreme head of the Church of England and Ireland', adopted a very different tone to Our Lady in his will:

> Also, we doe instantlie desire and require the blessed Virgine Marie his mother, with all the holy companie of Heaven, continually to pray for us while we live in this world, and in the passing out of the same, that we maie the sooner obtayne eternall life after our departure out of this transitory life, which we do both hope and claime by Christ's passion and word.[75]

CHAPTER 10

REMEMBERED WITH DEVOTION

It is impossible to imagine the crushing defeat felt by people in and around Walsingham, when the image of Our Lady was taken away to be destroyed, when the demolition of the Priory and Friary began, and their religious devotion and livelihood were swept away. In nearby King's Lynn there had been sixty or seventy priests to instruct and care for the people, reduced by the Reformation to three or four. The dreary reading of homilies was a poor substitute for the animated preaching of the friars. There had been about a dozen Religious Houses in Lynn, and as an early nineteenth-century clergyman remarked, with their demolition Lynn 'must have looked somewhat like a town that had undergone a close and successful siege, and which had been left half demolished and ruined by a victorious and exasperated enemy.'[1] We know that at Thetford, where there had been a popular shrine, the mayor lamented in 1539 that 'pilgrims were abhorryd, exesepulsyd and sette apart forever wherby a grett nombyr or peopyll … by idyllyd (unemployment) and lyke to be brought ynto extreme beggarye.'[2] Walsingham may have fared a little better for there was in the town a thriving industry growing saffron.

More than a year after Our Lady of Walsingham had been burned, people were still praying to her. On 20 January 1540, Sir Roger Townsend, the magistrate at Walsingham, who had uncovered the Walsingham Conspiracy, wrote to inform Cromwell about 'a woman of Well(y)s, beside Walsingham', who had 'imagined' a miracle wrought by the image of Our Lady at Walsingham. He set her in the stocks at Walsingham on the market day with a paper about her head, 'a reporter of false tales,' and then sent her round the town in a cart, the young people and boys casting snowballs at her. 'This was her penance, for I knew no law otherwise to punish her but by discretion … The said image is not well out of some of their heads.'[3]

It was not well out of their heads, nor ever would be.

Two nuns chose Walsingham for their home after the dissolution of their convent at Dartford. Elizabeth Exmew was the sister of one of the Carthusian martyrs, Father William Exmew, and daughter of Sir Thomas Exmew, Lord Mayor of London. The other nun was Elizabeth Seygood. The Report on Pensioned Religious in Norwich Diocese says of Elizabeth Exmew, she 'hathe an annuall pencon of fyve pound … she hathe nothinge more then the same pencon to lyve uppon, and she is of an honest conversacon and is reported to be a Catholick woman.[4] Elizabeth Seygood did nor fare anything like so well. She 'hathe an annuall pencon of fourtie shillings … and hath nothinge besids the same pencon to lyve uppon, she dwellithe at Walsingham and lyveth continentlye and is reputed an honest and Catholyck woman'. When Queen Mary sought to restore Religious Life in England, Elizabeth Exmew joined Elizabeth White, a half-sister of Bishop Fisher, and some others from Dartford in a community established at King's Langley. For a few months they actually returned to Dartford. With the accession of Queen Elizabeth the community dispersed, and Elizabeth Exmew, the last survivor, died in exile at the Flemish Convent of Val des Anges, near Bruges.[5] What happened to poor Elizabeth Seygood, we do not know.

Henry VIII was succeeded by his young son, Edward VI, whose guardians encouraged a more protestant direction in the Anglican Church, but his death, after only a six-year reign, brought his half-sister Mary to the throne, for another brief reign of but five years. Mary restored Catholicism, and Eamon Duffy has shown how welcome was the return of Catholicism in parishes all over the country, despite fierce and sincere opposition in some.[6] These opponents, like Catholic opponents in the reign of Henry VIII, suffered the inevitable consequence of those days. Two hundred and seventy-three chose to die rather than be Catholic, among them Archbishop Cranmer, and Bishops Latimer and Ridley. One of these was William Allen, burned at the stake in Walsingham, a labourer, who refused to follow in a procession after a cross. Whether he died on the Martyrs' Field, already hallowed by the two Catholic martyrs, is not known, nor whether or not he was a resident of Walsingham.[7]

Elizabeth inherited a bitterly divided country, a country weary of religious bloodshed and conflict. Her policy was to impose a religious settlement similar to that of her father, with herself Supreme Governor of the Church, rather than Supreme Head, a title she thought impious. By enforcing a *via media* Elizabeth wanted to join both Catholics and extreme Protestants in one national Church. Yet with so many changes in the previous twenty years there was huge confusion in peoples' minds about what they should believe. At Corpus Christi in Canterbury, in 1559, a crowd of three thousand turned out in a Procession, for them the last great act of Catholic witness in England.[8] The Commissioners of Elizabeth had their work cut out to eradicate the old Faith. People gave what Eamon Duffy called 'weary obedience to unpopular measures.' She at first pursued a tolerant policy, allowing Catholics to absent themselves from Anglican worship for the payment of a small tax, but this dramatically changed when Mary, Queen of Scots, who had a good claim to the English throne, arrived in England and became involved in plots to assassinate Elizabeth. In November 1569 the Earls of Westmoreland and Northumberland raised a rebellion to get rid of Elizabeth and establish the 'true and catholic religion', but the rebellion was quickly quelled with great severity. Pope Pius V was advised that England was on the verge of overthrowing the Queen and becoming Catholic again, and so, seventeen years after she became queen, in 1570 he excommunicated Elizabeth, and commanded all her subjects 'that they presume not to obey her or her orders mandates and laws', on penalty of excommunication.

It was a disaster for Catholics, now suffering severe consequences, as suspected traitors. They became recusants, keeping their heads down, most of them loyal to the Queen, but keeping the Faith as best they could. Sometimes it was a matter of paying heavy fines of up to £20 for each month's non-attendance at Anglican worship and suffering the confiscation of lands; at other times it meant death, especially when plots or the threat of a foreign invasion to unseat Elizabeth loomed large. Young men went abroad to be trained as priests, returning to serve recusant communities knowing they faced certain martyrdom when caught, as they mostly were. There is no record of any coming to Walsingham. Every time news of another martyr reached the English College in Rome, the students gathered in the Chapel to sing the *Te Deum*. More than three hundred Catholics died for their faith in the reign of Elizabeth, but the bloodshed continued long after her forty-five year reign. Had it not been for them it is possible that all Catholics would simply have conformed in the end to the Anglican settlement, as the majority did. The martyrs gave heroic witness, and strengthened the resolve of others to keep the Faith. From 1559 until the nineteenth century, Catholics were seriously disadvantaged and mistrusted, and a long-lasting and deep-seated antipathy to Roman Catholicism fell on Britain, which John Henry Newman grew up with, and called 'a kind of false conscience.' Inevitably, Catholics declined in numbers, in Norfolk down to an estimated one thousand in 1759, out of a county population of 237,000.[9]

The Queen's Progress in East Anglia

As a means of securing her throne and enforcing religious conformity, Queen Elizabeth enjoyed summer 'Progresses' around her realm to increase her popularity; wherever she went church bells were rung and the crowds gathered to see her.

In 1578, the Queen embarked on a Progress through East Anglia where many noble Catholic families wouldn't give up their old ways, and the Bishop of Norwich was said to be more sympathetic to Catholics than to Protestants. 'Mr Sidney's at Walsingham', the old Priory estate, was one of two-dozen houses earmarked for a visit, but the list was whittled down to a handful, and in the end she didn't go there. The country had to be governed during these travels, and her Privy Council trailed around too. In August it began the recusancy hearings. During the previous year the Bishop had submitted the names of fifty men and women who refused to attend Anglican worship, including three from Walsingham, Robert Sands, John West and Edward Mason. Seventeen of these, all wealthy, were examined. In 1588 the Bishop's recusancy return for Walsingham listed only Robert Drewrie, his wife, and four male members of his family. In 1595 only one Catholic recusant was recorded in Walsingham, William Seele, despite an estimated Catholic population of 11 per cent in Norfolk.[10] No more recusants were listed between 1664 and 1669, or in the census of 1676. The same absence is apparent in 1767.[11]

Sir Henry Bedingfeld of Oxburgh was a prominent Norfolk recusant. His family was firmly Catholic, with a long history of royal service. Henry VIII had entrusted his father with the care of Katherine of Aragon after the divorce, and with the arrangements of her funeral and burial in Peterborough Cathedral. Sir Henry, as Lieutenant of the Tower of London had held Queen Elizabeth I at Woodstock Palace during the reign of Mary. Their relationship seems to have been happy and she used to affectionately call him her 'gaoler' whenever they met in court. She granted him the manor of Caldecot, which is still part of the Oxburgh estate. He paid heavy monthly fines for not attending the parish church, and his servants were dismissed for refusing to conform. Oxburgh Hall has a priest's hole, but it was never found when the house was searched; whenever a priest was expected Sir Henry would signal to the neighbourhood by hanging items of laundry on a hedge. Two items meant a Mass in two days' time.

Oxburgh was on Elizabeth's original list for the 1578 Progress, but there is no record that she went there. Sir Henry was summoned to appear before the recusancy court in Norwich but refused to attend. The Council moved on to Woodrising, near Oxburgh, and examined him there. He would not conform, and was put under house arrest in Norwich against bail of £500. There he remained for some months, until, excused by age and ill health, he was allowed home to Oxburgh. His wife died two years later and Sir Henry was permitted to stay with his daughter at Wiggenhall St Mary, near Watlington, to recover from his loss, but in the following year he died.[12]

There were more recusants in Wiggenhall St Mary that in any other part of Norfolk.[13] Inside the church a very fine brass eagle lectern is to be seen, bearing the inscription, ORATE PRO ANIMA FRATRIS ROBERTI BARNARD, GARDIANI DE WALSINGHAM (Pray for the soul of Robert Barnard, Guardian of Walsingham). Brother Barnard died in 1518, and the lectern once graced Walsingham Friary in his memory. Less than twenty years later his friary was demolished, and it seems evident that the Kerville family of Wiggenhall St Mary purchased the beautiful lectern when the Friary's goods and contents were sold. The church also contains a medieval screen in which none of the saints are defaced, and carvings of saints on the pew ends, which they successfully protected. One can only wonder whether anything else from Walsingham was hidden and awaits discovery.

Sometimes the Queen deliberately stayed with Catholics in order to intimidate them, and ensure their support in the event of an invasion. While the Queen was staying at Euston Hall in Suffolk with Edward Rookwood, it appears by a ruse, a statue of Our Lady was found in a hayrick and carried into the presence of the Queen while she was watching some country dancing. In all the consternation the Queen ordered the image to be burned and watched as it was. Edward Rookwood was arrested and brought to Norwich for the recusancy hearings, imprisoned to receive religious instruction, but in October conformed, and was released on payment of guarantees. Like others, he soon returned to the Faith and was still paying heavy fines twenty years later.[14] The Rookwood family owned many properties in Norfolk and Suffolk, including at Egmere, close to Walsingham, where they were listed as recusants in 1680. According to the historians Francis Blomefield and Charles Parkin, Robert Sydney, Earl of Leicester, split up the Walsingham estate, and sold Walsingham Abbey (Priory) to Nicholas Rookwood in 1639. In 1666 it was sold to Dr John Lee, archdeacon of Rochester.[15] For this short time of twenty-seven years, assuming Nicholas kept up the family's faith, it was Catholic once more.

The Queen also stayed on her Progress with twenty-one year old Philip Howard, who became Earl of Arundel. Philip's grandfather, Thomas Howard, the Duke of Norfolk, and Thomas' own father, Henry, had fallen from favour in the reign of Henry VIII. Henry Howard was beheaded in 1547, but the day before Thomas was due to die he was saved by the death of Henry VIII. Philip was anxious not to share the fate of his father, and conformed to the Anglican Faith, going out of his way to ingratiate himself with the Queen. Both she and her Council stayed at his home in Kenninghall in Norfolk. From there she went with him to his house in Norwich. The enormous cost of all this, £10,000, crippled him.

By all accounts Philip Howard led a dissolute life and badly neglected his young wife. But when he was twenty-four he went, out of interest, to hear a disputation between St Edmund Campion and some Protestant divines in the Tower of London. This proved the first step in his conversion. He was reconciled to the Catholic Church and became faithful to his wife. She too came back to the old Faith. Attempting like many others to leave England, in order freely to practice their faith, they were arrested at sea. Brought back to the Tower and charged with treason that was never proved, he was sentenced to death in 1589, though it was not carried out. Feeling that his death was near in 1595 he petitioned the Queen to be allowed to visit his wife and their son whom he had never seen. The Queen responded that if he returned to the Anglican Church he could go free and all his titles and honours would be restored. He refused, and died alone in the Tower of dysentery, aged thirty-eight, and was immediately acclaimed as a Catholic Martyr. He was buried in the same grave in the Tower Church that had received his father, but in 1624 his widow took his remains to Long Horsley, and thence to Arundel, where they still rest. Canonised as one of the Forty Martyrs his shrine is a centre of pilgrimage today.

Among the other houses owned by St Philip Howard were Flitcham Priory, a former cell of Walsingham Priory, and Castle Rising, not far from Walsingham. It is likely that between his conversion and his imprisonment he may have visited Walsingham, for among his papers was found a *Lament for Walsingham*. Although unsigned, Leonard Whatmore concludes, for various reasons, that it was composed by St Philip Howard, though some have questioned it: but since it was found with his papers he clearly treasured it.[16] And it shows how Our Lady of Walsingham was still remembered:

> In the wracks (devastation) of Walsingham whom should I choose
> But the Queen of Walsingham to be guide to my muse?
>
> Then thou Prince of Walsingham, grant me to frame
> Bitter plaints to rue thy wrong, bitter woe for thy name.
>
> Bitter was it oh to see the seely (innocent) sheep
> Murdered by the ravening wolves, while the shepherds did sleep.
>
> Whiles the gardeners played all close rooted up by the swine.
> Bitter, bitter, oh to behold the grass to grow
>
> Where the walls of Walsingham so stately did show.
> Where the press of peers did pass while her fame far was blown.
>
> Such were the works of Walsingham while she did stand
> Such are the wracks as now do show of that holy land!
>
> Level, level with the ground the towers do lie,
> Which with their golden glittering tops pierced once to the sky.
>
> Where were gates no gates are now; the ways unknown
> Where the press of peers did pass while her fame far was blown.
>
> Owls do shriek where the sweetest hymns lately were sung;
> Toads and serpents hold their dens where the pilgrims did throng.
>
> Weep, weep, O Walsingham whose days are nights,
> Blessings turned to blasphemies, holy deeds to despites (outrages).
>
> Sin is where Our Lady sat, Heaven turned is to hell,
> Satan sits where our Lord did sway, Walsingham, oh farewell![17]

Devotion and Pilgrimage after the Reformation

Owls shrieked in Walsingham, and at all Our Lady's Shrines. So severe were the restrictions on Catholics that there could be no public devotion to Our Lady; for even the possession of a rosary or image was dangerous and could lead to dire consequences.[18] Yet, people took risks. Recusants living in exile in such cities as Antwerp, Paris, Rheims and Rome, translated some of the old primers, including Offices of Our Lady, printed them, and smuggled them into England at great personal danger. Pilgrims frequented shrines. Loreto was a particularly popular destination, where its resemblance to Walsingham would not go unnoticed. They also made pilgrimages to former English shrines. In 1616 the Archbishop of York sent spies to report on devotees of Our Lady of Mount Grace, near Osmotherley, who were gathering at this isolated Shrine in North Yorkshire, which had not been completely destroyed, and so he ordered the roof to be taken off it.[19]

Most remarkable of all was the seventh-century Shrine and Holy Well of St Winifred in Flintshire. St Winifred's was not destroyed like all the other shrines, probably because the chamber and chapel, which still survive today, were built in about 1500, under the patronage of the devout and formidable Margaret Beaufort, Henry VIII's grandmother. Catholics, and Anglicans too, continued coming from all over the country by sea and land to pray at the Shrine, and ask for healing at the Holy Well. The Jesuits set up a hostel in 1581 at the Star Inn, where Mass could be said in comparative safety, and secular priests built another. In October 1626 the Mayor of Poole (Welshpool) wrote to the Privy Council that he was trying to stop the pilgrimages, but he had little success for in 1629 there was an exceptional pilgrimage of fourteen or fifteen hundred, with a hundred and fifty or more priests, 'the most of them well known what they were.'[20] King James II and his queen visited the Well in 1686, to pray for an heir. Shortly afterwards her prayer was answered. Graffiti on the walls of the well chamber record those who have found answers to prayer and healing there.

Pilgrimages to St Winifred's have never ceased, and a Catholic church opened in the town in the 1840s. A pilgrims' hospice was erected, and in the 1890s pilgrims were coming in their thousands, necessitating a branch rail line into the town. The popular press gave accounts of each reported cure and in such numbers that Holywell came to be called the *Lourdes of Wales*. An anonymous rhyme written in the eighteenth century names St Winifred's Well as one of the Seven Wonders of Wales:

> Pistyll Rhaeadr and Wrexham steeple,
> Snowdon's mountain without its people,
> Overton yew trees, St Winefride wells,
> Llangollen bridge and Gresford bells.

Nothing like that is recorded of Walsingham; surveillance was too tight, and with the Priory land in Protestant hands, except perhaps during the brief ownership of the Rockwood family, it would have been impossible. Anecdotal evidence has been passed down, however, that people used to ask the farmer who owned the Slipper Chapel for permission to visit his 'barn', where they would kneel and pray. And confirmation of this came in a private pilgrimage of Bishop Hilton Deakin, the Auxiliary Bishop of Melbourne, in 2007. He related how his great grandfather, who died in 1896, possessed a copy of the popular prayer book, *Garden of the Soul*, in which on the front blank pages he had written a list of dates around 1847-8 when he had missed attending local Anglican Services. On pages at the back was a list of the same dates, and places where he had attended a Catholic Mass instead. Inside the book was a letter, written to his parents, telling of his decision to emigrate to Australia. He relates how his parents had encouraged him first to make a journey to the shrine of the Lady (sic) at Walsingham, Norfolk, to seek her help and guidance at the chapel (the Slipper Chapel). Both his parents had made this pilgrimage. In the letter to his parents, which he wrote in 1848, on his return from Walsingham, confirming his decision to emigrate, he mentioned that the Chapel was a barn, and some distance from the centre of the old ruins. Bishop Deakin wrote: 'It was enough to encourage me to follow in his footsteps, and seek Our Lady of Walsingham's blessings and prayers for my family, as he had done so long ago.'[21]

It shows, as Sir Roger Townsend told Cromwell, 'the said image is not well out of some of their heads,' even in the early years of the nineteenth century. It is remarkable that despite the prohibitions on worship, the absence of churches, the lack of priests to give instruction, the legislation, fines, and punishments, and the fear of possessing Catholic prayer books or objects of devotion, the Catholic Church survived.

As we have seen, many recusants caved in and conformed under pressure and heavy fines, only to repent and return, sometimes again and again. Those Catholics who conformed and attended Anglican Services were scornfully called 'Church papists' by true recusants. But it was one thing to make people conform and attend Anglican worship, quite another to make them believe in it. There remained the hint of a 'Catholic side' in Anglicanism. Anglicans erected the first image of Our Lady in England since the reign of Queen Mary. In 1637, a statue was placed above the 'Virgin Porch', in the University Church of St Mary the Virgin in Oxford, partly paid for by Dr Morgan Owen, chaplain to Archbishop William Laud of Canterbury. Archbishop Laud was involved in an attempt to reunite the Anglican Church with Rome, and the placing of the statue was held against him at his trial, along with other charges including 'treating with the Pope's men in England' and 'corresponding with Rome.'[22] He was convicted and beheaded, along with King Charles I. There are bullet holes in the statue made by Cromwellian troopers.

One Anglican bishop who extolled Our Lady was Bishop Ken, the Bishop of Bath and Wells (1684-1690), who wrote a most beautiful 186 line paean of praise to Mary's life, which include stanzas celebrating both her Immaculate Conception and her Assumption:

> The Holy Ghost His Temple in her built,
> Cleansed from congenial, kept from mortal guilt;
> And from the moment that her blood was fired,
> Into her heart Celestial Love inspired. (11-14)
> Heaven with transcendent joys her entrance graced,
> Next to His throne her Son His Mother placed;
> And here below, now she's of Heaven possess'd,
> All generations are to call her blessed. (183-186)

These last lines form part of a hymn in several Anglican hymnals.[23] There were some other writers who kept a thread of continuity,[24] but it would be misleading to think that such sentiments were in any way representative of seventeenth and eighteenth century Anglicanism. There was great wariness of any mention of Mary, for even the most restrained devotion to her was equated with 'Romanism.'[25] Devotion to Our Lady in England during that time was left to Catholic recusants.

Other Memories of Walsingham

Walsingham was not forgotten, even if people no longer remembered what it once had been. The Holy Wells remained, but they became wishing wells. There are many allusions to Walsingham in literature. In 1765, Thomas Percy, the Anglican Bishop of Dromore, a companion of Dr Johnson, published what is now known as the *Percy Folio Manuscript*. Astonishingly, Percy found it 'lying dirty on the floor, under a bureau in ye parlour' in his friend Humphrey Pitt's residence at Shifnal in Shropshire, 'being used by the maids to light the fire.'[26] The manuscript, which seems to have been compiled about 1650, contained nearly two hundred texts, among them two Walsingham ballads and some verses of a third. The two are to be found in Appendix 3. *Gentle Herdsman* has already been quoted in Chapter 7, while the second is a love ballad convincingly attributed to Sir Walter Raleigh, who lived from 1552 to 1618.[27] This is of exceptional interest because Raleigh came from a strongly Protestant family, but in the late 1570s mixed with a number of Catholics at court, including Thomas Howard, Sir Philip Howard, and Francis Southwell. His official duties involved the execution of Catholics, but he tried to save the life of Fr Polydore Plasden, one of the Forty canonised martyrs, which did not endear him to his chiefs. Failing to save him, Raleigh gave orders he was to be hanged, and the sentence for him to be drawn, and quartered was carried out upon his lifeless body, saving him the most appalling agony. That he had grown more sympathetic with Catholics is evident from the Ballad attributed to him, which, although it is simply a love poem, speaks of 'the holy land of blessed Walsingham':

> As you came from the holy land of blessed Walsingham,
> Met you not with my true love by the way as you came?
>
> How shall I know your true love, that have met many one,
> As I went to the holy land, that have come, that have gone?[28]

There are fragments of a third Walsingham Ballad in Bishop Percy's collection:

> As I went to Walsingham to the shrine with speed,
> Met I with a jolly palmer (pilgrim) in a pilgrim's weed (garb)
>
> 'Now God you save, you jolly palmer! Welcome, lady gay.'
> 'Oft have I sued thee for love, oft have I said you, nay!'[29]

176

And two verses of another are quoted in John Webster's *The Weakest goes to the Wall*, dated around 1600:

> King Richard's gone to Walsingham, to the holy land;
> To kill the Turk and Saracen, that the truth do stand.
>
> Christ His cross be his good speed, Christ His foes to quell;
> Send him help in time of need, and to come home well.[30]

These Ballads have a fairly similar metre, and with a little adjustment can be sung to a well-known melody called the Walsingham Air. No one knows who composed it but it appears in several Elizabethan Virginal and Lute books and is easily found today.[31] Both William Byrd and John Bull wrote variations.

The Elizabethan rector and physician, William Bullein, no friend of Catholics, who was buried in the same grave as John Foxe, wrote cattily, 'He playeth Our Lady of Walsingham, giving as much health for a penny as she did holiness.' Mocking it may be, but 'the said image is not well out of some of their heads.'

The comedy, *Misogonus*, perhaps written about 1560, has a more reverent recollection: 'Our Sweet Lady of Walsingham be with her sweetly sweet soul.' Later still, Michael Drayton in an Ode, of 1619, eighty years after the shrine was destroyed, writes:

> Had she been born to former age
> That house had been a pilgrimage;
> And reputed more divine
> Than Walsingham and Becket's shrine.[32]

In 1781 John Wesley, the founder of Methodism, came to Walsingham on 30 October. He wrote in his journal:

> At two in the afternoon I preached at Walsingham, a place famous for many generations. Afterwards I walked over what is left of the famous Abbey, the east end of which is still standing. We then went to the Friary; the cloisters and chapel whereof are almost entire. Had there been a grain of virtue or public spirit in Henry the Eighth, these noble buildings need not have run to ruin.

It is likely he preached in Friday Market by the remains of the village Cross. Two years earlier a Methodist Society had come into existence, and the present Methodist Church in Walsingham, which opened in 1794, is the oldest still used in Norfolk. The church, manse and garden occupy part of what had been the church of the Friary. Of the Marian devotion of Wesley there is no evidence, but he was friendly with individual Catholics, particularly religious, and in his *Letter to a Roman Catholic* affirmed that Jesus was 'born of the blessed Virgin Mary, who, as well after as before she brought Him forth, continued a pure and unspotted virgin.'[33] A rosary sometimes said to have belonged to Wesley, passed down from his family, actually contains a Miraculous Medal, indicating a nineteenth century origin.[34]

The nineteenth century witnessed a reawakening of historical interest in Walsingham. At the turn of the century Charles Parkin wrote in great detail about Walsingham for Blomefield's *History of Norfolk* he was completing. This may have drawn the attention of the Victorian novelist and poet Agnes Strickland, who in 1835 wrote three volumes entitled, *The Pilgrims of Walsingham; or Tales of The Middle Ages: An Historical Romance*. It has recently been republished. A curious work, and quite well researched, she purportedly based it on Chaucer's *Canterbury Tales*. But her pilgrims are historical characters who include Henry VIII, Cardinal Wolsey, Queen Katherine, Anne Boleyn (!), Emperor Charles V, Sir Thomas Wyatt, and more, who are travelling incognito.

The nineteenth century also saw an enthusiasm for archaeology. The Revd James Lee Warner of Walsingham Abbey carried out a series of excavations in 1853-4.[35] While not as complete and accurate as the 1961 excavations, he did locate the site of the Holy House, though Henry Harrod, who had collaborated with him for a time, disputed this.

According to Blomefield, in his day, around 1740, the Milky Way was still spoken of as 'the Walsingham Way' by older Norfolk folk,[36] while Kelly's Directory for Cambridgeshire, Norfolk and Suffolk, which was published in 1883, says the expression was still used then. The memory of Walsingham had never died away completely, and it was waking up from its long sleep so that gradually, though no one could have guessed it at the time, the way was being prepared for the restoration of devotion to Our Lady of Walsingham.

Devotion and Pilgrimage in the Nineteenth Century

From the passing of the Roman Catholic Relief Act of 1791, which gave Catholics freedom to practise the Faith, and allowed registered churches, chapels and schools, the legislation against Catholics in England began to be dismantled. Earlier than that, judges had been unwilling to exact penalties, and many turned a blind eye to discreet churches in the shape of warehouses, or upstairs rooms or in courtyards. In Osmotherley, where there was a considerable recusant population, as early as 1665, Franciscan friars had a house, and the Old Hall was a place of Catholic worship. In 1745 the friars invited John Wesley to the village where he preached in the Old Hall and in the parish church. Catholics had learned how to survive. In 1832 the Catholic Emancipation Act came into force and, despite vociferous opposition in the country, dioceses were re-established by Pope Pius IX in 1850. Little by little the discriminations against Catholics serving in the armed forces, in the legal profession, against taking degrees at Oxford and Cambridge were removed, all except the bar on the monarch being, or being married to a Catholic.

Remnants of the Catholic Faith were still found in Norfolk, as Frederick Hibgame observed: 'I travelled much about Norfolk about 1890, and was surprised to find many traces of the old Jesuit missions of the seventeenth and eighteenth centuries in pictures and rosaries still preserved by the descendants of those who first received them. I was a pupil of two different Church of England clergymen when I was a boy, and the sexton to one of them had three pictures, on glass, of Our Lady of Sorrows, The Sacred Heart, and the Immaculate Conception, which, he told me, were "from the Romans when they came about these parts".' But for most Norfolk people 'the idea that his ancestors had been Catholics was as remote as the idea that dinosaurs had once roamed the land.'[37]

These new-found freedoms for English Catholics, together with the immigration of poor Irish Catholics after the potato famines of 1845-1849, the flow of converts from the Church of England, and the arrival of Italian missionaries, were strengthening devotion to Our Lady during the nineteenth century amongst Roman Catholics, while in the Church of England the same eventually happened through the Oxford Movement.

An example of an enthusiastic convert was Father Frederick Faber, son of the Vicar of Calverley, who joined the Oratory founded by Newman, but who fell out seriously with him, becoming Superior of the London Brompton Oratory, while Newman remained in Birmingham. Newman was much more in line with the old English Catholicism. Faber was personally flamboyant, and that is how he liked his Faith. He launched a scathing attack on what he perceived as the lack of devotion to Our Lady in England. In his preface to his translation of St Louis Marie Grignon de Montfort's *Treatise on True Devotion to the Blessed Virgin*, with which he was seeking to remedy the situation in 1862, he wrote,

> Here in England Mary is not half enough preached. Devotion to her is low, thin and poor. It is frightened out of its wits by the sneers of heresy. It is always invoking human respect and carnal prudence, wishing to make Mary so little of a Mary, that Protestants may feel at ease about her. Its ignorance of theology makes it unsubstantial and unworthy. It is not the prominent characteristic of our religion which it ought to be. It has no faith in itself.[38]

By translating and publicising the Treatise of St Louis Marie Grignon de Montfort, Faber was certainly promoting a great classic. But his polemic has been seen as part of the tensions between old English Catholics who kept the Faith with their quieter devotion, and more intense piety favoured by Italian missionaries like Fr Luigi Gentili, supported by the Irish poor, and by some of the converts. This perception that devotion to Our Lady was shallow in native English Catholicism has been firmly challenged by John Bossy and others.[39] And Mary Heimann has shown that the advent of outdoor processions, public witness, plays and missions and other manifestations of faith and enthusiasm was common to all the churches, including the nonconformist, and was more to do with countering the process of secularisation which became apparent from the 1880s.[40] In fact, far from lacking in devotion to Our Lady, from 1750 when Bishop Richard Challoner published it for the old Catholics, *The Garden of the Soul* remained the most popular book of prayers throughout the nineteenth century, followed by the *Raccolta*, the *Key of Heaven,* and *Manual of Prayers*. All of these contained devotions to Our Lady, and *The Garden of the Soul* included everything from the Angelus, Anthems of Our Lady, the *Salve Regina*, invocations to Our Lady before and after Communion, Hymns to the Virgin, the *Litany of Loreto*, the Rosary, and a huge section of Offices of Our Lady covering Mattins, Lauds, Prime, Evensong, Compline and other Hours.

A ground-breaking publication aimed at reminding the faithful about the once-famous love for Mary in England was *Pietas Mariana Britannica: A History of English Devotion to the Most Blessed Virgin Mary Mother of God, with a Catalogue of Shrines, Sanctuaries, Offerings, Bequests, and Other Memorials of the Piety of Our Forefathers*, by Edmund Waterton, printed in 1879, and recently re-published.[41] Edmund Waterton was educated at Stonyhurst, a Knight of Malta, and Fellow of the Society of Antiquaries, and in his book sought to recover medieval Catholic traditions. The first part of *Pietas Mariana* traces the history of English devotion to Our Lady from the time it was designated 'Mary's Dowry' with all the homage she received from everyone from kings to innkeepers. The second part relates the ways in which people paid homage, through shrines and churches, organs and bells, Loreto Chapels and other Lady Chapels, with altars, inscriptions, relics, guilds, sodalities, pilgrimages, processions, Masses and offices of Our Lady, the angelus, rosary, litanies, and through the naming and consecration of things to her like cities, land, wells, flowers, even furniture. The third part deals with iconography, the crowning and dressing of statues, and such like. He gives accounts of the more important shrines of Our Lady in England, with a long section on Walsingham. Not accurate in every detail, it nonetheless reveals painstaking research, and was very influential in attempting to revive a medieval past and increase devotion to Our Lady.

Pietas Mariana Britannica was first published by instalments in the *Month*, and just as the first one appeared, Fr Thomas Edward Bridgett produced the first edition of *Mary's Dowry; how England gained and lost that Title*. He was a convert, a student at St John's College, Cambridge, which he left without a degree in 1850, because graduation was open only to those who subscribed to the Anglican Thirty-nine Articles. He had attended and been convinced by Newman's lectures at the London Oratory on *Difficulties of Anglicans*. After being received he became a Redemptorist priest. *Mary's Dowry* covers some of the same ground as *Pietas Mariana*, and caused him much embarrassment. Bridgett confirmed that had he known of Waterton's research he would much preferred to have handed all his notes over to him, for he recognised that Waterton 'was entitled to be the Knight of Our Lady, as representing the old English Catholic traditions.'[42] They became firm friends, however, for their common purpose was to remind the faithful of England's Marian history and arouse in them a true and deep devotion to Our Lady. By their researches they were unwittingly preparing the way for the restoration of England's greatest Shrine, Our Lady of Walsingham, as more and more people came to hear of its glorious past.

While this was happening in the Catholic Church a deepening devotion to Our Lady was emerging in the Church of England. From about 1828 a movement was beginning at Oxford where a group of scholars were seeking ways of renewing the Church of England, and making her aware of her Catholic heritage. Their leader was John Henry Newman, a tutor at Oriel College. Others included Richard Hurrell Froude, Edward Bouverie Pusey, and John Keble. Newman acknowledged that Froude, the son of the Archdeacon of Totnes, 'fixed deep in me the idea of devotion to the Blessed Virgin and led me gradually to believe in the Real Presence'.[43] This was when Newman was in his mid-twenties and before he became Vicar of the University Church of St Mary the Virgin, Oxford, where the statue of Our Lady had been erected. Later, he wrote, 'I had a true devotion to the Blessed Virgin, in whose College I lived, whose altar I served, and whose Immaculate Purity I had, in one of my earliest printed Sermons, made much of.'[44] This was a sermon he preached in St Mary's on the Feast of the Annunciation, 1832, entitled 'The Reverence due to the Virgin Mary', in which he lyrically asked,

> Who can estimate the holiness and perfection of her, who was chosen to be the Mother of Christ? If to him that hath, more is given, and holiness and Divine Favour go together (and this we are expressly told), what must have been the transcendent purity of her, whom the Creator

Spirit condescended to overshadow with His miraculous presence? What must have been her gifts?[45]

When at length Newman came into the Catholic Church he brought with him and developed all that he had come to understand about Our Lady during his Anglican days, especially from the depths of his studies in the Scriptures and the Fathers. Soon the Oxford Movement spread far beyond Oxford. Even when Newman and many others became Roman Catholics, the Movement went on, until it changed the Church of England almost beyond recognition. Religious orders for women, then for men were founded, daily mass and devotion to the Blessed Sacrament was fostered, confession and the anointing of the sick were restored, retreats were organised, devotional societies, confraternities, and parish missions, in a widespread emphasis on the spiritual life, holiness, and discipline. Devotion to Our Lady was much slower to develop, because the followers of the Oxford Movement, Anglo-Catholics as they came to be called, were very anxious about the accusations of 'Romanism' levelled against them. Even as late as 1869 a popular prayer book, *The Treasury of Devotion*, was very muted on Our Lady, and the Hail Mary only included the first Scriptural part, omitting 'Holy Mary, Mother of God, pray for us sinners now, and at the hour of our death.' It did, however, include mediations of the Rosary, with 'The Triumph of the Church in the Saints' and The Beatific Vision, replacing the Assumption and Coronation of Our Lady. The breakthrough came in 1893 with the publication of *Catholic Prayers for Church of England People*, later just known as *Catholic Prayers*. It was written anonymously by, it is now believed, a curate of St Alban's Holborn. Running into numerous editions it was the most widely-used devotional prayer book for the next fifty years. Anglican clergy and people now had access to most of the popular Catholic devotions to Our Lady, Vespers, the *Litany of Loreto* in both Latin and English, the full Hail Mary and Rosary, as well as many Marian hymns and prayers. Some of the Marian hymns found their way into Anglican hymnbooks for the first time. Other prayer books followed, like the *Anglo-Catholic Prayer Book* and *St Swithun's Prayer Book*; devotion to Our Lady was becoming firmly entrenched among Anglo-Catholics.

Statues and pictures of her began to be placed in churches, despite furious protestant opposition. In 1885 the *Confraternity of the Children of Mary*, founded in Madras, reached England, where it became known as the

Confraternity of Our Lady. The Union of the Holy Rosary, whose members undertook to pray it daily, came in 1886. *The League of Our Lady* followed in 1904, and these Marian organisations merged together as the *Society of Mary* in 1931. The aims of the Society are to love and honour Mary, to spread devotion to her in reparation for past neglect and misunderstanding and in the cause of Christian unity, and thirdly to take Mary as a model in purity, personal relationships and family life. The Society is dedicated to the glory of God and in honour of the Holy Incarnation, under the invocation of Our Lady, Help of Christians, and members are called to keep a Rule of Life, including such devotions as the Angelus, the Rosary, the Litany and Anthems of Our Lady. They pray for departed members of the Society and offer Mass for them, take part in the Mass on the principal Feasts of Our Lady, and engage in apostolic and pastoral work.

Pope Paul VI paid tribute to Anglican devotion to Our Lady in his Apostolic Exhortation, *Marialis Cultus,* of 2 February 1974:

> Catholics are also united with Anglicans, whose classical theologians have already drawn attention to the sound scriptural basis for devotion to the Mother of our Lord, while those of the present day increasingly underline the importance of Mary's place in the Christian life.[46]

The idea of pilgrimage was also being recovered. Catholics, unable to go on pilgrimage in England, had long travelled abroad. Loreto was a favourite destination. But Anglicans too revived the devotion and from 1877 a series of books on the Pilgrim Way to Canterbury led some cathedrals to promote themselves once again as centres of pilgrimage.[47]

The second half of the nineteenth century witnessed the building of some very fine churches, Roman Catholic, Anglican and non-conformist. Anglo-Catholics employed some of the best Victorian architects who shared their faith, and through inspiring work were able to draw ever more disciples to their cause. Wealthy families, whether Catholic, Anglican or nonconformist, loved to build churches, many of them for the poor, none more so than the Wagner family. The Revd Henry Michell Wagner, who became Vicar of Brighton in 1824, built six churches, among them, in 1848, St Paul's.

The First Walsingham Chapel

Henry's son, Fr Arthur Wagner, became perpetual curate, then vicar of St Paul's in 1850, remaining there for the rest of his life. A great friend of Newman he attended the ceremony in Rome when he was made a cardinal. He continued the family tradition, and in the poorest parts of the town he built five churches, including St Bartholomew's, a huge church seating 1500, said to have the same dimensions as the nave of Westminster Abbey. To each of these churches he gave a personal gift, a copy of the venerable icon of Our Lady known as *Salus Populi Romani*, the Protectress of the City of Rome, and the most sacred icon in the city. A statue in an Anglican church in those days would have invited fury. Fr Wagner's care for the poor also led him, at his own expense, to build some 400 houses for them, and to assist in his pastoral work he founded the Community of the Blessed Virgin Mary in 1855. A terrible event caused immense distress. A girl taken in by the Community, Constance Kent, who gave herself up to the police in 1865, admitted in court that when she was sixteen she had murdered her half-brother. Fr Wagner refused to reveal what she had told him in the confessional box, was accused of forcing her to confess, and as a result he was assaulted in the streets of Brighton, and objects were thrown at the windows of the Community's Home. Constance was sent to prison, the judge in tears. The story is beautifully told in *The Suspicions of Mr Whicher*.[48]

In 1873 Fr Wagner had acquired a house in Buxted, a small town twenty miles north of Brighton, which he used as a retreat from the controversies, and allowed the sisters to use as well. Five years later he built them a convent in Buxted, where Constance, after her release, spent some time with the sisters again before making a new life in Australia as a nurse, for many years nursing lepers. True to form, Fr Wagner also built a church there. On 27 January 1885 the foundation stone was laid and on 12 March a schoolroom was opened to serve as a temporary church, until St Mary's was ready for use on the Feast of Pentecost in 1886. It was consecrated a year later. The Community of the Blessed Virgin Mary remained in Buxted until 1912, when their house passed to the Community of St Mary the Virgin of Wantage.

It was in the Church of St Mary's Buxted that the precursor of both the Catholic and the Anglican Shrines at Walsingham is to be found. For in the early stages of building St Mary's Fr Wagner heard about the 1854 excavations in Walsingham that had located the site of the original Shrine, and he at once ordered the building plans to be changed so that within the church, on the south side, he created the 'Walsingham Chapel,' to the exact dimensions of the original Holy House.[49] Fr Wagner must be credited with being the first to restore devotion to Our Lady of Walsingham, although a statue was not put into the Chapel until 1932. Not only that, but Fr Wagner had a curate, Fr Philip Fletcher from 1872–1874, and almost fifty years later there was another curate at Buxted, Fr Alfred Hope Patten, both of whom were destined to take it much further.

CHAPTER 11

RESTORATION

Unlikely as it may seem, although one king of England was responsible for the destruction of the Shrine, another king of England, or at least a future king, unwittingly prompted its restoration. The Mission Rector (as he was known) of King's Lynn, Fr George Wrigglesworth, had only been in King's Lynn for two years when, on 6 December 1889, HRH Edward, Prince of Wales, the future King Edward VII, invited him to Sandringham House, which he had recently built.[1] Catholic guests staying at Sandringham, who included the Comte and Comtesse de Paris, the King of the Belgians, the Duke of Chartres, the Duchess of Mecklenburg, and the Duke of Norfolk, had attended Mass in King's Lynn, and drawn the Prince's attention to the condition of the church. Parts of the roof were open to the sky and rain poured in, and there were cracks in the walls so wide that draughts blew through them. It was indeed in a sorry state, all the sadder because it had been standing for little more than forty years and had been designed by Augustus Welby Pugin. If the Rector would launch an appeal, the Prince would help with the cost of repairs.

Fundraising began, but Fr Wrigglesworth's priority was the building of a school, and only when this was opened in 1894, did he turn his full attention to the church. No doubt the building would have been listed today, and it would have been underpinned, but an inspection revealed inadequate foundations on the soft marshy ground of the seaport, and it was condemned as unsafe. Demolition was advised and a new church had to be built. This was a disaster for the priest and his congregation of but a hundred and fifty, all of them poor. The Bishop of Northampton, Arthur Riddell, was supportive at first and in his 1895 Advent Pastoral wrote, 'Next year we hope to rebuild the church at King's Lynn which is past repairing.' In less than a year he apparently went back on his word, for Fr Wrigglesworth wrote a long and heartfelt letter to him:

> I cannot express the crushing effect of your letter to hand. Especially as I had hoped and prayed that St Joseph, on the anniversary of my paying off the debt on the school, would give the new church. Since last December I have been living in hope of at least seeing the new church before I die. But that hope is now gone. When I came to Lynn it was my boast that I was the strongest priest in the Diocese. Now I do not think there could be a weaker. Indeed, had it been a severe winter, in all probability, I should have been in my grave ere this. And this has been brought about by the condition of the church. Unless you had the experience I have had, your Lordship could not realise what it is, especially in winter. It would be safer to be out in the open field.[2]

Pugin Church, Kings Lynn

The reply from the Bishop 'caused hope to revive in me,' and on 12 July the Bishop wrote formally to approve the demolition of the church and the building of another. On hearing the news, the Prince, who was a notable benefactor of churches in Norfolk, promised to donate the princely sum of fifty guineas, and was as good as his word.

Fr Philip Fletcher

Fr Wrigglesworth appealed for help, and placed an advertisement in a London newspaper, which is where Fr Philip Fletcher, a former curate of Fr Wagner at St Bartholomew's Brighton, from 1872–1874, comes in. St Mary's Buxted was not built until 1886, but of course Fr Fletcher knew of it, and it was from Fr Wagner, he always said, that he first heard about the great medieval shrine in Walsingham. On leaving Brighton Fr Fletcher became a Roman Catholic and in due course parish priest of nearby Uckfield in Sussex, where he founded the *Union of Intercession for the Conversion of England*. This attracted the attention of a lay convert and barrister, Lister Drummond, who convinced Fr Fletcher that action was needed as well as prayer, and in 1887 the *Guild of Our Lady of Ransom* was founded, inspired by two orders that have already been mentioned, the Trinitarians and the Mercedarians, who had a particular devotion to Our Lady of Ransom. Fr Fletcher spent the rest of his life travelling all over the country, preaching and speaking. Drummond preached out of doors and was frequently heard at Hyde Park Corner, paving the way for the *Catholic Evidence Guild*.

The Guild of Our Lady of Ransom published journals, *Faith of Our Fathers*, *The Catholic Standard*, *Ransomer*, and *The Second Spring*, and although arguing the case against Anglicanism, Fr Fletcher never lost his affection for the Church of England or tired of acknowledging the sincerity of Anglo-Catholics. In some respects he was like Fr Patten. Both were persuasive and full of charm. They both had a desire to promote pilgrimages and work in their different ways for the conversion of England to Catholic Faith. They also had a highly developed spiritual sensitivity. Fr Fletcher never forgot a strange experience when he was staying at St Vincent's Home for Boys in London, when a little boy had been brought in off the street dying. They baptised him conditionally and he was sleeping peacefully. 'Before I went to bed I asked the little boy to visit me when his soul left his body. At two o'clock I was awakened by a boy's face, brilliant with glory, so bright that I was obliged to cover my face with the clothes. In the morning they told me: "He died at two o'clock".'[3] Fr Patten had similar spiritual awareness, and was sensitive to supernatural presences.[4]

The Guild of Our Lady of Ransom works and prays for the conversion of England, and seeks to revive pilgrimages and processions. But part of their work was to assist poor parishes with the building of churches, and it was this that attracted Fr Fletcher to Fr Wrigglesworth's appeal. 'My attention (was) arrested by a pleading advertisement, "Help! Help! My church is falling down".'[5] Fr Fletcher came to King's Lynn to discuss a new church with Fr Wrigglesworth and, following the model of St Mary's Buxted, they decided to restore inside it the Shrine of Our Lady of Walsingham. As at Buxted, the Chapel, a small-scale copy of the Holy House of Loreto, stands on the south side of the new Church of Our Lady of the Annunciation. Fr Wrigglesworth had visited Loreto, and noted the wavy patterns on the brickwork, which were reproduced in King's Lynn. The Bishop of Northampton fully approved, and not withstanding that only a quarter of the necessary money had been raised, he ordered the work to begin, and Mr W. Lunn of Great Malvern was the appointed architect.

He was able to save some of Pugin's work. The rood and font were retained, together with six silver candlesticks, and also a panel of the Annunciation, which had formed part of the reredos in the earlier church. A Pugin window, featuring Our Lady, St Thomas of Canterbury, and St George, a rare early work made by the great William Wailes, was also preserved. Of unique interest is the coat of arms of the King of Spain commemorating a Sunday in 1907 when King Alfonso XIII and Queen Victoria Eugenie, a granddaughter of Queen Victoria, went to Mass there.

On 6 February 1897 Pope Leo XIII issued a rescript for the reconstitution of the ancient Shrine of Our Lady of Walsingham, and blessed the statue chosen by the Cardinal Vicar. Perhaps neither Fr Fletcher nor Fr Wrigglesworth knew what Walsingham's original image looked like, but the chosen statue is a standing Madonna and child, copied from a picture of

Our Lady in Santa Maria Cosmedin in Rome, the titular church of Cardinal Pole, the last English cardinal before the reign of Elizabeth. (Pilgrims to Rome no longer see it because the church was given to Greek rite Catholics who use icons, and its statues and pictures languish in a room beneath the Church). The statue was carved in Oberammagau, and Fr Fletcher said that the Pope told him, 'When England comes back to Walsingham, Mary will come back to England.'

The Chapel was presented with a pair of candlesticks believed to have belonged to the Priory in Walsingham.[6] Fifteen lamps burned in front of it, one for each mystery of the rosary, and the chapel was enclosed with a little wooden screen in medieval style, like the one in Buxted, with six panels depicting the Annunciation. In 1961 a fine window by Lily Dagless, depicting Richeldis with Our Lady holding the Holy House, was put in the Chapel to celebrate the 900th anniversary of her vision.

In a lovely letter to the Bishop, Fr Wrigglesworth told him that the Holy House 'is a little gem, and the architect was quite "touched" when he saw how it had turned out. And Fr Freeland declared that it would be said the angels had transported the Holy House from Loreto to Walsingham.'[7] The Bishop blessed the foundation stone on 29 September 1896, and on 2 June 1897 he celebrated its opening Mass. The church, which had been dedicated to St Mary, was renamed Our Lady of the Annunciation.

On Thursday 19 August 1897 the first pilgrimage to the Holy House was made. Fr Fletcher celebrated Mass in the Annunciation at 11.15 a.m., and after Mass a long procession was formed, with thirty girls in white dresses and sashes, innumerable Ransomers, clergy and hundreds of people, who passed along London Road, through The Walks, to the Railway Station.

> The new statue of Our Lady of Walsingham, designated by the Holy Father and carved at Oberammagau had arrived from London. After the statue had been placed on the bier it was carried shoulder high by the maiden bearers, and the procession, singing the Pilgrim's Ave, and reciting the Rosary, returned by the same route, with the exception that a detour was made round that exquisite gem of fourteenth century work, the octagonal Chapel of Our Lady of the Mount, where pilgrims on their way to Walsingham used to stop. The demeanour of the dense crowds that witnessed it was most attentive, respectful, and in several instances reverential, not an unpleasant remark being made throughout

its course. Arrived at the church, the statue was blessed and enthroned in the new Shrine.[8]

In the afternoon, before Benediction, Fr Arthur Whelan, Rector of the Church of Our Lady, Little Albany, preached a fervent sermon:

> You have, my dear Brethren, a great treasure, a precious inheritance. Guard it, preserve it; let no enemy take it from you. Increase your love for Mary. The measure of your love for the Mother is the measure of your faith in her Son. Be loyal to his Church, be faithful Catholics. All past Christian glories are ours, renew them, create others. The future of the Church in this land depends upon the seeds which are now sown: seeds of faith, zeal and enthusiasm.[9]

Fr Wrigglesworth shared the vision that one day the streets of King's Lynn would be thronged with colourful processions and singing, in a glorious revival of medieval days. But he also shared the hope of many that the Shrine would one day be restored in Walsingham, and next day he and Fr Fletcher, the Duke of Norfolk, the Prior of Downside, and a Miss Charlotte Boyd, gathered with forty or fifty Ransomers and other pilgrims at Walsingham Station, from where they were led by a crucifer and acolytes to the Slipper Chapel, to sing the Litany of the Holy Name, the *Litany of Loreto*, the *Ave Maris Stella*, and an act of reparation for the sacrilege which had destroyed the ancient Shrine. This was the first pilgrimage to come back to Walsingham since the Reformation. Afterwards they dispersed and went in small groups to pray at the site of the ancient shrine in the ruins of the Priory, and Friary.

Both priests felt called to restore devotion and pilgrimage to Our Lady of Walsingham, and saw King's Lynn as an interim measure. Fr Fletcher wrote:

> I do not think there would be any difficulty in restoring the shrine to Walsingham eventually … The reason why King's Lynn was chosen some years ago was that there was a resident priest and congregation there, who could keep up the devotion and guard the shrine … Nothing of this kind was possible at Walsingham when Fr Wrigglesworth and I began the restoration … we must keep to King's Lynn for the present but may hope and pray to see Walsingham restored when a mission can be established there.[10]

47.

The Slipper Chapel as Charlotte Boyd found it, used as a cow shed, its windows blocked in, a chimney on top, and an old cottage attached. She restored it in 1897, had great plans for it, and sent a lithograph to the Bishop of Northampton to show him her idea. But it was not furnished until 1934 when it become the National Roman Catholic Shrine. Soon pilgrims began to come in great numbers to pray there beside the statue of Our Lady of Walsingham designed by Professor Tristram. This was replaced in 1954 by the present one carved by Monsieur Marcel Barbeau.

RESTORED PILGRIM CHAPEL AT HOUGHTON-LE-DALE, NEAR WALSINGHAM.

48.

49.

50.

The Shrine of Our Lady of Walsingham, facing the ruins of the Priory, set up by Fr Patten in St Mary's on 6 July 1922, on a pillar in the Guilds Chapel, shown here on the north side of the church. It soon became a place of great prayer, and was surrounded by candles, flowers and votive offerings. The sacred image remained there until the building of the Holy House in 1931, when it was replaced by a picture, which was destroyed in the fire of 1961.

51.

52.

On Thursday 15 October 1931 the Sacred Image of Our Lady of Walsingham was carried in a procession through the village from St Mary's to the newly built Anglican Shrine and Holy House.

53.

54.

55.

The Procession halted outside the new Sanctuary before the Image of Our Lady was enthoned in the Holy House.

56.

57.

Whit-Monday 6 June 1938. The extension to the Shrine (the roof line clearly seen in the photograph) was blessed by Bishop O'Rorke, attended by two priests of the Community of the Resurrection, Mirfield, in the presence of 150 priest associates and between 3,000 and 4,000 pilgrims.

58.

59.

The Procession of 15 October 1952, marking the 21st anniversary of the translation of the image from St Mary's to the Holy House, passing the Bull, with the Guardians flanking the statue, and Sister Julian, Mother Margaret, Sister Barbara, and Miss Struggles supervising the petal girls. Fr Patten, preceded by the young John Shepherd, in the procession.

60.

61.

Kensit's Wycliffe Preachers disturbed Services in St Mary's, and their successors still protest at the Anglican National Pilgimage. Christmas 1957 in St Hilary's, with Fr Patten at one end of the table, and Mr Stanley Smith at the other, and Miss "Will" (left) and Barty, who ran the home for 21 years.

62.

63.

Both Catholic and Anglican pilgrims drank water from the twin wells in the Priory grounds. 63. An early Anglican Pilgrimage. 64. A Catholic Pilgrimage from Roehampton on the Feast of the Annunciation, 1936. Many early pilgrimages arrived by train, and there was a halt by the Slipper Chapel. Girls from London Oratory School on pilgrimage in 1938.

64.

65.

After being neglected for more than 25 years, the Slipper Chapel was at last opened and furnished in 1934.

66.

On the Feast of the Assumption, 1934, Bishop Youens of Northampton celebrated Mass in it, assisted by Canon Francis Sammons of Fakenham (left) the first public Mass since the Reformation.

67.

It was consecrated on Our Lady's Birthday, 1938.

68.

69.

70. On Sunday 19 August 1934, Cardinal Francis Bourne, though very ill, led a Pilgrimage of 12,000 in reparation for the destruction of the Shrine. With the approval of the Pope, and on behalf of all the Bishops of England and Wales, he declared Walsingham to be the National Shrine of Our Lady. 69. In the afternoon, Fr Vernon Johnson preached to the vast crowd gathered in the meadow by the Slipper Chapel. 71. In 1938, to mark the 400th anniversary of the desecration of the Shrine, Cardinal Arthur Hinsley led a pilgrimage of 10,000 young people on another pilgrimage of reparation and to pray for peace.

70.

71

Fr Bruno Scott James welcomes Father Paul O.S.F.C. (left) and Brother Andrew O.S.F.C., in 1937, to their Friary in Friday Market, Aelred House, which they renamed Greyfriars. Their Chapel of St Aelred served as the village 'parish church' until the Church of the Annunciation was built. Fr Bruno and his Siamese, which often perched on his shoulder when he preached in the open air.

72.

73.

74.

The Friars demolished with their own hands the two cottages that stood between the Old Grammar School (now the Pilgrim Bureau) and the Black Lion.

75.

The Church of the Annunciation was blessed on 2 July 1950 by Bishop Parker.

76.

Enid Chadwick, the gifted Anglican artist, designed the façade as a gift to the church.

77.

1948 was the great Cross-carrying Year of Pilgrimage at the Catholic Shrine. Over 400 men with heavy crosses walked from all over England as an act of reparation for the war and a prayer for peace. They were placed around the grounds of the Shrine where they serve as Stations of the Cross. A notice tells where the walkers came from and how many miles they walked. This inspired the annual Walk by the Guild of Our Lady of Ransom, which continued for 50 years.

78.

On 16 July 12,000 pilgrims saw Cardinal Bernard Griffin consecrate England to the Immaculate Heart of Mary at the site of the ancient Shrine.

79.

Also in 1948 was the first Student Cross Pilgrimage. Here the London leg is walking through Smithfield, where both Catholics and Protestants were put to death in the Reformation period. Now an ecumenical pilgrimage, students walk in Holy Week to arrive in Walsingham on Good Friday.

80.

81.

On the Feast of the Assumption, 1954, a Marian Year, 15,000 pilgrims witnessed Our Lady of Walsingham being solemnly crowned by the Apostolic Delegate, Archbishop O'Hara, on behalf of Pope Pius XII, in the Abbey grounds. Two white doves settled on the statue and remained there on the procession along the Holy Mile, and overnight in the Slipper Chapel. Mysteriously, the same phenomenon had occurred to the statue of Our Lady of Fatima after it was crowned on 13 May 1946.

82.

On 12 August 1958, Fr Patten sings the Collect in Benediction at the end of the Saturday evening procession, during the first Bishops' Pilgrimage. The occasion crowned his life's work. No sooner had he replaced the Blessed Sacrament in the tabernacle than he collapsed and died.

83.

84.

Fr Patten wearing his Guardian's mantle, and his chain of office as Master of the College of Guardians.

85.

St Mary's, as it was in Fr Patten's day. Tragedy struck on 14th July 1961 when the church was gutted by fire.

86.

The famous font was saved, and the tower and outside walls. Laurence King was the architect who rebuilt it, with support from all over the country.

87.

Fr Wrigglesworth died suddenly only three years after restoring the Shrine, and he was remembered with great affection:

> His priestly form was well-known in the streets, lanes and alleys in and around Lynn. He has been known to take a journey of 23 miles in the hope of getting one Catholic woman to her duties. And Sunday by Sunday he spoke to his flock with a force which constitutes true Christian eloquence. His tact, courtesy, kindliness, and the power of imparting to others the piety, of which his own life was a striking example – all made him a true father and pastor to his people, to whom he was devoted heart and soul.[11]

The Catholics in King's Lynn had a parish priest and people working together in the restoration of the Shrine, but in Walsingham there was neither a priest nor any people. No bishop was going to allow a church or shrine to be built with no Catholics to use it. The fact that it happened eventually is due to a remarkable Anglican lady.

Miss Charlotte Boyd

Miss Charlotte Boyd was born into a particularly wealthy family, descended from the Earls of Kilmarnock on her father's side and on her mother's a sixteenth-century Lord Mayor of London. She had an extraordinary experience during a visit to the ruins of Glastonbury Abbey, when she was but a child of thirteen. Much later she wrote of herself in the third person:

> a young girl at the time, sat alone on that summer afternoon, sadly contemplating the ruins in their desolation and desecration. Impelled by a sudden impulse, she knelt and offered herself to the work of Restoration, if God would accept her. Quickly and silently the years passed by, while the desire then kindled in her heart was meantime only mentioned to God in prayer; till in 1865, when Dr Neale was sought as a counsellor, his words, 'I would have you take this as your work in life,' encouraged and confirmed the purpose formed so long ago.[12]

Dr Neale was the Revd John Mason Neale, the founder of an Anglican religious community, the Society of St Margaret, who work in the Anglican Shrine today. He was also the author and translator of very many well-known hymns including *All Glory, Laud, and Honour*; *O Come, O Come, Emmanuel*; *Of the Father's Heart Begotten*; and the legendary Boxing Day carol, *Good King Wenceslas*.

Charlotte Boyd enlisted the help of three Anglican Religious of the Society of St John the Evangelist, Cowley, and founded the *English Abbey Restoration Trust*, with the aim of purchasing and restoring the ruins of Religious Houses destroyed by Henry VIII, and putting them back into the hands of religious. Before long the Trust had a thousand members, including thirteen Religious Communities. Interestingly, one of her forebears had been William Boyd, an Abbot of Kilwinning in Ayrshire in 1451. This work, of course, did not occupy all of her time, and in 1866 she founded the *Orphanage of the Infant Saviour*, in Kensington, before moving it to Kilburn. She built a school and remained as head of the orphanage for the next forty years until her death. Not only did she care for orphans, but in the Annual Report of 1902 it was recorded that

> Six gentlewomen have received hospitality in time of distress, and remained with us until suitable employment was found for them. Servants out of work or in bad health have been taken into the Home for rest and care. Children have been temporarily sheltered while their mothers were in various hospitals.

Pastoral care for the poor was a hallmark of the Anglo-Catholic Movement in the Church of England, and Charlotte's work was inspired by the often heroic labours of the so-called 'slum priests' who devoted their lives to the poor, as well as taking social and political action to improve their lot.

In 1883, the owner of Malling Abbey in Kent, an eleventh-century former Benedictine convent offered the use of the gatehouse and chapel to the *English Abbey Restoration Trust*, and Charlotte loved to take her orphans there, away from the noise and unpleasantness of London. Nine years later the *Trust* was able to buy the Abbey itself, by which time she had taken a poor community of Anglican sisters under her wing, and so she gave it to them. Benedictines were once again singing the praises of the Lord in Malling Abbey, and still are. This community left Malling Abbey in 1911 and joined the Roman Catholic Church, but another community of Anglican sisters, the Order of St Benedict, replaced them. Charlotte had fulfilled something of her girlhood aspirations.

In 1893 Charlotte was looking for another monastic ruin to buy, and approached Henry Lee Warner of Walsingham Abbey for the old priory. He was unwilling, it was after all his home, but he did agree to sell the Slipper Chapel for £400. Having been used as a cowshed, barn, and cottage, it was in a terrible state, but she was delighted to have the chance of rescuing it.

The legalities were complicated and dragged on for two years, during which time Charlotte's life took a new turn. She went on retreat to the English Catholic Convent in Bruges in September 1894. She went there an Anglican, but by the end of the week she had been received into the Catholic Church, not a sudden impulse, as it may seem, but the culmination of a long desire which some of her Anglican priest friends had understandably discouraged.

Now she had problems. The first was that she had set up her *Abbey Trust* to buy monastic buildings for Anglicans, and the Trustees were regretfully unable to purchase the Slipper Chapel for a Catholic, so Charlotte had to buy it herself. Another problem was that she was head of an Anglican orphanage and school, with Anglican staff and children. Local Catholics, initially delighted, became disagreeable when it became clear that Charlotte was not going to instantly dismiss all the Anglicans in her charge and replace them with Catholics. But her way was always one of compassion and love, so she allowed it to happen by a gradual process, thus no doubt breaking down a lot of barriers as she did so. Not until four years later was the orphanage Chapel licensed for Catholic Mass, and a local priest of the Order of Mary Immaculate was appointed Chaplain, and Manager of the orphanage school.

For Walsingham, so far as its Catholic future was concerned, the reception of Charlotte into full communion was a huge blessing, for it meant that the Slipper Chapel came back into Catholic hands. Charlotte wanted to return it to Benedictine monks, because she thought that it was originally owned by the Benedictines who served St Giles' Houghton, (though it may, in fact, have belonged to the Augustinians at the Priory). She did not appreciate that, unlike the Church of England where she had restored an abbey and given it to a community, in the Catholic Church a community would not come into a diocese without the authority of the Bishop. Fr Ethelbert Taunton in Bruges explained this to her and wrote on 29 July 1895 to Bishop Riddell of Northampton on her behalf, telling him that Miss Boyd had purchased the Slipper Chapel with about one and a half acres of land.

> I fear it is somewhat of a white elephant. She desires me to ask your lordship whether it would serve as a Mission. Her real desire is to have it in the hands of the Benedictines (in which order she is an oblate).[13]

Bishop Riddell's reply has been lost, but it caused Fr Taunton to respond on 3 August:

> I may as well give your lordship a word of warning that she is very timid and easily frightened. But like many of this sort of character she has a decided will when once she makes up her mind. She is full of faith and full of the love of God and her heart is all gold. At the present moment she has a decided desire that the Benedictines have the property.[14]

A week later Charlotte wrote to the Bishop herself, asking

> It is old Benedictine ground and I had a great wish to restore it to them … Would your Lordship accept the Benedictines should it be possible for them to take a Mission near Walsingham, or have you any other suggestion to make regarding the Chapel?[15]

Bishop Riddell responded on 13 August 1895 that

> For years I have longed to do something for the North district of Norfolk and I begin to see in your work the realisation of my hopes … In answer to your questions I may say that I should like to place a good missionary priest at the Slipper Chapel … who might in time establish little missions at Dereham, Fakenham and Wells.[16]

The Slipper Chapel after restoration

He also said he wished to visit the Chapel with Fr Wrigglesworth. But Charlotte wanted it to be more than a Mission, she wanted it to be Benedictine and she wanted it to be a shrine, and so she did, in fact, hand the Chapel over to Downside Abbey in June 1897. She had appointed an eminent architect, Thomas Garner, to restore the Chapel and build a cottage beside it, work that was completed in 1900. A pupil of Sir George Gilbert Scott, Garner worked for some years in partnership with George Frederick Bodley.

Thinking he would be interested, on 27 July 1897, Charlotte sent the Bishop a lithograph of the Chapel 'as it is to be'.

> At present only a plain stone Altar and the Shrine of Our Ladye of Walsingham is promised … The property is invested in the names of three of the Downside Benedictine Fathers – it is hoped in time to endow a Mass there for the conversion of England and to form it, with your kind permission into a Mission Station. But this is in the far distance and the Chapel can only be a place of pilgrimage at present.[17]

We do not have the Bishop's reply but he cannot have been very pleased. Only a month earlier he had blessed the new church and Shrine of Our Lady of Walsingham in King's Lynn. An insight into his attitude comes in his reply to a letter from the Abbot-elect of Downside, Dom Edmund Ford, a great friend and adviser of Charlotte, who wrote,

> I am thinking of arranging a pilgrimage from Beccles (a parish near Norwich served by Benedictines) to Walsingham in August, but I am told that your Lordship would not approve of it. Will you send a line to say if this is so, for I should not move any farther in the project unless I was sure of your approval.

The Bishop replied tersely on 27 May 1900:

> There is only one pilgrimage approved by me, that to the Shrine of Our Lady of Walsingham at Lynn. I cannot approve of any other.[18]

Next year, another convert and close friend of Charlotte, Dom Philibert Feasey, a monk of St Augustine's Abbey, Ramsgate, as though preparing for the future, published a book entitled 'Our Ladye of Walsingham,' which included the lithograph of the Shrine in the Slipper Chapel.

Neither Charlotte nor Downside knew what to do. Here was a disused chapel in the countryside and a house with no one to live in it. Charlotte thought she found the answer. Dudley Baxter, another convert, and the founder and secretary of the *Catholic Newspaper Guild*, was the author of a pamphlet on Walsingham, for which Bishop Riddell wrote a preface. It was planned he would live in the cottage. The Bishop wrote to him on 12 April 1901:

> I have been informed that you have an intention of taking up residence at Walsingham in the belief that a mission may be opened in that town. As there is no prospect of that being done soon I write to advise you not to go there. Of course I should be only too pleased to have a mission there, but my efforts now are to open Cromer, Fakenham and Aylsham, also Hunstanton, and so gradually approach Walsingham. At Fakenham we already have Mass once a month. As means are sadly lacking in this diocese we have to march with great caution.[19]

In a further letter to Mr Baxter dated 16 October 1901, the Bishop revealed more of his thinking.

> The only reason to my mind for translating the Shrine from Lynn would be the recovery of the *exact spot* of the ancient shrine and the reconstruction of the old Loreto … As you know I am endeavouring to establish missions at Cromer, Aylsham and Fakenham and so gradually approach Walsingham: Fakenham would be a good centre. My successor may have an opinion different to mine and may consider that the Shrine might be translated to a Secular Catholic church and not necessarily to the old hallowed spot: he will be free to act upon it. We must wait patiently for better times in North Norfolk.[20]

Just how close the Bishop came to recovering the exact spot of the ancient Shrine, is revealed in letters from Launcelot Lee-Warner, the cousin of Henry, who lived at the Abbey. Launcelot was received into the Catholic Church on 7 September 1907, and after coming across Dudley Baxter's pamphlet, entered into correspondence with him.

> I am, under certain contingencies, certain to inherit the Walsingham estates … I can truly say that if God so wills it, and I do become possessed of Walsingham, I shall make every effort to return the sacred precincts to the true Church… My vow is a solemn one, and it is in God's hands solely whether He permits and honours one so unworthy as myself to be mainly instrumental in this restoration, so glorious and so much longed for by all Catholics who are fully acquainted with the history and facts relating to this most ancient shrine of Our Blessed Lady.[21]

In a later letter, after consulting lawyers, he wrote back confidently:

> It is so near my heart, dear Mr Baxter. Gladly, if I was life tenant of Walsingham would I deny myself to be able to make a present of this most sacred spot to Our Lady, and then rebuild the Church.[22]

In the event, Launcelot was disappointed. The family was already burdened by serious debts, his elder brother Chandos Brydges Lee-Warner inherited the Abbey, and it passed to Sir Eustace Gurney, of Gurney's Bank, who in 1904 married Anne Agatha, the daughter of John Lee-Warner.

Charlotte, nonetheless, had the Slipper Chapel and really wanted a Mass to be celebrated in it daily for the conversion of England, having made an endowment for this purpose. The Abbot had asked the Bishop for permission to celebrate Mass there, but he would not allow it. So she suggested to the

Abbot that 'the Slipper Chapel must be rather a white elephant to you and is only one of my fads! Why not offer it to my Lord of Northampton for a 'consideration' and apply the funds to your poor missions?'[23] Charlotte had concluded, perhaps rightly,[24] that the Bishop had a 'known dislike' of religious, especially Benedictines. On 5 June 1903 she wrote to the Bishop to ask if he would buy it.

> Your Lordship may remember that some years ago I bought and restored the Slipper Chapel near Walsingham in the hope that Holy Mass might again be offered there. The Benedictine Fathers to whom I looked to carry out this desire seem unable to meet my wishes – at least so far they have not done so, and I therefore now write to offer the property for sale, and venture to give your Lordship the first refusal. The site, ruins, restoration and priest's house have cost me over £2000 and I am naturally anxious not to sell it at a loss.
>
> I thought that perhaps these days when so many foreign Communities are in search of a home that there might be a better opportunity of disposing of this property as the place is well fitted for an enclosed order.

The Bishop replied,

> I am obliged to you for offering the Chapel near Walsingham for £2000, but of this I am quite unable to avail myself. Should I hear of a community desirous of settling there I will not fail to let them know that the property is for sale.[25]

In a further letter on the subject to Mr Baxter, the Bishop noted that there were some French nuns at High Wycombe but that a community would need at least £120 salary. 'If this were guaranteed I would make an effort to find a community. At present I am weighed down by costs at Cromer and at Hunstanton.[26] He could not afford to buy the Slipper Chapel and a year later, in 1904, confessed to Mr Baxter that 'if the Slipper Chapel had been given to the Bishop something might have been done there.'[27]

The only thing to be done now was appoint a caretaker to live rent-free in the cottage and look after the Chapel. Despite the best efforts of Mr George Hunt, who was appointed and lived there for thirty-four years, until ill health compelled him to retire in 1935, its state became 'deplorable,'[28] and needed further restoration. In his agreement he was to show the Chapel to anyone who had the Abbot's permission, and to keep a bedroom and sitting room for a monk making an occasional visit for a night or two. George Hunt had seen his father threshing corn on the old chapel floor when it was a barn seventy years before. But he lived to see Cardinal Bourne visit it and declare it to be the National Shrine of Our Lady in 1934.

Charlotte was probably right to think she was 'unsavoury ... in the Bishop's nostrils,'[29] but for all her disappointment she was never angry or disrespectful to him. She continued to devote her life to the orphans, and in 1904 opened a second home, the *Orphanage of Our Lady of Walsingham*, in Ealing, in the same year purchasing a house, which was used by Benedictines for their Ealing Mission before their Abbey was built. Her circle of friends was wide, and many of them became Roman Catholics, from an engine driver in Kent and her architect Thomas Garner, to innumerable priests, and even the Archbishop of Canterbury's son, Robert Hugh Benson.

She never lived to see Mass celebrated in the Slipper Chapel and her work for Our Lady of Walsingham was incomplete. But it had begun, and she never lost faith that 'the shrine will be restored and we have only need of a little more prayer and patience and Walsingham will have a Catholic centre and Holy Mass will be restored.'[30] Charlotte died in her Kilburn orphanage on 3 April 1906. But in the end her hopes bore fruit.

For many years her grave in Kensal Green Cemetery was sadly neglected but in 1962, a great devotee of hers, Mr Martin Gillett, persuaded the Abbot of Downside to give an iron cross of the type used for oblates in the monastery cemetery. This cross now records her memory at the Slipper Chapel. Cardinal Godfrey of Westminster paid the expenses and gave the gravestone. And on the anniversary of her death in 1962 it was blessed by Canon Flood, representing the Cardinal, in the presence of the Abbots of Downside and Ealing, while the Bishop of Northampton was represented by Fr Gerard Hulme, the priest in charge of the Shrine. Sadly the grave became neglected again over the years until Mgr George Tüttõ paid for its restoration. A prayer for Charlotte's beatification was approved in 2002, and the hope has been expressed that one day her mortal remains may be moved to Walsingham, beside the Chapel, which, but for her, would never have become England's National Shrine of Our Lady of Walsingham.

The National Shrine

In May 1922 the Downside Chapter considered handing the Chapel over to the Diocese, but chose not to do so, even though Bishop Dudley Charles Cary-Elwes was keen on the idea. Cardinal Bourne, who had consecrated England and Wales to the Sorrowful and Immaculate Heart of Mary during the First World War, in 1928 expressed sadness at the state of the Slipper Chapel but 'I fear I can do nothing except by the Bishop of the diocese, but I will certainly help in the restoration of the pilgrimage if and when I have an opportunity to do so.'[31] An Archbishop with vision, he expressed the desire for there to be a Catholic church in every town and large village in the country.[32] This same year Fr Fletcher died, and his successor, Fr Filmer, was opposed to any move that might detract from the Shrine at King's Lynn. But in 1931 the Community at Downside gave the Chapel to the Diocese of Northampton and when, in 1933, Bishop Laurence Youens was consecrated Bishop of Northampton, he turned to his MC and close friend, Fr Squirrel, to thank him, and said, 'Well, I'm Bishop of Northampton; what do you want?' 'My Lord, open the Slipper Chapel,' was the answer. This coincided with the appointment of Fr Francis Sammons as parish priest of Fakenham, who was just as enthusiastic.

A beautiful Shrine was created. The statue of Our Lady and Child remained in what is still the Pontifical Shrine at King's Lynn, and a new statue, modelled from the Priory Seal, was designed by Professor E.W. Tristram, above it a canopy (now in South Creake Church), designed by Lily Dagless, who also painted the reredos depicting the patron saint of pilgrims and the Chapel, St Catherine of Alexandria, and St Lawrence. The statue, canopy and a lamp were given by Miss Cary. The statue was never popular and Miss Cary herself never much liked it.[33] Two fine Florentine candlesticks were given by Mrs Chapman in memory of her son. A stone from the Holy House of Loreto in a silver casket was presented in 1972 by Fr Modestus Papi of Loreto.[34]

The great day arrived. On 14 August 1934, Canon Squirrel privately blessed and celebrated the first Mass in the Slipper Chapel since the Reformation, and Fr Sammons celebrated the second after him. Next day, on the Feast of the Assumption, Bishop Youens offered the first public Mass in it for 400 years. The next Sunday, 19 August, Cardinal Francis Bourne, accompanied by most of the bishops of England and Wales, led 12,000 or more people on a Pilgrimage of Reparation, beginning with a Mass in what is now the St John the Baptist's Catholic Cathedral in Norwich, celebrated by the Archbishop of Cardiff in the presence of the Cardinal, and Bishop Youens, who preached declaring he saw the finger of God in the recovery of the ancient chapel. Travelling by train to Walsingham the huge procession walked to the Slipper Chapel for a sermon in the meadow by Fr Vernon Johnson, and Benediction, where with the approval of the Pope, and in the presence of the Bishops, Cardinal Bourne declared it to be the National Shrine of Our Lady in England. It was a tremendous effort for Cardinal Bourne, who was seriously ill. But such was his devotion and conviction of the importance of the Shrine for England that he had a beautiful mosaic panel of Our Lady of Walsingham made for the restored pulpit of Westminster Cathedral.

It now became necessary for a resident priest to be appointed to live at the Slipper Chapel and develop the pilgrimages. So it was that Bishop Youens made Walsingham an episcopal parish and in an inspired choice appointed a former Anglican, Fr Bruno Scott James, immediately following his ordination in Rome, after six months at the Beda. In November 1935 he became custodian of a Shrine that had no pilgrims, and priest of a village that had but two Catholics, both converts, Mr Arthur Bond, and Mr Claude Fisher, who moved into Walsingham in November 1934 and had been asked by Bishop Youens to be the first Pilgrimage Secretary.[35] Described by the Abbot of Downside as an 'independent-minded, freelance priest,'[36] few others would have succeeded in such a bewildering task, and if he hadn't gone to Walsingham it is hard to see how he would have fitted into a conventional Roman Catholic parish. He was, in fact, a highly intelligent and prayerful young man, who had spent some years at Pershore Abbey, the forerunner of Nashdom, and it was at the Slipper Chapel that he decided to become a Catholic. In typical dramatic fashion, he describes how

> One day, driven to the verge of desperation by the awful choice that seemed to lie ahead of me, I walked out to the Slipper Chapel and, having obtained the key from the custodian, threw myself on my knees and implored God to give me the grace to follow his will whatever the cost might be and wherever it might lead me. I then vowed, hardly realising what I said, that if Our Lady would obtain from her Son this grace for me I would devote my life to her service at Walsingham.[37]

It did not actually take up the whole of his life, for his life after Walsingham was, if anything, even more interesting than his time there, as we shall see later.[38] His work is best described in his own words:

> The first pilgrimage to come after my arrival was led by Bishop Craven, then Father Craven of the Crusade of Rescue. It amounted to some hundred persons and seemed enormous, but the time was to come when I would think nothing of a thousand. At first the pilgrims came in dribs and drabs. Not until the middle of my second year at Walsingham did they begin to come in real crowds. From then until the war, I was busy preaching sometimes as often as eight times a day and hearing confessions not infrequently from six in the evening until midnight. Some would come on foot, some by bicycle, some by special trains and very many by buses. They came from all over the country and sometimes from France, Italy and Belgium. By the outbreak of the war a conservative estimate of the numbers was fifty thousand a year, but they were difficult to assess because so very many came on their own and went away without leaving any record. Private cars were arriving all day.[39]

In November 1937 Franciscans returned to Walsingham, Capuchins, living in Aelred House in Friday Market, to provide accommodation for the growing number of pilgrims, and Fr Scott James hoped they would take over the running of the Shrine. However, this was not the idea, and in the same year he began to develop another ministry, which he said appealed to him much more than organised pilgrimages, the arrangement of which he left to Claude Fisher.

> It began with my preaching every day from the steps of the Slipper Chapel to any who might be passing. Even when there was no formal pilgrimage, a large crowed overflowing on to the road never failed to collect. Nearly always the crowd contained persons in need of help; quite often men and women who had lapsed for years from their faith, to find it again at the feet of Our Lady at the Slipper Chapel. From this developed my plan of giving retreats to men, so that before long there were young men of every kind and class coming to Walsingham to learn how to be still and know God. Since my house had only one spare room, I built for them at the end of my garden small one-roomed houses or huts of cedar wood. With their high-pitched shingle

roofs they looked not unlike tiny alpine cottages. Within there was a bunk, a bookshelf, a table and a chair. It was my dream that Walsingham should become not only a place of pilgrimage, but also a power-house of prayer – the two do not necessarily go together. It was for a group of young men who came to Walsingham regularly for this purpose that I wrote my first book, *The One Thing Necessary*. I wrote it at their request after the war had broken out, so that while they were fighting they might have something they could keep in their pockets and read at odd moments to remind them of what they had learned at Walsingham.[40]

Fr Scott James arranged the purchase of a meadow beside the Slipper Chapel, and as well as the huts, he erected a wooden altar and outdoor shelter because of the crowds of pilgrims. He also built a sacristy on the Chapel, and another Chapel, the Chapel of the Holy Ghost, where priests could say Mass. Bishop Youens and Bishop Myers, an auxiliary bishop in Westminster, consecrated both Chapels on Our Lady's Birthday 1938. As soon as it was known that he intended to build on to the Slipper Chapel, Fr Scott James said

> there was an immediate uproar amongst those, mostly Anglicans and archaeologists, who thought the Slipper Chapel too perfect to be touched. Every post brought letters of protest, some anonymous and one, strongly worded, from the Anglican Dean of Norwich, no doubt written in the utmost good faith. To the Dean I simply replied that when the Slipper Chapel was in Anglican hands and used as a barn for the storage of crops I could understand that there would not have been any compelling need to build, but now that it had come back to our hands and was being used once again for Divine Worship some development was necessary and inevitable. I understand that this letter of mine was widely quoted as a blatant example of Roman Catholic intolerance. In fact, the whole addition was so planned as to detract as little as possible from the fine proportions of the original.[41]

These comments reflect the background of polemic, suspicion, and rivalry there was in those days, long before ecumenism transformed the relationship between the two Shrines.

Earlier in 1938 had come the first National Pilgrimage of Catholic Youth, when Cardinal Arthur Hinsley led 10,000 young people on a Pilgrimage of Reparation and prayer for peace on 2 July, the 400th anniversary of the Shrine's desecration. After the outdoor Mass the pilgrims processed to the Abbey grounds where the Cardinal presented a bouquet of flowers to Lady Agatha Gurney, and laid another on the site of the Holy House. Later, Lady Agatha was observed placing her own on the site too. Next year the country was plunged into war, and many of those Catholic youth would be serving their country, some of them with Fr Bruno Scott James' book for company.

Fr Alfred Hope Patten

It is time now to turn to that later and most remarkable curate of Buxted, Fr Alfred Hope Patten, for the restoration of the Anglican Shrine was entirely the work of this priest and those he drew in to work with him. He was, as his biographer, Michael Yelton described him, 'one of the most significant figures in the Church of England in the twentieth century.' [42] Or, as one who knew him very well wrote, 'a model priest.'[43]

Born in 1885, Hope Patten's parents went to live in Hove around 1902, where their only son soon became acquainted with Fr Wagner's Anglo-Catholic churches of Brighton. As his biographer observed, he 'absorbed the ethos and beliefs of Anglo-Catholicism as a choate whole.'[44] Far from being interested only in ceremonial, as some 'ritualists' were said to be, a close friend of those days recalled how he went to Mass almost daily, to confession most weeks, and observed days of fasting and abstinence with great severity, in a growing and deepening spirituality. It was in Brighton that Hope Patten met some people who would be his friends and collaborators for the rest of his life. The closest was Wilfred Leeds, with whom he travelled around a good deal as a young man, and who would one day be his curate in Walsingham. Another was Fr Charles Roe, the curate of St Paul's, Brighton. The most distinguished and important friend Hope Patten made was Fr Henry Joy Fynes-Clinton, who arrived in Brighton in 1904 for a curacy at St Martin's, and who became a most influential Vicar of St Magnus the Martyr London Bridge, an early ecumenist, and a close supporter and adviser to Hope Patten in Walsingham.

Hope Patten was ordained priest in 1914, and served several curacies in parishes with a firm Anglo-Catholic tradition, like the ones he knew in Brighton. One was at Holy Cross St Pancras, where he had a famous vicar, Fr Francis Baverstock, brother of the even more notable Alban Baverstock, another one who became a trusted collaborator in Walsingham. Francis had been Fr Edgar Reeves' curate at St Michael's Islington, from where Fr Reeves had gone in 1904 to be Vicar of Walsingham. One morning at breakfast Fr Baverstock produced a small statue of Our Lady provided by the new *League of Our Lady*, with which Francis was involved, and which was to be sent to Fr Reeves in Walsingham. Years later Fr Patten commented that Our Lady had gone to Walsingham before him. That small alabaster statue remained in St Mary's and even survived the fire that devastated the building in 1961.

From Holy Cross St Pancras Fr Patten moved in 1915 to be curate at St Alban's Teddington, another church of 'advanced' Catholic tradition. Two laymen he met here would feature prominently in the Walsingham story. One was Oliver Richards, a gifted musician, who went to Walsingham with Fr Patten, and lived in the vicarage for some years. Another was Thomas Tapping, who also went to live with him, and in due course became headmaster of a school Fr Patten opened in the village.

Fr Patten left Teddington in 1919 to help out for a few months at St Michael's Ladbroke Grove, before spending a year as the curate of St Mary's, Buxted, with its Walsingham Chapel, where Fr Roe was now Vicar. It is certain that Fr Patten would have known all about the Chapel when he lived in Brighton as a young man, but if there were any gaps in his knowledge of Walsingham Fr Roe would have filled them in, just as Fr Wagner had taught Fr Philip Fletcher all he knew about Walsingham nearly fifty years earlier. Here in the Chapel, the Angelus was recited at noon each day. Many years later, when he built the Shrine in Walsingham, Fr Patten put a brass in the floor to commemorate Fr Roe.

A brief locum may have followed Buxted at St Michael's, Edinburgh, in 1920, and then a short curacy at Carshalton in charge of the daughter Church of the Good Shepherd. Here again, Fr Patten's personal magnetism resulted in two sisters, the Misses Lloyd, following him to Walsingham, where they helped with the organisation of pilgrimages. Fr Patten was a man who saw God's signs and intimations where other people see only coincidences. It is rather mysterious how so many things were coming together, as though preparing him for his life's work.

Anglo-Catholicism

To understand Fr Patten's convictions it is essential to have some grasp of Anglo-Catholicism, which began in 1833 with the Oxford Movement (when it was called 'Tractarianism' because it was largely driven by tracts and articles of a doctrinal, spiritual, and historical nature). The Movement reminded the Church of England of its Catholic heritage, and worked to restore and reintroduce elements of faith, spirituality, and practice that had been lost. Gradually came the foundation of Religious Communities for women and for men, the restoration of Sunday and weekday Mass, the revival of the sacraments of confession and anointing the sick, the practice of retreats and spiritual direction, devotion to the Blessed Sacrament, Our Lady and the Saints, as well as the gradual recovery of catholic liturgy and ritual.

Central to Anglo-Catholicism is the conviction that the Church of England is the Church that was planted in England by St Augustine, the first Archbishop of Canterbury, with the essential apostolic succession in the Catholic Orders of bishops, priests and deacons. It remained the 'Catholic Church of the land', despite the distortions and doctrines introduced by the Reformation, and notwithstanding the recusant Roman Catholics who kept their faith alive in the centuries of persecution.

Yet within this broad spectrum of Anglo-Catholic agreement there are a number of different emphases. Some have been quite hostile to Roman Catholicism, though less so in recent times, calling it the 'Irish' or 'Italian' Mission. Others argued that the Roman Church had added unwarranted doctrines like the Immaculate Conception and Assumption of Our Lady and the Infallibility of the Pope to the Catholic Faith. 'High Church' was often used as a derogatory term for those who were more interested in ceremonial than Catholic Faith and discipline. One section introduced English medieval liturgy and ceremony, like the Sarum Rite, while others preferred to introduce all or part of the Roman Missal in English. Others were strictly 'Prayer Book Catholics.'

Fr Patten and his supporters belonged to a small but highly influential grouping called 'Anglican Papalists.' They believed all the doctrines and moral teaching of the Roman Catholic Church, including the primacy and infallibility of the Pope and the Magisterium of the Catholic Church and all its Councils, apart from its ruling on Anglican Orders which they thought mistaken, and which, it was argued, did not constitute an infallible decree. Their convictions were set out in the *Oxford Movement Centenary Manifesto*, in 1933, which was signed by Fr Patten, Fr Fynes-Clinton, and all the leading Papalists of the day.

> Our Lord set up but One Church, the members of which were to be in communion one with another. This One Church was constituted with St Peter as its Foundation and Head, and for ever has as its Centre and Guide on earth the successor of St Peter. [45]

The Church of England is a schismatic body, having been forced into schism from the rest of the Catholic Church by King Henry VIII and Queen Elizabeth. 'Two provinces', 'a severed limb,' they called it, which must be brought back into communion with the Pope and the rest of the Catholic Church. The Manifesto was unambiguous:

> The existence of the Church of England as a body separate *de facto* from the rest of the Catholic Church is only tolerable when it is regarded as a temporary evil, destined to disappear when God shall be pleased to restore us to our normal place among our brethren.

All Anglo-Catholics considered the Church of England to be the 'Catholic Church of the land', but for the Papalists this claim was conditional:

> We affirm that the claim of the Church of England to continuity with the Church of St Augustine and St Theodore, constantly maintained by the Oxford Fathers, involves oneness of Faith and Practice with the historic Church of the past … That succession is not maintained by a mere succession of property, nor by the revival of ceremony, nor by the use of words, but only by complete identity of Faith, the possession of which is the sole justification of her existence.

The vocation of Anglo-Catholics was to promote a Catholic Revival, a 'steady and progressive return to the faith and practice of historic Christendom', but Papalists recognised an inherent fragility in the Catholic Movement:

> It is well to bear in mind that the Catholic Revival in the Church of England will only be safeguarded and made permanent by the recognition of that Authority (the Pope), whose divinely-appointed office it is to 'strengthen the brethren' and who always and everywhere preserves the one Faith in its integrity.

This barely concealed fear that the Church of England might abandon Catholic Faith and practice Fr Patten expressed in a letter to Fr H.K. Pierce in 1930:

> I am more and more coming to the opinion that Catholics in the Church of England in communion with Canterbury must consider the example of the Wee Frees of the Scots – the day cannot be far off when some of us will have to go out into the desert – and there prove our catholicity – after which perhaps a united body may be formed as the link.[46]

In 1947 a crisis blew up with the South India Unity Scheme which Fr Patten called a 'greater crisis than the Reformation', since it involved 'invalid orders' in which 'the Anglican laity will be in danger of being in the invidious position of scarcely ever knowing if they are receiving the Bread of Life, or absolution, or the blessings of Christian marriage.'[47] The storm died away when the Church of England made it clear it was not in full communion with the Church of South India.

Few Anglicans, let alone Roman Catholics, understood the Papalist position. Most people speak naturally of 'Anglicans and Catholics', but with Fr Patten the Anglicans became 'Catholics' and the Catholics became 'Romans', a word Roman Catholics especially resented, retorting that they did not wear togas. When Fr Patten wrote in the Pilgrims' Manual that membership of the *Society of Our Lady of Walsingham* was open to 'Practising Catholics', and that 'Catholic Priests' (with no mention of 'Anglican' or them being 'in communion with Canterbury') were eligible to become *Priest Associates of the Shrine*, to Roman Catholics it sounded like a deceit. Yet, this was Fr Patten's sincerely held conviction. First and foremost he was a Catholic.

Despised and misunderstood as Papalists were, Fr Patten would have been delighted had he lived to read the appreciation of a Mirfield Father, Geoffrey Curtis:

> We are beginning to see that Anglican Papalists have been unfairly judged … They are a small group with a long lineage in our Church, and many of them are the salt of the earth. Their particular standpoint many of them have recognised as involving a call to a life of reparation. Contrary to average opinion this small group is notable for its intellectual power as well as for its holiness. Perhaps the books of Anglican theology of this century that have been most widely read abroad have been books by Papalists – Spencer Jones' *England and the Holy See* and Gregory Dix's *The Shape of the Liturgy*.[48]

The Week of Prayer for Christian Unity was started by Papalists under the name *Octave of Prayer for Christian Unity*. They had several societies to promote their teachings, which merged into the *Catholic League* in 1913. Fr Patten was an early member of the *Catholic League*. Many Religious Communities were Papalist, notably the Benedictines of Nashdom Abbey. They were well ahead of their time. When few in the Church of England cared anything about Christian Unity, least of all with the Roman Catholic Church, the Papalists prepared the ground with prayer and scholarship, until eventually after the visit of Archbishop Michael Ramsey to Pope Paul VI the Anglican-Roman Catholic International Commission was formed in the 'quest for the full, organic unity of our two Communions.'[49] Among their joint Declarations was an Agreed Statement entitled *Mary, Grace and Hope in Christ*.[50]

Vicar of Walsingham

The appointment to parishes in the Church of England has never been simply the responsibility of bishops. The family of the Abbey are the patrons of Walsingham. Moreover, priests can always refuse to go to a parish. By all accounts this is what happened at Walsingham. More than twenty priests had been invited to be the vicar and had turned it down. The problem, in those days, was the income, £197 a year net, which they considered inadequate. On 19 January 1921 Fr Patten was inducted, and rang the Angelus on the church bell.

Not only had the small alabaster statue of Our Lady gone before him to Walsingham and prepared the way, but in 1916 a temporary headmistress at Walsingham Primary School produced a pageant in which the children dressed as kings and queens and pilgrims, some of them on horseback, so that if they hadn't known before, everyone in the village knew about its famous history before Fr Patten arrived to teach them. It was intended as a morale-booster in a village made all too aware of the horrors of the War, because Berry Hall in Great Walsingham and Oddfellows' Hall in Little Walsingham had been used to receive some of the first casualties. Fr Patten came to a parish in which twenty-eight men from Little Walsingham alone had been killed.

In their biographies of Fr Patten, Colin Stephenson and Michael Yelton give good accounts of Fr Patten's years in Walsingham, both as vicar and as restorer and first administrator of the Shrine. A brief account is needed here, and much of it relies on their work. Fr Patten came to a village in which the Anglo-Catholic tradition was well established. The Revd James Lee-Warner, vicar of Walsingham in the mid-nineteenth century, had been tutored by

Newman at Oriel College in 1827, and actually visited him in Rome in 1847.[51] He was the first to publish an engraving of the seal, from which we know the form of the original statue of Our Lady of Walsingham, in his report on the excavations he made in the abbey grounds in 1856. Fr George Ratcliffe Woodward was vicar from 1882-89, and he had come from the notable Anglo-Catholic parish of St Barnabas, Pimlico. He began a daily Eucharist in St Mary's; a noted musician and expert on plainsong, he also introduced daily Sung Evensong to St Mary's, which the squire, Mr Henry Lee-Warner accompanied on the 'cello. He is best remembered as a prolific writer of hymns including *This Joyful Eastertide* and *Ding, Dong Merrily on High*. His successor, Fr Wansbrough, maintained the Catholic tradition, and then there was Fr Reeves, the immediate predecessor of Fr Patten, who installed the statue of Our Lady. Having such forerunners Fr Patten encountered none of the opposition that other priests often did when they began to introduce a Catholic tradition.

He at once set to work, visiting, teaching and endearing himself to the villagers. Very successful with young people, soon a large band of servers with their girl friends were at home on Friday evenings in the vicarage with its old stables and extensive grounds, where they were fed well and often enjoyed riotous games. Norfolk people had never seen anything like this bright young vicar. Soon, young and old were devout Anglo-Catholics. Women queued for confessions on Saturday evenings, and men on Sunday morning before the 8.00 Mass. The 11.00 am Mass, in the tradition of those days, was non-communicating. An old parishioner recalled that when the ten-minute bell sounded, all the doors on the High Street would open and the people streamed to Mass together. A parishioner who remembered the early days told the writer how people from neighbouring villages would walk over the fields to hear him preach at Evensong and Benediction on Sunday evenings. Sir Eustace Gurney, the squire, was Low Church, and attended Matins at Little Snoring, but his brother Sam Gurney had become an Anglo-Catholic. Having heard some criticism of Fr Patten, presumably from his brother, he decided to make a discreet enquiry of Canon John Blake-Humfrey, his uncle, who had retired to the charming Church House just outside St Mary's. From Canon John Blake-Humfrey we have the following testimony, written in 1926, which is worth quoting in full:

My dear Sam,

I am in a position to know very well both the inward and outward church life here at Walsingham, and its very great influence over all conditions of people - young and old - under the guidance and teaching of Fr Patten. Since his advent, Church doctrine, life and 'go' have grown enormously in the parish, and his teaching, both amongst the young and old, has sunk in and 'holds' them in their lives. What makes people 'catch on' with him (humanly speaking) is his loving sympathetic manner; in spite of interruption, or being stopped, he is always ready to give a listening ear, always ready to give up his time to people. I have never known anyone so approachable, so winsome. Hence through God's Grace his power of attraction, his influence and faculty of imparting his Creed and Gospel.

The whole spiritual atmosphere of Walsingham and church life here is of the very highest order. I cannot speak of it too highly. To sum up: the congregations at all the services are always large and have vastly increased and are increasing.

The attendances at Holy Communion are wonderful both by the old and the young. Old men and women, and women, girls and boys: they all come.

I should say that the influence of Church Life in Walsingham is very great, extending to the whole Parish and in consequence the Moral Tone is high. We certainly have

> a Model Priest in Fr Patten
>
> a Model Church
>
> Model Services in Church
>
> Model Congregations
>
> Model outside influences bearing fruit.

This is something to be optimistic about.

Yours affectionately,

Uncle John.[52]

Restoring the Shrine

Fr Patten went to Walsingham determined to restore the medieval Shrine. And he wasted no time. Through the Art and Book Shop near Westminster Cathedral, a Carmelite nun, Sister Catherine, was commissioned to carve an image of Our Lady of Walsingham copied from the Priory Seal. On 6 July, 1922, the year following his induction, he set up the statue in the Guilds Chapel, on a pillar, so that it faced the ruins of the Priory and site of the ancient Shrine. The church bells were rung, village girls in white dresses and veils, carrying sprays of syringa, accompanied Our Lady in procession, and the distinguished scholar, Fr Archdale King, preached the sermon.

Every day since then, at 6.00 p.m., the Rosary has been prayed before the Image, followed by intercessions, a devotion that came to be called 'Shrine Prayers.' Fr Patten very carefully saved letters and testimonies to healings and answers to prayers.

Now came the first pilgrimage. The *League of Our Lady* in London, already mentioned, whose President was Lord Halifax, arranged this auspicious event from 24-26 October. The rather inconvenient mid-week days were chosen because Wednesday was the only day in the week when the Abbey grounds were open, and Fr Patten wanted the pilgrims to pray at the site of the ancient shrine and drink water from the twin holy wells. The organiser was William Milner, the secretary of the League, and destined to have a huge role in the growth of the Shrine, but unfortunately he was taken ill and dropped out of the pilgrimage. He was not the only one.

The villagers were excited and arranged to welcome them, the Black Lion was booked to provide accommodation and meals, the choir and servers were drilled, but when Fr Patten and some of his helpers went to the Station to meet the train, the only ones who got out were Fr Hibbs, vicar of St John's Balham, and two elderly ladies. A lesser man would have been distraught, but not Fr Patten who took it as a sign that the village people themselves should make the first pilgrimage to their Shrine. So, parishioners were rounded up. They celebrated Vespers and Mass, and took part in all the pilgrimage devotions, and enjoyed the meals that had been arranged. From that moment they were involved with the Shrine, and supported Fr Patten to the hilt. A local Guild was formed.

The second pilgrimage was far better organised. Elsie Lloyd, who had followed Fr Patten from Carshalton, was the local organiser. Forty people, under the auspices of the *League of Our Lady*, started off together on 22 May 1923, from St Magnus the Martyr, where Fr Patten's great friend and supporter, Fr Fynes-Clinton, was now vicar. Here he re-founded the *Fraternity of Our Lady de Salve Regina* (dating originally from 1343), which held devotions at midday every day.[53] Soon the League was bringing two pilgrimages a year, in May and August. Other small groups came from time to time from Norwich and whereabouts, and the pilgrimage programme evolved. First the pilgrims went to pray at the Shrine in the Guilds Chapel, and then attended Vespers of Our Lady, beautifully sung to plainsong by the choir under the direction of Oliver Richards. Then they enjoyed Supper at the Black Lion, before returning to St Mary's for confessions, always an essential sacrament on the pilgrimage. Next morning the priests said Mass at the various altars that Fr Patten had by now put in St Mary's. Then came Stations of the Cross and a Sung Mass, followed by a walk up to Houghton to pray in St Giles, and down to the Slipper Chapel for prayers. After lunching at the Black Lion they visited the site of the Priory and Holy House, praying in reparation of its destruction, and then drank water from the holy wells. Tea was served on the vicarage lawn, and Fr Patten was remembered as always the perfect and generous host. Then came supper at the Black Lion, followed by Vespers and Benediction, and the pilgrims departed next morning after Mass on their long train journey back to London.

Pilgrims often stayed with local people who welcomed them into their homes and received a small payment in return, but Fr Patten realised that for pilgrimages to expand more accommodation was necessary, so that when in 1924 The Beeches in Holt Road came up for sale, along with its garden, land, a barn, cottages and outbuildings, he was keen to buy it. The cottages were restored and in due course became St Augustine's, while the barn, formerly used by the Salvation Army and then by the Quakers, served for many year as the pilgrims' refectory, later the Pilgrim Hall. Bidding for him at the auction was George Back, the organist of St Mary's, and the money was lent by William Milner, who by then was a close friend and admirer of all that Fr Patten was doing, He was repaid after a fund-raising appeal sponsored by Lord Halifax and Dame Sybil Thorndyke. Fr Patten was attracting the support of prominent and well-to-do patrons.

Now, he needed a Religious Community of women to look after the pilgrims, and approached the Community of St Peter in Horbury, who sent three sisters. They moved first into a cottage attached to the vicarage, and when it was ready, into The Beeches, which was renamed The Hospice of Our Lady, Star of the Sea. The villagers were agog. They were learning never to be surprised at what this extraordinary vicar would do next. Nuns in a Norfolk village were unheard of, but soon the sisters endeared themselves to everyone, and were admired as they sang their offices beside the Shrine each day.

The policy of purchasing property went on, and within a short time Fr Patten had soon purchased the whole street. Long before the word 'conservationist' was used, Fr Patten had shown a genius for seeing the potential in dilapidated old buildings, and persuading the local builder and undertaker, Tom Purdy, that he could restore them. The shrine side of Knight Street was more or less all condemned and the Mount Pleasant Estate was built to house the residents. Half Knight Street would have been lost without the intervention of Fr Patten.

Medieval pilgrims had more than one focus of devotion in Walsingham, and Fr Patten was soon to provide another. In 1924 he went to Assisi and there found a relic, which the Bishop authenticated as a relic of St Vincent. Fr Patten brought it back in triumph, put it in a place of honour in the church, and from henceforth the Veneration of St Vincent became a necessary devotion in the pilgrimage programme. He founded a servers' *Guild of St Vincent* in the parish, for in all he did to promote pilgrimages, the village remained his pastoral care. Before long there was a considerable collection of relics. The Shrine became indistinguishable from any Continental Catholic Shrine, with candles, votive offerings and flowers. Visitors, parishioners and pilgrims were making it a place of prayer, and people remarked on the special atmosphere the church took on.

In 1925 the local Guild became the *Society of Our Lady of Walsingham*, and its members, who promised to live by a Rule of Life, which included devotion to Our Lady, were invested with a blue scapular. In 1926 he began producing the quarterly *Our Lady's Mirror*, which continued to the end of his life. Sent to all members of the Society, it brimmed with interesting articles and news, teaching and descriptions of shrines all over the world, adding to the impression that Walsingham was now taking its perfectly normal place in the Catholic world. The first issue, January 1926, included an article by Fr Archdale King who had preached at the Shrine's inauguration. Under A Return to the Ages of Faith, he declared:

> To my mind, nothing could restore Faith to the waverer and the doubter more than a pilgrimage to Walsingham, where controversy, discussion, and argument are non-existent, and where the Seven Fruits of the Holy Spirit take their place.

1926 was a great year in another important aspect. There came a new vicar to Blakeney, not far from Walsingham, on the coast. He was Bishop Mowbray Stephen O'Rorke of Accra, who had retired from there a little early. He was a

218

doughty Anglo-Catholic and strong supporter of the Shrine, where he used to enjoy celebrating Pontifical Mass and Vespers for pilgrimages. There is no doubt that as well as adding solemnity with his exceptionally tall Roman mitre, gloves, and all the accoutrements, he seemed to add the official seal of approval, the more so since the Bishop of Norwich had not come anywhere near. In fact when that Bishop suggested to Bishop O'Rorke, who acted as his assistant bishop, that he might spend less time at Walsingham, he replied that since God had magnified Mary he would do the same!

In London, Fr Fynes-Clinton, knowing how poor the stipend was, started the 'Walsingham Clergy Fund' to supplement the living and provide a curate. In 1926 Fr Patten's old friend, Fr Leeds and his wife Dolly, joined him, and came to live in the parsonage at St Giles, where they stayed until 1932. Fr Patten strongly disapproved of married priests, but this didn't get in the way of either friendship or working together, and he was always kind to Dolly and enjoyed her company. A great supporter of Fr Patten from those early days was Derrick Lingwood, son of the local baker, in whom Fr Patten discerned a vocation. In return for helping with his education Derrick took over all the financial affairs, both personal and parish, from Fr Patten, who by his own admission was hopeless with money, and in due course, in 1934, he was ordained and stayed with Fr Patten until 1956.

In 1927 Fr Patten founded the *Priest Associates of the Holy House* who promised to say Mass for the intentions of the Shrine on Saturdays, which later was reduced to once a month, on which day they would be prayed for by name in Shrine Prayers. One of the first to be an Associate was Fr George Woodward. In that year the *Catholic League*, another of Fr Fynes-Clinton's societies, organised its first annual pilgrimage. There were still only four or five organised pilgrimages a year, apart from small groups and individuals, but in 1928 there were more. Anglo-Catholic Congresses were held in Kettering and Norwich, and they came, plus the usual two from the *League of Our Lady*, the *Catholic League*, and other groups from London and Yorkshire.

In 1929 Fr Patten started the May revels, which became a feature of the village life. Combined with May devotions to Our Lady, the May Queen was crowned in the vicarage garden after a procession of the trades around the village, dancing around the maypole and sports. The day ended with a masked ball in the Parish Hall and the Queen was conducted home in a sedan chair with a torchlight procession. It was no doubt because he heard so many good things about the work of Fr Patten in the village, that the Bishop of Norwich, Dr Bertram Pollock, left him undisturbed. And also because of an alliance between them over the controversial 1928 Prayer Book, which they both strongly opposed. The Bishop even wrote letters on black-edged notepaper to Fr Patten about it, generally marked 'Private and Confidential', 'Personal and Private'. In a letter dated 24 February 1928, the Bishop told him 'I have no doubt at all that the step you took after, or because, of our talk together in the Summer played a considerable part in the rejection of the book last winter.'[54] This certainly stood Fr Patten in good stead.

But the Bishop was not unaware of what was going on in Walsingham. In the House of Lords he had been heckled by peers wanting him to take action against the 'excesses' at Walsingham. John Kensit (the originator of the group that even today makes a nuisance during the Anglican National Pilgrimage) had disrupted services at St Mary's, and no doubt the Bishop had been assailed by letters. The Bishop of Durham, Dr Hensley Henson, while on holiday in the area, came to see St Mary's. He wrote about it in the *Evening Standard* on 1 September 1926:

> Walsingham is as complete an example of triumphant Anglo-Catholicism as the country can present. The parish Church might be taken for a Roman Catholic Church: there was nothing Anglican about it except the fabric (sic). Perhaps it is inevitable that the revival of pilgrimages should be included in the general policy of 'undoing the Reformation' which the Anglo-Catholics have adopted and are pursuing with such remarkable vigour, pertinacity and success, for the abolition of pilgrimages and the demolition of the Shrines to which pilgrims resorted were conspicuous features of the religions revolution which the Reformers effected.[55]

Dr Henson was quite right. 'Undoing the Reformation' was exactly what Anglo-Catholics like Fr Patten were about. So, eventually, the Bishop of Norwich decided to visit St Mary's. Accounts of his reactions vary, but according to Fr Stephenson, the Bishop said, 'It is far worse than I expected, far worse; all the things which you have put in must be cleared away.'[56] In *Our Lady's Mirror* for Spring 1931, Fr Patten broke the bad news:

> The Bishop of the Diocese demanded that the images should be taken away and that many other matters should be 'reformed'.

Building the Shrine

Anglo-Catholics were used to such demands. They were under frequent attack as 'Papists' in the deeply prejudiced atmosphere of nineteenth and twentieth century England. In a vain attempt to control the movement, five priests were put in prison and dismissed from office under the *Public Worship Regulation Act* of 1874 for such offences as wearing vestments during the Eucharist and having lighted candles on the altar. One of these was a former curate of Fr Wagner at St Paul's Brighton, Fr Arthur Enraght, whose daughter married Fr Reeves, the predecessor of Hope Patten at Walsingham. Another was Fr Arthur Tooth. Even after the repeal of that notorious Act, diocesan courts and bishops continued to 'persecute' Anglo-Catholics, who in turn became very adept at getting their own way. One ruse adopted by many, including Fr Fynes-Clinton, when he was ordered to remove the six candlesticks from the high altar of St Magnus the Martyr, was to substitute six wooden candlesticks for the fine renaissance ones. The officers removed the substitutes and Fr Fynes-Clinton promptly replaced them with the originals. Other parishes were not so lucky and were stripped of Catholic ornaments.

Fr Patten was fortunate that his relations with the Bishop of Norwich were friendly and respectful, and he traded on his good name and charm to get his own way. Concerning the images, he told the Bishop that other churches in his diocese had them and he would call a meeting of the clergy to discuss the whole matter. This never happened and it was all dropped. So far as the image of Our Lady of Walsingham was concerned, Fr Patten had already conceived the idea of a separate shrine, and had the land on the corner of Holt Road and Knight Street on which to build it. He agreed with the Bishop. The image had never been in St Mary's in medieval days and shouldn't be there, and the best solution would be to find somewhere else for it. With pilgrimages already arranged, perhaps the bishop would give him a year to sort it out. And the bishop was delighted by Fr Patten's willing agreement.

When he got home he began to wonder, as well he might, and so he wrote to Fr Patten, expressing his pleasure that he had agreed to move the image out of the church, but asking for clarification. 'I have not got it quite clear in my mind where the image would be placed … not, I suppose, in any consecrated building.' Fr Patten went to see him and we don't know what transpired, except that he wrote to the Bishop afterwards saying, that 'we all hate and are grieved by the prospect' of moving the image but adding, 'People who really mind and understand have all been very touched by your great kindness and consideration in this affair,' and telling him that he had obtained the land for the new Chapel and that the money was coming in well. The Bishop replied that he quite understood the present position, and 'I am always so glad that our personal relations together offer a conspicuous illustration, of what I always say, namely that good men can differ without quarrelling.'[57]

The Bishop had unwittingly given Fr Patten everything he wanted. The Anglo-Catholic position was always precarious. Bishops and consistory courts could inflict great damage. Bishops put some parishes 'under the ban' for having services like Benediction, and refused ever to visit them or accept candidates for confirmation or ordination. This was the last thing Fr Patten wanted to happen. A change of Vicar was also hazardous, for a bishop or patron could very easily install a new vicar to remove all traces of Anglo-Catholicism, and Fr Patten's patron was not at all well disposed to what he was doing. Setting the image in a building on private property would put it beyond the control of both the bishop and the patron. Wasting no time he embarked on fund-raising. In *Our Lady's Mirror* for Spring 1931 he set out his vision:

> This chapel will be as near as possible an exact reproduction of the original shrine – founded here by Richeldis in obedience to Our Lady's request – as it is possible without seeing the Sancta Casa in situ. But we have the Holy House of Loreto, which is claimed to be the actual cottage in which the Annunciation took place, where Our Lord was incarnate and lived his days on earth, and we know that the Shrine at Walsingham was supposed to have been a copy of this building although – according to William of Worcester – slightly smaller in dimensions. So we have much to go on. In this little chapel was originally the image of Mary of Walsingham, and in this reconstructed sanctuary the statue we all love so well will find its new and, we hope, permanent home.
>
> But at the time of the dissolution, this 'English House of Nazareth' was itself enclosed in yet another chapel, called variously 'The Church of St Mary' and the 'Novum Opus'. It was only a small building, when all was said, but sufficient to preserve the Sancta Casa and to enable

pilgrims to circulate under cover from our variable and inclement weather. We propose erecting a similar building.

He makes the point that the Holy Sacrifice could not be offered there unless it is licensed by the Bishop, and asks members of the Society to pray that 'the bishop may grant us the privilege of having holy mass at the shrine', which he thought might be possible as the outer chapel would serve as the chapel for the sisters. With an oblique reference to the uncertainty of the Catholic tradition continuing in the parish church, he concluded:

> This little pilgrimage church will always be open to the public although on private property, and whatever the parish church may be in years to come, its doors will always be open to the servants of Mary who will seek her in the sanctuary of her choice.[58]

Romilly Craze, the partner of William Milner, was the chosen architect, the money began to come in, and work proceeded at speed. In *Our Lady's Mirror* for Autumn 1931 Fr Patten announced that the sanctuary would be placed in the hands of trustees and a body of twenty-four Guardians, half of them clergy and half laymen. In the event there were eighteen, very carefully selected. The clergy and most, if not all, of the laymen, were Papalists. The laymen were mostly prominent and powerful, including the Duke of Argyll, Lord Halifax, Sir William Milner (as he became), Sir John Best-Shaw, Mr (later Sir) Eric Maclagan, Director of the Victoria and Albert Museum, and Major Arthur Bowker, and the churchwardens. He was making the Shrine very secure.

On a number of occasions religious sisters and brothers met at the chosen site to pray for a sign from God to confirm it. Fr Patten was especially looking for a source of water, as with the original shrine. He ordered some exploratory excavations. And he was not disappointed. Water began to gush out from a well that had been blocked up with clay, deliberately it seemed, at the time of the Dissolution, because at the bottom of it were some soles of early sixteenth-century shoes. The excavators also found a cobbled area, and it is said there was a cobbled area around the original Shrine. Then they found the footings of a rectangular building, with turret-like foundations at the corners. These were kept exposed and may be seen in the little garden by the first Station of the Cross. Fr Patten wondered if they had found the site of the original shrine. In a pamphlet of 1934 *The Site of the Shrine of Our Lady of Walsingham* he wrote:

> We make no claim, but we do consider that these discoveries are very extraordinary and, remembering that there is an old tradition that the Holy House was moved some time during the course of its history, it seems more than probable that the present Shrine may be on the site of one or other of these sites.

In a later pamphlet, published after further excavations during the building of the 1938 extension of the Shrine, he was more positive, asserting,

> there is adequate ground for believing that the site has a better claim than any other to be regarded as that of either the earlier building in which the Holy House stood (assuming, that is, that the legend which mentions two sites contains a background of fact), or the 'Novum Opus' described by William of Worcester and Erasmus.[59]

Fr Patten died in 1953, but in 1961, as we have seen, the site of the original shrine was confirmed beside the Priory as Lee-Warner had thought, and where until the interesting discoveries on the site of the Anglican Shrine, Fr Patten too had believed it to be, and where he had encouraged pilgrims to pray. And, of course, in the Ballad, the first site of the Holy House was close by the twin wells. So what are the remains beneath the Anglican Shrine? Dickinson thinks it is quite likely they are the remains of a medieval Elymosinarium or Almshouse, and that the well is the 'well called Cabbokeswell' referred to in a note of 1387 on a flyleaf of the Walsingham Cartulary. The Prior of Walsingham, John Snoring, was given the right of way to a well that belonged to Nicholas Black and later to James Cabbok, and also the vacant parcel of land between the Elymosinarium and the Priory.[60] There were many wells in Walsingham, for piped water only came to the village in 1955, but it is still a holy well because it was discovered when Fr Patten was praying for a sign of water to appear, and remarkable healings have occurred there.

Building commenced. The outer chapel corresponds to the measurements of William of Worcester's *Novum Opus*, and the plans were modified to allow the newly discovered holy well to be cleverly included inside it. The Holy House was built to the same dimensions as Loreto, and has two doors facing each other. The altar was constructed of stones from the ruined priory and from other religious houses destroyed at the Reformation, an idea Fr Patten got from Caldey Abbey. In the walls of the Holy House itself were embedded about 170 stones making almost a catalogue of the houses destroyed by Henry VIII, and other places including Chartres and Patmos. On the south wall are stones from Augustinian ruins, with Benedictine stones on the north wall. 'No gesture could more visibly, rhetorically or liturgically pronounce Walsingham's purpose as an expiation of the sins of Reformation and as a reversal of the thrust of Protestantism in the Church of England.'[61] The building was small, but it did allow for an extension.

The great day arrived. On the eve, a carillon of nine bells, hung in a wooden frame, was baptised. On Thursday 15 October 1931, known ever after as the Feast of the Translation of Our Lady of Walsingham, the sacred image of Our Lady was carried through the village from St Mary's with three thousand people, including monks, nuns and friars, thronging the streets. The dreary days of the Reformation were being rolled back and once again the village was filled with happy pilgrims. Bishop O'Rorke presided in his tallest mitre, accompanied by the Abbot of Nashdom and over a hundred priests. Lay people carried candles and rosaries, many women wore blue veils, and children in white cast flowers on the way. The crowned statue of Our Lady in cloth of gold, under a gold and blue canopy, was lifted high on the shoulders of four priests in dalmatics.

The day had started at 7.00 a.m. with a few parishioners and others present while Fr Patten blessed the new Shrine and celebrated the first Mass there. Bishop O'Rorke sang Pontifical High Mass in St Mary's at 11.30 a.m., and the procession began. When they reached the Shrine they sang the Magnificat, the sacred image was censed, and during the *Salve Regina* it was carried into the Holy House and enthroned above the altar within gold hangings and rays of glory. Finally, the *Te Deum* was sung by everyone inside and around the Shrine. At 6.00 p.m. Shrine Prayers, with Rosary and Intercessions, were offered before the image, as from the beginning in St Mary's they had been and have never ceased, 'for the conversion of England, the return of the lapsed, the sick and the whole, the living and the dead and on behalf of all who visit the Holy House each day.'[62]

One person not present, however, was the Bishop of Norwich. Well aware that his demand for the statue to be removed was not being met in the way he expected, he had come one day to Lady Agatha Gurney, and from an upstairs window in the Abbey House gazed through binoculars at the building operations, muttering, as he went away, 'Deplorable, deplorable!' Worse was to follow. Fr Patten had the Foundation Stone of the Shrine inscribed in Latin. Translated it reads:

> This Shrine, founded in the year 1061 at the will of the Blessed Virgin Mother of God in honour of the mystery of the sacred Incarnation, St Edward, King and Confessor and the Lord of the Manor having reigned nineteen years, and afterwards utterly overthrown by the King who raged with the most foul love of gain (on whose soul may God have mercy) now for the first time in the year 1931 and the ninth year of the pontificate of our most holy Lord Pius XI. P.M. was restored, Bertram Bishop of the Church of Norwich, and Hope Patten parish priest of Walsingham holding office. A.M.D.G.[63]

Fr Patten was simply being true to his Papalist beliefs. He had restored the Catholic Shrine, to be held in trust by Anglicans pending the day when the two Provinces of Canterbury and York would be united with the Holy See. He was simply stating his conviction on the stone. Fr Patten would never allow it to be called the 'Anglican Shrine.' He only used the words 'Anglican' and 'Church of England' when he had to, and they were not mentioned in the Constitution he drew up. He simply called himself 'a Catholic.' As Michael Yelton wrote, 'There was perhaps no statement which more adequately set out the Anglican papalist position with succinctness, and conversely no statement that was more alien not only to most Anglicans but also to virtually all Roman Catholics.'[64] Roman Catholics were confused and annoyed, as he anticipated they would be. Someone sent a cutting from the Catholic Herald to the Bishop of Norwich, which he forwarded to Fr Patten with an amusing comment:

> My dear Vicar,
>
> If this is true, is there any need for my name to appear? Would not the date be adequately given otherwise, without my appearing as a kind of Consule Manlio!!
>
> With kind wishes,
> Yours sincerely,[65]

In his reply Fr Patten played on the Bishop's own bias. The inscription has been inserted in the wall as a witness to the claim of Anglicans, which claim our English Roman 'friends' will not allow, namely that we (the donors) believe that in this year of grace 1931 the rightful parish priest of Walsingham is Hope Patten, *not* Fr Grey of Fakenham – and that the true bishop of the diocese is Dr Pollock and not the Bishop of Northampton.[66]

Dr Pollock was unlikely to have had any doubts about who was "the true bishop of the diocese", and he was unimpressed by Fr Patten's explanation, but Fr Patten obliged by filling the engraved letters of the bishop's name with plaster of Paris, now long since fallen out.

Fr Patten was, however, heading for a serious confrontation with the patient Dr Pollock. Before the blessing of the Shrine, Fr Patten wrote to the Bishop in a very ingratiating way:

> I feel I must write, as you have been so kind all the time I have been in Walsingham, and I hate not being quite open with you. On Thursday morning quite early I am going – as parish priest – to bless the new Chapel in the Sisters' grounds (the new Shrine) and I propose celebrating their Mass. Many of my friends tell me I ought to do so and that there is no need to trouble you about it, but I feel I cannot do that. I am not happy about it as I know you will not personally approve; at the same time you will not positively forbid me and then put us under a ban. I think I shall be much blamed for writing – but I just feel I must.[67]

'Positively forbidding him' was what the Bishop thought he had expressly done. He replied immediately, and the letter begins, not 'My dear Vicar', but 'Dear Mr Patten.'

> I am a little surprised to have your letter after our long conversation. It proves to have been rather a waste of time to talk as we did if your mind is made up or if I failed to make it clear that I do not think it proper for the Holy Communion to be celebrated publicly except in a chapel licensed for the purpose.

And then he continues in his customary kind and warm-hearted way:

> However, this waste of time does not mitigate my appreciation of those respects in which, at a real cost to yourself, you have conformed,

and have come into line with the general worship of the Church of England, as set out in the Book of Common Prayer.[68]

From time to time over the next few years the Bishop wrote to ask Fr Patten how many times he had celebrated in the Shrine, and Fr Patten was able to assure him that it was not often (though priests on pilgrimage did so). The Bishop kept reiterating his desire or demand that he should stop, and Fr Patten pleaded that the spiritual needs of pilgrims required it, the physical needs of elderly and sick parishioners made it desirable, and how difficult it was for him to have the Guardians on one side saying Masses should continue and on the other his desire to please the Bishop who was unhappy about it. In 1938 the Bishop wrote in the Diocesan Gazette that 'The new Chapel at Walsingham is not licensed by me and no priest in this diocese or any other has my permission to celebrate Holy Communion there.' Fr Patten told the Bishop he was displeased by this and the Bishop wrote to say he was sorry 'if I have seemed discourteous … I should be so sorry if you considered that the notice in the Diocesan Gazette had spoilt the situation.' But he reiterated his desire for Holy Communions to stop. Neither the determined parish priest nor the reasonably tolerant bishop could reach an amicable agreement. Something was needed to get them both off the hook, and one of the Guardians, Fr Whitby, found it.

This is where the ancient foundations under the Shrine came in. If they were indeed the footings of the medieval Shrine then the new Chapel could be regarded as consecrated since it was a rebuilding of the original. Counsel's legal opinion was sought, and Mr Marshall Freeman declared that as the original Shrine had been a 'peculiar', (i.e. extra-diocesan) a right that had never been taken away in law, a reconstruction on the same site might be considered to be in the same position. When this was put to the Bishop, who came from a distinguished family of lawyers, he was intrigued:

> I shall be interested in due course to see the actual quotation and extracts from the opinions when you are able to send these along. I shall carefully consider what you send, which will, of course, be germane to our talk on Saturday and I am bearing in mind all that you mention in connection with the foundations that you have discovered.[69]

Although he was too astute to put anything in writing, the Bishop withdrew his objections, and never again opposed Mass being said in the Shrine.

Fr Patten, meanwhile, had his mind on other things. Work was already in progress to complete the Shrine or Pilgrimage Church, as the Chapel soon came to be called. Increasing numbers of pilgrims were arriving. During 1935 there were 30,000 (including the first Anglican walking pilgrimage, when five men started from the Church of the Most Holy Trinity, Hoxton, on 26 August 1935), and it was essential to expand. Fr Patten envisaged not only an extension to the Chapel but domestic buildings to accommodate a community of priests and laymen to serve the Shrine, with a substantial library, cloistered court and museum area. There was to be a new pilgrims' refectory, kitchens, offices, gardener's cottage and other buildings, including an Orthodox Chapel. Fr Fynes-Clinton pioneered ecumenism with the Orthodox and received decorations from both the Russian and Serbian Orthodox Churches.[70] Through his influence the Orthodox showed great interest in the Shrine. The first Orthodox clergy came on pilgrimage in May 1937, and in November Russian Orthodox Archbishop Seraphim came from Paris to bless the land on which the Church was to be built. In the event it never materialised, but the small Orthodox Chapel of the Theotokos was incorporated into the Shrine Church, and at Pentecost 1944 was consecrated by Archbishop Sava of Grodno, the Orthodox Chaplain General of the Polish forces in this country. This continues to be used by Orthodox pilgrims. A two centuries old copy of the ancient and revered icon of Our Lady of the Gates on Mount Athos is venerated in the Anglican Shrine.

Much of the interior painting was done by the gifted artist Enid Chadwick who came to live in Walsingham, had a studio near the Pilgrim Hall, and became well-known as an illustrator of children's books about the Faith. Other Walsingham artists who worked in the Shrine were Lily Dagless and her brother James, whose latent talent had been discovered by Fr Patten. They fashioned the beautiful statue beside the Holy Well, which is of Our Lady of Sudbury. Another is to be found in the restored Shrine of Our Lady of Sudbury in the Catholic Church there, and a copy in St Mary's South Creake. For some years James and Lily had a church arts and craft shop in Walsingham before moving to King's Lynn. Sir Ninian Comper was commissioned to design several stained glass windows in the Shrine Church, and at a later date in the Holy House the altar, reredos and mandorla. Great care was taken to find and create art of good quality in the Shrine.

Outside the Shrine Church, Sir William Milner, a noted garden designer, created an attractive garden, which remained until the fine landscaped garden was made in 2005. Stations of the Cross were erected, with three full-size crosses on a mound, and a replica of the holy sepulchre of Jesus in Jerusalem. A Statue of St Thérèse of Lisieux, to whom Fr Patten had great devotion, was placed in a corner of the garden, close by the 'Hatcham Crucifix' said to have come from St James' Hatcham, the church of Fr Tooth, who was one of the priests imprisoned for ritual offences and whose effigy was placed in the Pilgrimage Church in his memory.

The Blessing of the Shrine Church took place on the Whit Monday Bank Holiday, 6 June 1938, and was annually commemorated by the National Pilgrimage on that day, until 1970 when the Bank Holiday no longer always coincided with Whit Monday. Bishop O'Rorke returned for the celebrations and preached in St Mary's on Whit Sunday and later consecrated the high altar of the Shrine Church. Fr Alban Baverstock preached at Evensong and Benediction, which was attended by exiled Archbishop Nestor of Kamchatka and Petropavlovsk with Archimandrite Nicolas Gibbes and other Orthodox clergy. The impact all this made on the villagers can scarcely be imagined, and they festooned the village with flags and bunting.

At noon on the Monday the Angelus was said in St Mary's and the Procession to the Shrine was led by the scouts, servers, Religious men and women, including the Abbot of Nashdom. Girls in white carried streamers, flowers, and the banner of Our Lady of Walsingham, and these were followed by a hundred and fifty Priests Associate of the Holy House, and the Orthodox. The Guardians came next, and behind them Bishop O'Rorke, attended by two priests from the Community of the Resurrection, Mirfield, then the architect, the wives of the Guardians, and three to four thousand pilgrims. The Bishop blessed the Shrine Church inside and out with holy water accompanied by litanies and *Faith of our Fathers*. He then presided at the throne while Fr Patten sang the Mass, and for the crowds outside Fr Raybould of St Julian's Norwich simultaneously sang Mass at the Hickleton altar (which had been built for the Anglo-Catholic Congress at Lord Halifax's seat, Hickleton, in Yorkshire). In the afternoon the Orthodox sang a solemn Te Deum in the Holy House and Fr Frank Biggert of Mirfield preached.

Next day Bishop O'Rorke and others attended the Liturgy celebrated by Archbishop Nestor at the high altar, assisted by two archimandrites, one of whom was Fr Nicolas Gibbes, who had been tutor to the Imperial family.

Prince Vladimir Galitzine served the lavabo. Every year a contingent of Orthodox clergy and people loved to come to the National Pilgrimage, where they were warmly welcomed, sometimes arriving in a colourful little procession after the Mass had started, until they decided they could no longer attend after the Church of England's decision to ordain women.

Those familiar with the Shrine Church know that it is a building designed to be conducive to devotion and personal prayer, with quiet corners and small spaces, 'full of reminders that the Church on earth is but a colony of the Church in heaven', as Archbishop Michael Ramsey once described a church full of statues in Hull. Fifteen altars dedicated to the mysteries of the rosary, and to different saints, are around it, where priests can, as they did in those days, celebrate their private masses with perhaps a few pilgrims. As with the altar of the Holy House, the House itself, and the altar in the Chantry Chapel of King Edward I, the high altar of the Shrine Church is built with stones from many cathedrals and religious houses. A campanile was built for the carillon, which was rung every evening, its sweet sound still heard all around the village, playing hymns.

In 1933 Fr Patten had obtained a beautiful book on the Holy House of Loreto,[71] in which he carefully annotated in pencil devotions and ideas he introduced at Walsingham. Pilgrims in Loreto often went around the Holy House on their knees, and Fr Patten similarly instituted a devotion known as *The Effective Prayer*. After kneeling in the Holy House to pray the Creed, Our Father and three Hail Mary's, the pilgrim walks round the outside of the Holy House three times saying the Rosary, kneels by the Holy Well and ascends the steps on his knees with a Hail Mary on each.[72] He noted that the robes worn by Our Lady of Loreto represented the robe Our Lady had worn at Nazareth, and that it was long and reached to the base of the pedestal. He underlined too that 'A pilgrimage to the Holy House is equivalent to one to Palestine.' He noted that pilgrims were to visit the Basilica three times on their pilgrimage and 'pour forth devout prayers to God.' He underlined 'the ceiling is studded with stars.' He took note of the *honorary chaplains,* and the *Confraternity of the Holy House* whose members (like Fr Patten's Society of Our Lady of Walsingham) prayed the Angelus every day and could form branches affiliating other Loreto shrines to the Holy House. He noted all the lamps (over fifty) that burned in the Holy House.

Friends warned Fr Patten that the Shrine Church, although it was the size of St Mary's, was too small, but funds were limited and Fr Patten was in a hurry. Events in Europe were to prove him right, for in a just over a year the country was at war, activities at Walsingham came almost to a halt, and no building could be done. And Fr Patten saw some significance in the year 1938, for in his Loreto book he underlined thus: 'The Basilica was completed under the pontificate of Paul III, 15<u>38</u>.'[73]

Walsingham in the War Years

Situated but five miles from the coast, and with many military bases in Norfolk, Walsingham was a restricted zone during the war. There were times when travel into the area was permitted, and the Anglican Guardians met occasionally, but although the *Catholic League* did manage one pilgrimage in the winter of 1943, pilgrimages to Walsingham were all but impossible. Members of the armed forces were, of course, allowed entry, and Catholic Chaplains were able to organise pilgrimages of soldiers, sailors and airmen, with processions bearing the Blessed Sacrament from the Chapel in Aelred House along the Holy Mile to the Slipper Chapel. Some of them were confirmed in the Slipper Chapel. Walsingham thus became known to Canadians, Poles, Frenchmen, South Africans, Dutch and Belgians, and even to Italian prisoners of war, some of whom returned in later years. And most of them visited the Anglican Shrine as well.

By then, Anglican shrines of Our Lady of Walsingham had been established in parish churches around England, and Fr Patten encouraged devotees to make private pilgrimages there. It was, however, the village people who found great solace and refuge in the Shrine, not least because so many men from the village were away in the war. Shrine Prayers (rosary and intercessions) were faithfully said every day. Each Friday a Holy Hour was kept to pray for peace and victory. A Triduum of Prayer was held most weeks, with special early Masses in the Holy House, the rosary around the altars of the Church, Benediction, Stations of the Cross, and confessions. In *Our Lady's Mirror* for Spring/Summer 1947, Fr Patten wrote:

> Those dark and frightful nights, when almost without exception after the enemy aircraft started crossing our coast line they moaned over the

Stiffkey Vale, constantly dropping bombs in places around the sanctuary. Every village was damaged by the enemy except Walsingham. By day they came over – hedge-hopping over the vicarage. Often and often, when the rosary was being said in the winter evening, the shrapnel would rattle on the roof and the Church rock like a ship at sea. But within the Shrine there was always a wonderful peace and calm – Our Lady's Mantle was spread over it.

In December 1942 Fr Bruno Scott James left Walsingham, and the next few years were difficult for the Catholic Shrine. Fr Arthur Brewer came for short while, then Fr Gerard Roberts, the parish priest of Fakenham took over as custodian of the Shrine in 1944. He and the Franciscans departed in 1948, and Fr Gerard Langley was appointed. A year later Fr Roberts came back, and on his departure in 1951 Fr Gerard Hulme became both missionary rector and custodian of the Shrine. Life was getting back to normal, the pilgrims were returning, and Fr Hulme, like Fr Patten, bought up properties in order to expand the ministry of the Shrine. Unfortunately, unlike the houses bought by Fr Patten, which allowed a huge site to be developed in the heart of the village, these were scattered around, and most of them in the end were sold to raise capital.

On the day after V-E day Fr Patten celebrated a High Mass of Thanksgiving in St Mary's, and history was made a week later, on 17 May 1945, when the first Catholic Mass in the Priory grounds since the Reformation was offered in the presence of the Bishop of Northampton, for American Servicemen. The altar stood on the site of the Priory's original high altar. Since then the grounds have been used by very many pilgrimages, both Catholic and Anglican, by kind permission of the family who live in the Abbey. Fr Patten tried to organise a Pilgrimage of Thanksgiving after V-J day, and was disappointed few took it up. Perhaps this sadly reflected the way it was with the forgotten army.

As the war ended, small pilgrimages gradually began to return, but transport was difficult, for not until 1950 did petrol rationing end. Many pilgrims came by rail, because there was a station at Walsingham with a halt at the Slipper Chapel. The Wells & Fakenham Railway, later part of the Great Eastern Railway, opened in 1857. Its closure in 1964 was a monumental mistake, though there are now plans being mooted to lay new track and reopen the station.

Fr Patten's Death

1958 was a Lambeth Conference year, and although most Anglican Diocesan Bishops in England had shown little approval of the Shrine, many overseas bishops were far more Catholic-minded, so it was decided to arrange a Bishops' Pilgrimage on 11 August. There were not many, just the Bishops of Barbados, British Honduras, Kalgoorie, South West Tanganyika and Zanzibar, but nothing like this had happened before, and a number of Guardians came to welcome them. After Shrine Prayers they all had dinner at the Knight's Gate Café with Fr Patten, who was in good form, and returned to the Shrine Church for the torchlight Procession of Our Lady and Benediction. There was nothing untoward, though Mrs Ferrier told the writer that she had looked up as Fr Patten was singing the Benediction collect because 'his voice was so strong, like it had been when he was young.' Fr Patten carried the Blessed Sacrament up the stairs to the Chapel in the gallery, replaced the pyx in the tabernacle, and arranged the veil, before turning and collapsing. He was assisted back to the College, the doctor came, but shortly afterwards he died in bed, surrounded by the Guardians. It was a perfect way for him to die, on that first pilgrimage of Bishops, giving the Church's seal of approval to his life's work. A muffled peal was rung on the bells, and by an instinct those villagers who heard it knew their beloved priest of thirty-seven years had died, and late as it was they began to fill the Shrine to pray.

With the approach of the Assumption and so many Guardians being already in Walsingham it was decided to have the funeral only two days later, on the 13 August, and word got round so quickly that nearly a hundred priests arrived from all over the country. Neither the Bishops of Norwich nor Thetford were able to attend, but in the Church of St Peter Parmentergate, Norwich, at a Requiem for Fr Patten, Bishop Leonard of Thetford paid his tribute:

> Father Hope Patten stands among the great benefactors of the spiritual life, as one who by his vision revealed to an innumerable company of Christian people the hunger in their souls for the Catholic Devotion to Our Lady and the healing power of childlike faith in prayer, and by his enterprise and constructive genius has created a centre of national pilgrimage on the site of an ancient and historic shrine.[74]

Developments at the Anglican Shrine

After Fr Patten's death, the work of both Shrine and parish being too heavy, it was decided to separate them; Fr Alan Roe was appointed vicar, and Fr Colin Stephenson became Administrator of the Shrine. From the start he was determined to broaden the appeal of Walsingham and fully integrate it into the life of the Church of England. For the first time, in 1959, the Bishop of Norwich was represented at the National Pilgrimage, as from that year the Whit-Monday pilgrimage was known, and soon the Diocesan Bishop himself came every year. In 1965 Bishop Mervyn Stockwood of Southwark preached at the National Pilgrimage, the first diocesan bishop to do so, and in 1972 it was the turn of the Bishop of Norwich. The Archbishop of Canterbury, Michael Ramsey, came after he retired in 1978 and Archbishop Runcie in 1980. Since then every Archbishop of Canterbury has been on pilgrimage, and an Archbishop of York, David Hope, was for many years Master of the Guardians.

An indication of the growth of the Anglican Shrine is that in 1948 twenty-one parish pilgrimages booked in, and in 1998 there were three hundred and sixty.[75] By the 1960s the Shrine Church was already too small, and so in 1964 the North Cloister was added as a memorial to Fr Patten, and in 1972 the South Cloister was built to celebrate the 50th anniversary of the Shrine in the parish church. In 1965 the *Guild of All Souls* built the Chantry Chapel of St Michael and the Holy Souls in the grounds.

Successive Priest Administrators improved the facilities and developed the pilgrimage programme as the numbers increased. A landmark was St Joseph's House, expertly equipped for pilgrims with special needs, opened in 1985 by HRH the Duchess of Kent. Richeldis House opened in 1990 to provide more accommodation, revealing as it was built a medieval shop front in Bridewell Street, a rare survival from the late fifteenth century.

A major development was the Education Department, opened in 1996, with full-time staff, providing a pilgrimage experience and teaching for the more than five thousand primary and secondary school children each year who come to visit both Shrines. As well as organising national Children's and Youth Pilgrimages, the department offers pilgrimage days and residential faith schools incorporating a Holy Mile walk, creative prayer, lively worship, optional healing ministries, workshops and fun. Schools for children with special needs are encouraged and come together for Pilgrimage Adventure

Days. The Christian Year comes to life with Bethlehem Days, and dramatic meetings with Bible characters, and Easter Trails that re-enact the Last Supper. The Department also takes a 'roadshow' to schools for a whole day, around Norfolk and Lincolnshire.

St Anne's was refurbished to provide facilities for educational and creative courses. And the Barn Chapel with its striking crucifix by David Begbie, quietly apart, is perfect for a small group. Conferences for clergy and laity on Church growth and evangelism and many other topics are hosted and encouraged.

A magnificent new Refectory was opened it in 2001 by HRH Princess Alexandra, replacing the prefabricated building, which had served for many years, but was far too small for the crowds it fed. In 2005, the Shrine gardens were opened-up and replanted to a design by Tessa Hobbs, completed by the building of the new Altar of the Mysteries of Light to replace the very old Halifax altar, now enabling thousands to gather around in worship. The piazza at the front of the Shrine was remodelled and the small garden at the side re-designed with a fountain.

In October 2008 the whole of the side of the Hospice of Our Lady along Holt Road was pulled out, not only making it safer and far more attractive, but allowing a state-of–the-art Visitors Centre along the roadside. Known as the Welcome Centre it is staffed all day by a team of volunteer stewards and even in the winter months a stream of visitors to Walsingham pass through the doors.

Four large panels explain the foundation, destruction and restoration of both the Anglican and Catholic Shrines, and the latest interactive technology invites both children and adults to explore topics of interest about the village and the Shrine, while in a small video room a short film traces the history and meaning of the Shrine from 1061 to the present day. This Welcome Centre formed part of a major building programme to celebrate the Millennium, and was opened by HRH the Duke of Edinburgh in 2009. It includes more accommodation called the Milner Wing, a Reception area and Hospitality Office to receive pilgrims, public lavatories with facilities for disabled people and a baby-changing room.

Throughout the work great attention has been paid to use good materials, well-designed decoration, and symbolism, in the long Catholic tradition, especially associated with devotion to Our Lady.

Developments at the Roman Catholic Shrine

In 1948 a great cross-carrying Catholic pilgrimage was organised, similar to the one to Vézélay in France in 1946. Fourteen groups of about thirty men walked with heavy crosses, as an act of reparation for the war and a prayer for peace, from all over the country, from as far north as Middlesborough and as far south as Canterbury, arriving outside Walsingham on 15 July. The night was illumined by the light of their campfires in a circle around the village, as the men kept a vigil of prayer before their crosses. Next day they processed to the Slipper Chapel where Cardinal Bernard Griffin celebrated Mass at the open-air altar with them and with the Union of Catholic Mothers on their annual pilgrimage, which had been inaugurated in 1946. Over 12,000 pilgrims took part, and after welcoming them all the Cardinal told them, 'Today, at the request of the Archbishops and Bishops of England and Wales, I am to dedicate this country to the Immaculate Heart of Mary.' This he did in the afternoon when they processed with the Cardinal and Bishop Leo Parker of Northampton to the Abbey grounds for the Blessing of the Sick and Benediction. The crosses were later arranged in a circle in the grounds of the Shrine to form a permanent Way of the Cross. A notice explains where each came from.

These cross-bearing soldiers were not the only cross carriers in 1948. On 20 March a group of about thirty Catholic students from various British universities accompanied by two priests, later three, set out to walk the one hundred and twenty miles from London to Walsingham. This was the first Student Cross Pilgrimage, which has taken place in Holy Week every year since. With the impact of the Second Vatican Council, Anglicans and others began to join in, and it officially became an ecumenical pilgrimage in 1972, with both Catholic and Anglican chaplains. The various legs from different starting points at the beginning of Holy Week sleep in halls, celebrate Mass, pray, sing, and visit hostelries on the way, like pilgrims of old, converging on Good Friday afternoon at the Catholic Shrine, some suffering and sore, for the journey is not always easy, and the crosses are heavy. Staying up late into Saturday night to celebrate the Easter Vigil, blessing the new fire in the grounds of the Anglican Shrine, the students process through the quiet village to the Catholic Church for the first Mass of Easter, full of excitement and joy, their crosses by then beautifully decorated with greenery and flowers.

The Guild of Our Lady of Ransom continued to support the Pontifical Shrine in King's Lynn, maintaining the fifteen lamps before Our Lady, organising the annual Whitsuntide pilgrimage, and encouraging other groups to go on pilgrimage too. But inspired by the walking pilgrimage of 1948, and to strengthen the Guild's links with Walsingham, the new Master, Monsignor Laurence Goulder, announced his intention to walk from London to Our Lady's Shrine in Walsingham, laying 'a Rosary of Masses' along the way. In September 1952, timed to arrive for the Feast of Our Lady of Ransom, Mgr Goulder and a small group of men set out on the Walsingham Walk. There had been no intention to repeat it, but the hardships endured being so severe, the men were convinced, like penitential pilgrims of old, of its spiritual value, and the Walk continued for fifty years. By contrast that year came a transatlantic pilgrimage from Washington D.C.

In 1948 the Franciscans left Walsingham and that allowed Aelred House to become the Pilgrim Bureau for a while. In 1973 a generous benefactor enabled the Oddfellows' Hall to become a Pilgrims' Hall, and the inadequate facilities in Aelred House to be improved. Walsingham Grammar School, which had been founded in 1639, closed after the Second World War; and after being briefly used as a Catholic Choir School and private Preparatory School, it was sold by Walsingham Estate Company to artist Michael Chapman, before being purchased by the Diocese of Northampton in 1971 and named Elmham House. It became the present Pilgrim Bureau in 1986. The accommodation of Catholic pilgrims had always been a problem, for they used several houses around the village, but now Elmham House was developed with the building of a new wing. It also enabled a refectory and kitchen to be built, with rooms upstairs.

In 1953 the Pope solemnly proclaimed Our Lady's Assumption, and Bishop Parker came to bless a new East window in the Slipper Chapel, which commemorates the mystery, a particularly fine work by Geoffrey Webb, and his last. The statue of Professor Tristram, although it fitted Erasmus' description of the original as small, was replaced in 1954, much to the scorn of Fr Bruno Scott James who described it as 'too austere for tastes formed on the mass-produced *bondieuserie* of the Place S. Sulpice, or what is called Catholic repository art. It has now been replaced for one of more sentimental appeal.'[76] Miss Cary, who gave the earlier statue, readily gave permission, for she had never cared for it. The new statue is actually very beautiful, and was carved by

Monsieur Marcel Barbeau, modelled on a Mme. Marcelle Mandar, quite appropriately since the medieval image had French provenance. That year was a Marian Year, and on the Feast of the Assumption, in the old Priory grounds, 15,000 pilgrims witnessed the new statue being solemnly crowned by the Apostolic Delegate, Archbishop O'Hara, on behalf of Pope Pius XII, with a gold crown encrusted with 118 precious jewels, all of which had been generously given. Two white doves settled on the statue and remained there on the procession along the Holy Mile, and overnight in the Slipper Chapel.[77] Mysteriously the same phenomenon had occurred to the statue of Our Lady of Fatima after it was crowned on 13 May 1946, and the doves remained close to it on a national tour.

The Silver Jubilee of the opening of the Slipper Chapel and the restoration of the National Shrine was commemorated in 1959 with three days of celebration. Bishop Parker of Northampton, the Bishop of Nottingham and the Archbishop of Malta led thousands of pilgrims. On the final day, 7 July, Cardinal Godfrey of Westminster preached in the Abbey grounds with three thousand members of the Union of Catholic Mothers on their annual pilgrimage adding to the crowd. The 900th anniversary of the founding of the Shrine was celebrated in 1961 with several events, notably with a Pontifical High Mass celebrated by Archbishop Cyril Cowderoy of Southwark on the site of the high altar of the original Priory, and on the Feast of the Assumption Bishop Parker brought 7,000 pilgrims, telling them that he hoped the Shrine in the Slipper Chapel would only be temporary, pending the building of a great basilica on the site of the original shrine.

In 1968 the arrival of the Marists to look after both the parish and the Shrine gave a huge impetus to providing better facilities for the increasing numbers of pilgrims. Fr Roland Connelly wasted no time in building a much-needed Pilgrim Centre at the Slipper Chapel with a café, toilet block, and repository shop. Pope Paul VI contributed £1000 towards it, along with his Apostolic Blessing on the pilgrims.[78] By Easter 1973 an open-sided church had replaced the old wooden structure of Fr Bruno Scott James. An Altar of polished Aberdeen granite was a gift from the Union of Catholic Mothers, who were on their annual pilgrimage when Bishop Charles Grant consecrated it and sealed in it the relics of St Laurence of Rome, St Thomas Becket, and St Thomas More. In 1974 the first Pilgrimage came from the Channel Islands.

In 1978 Sister Kathleen Moran S.M. succeeded Fr Connelly S.M. until Fr Clive Birch S.M. was appointed in the following year, and at once set about replacing the open-sided church with the new Chapel of Reconciliation, under the direction of architect Michael Wingate. Blessed by Cardinal Basil Hume in 1981 at the National Pilgrimage, it was consecrated by Bishop Alan Clark of East Anglia on 22 May 1982. In those ecumenical days a Bible Service of praise and prayer was accompanied by a talk from Fr Christopher Colven, the Administrator of the Anglican Shrine. From the outside, viewed from a distance, the sweeping roof makes the Chapel resemble a Norfolk barn, the intention being to blend in with the simplicity of local farms around the Shrine. Deliberately open and uncluttered, people frequently mention its quiet dignity, simplicity, and atmosphere of prayer. The altar of Aberdeen granite was reconsecrated, and a relic of St Peter Chanel, the Marist martyr, was sealed with those already enclosed. Although it can seat up to 400, many more regularly fill the outer aisles of the Chapel, but when there are more pilgrims the sanctuary can be opened and the altar becomes the focal point for thousands of pilgrims outdoors. Wooden shutters opening to the grounds were replaced in 2011 with stunning panels of engraved glass, designed by Sally Scott. Pilgrim facilities were improved in the late 1980's with a new café, toilet block, repository shop, and office, and a small covered way with a frieze depicting the history of the Shrine from the beginning until the restoration of both the Anglican and Catholic Shrines, enclosing a fountain of blessed water engraved by Jane Quail.

Catholic Schools and Religious Communities frequently come on day pilgrimages, and many parishes, groups and individuals spend several days in Walsingham on residential pilgrimages. The *Walsingham Association* promotes these. Diocesan pilgrimages, and various national pilgrimages, sometimes numbering thousands, occupy most weekends in the pilgrimage season. They include the Union of Catholic Mothers, the East Anglian Diocesan Schools' and Children's Pilgrimages, Aid to the Church in Need, the Association of Sri Lankan Catholics, the Caribbean Pilgrimage, the Nigerian Pilgrimage, the Day with Mary, Divine Mercy Day, Dominicans, the Order of Malta, Our Lady Queen of Peace, the Divine Mercy Pilgrimage, Padre Pio Pilgrimage, a Pilgrimage for Children, Parents and Grandparents, the Pilgrimage for the deaf, Pilgrimages of Reparation and Consecration, Pro-Life pilgrimage, the Society of St Vincent de Paul's pilgrimage for the sick, St Patrick's Missionary

Society, Syro-Malabar pilgrimage, several all-night vigils in the year, the Latin Mass Society, the Travellers at the Assumption, and the Vocations pilgrimage, an ever-increasing list. In the summer, the fields around are filled with marquees and tents, music and laughter for the New Dawn Pilgrimage Conference of Charismatic Catholics, Catholic Families, Children's Pilgrimages, and for Youth 2000. Quiet Days and Retreats feature in the programme, the latter especially encouraged by Fr Alan Williams S.M.

The former National Pilgrimage in September, on the nearest Sunday to Our Lady's Birthday, became the Dowry of Mary Pilgrimage in 1989, in the tradition of prayer for the conversion of England, with a Mass at the Shrine and procession to the Abbey grounds, concluding with Benediction below the Priory arch and prayers at the site of the ancient Shrine. From 2007 it became representative of the many Catholic people from around the world who live in Britain. Bearing national flags, with many in national costume, this pilgrimage, numbering thousands, is the most colourful of the year. The largest pilgrimage, numbering over 7000, stretching the Shrine's capacity almost to the limit, is the annual pilgrimage of Tamils. This noteworthy pilgrimage includes large numbers of Hindus who happily join in the prayers and the singing, venerate Our Lady, and seek blessings and healing, a beautiful example of two faiths celebrating their joy together, cooking food and sharing it with one another.

The Mission of Our Lady of Walsingham

As an indication of the importance Pope John Paul II attached to Walsingham, in 2001 he approved the new Feast of Our Lady of Walsingham to be observed on 24 September, formerly the Feast of Our Lady of Ransom. Celebrated as a memorial throughout England and Wales, it is a feast in the diocese, and a solemnity in Walsingham. Many dioceses now celebrate Walsingham Festivals on the day. Both Shrines observe it, and on the Eve, starting with a procession from either the Chapel of Reconciliation to the Anglican Shrine Church, or in the opposite direction, Catholics and Anglicans gather for Vespers together. This feast has brought Our Lady of Walsingham to the attention of the people of England once more, recalling England's title as Mary's Dowry, and the consecration of England to Our Lady at Walsingham on 16 July 1948 by Cardinal Bernard Griffin and all the Bishops of England and Wales. The feast enables thousands throughout the country to seek her intercession, and gives Walsingham a special vocation in the life of faith in our country, as its National Shrine of Our Lady. It also provides a chance for Anglican and Roman Catholic parishes around the country to celebrate Vespers of Our Lady and the rosary together.

A Pilgrim Statue of Our Lady of Walsingham, under the title, Our Lady of Reconciliation (to whom Cardinal Hume dedicated the Chapel of Reconciliation) was blessed in Rome by Pope John Paul II, remarkably on 24 September 1997, before it became her feast. Ever since that day, through the initiative of Antonia Moffat, the statue has been travelling through the dioceses of England, Wales, Ireland (it was there when the *Good Friday Agreement* was signed), and Scotland, around parishes, religious houses, and schools, where it becomes the centre of devotion and prayer. 2001 was a year of outreach for the Anglican Shrine when the statue of Our Lady of Walsingham left the Shrine to visit five cathedrals in Britain for a series of regional festivals. In 2004 the statue visited a variety of different venues - a hospital, a prison, an army barracks, an Oxford college, a school, and even an airport – in an outreach called *Magnificat*. The two months of travelling culminated in a celebration in York Minster.

Our Lady of Walsingham has travelled beyond our shores. There are statues of her in Santiago de Compostela given by Cardinal Godfrey, and at Lourdes by the Anglican Society of Mary. In the United States, at Williamsburg, is the National Catholic Shrine of Our Lady of Walsingham and the Walsingham Academy, and there are Shrines in both Anglican and Catholic parishes in the States.

The Shrine at Walsingham exists to bring Mary to the waiting world as she brings Jesus to the waiting world. 'Many people find it easier to walk rather than talk their faith and find encouragement in treading in the footsteps of countless pilgrims before them,'[79] wrote Ian Bradley. Mission is part of Walsingham's huge appeal, because Mary is revealed in the Scriptures as one who listened and 'pondered these things in her heart.'[80] She silently reflects upon the Word of God, and carries within her the Word of God as she travels to her cousin. In the image of Our Lady of Walsingham Mary holds Christ to the world – and he holds the Book of Life.

CHAPTER 12

ANNUNCIATION AND INCARNATION

The Ballad relates that Our Lady asked Richeldis to build the Chapel in Walsingham 'where shall be had in memorial the great joys of my salutation.' The picture of Mary listening and responding to God's call coming to her through the angel has inspired art and poetry throughout the ages, and a spirituality which is at the heart of the Faith. When a devout woman in the crowd, overcome with the preaching of Jesus, raised her voice to shower praise on his mother, 'Blessed is the womb that bore you and the breasts you sucked,' Jesus recalled her to the secret of his mother's blessedness, and invited her to share it. 'Blessed rather are those who hear the word of God and keep it.'[1] A little earlier in the Gospel Jesus had commented, 'My mother and my brothers are those who hear the word of God and put it into practice.'[2] Mary exemplifies all the faithful who respond to the call of the prophets to 'hear the Word of the Lord.' The Shrine at Walsingham exists to recall Mary's total surrender to the word and will of God, and her willingness to believe it. Pilgrims come to Walsingham to share in this, and many seek the will of God to find their vocation or a new direction in life.

It was Mary's attentiveness to God, and her obedience, that made possible the incarnation of the Son of God. The Word was made flesh in her, but in as much as she is our pattern, the Word is made flesh, in a sense, in all believers. Through the 'incarnate' life of Jesus, God entered into the world and is visibly seen by those with eyes to see him, especially amongst the sick, the poor, the rejected and the 'sinners'. Nowhere is the incarnation more visible than in the lives of men and women who hear and respond, as did the first disciples, to the call to 'leave everything behind and follow him.' Some Jesus calls to sell everything they own and give to the poor. Others respond to his call to leave 'house, wife, brothers, parents and children.'[3] Unsurprisingly, Geoffrey de Favarches wanted a community of men, who lived this kind of life, to care for his mother's Chapel in Walsingham. For centuries there were Augustinian canons in Walsingham, and Franciscans, till all were swept away. But they were bound by the power of this place to come back.

Religious Communities in Walsingham

The first Religious to live in Walsingham, after their convent at Dartford was dissolved in the reign of Henry VIII, were, as we have seen, Sisters Elizabeth Exmew and Elizabeth Seygood. Nearly four hundred years had to elapse before there were any more, and these were, as we have noted, the Sisters of the Anglican Community of St Peter in Horbury, who came at Fr Patten's invitation in 1924 to look after pilgrims. Founded in 1858 to care for unmarried mothers and girls in distress, the community split in 1932 and half of them established a Mother House in Laleham from which they worked in many parishes closely associated with Walsingham. The sisters in Walsingham, who usually numbered around five or six, were attached to Laleham. However, in 1941 the Reverend Mother Sarah reduced the number to three, which did not seem unreasonable during the war when there were virtually no pilgrims to care for, and there was great need in cities like London and Manchester, but it caused Fr Patten to think that Walsingham ought to have an autonomous House over which he and the Guardians could have more control. There followed a difficult period during which the numbers in Walsingham varied from three to a dozen, and in the end with only one left, Laleham withdrew early in 1947.

In April that year the Society of St Margaret came from Haggerston, where it had been founded in 1855 by the Warden of Sackville College, East Grinstead, Dr John Mason Neale, who has already been mentioned. The sisters nursed the sick and cared for the poor in East Grinstead, and in the dreadful slum of Haggerston, as it was in those days; they alone among the terrified people went into the streets during a smallpox epidemic, looked after the sick, laid out the dead, destroyed infected bedding, and gave out food. From there the sisters have worked in many parts of the world including America, Canada, Haiti (where they survived the earthquake of 2010 despite losing their convent and school), Sri Lanka and South Africa. The distinctive cross worn by the Sisters is a central symbol of their life, expressing outwardly that intense love of the Saviour, and the mystery through which they enter into the life of Christ.

In their early days in Walsingham, the Sisters looked after the Hospice, made the bookings, coped with the Shrine finances, cooked the meals, and ran the sacristy, huge tasks now undertaken mainly by paid staff. The Sisters have always worked in the parish where they quickly became deeply loved and respected. As religious life has changed so has their work, which now includes pastoral and spiritual work among pilgrims, ministering and teaching in the Shrine, conducting Quiet Days, all the while maintaining for more than sixty years in Walsingham a joyful, disciplined, and prayerful way of life centred on Adoration. The House became autonomous in 1955, which no doubt pleased Fr Patten, and remained so apart from a few years between 1984 and 1994, and it has been blessed with new vocations.

Fr Patten always envisaged a community of priests and lay brothers in Walsingham, and in late 1929 announced that a 'cell or rest house' of Benedictines from Nashdom Abbey would open a guest house in St Augustine's, one of the cottages close to the Shrine. The biographers of Fr Patten seem to agree that he had insufficient understanding of the Religious Life, for either men or women, and that he expected to be, if not their Superior, then in charge of them, with unrealistic expectations of how Religious could combine their life of prayer with duties in the Shrine, not to mention pastoral work in the village. So far as the Benedictines were concerned the Abbot thought it was to provide a 'rest' for monks (as they called their annual break), but Fr Patten expected them to look after guests in a dilapidated cottage lacking a bath or indoor sanitation. When Abbot Denys died in 1934 his successor Abbot Martin closed the house.

Fr Patten now turned his attention to the idea of founding a College of Augustinian canons. Curiously, even before he came to Walsingham he had been interested in their life and in 1913 had written some notes about an Augustinian revival in England. The College began in the vicarage, and continued more or less until the end of his life. However, it was never approved as a Religious Community. The Bishop of Norwich wrote to Fr Patten on 25 November 1952 to say that 'I have heard from the Bishop of Oxford following a meeting of the Advisory Council which discussed the question of the College at Walsingham. He says that there is no question of the College being or becoming a Religious Community.' Knowing that Fr Patten's real concern was the future of the Shrine, which he thought would best be secured by a recognised Religious Community, the Bishop reassured him by adding,

> I am writing to state that on any change of incumbency I should be ready to regard the College and Shrine as coming within the provisions of the Private Chapels Act, 1871, and to license as Warden a priest of the Church of England nominated by the Trustees and approved by me in the usual way.'[4]

The College rarely had more than three or four members, never the same ones for long, and it cannot be counted a success, simply because there was no adequate formation for novices, and not even Fr Patten could combine the roles of Prior, Administrator of the Shrine, and Vicar. After the war Fr Patten left the Vicarage and the College moved with him into the cottages beside the Shrine. In 1955 he wrote rather sadly that sixteen men had come forward since the inception of the Community, twelve of whom decided after a six month postulancy to continue, eventually being reduced to five who renewed their vows every three years, of whom just two had continued. Fr Colin Stephenson says that Fr Patten's perseverance in spite of continual disappointment, as men left, is most impressive, and that when anyone suggested he should abandon the idea he replied, 'But God has never left us without anyone, that must mean that he intends it to continue.' 'He himself was the only member of the community who persevered unto death, and richly deserves the initials C.S.A., which are carved after his name upon his tomb.'[5]

Just three years after Fr Patten had restored Augustinians to Walsingham, it was perhaps appropriate that the Roman Catholic Bishop of Northampton, Bishop Laurence Youens, should invite Franciscans back to Walsingham in November 1937. The Bishop provided a house in Friday Market, Aelred House, which they renamed Greyfriars, and their work was to look after pilgrims, as they had done before the Reformation. They bought Falcon House, the old inn on the High Street, and called it St Francis, so that it was being used once again as a pilgrim hostel for men, while behind it they opened St Clare's (off Almonry Lane) for women. Sadly, the hostels were short-lived and when war broke out the houses were let to tenants. On one occasion all the friars came from their English friaries for a celebration together in the Friary ruins, the first time they had been there since its dissolution.

The Capuchin Friars, in their brown habits and sandals, were popular figures in the village. There were still only three Roman Catholics living in the village in the 1930s, and successive bishops of Northampton, Bishop Arthur Riddell, Bishop Frederick Keating and Bishop Dudley Carey-Elwes had resisted any idea of building a parish church. All there was in Walsingham was a chapel that Bishop Youens had blessed in Aelred House. The great hope of the friars was to build a huge church stretching from Falcon House the length of Almonry Lane, where Mass would be offered and the Office chanted by night and day. They had considerable success fund-raising in a scheme known as 'Marypence', but Bishop Youens died in 1939 and his successor, Bishop Leo Parker, did not approve of their plans. Nor did Cardinal Arthur Hinsley, who declared, 'I would never be party to any church being built in Walsingham except on a scale worthy of its past.'[6] Undaunted, the Capuchins acquired land beside the Black Lion with cottages in front, which they began to demolish with their own hands, but the war brought their plans to an end, and the community became reduced in number until only one, Father Pacificus, remained. He was loved in the village, a tall character with a long white beard, and for a time he carried on the work of the parish and the Shrine. But Bishop Parker thought that with only one friar the situation was 'pitiful' and suggested they should withdraw, which they did in 1948.

Bishop Parker was nonetheless in favour of building a parish church. Fr Gerard Langley came for a year, and began the building of a church on the site beside the Black Lion. Fr G. E. Roberts from Fakenham took over in 1950, and although there were still only about twenty Catholics in the village, the temporary parish Church of the Annunciation was blessed on 2 July by Bishop Parker. It was a poor sort of building, though it did over the years develop a beautiful prayerful atmosphere. Lily Dagless, by then a Catholic, assisted with the decoration, and the gifted Anglican artist in Walsingham, Enid Chadwick, was generous enough to design a façade, which greatly enhanced its appearance. It was further improved when a sanctuary was added in 1982. 'We intend this shall be purely temporary until the time comes when we are able to set up a great basilica worthy of Walsingham and surpassing even the Priory of old,' Bishop Parker loftily declared.[7]

In 1954 Miss Mary Garson founded the The Congregation of the Sisters of Our Lady of Grace and Compassion, which in 1978 became part of the Benedictine family. Miss Garson and two others came to Walsingham as a fledgling community in January 1958 to run a Pilgrim Hostel named St Joseph's, occupying the High Street part of Aelred House (now St David's and a Gift Shop). They had hoped to purchase it, but the Diocese was unwilling to sell it, and they left after four years, nonetheless grateful for the privilege of living in Walsingham. The Sisters, who now number more than 200, work in England and also have foundations in India, Sri Lanka, Kenya and Uganda, mainly looking after the old, the sick and the poor.

Not until 1968 did any more Catholic Religious come to work in Walsingham, and it fell to them, if not to build a basilica exactly, then at least a worthy church. Bishop Grant entrusted the care of both the Shrine and the parish to the Society of Mary, and Fr Roland Connelly S.M. arrived as Administrator and Priest Custodian. Fr Walter Symes S.M. became the first parish priest. In 1979 they bought Falcon House and used it for many years as their home, with a chapel in the cellar. The Society may be traced back to 1809 when Jean-Claude Courveille, at the age of ten, bathed his eyes, which had been severely damaged by smallpox, in oil from a votive lamp in the Cathedral of Le Puy. He was cured, and when he returned to give thanks he heard 'with the ears of his heart' the voice of Our Lady saying, 'here is what I want…a Society which will have my name, which will call itself the Society of Mary, whose members will call themselves Marists.' A few years' later twelve seminarians of Lyon, one of whom was Fr Colin, made a pilgrimage to the Chapel of Our Lady at Fourvière in Lyon, and committed themselves to this foundation.[8] It was not to be hierarchical, not a clerical congregation like the Jesuits and others, but a 'tree with three branches' with men and women, priests and laity working together in a new way, looking back to the early Church where Mary was at the heart of the disciples. The Curé d'Ars was an early Marist. Their devotion is to Our Lady of Mercy, and they seek to be instruments of mercy 'to portray the "feminine features" of God, and to help to build a church which is not perceived in terms of power, planning, control, administration and competitiveness, but rather in terms of community, compassion, simplicity, mercy and fellowship.'[9] They live out their vocations as missionaries, notably in Oceania where St Peter Chanel was martyred, and in schools and parishes around the world.

The Marist Fathers in Walsingham were joined by a small community of Marist Sisters, who live in the High Street in what in the Middle Ages was the Swan Inn, serving the pilgrims in different capacities. The Marists brought stability both to the parish and to the Shrine, and under their care its work has expanded remarkably, as has already been noted, both in terms of the facilities they have provided, and in the increasing numbers of pilgrims who come. Each year the Marist family from all over England, and sometimes beyond, gathers at the Shrine for a great Marist Pilgrimage Day.

One of the major achievements of the Marists in the parish has been the replacement of the temporary church with a parish church designed by local architect Anthony Rossi, under the direction of parish priest Fr Michael Simison S.M. and Shrine Director Fr Noel Wynn S.M. Bishop Peter Smith oversaw the planning and the church was consecrated by his successor, Bishop Michael Evans, on 26 March 2007. Built of traditional Norfolk brick and flint, with a round tower evoking medieval Norfolk churches, it is designed as Britain's first carbon-neutral church, heated not only by solar panels but by pumps circulating water drawn from deep within the earth.

Following hard on the heels of the Marist Sisters came the Little Sisters of Jesus, another community with French roots, founded among Moslems in Touggourt in the Sahara by Little Sister Magdeleine of Jesus, in 1939. They turned two small cottages in Egmere Road into a convent, largely with their own hands, trundling barrow loads of stones up the hill. Vowed to earn their own living, either outside the convent or in their own little pottery, with usually three or four in number, they live a life of Adoration, and their chapel is open to all who wish to pray. Their gift to Walsingham is perhaps best summed up by their foundress: 'Immerse yourself deeply among people by sharing their life, through friendship and love. Give yourself to them completely like Jesus who came to serve and not to be served; you too become one with them. Then you will be like leaven which must lose itself in the dough to make it rise.' The elderly and the needy in the village, whether belonging to a Church or not, are the ones who have the most to tell of them.

The Orthodox Brotherhood of St Seraphim of Sarov was formed in the former railway station, when Leon Liddament and Father David came to Walsingham in 1966, and established in it an icon studio. Above the entrance is a little golden dome, and the old waiting room, divided by the iconostasis, their earliest work, is the monastery chapel of St Seraphim, a place of mission and prayer, always open to welcome pilgrims. In the entrance is a small shop where the visitor and pilgrim can buy icons written in the studio and some imported works, as well as cards, Chotki, incense and other Orthodox items. Father David died in 1993.

Between 1973 and 1983 the Focolare Movement had a House in Walsingham. Formerly the Guild Hotel, 51 High Street, they renamed it Loreto. Clergy and laity from different churches, including Catholics, Anglicans, Methodists, Baptists and others, met for retreats and conferences, and it was often full of young people. An international community inspired by the Gospel, the Focolare Movement draws together people of all Christian traditions and from many of the world's religions, alongside people with no formal faith, to work for unity in all spheres of life.

In 1982 the Carmel of Our Lady of Walsingham was established in the village of Langham, near Walsingham, at the invitation of Bishop Alan Clark. They had been unsuccessful in finding suitable premises in Walsingham for their enclosed and contemplative life, but they were very much part of the life of the Shrine, and it was a sad day in October 2008 when the shortage of vocations caused them to leave. Sister Elizabeth Ruth Obbard, O.D.C. wrote a beautiful book on Walsingham's history and spirituality, which includes these lines that perhaps sum up the Carmelite calling as well as the vocation of all.

> Walsingham exists to remind us of the mystery of Mary's silent surrender, her self-sacrificing love, her joy and humility in bearing and believing the Word of God. In this lies Walsingham's power and its challenge. In this too lies its open-ness to an ever new and unexpected future, because the Spirit is ultimate freedom, total unpredictability. God lives not in a 'house made with hands' but in hearts that are, with Mary, ready for *anything* – 'Be it done to me according to *your* word.'[10]

In this spirit a new community within the Carmelite tradition, the Community of Our Lady of Walsingham, was founded in the Slipper Chapel on the 6th January 2004. At present they look after Abbotswick House of Prayer in Brentwood Diocese where they lead a life of prayer and outreach centered on Eucharistic adoration. They are developing a vocational spirituality, rooted in a devotion to Our Lady expressed in the Fiat Rosary and Angelus.

At the Anglican Shrine there have been anchoresses. From 1933 there was Sister Mary Phillida, who before she entered the religious life, was Lady

Phillida Shirley, and who in early life had been a pianist talented enough to give recitals at the Wigmore Hall. Fr Patten was heard to say 'If God has achieved anything in this place it is because Sister Mary Phillida has been and is a silent centre of the ongoing miracle.' She became a solitary, a hermit, in a silent life of prayer, living for many years, close to the Anglican shrine, in a cell with a small garden enclosed by wattle hedges, yet few pilgrims were aware of her existence. Occasionally Fr Patten would issue warnings that pilgrims were to respect her vow of silence if they saw her, and under no circumstances speak to her. She died in 1985.

Then there was Sister Mary Lioba a former nun from West Malling, who for ten years from about 1950, lived in Walsingham in an anchorage in the garden of St Anne's. When she became ill her friend Bridget Monahan took her to live with her in Worcester until she died, and little is known about her quiet life in Walsingham. Her vacant anchorhold was subsequently used by Mother Mary Magdalene from 1973 to 1995. Mother Mary Magdalene's vocation was different. She had been matron of a large hospital before spending time with the Order of the Holy Paraclete, which included assignments in Guyana and also at Burswood Home of Healing. Here she became aware of her vocation to be a solitary. Speaking at her funeral, Sister Teresa said, 'She had a very deep devotion to the Sacred Heart of Jesus and it was there that she placed everything in trust and love . . . without doubt she had been graced with the gift of healing – some of these were truly remarkable with no purely human or medical explanation.' Living a less secluded life than the other anchoresses, she was in great demand by people seeking spiritual guidance and healing.

In April 2008 Franciscans returned to Walsingham, Anglicans, who belong to the Society of St Francis, which traces its origins to Brother Giles, a member of the Society of the Divine Compassion, who in 1913 found his vocation living as a friar with tramps and outcasts. Other young men joined him, and they lived with the 'wayfarers' in a farm they were lent, but 'often the brothers would leave the Friary and themselves tramp the roads, sleeping under the hedges, in casual wards, or in common lodging houses.'[11] In Walsingham they live in a small friary, 'Our Lady of the Angels', in Knight Street close to the Anglican Shrine, where two brothers share fully in its liturgical life and ministry to pilgrims.

As well as these communities Walsingham has been a home for many individual Religious and consecrated men and women who find a blessing in the place and give many in return.

Living out Christ's Incarnation

Walsingham is a Shrine honouring the incarnation of Jesus, so it is not surprising that people find there an inspiration and vocation to live out the meaning of the incarnation of God immersed in human life, especially with the poor.

When Fr Bruno Scott James left Walsingham in 1942 he was seriously ill, having lived almost exclusively on a diet of bread and milk except when he was entertaining guests, and because 'the senseless slaughter of the flower of England and other countries, haunted me so that even sleep became impossible.'[12] In a strictly confidential letter to the Bishop he told how after 'eight major operations and every sort of treatment' he was only getting worse.[13] Over the next few years, which he called his 'Fallow Years,' he rested, founded the Virgil Society, translated and edited the Letters of St Bernard, travelled around Europe and stayed in various monasteries. He relates how he was enjoying a glass of his rapidly diminishing Cockburn 1912 port and reading his latest Virgil when the call came, and it was from Fr Mario Borelli, the founder of the *Casa dello Scugnizzo*, inviting him to help him in his work among street children in Naples. Immediately, to the consternation of his friends who thought him quite mad and likely to stay three weeks at the most, he gave away his library, wine cellar, and furniture, and left at once for Naples. 'In the fetid and crowded slums of Naples I found a solitude more creative and positive than I was able to experience in the cell of a Carthusian monk.'[14]

After four years Fr Bruno helped to found the John Henry Newman College, a student hall at the University of Naples, having come to the conclusion that he might be able to shape the minds of young university men who would be the ones to influence for good the society where so many children were in need. Over the years, the name of 'Padre Bruno' came to be known and loved, and when the time came for him to leave Naples he did not come back to England, for he was appointed by Pope Paul VI as canon of the Basilica of Santa Maria in Trastevere in Rome, with the title of monsignor. His new responsibilities required him to reside in Rome, but he frequently visited his friends in Naples. Finally, failing health compelled him to retire, and he returned to England, to Brighton, where he died on 16 March 1984, at the age of 77. He is buried at his beloved Downside Abbey.

His obituary in the Times was written by Bishop Gordon Wheeler, who knew him well, and first met him at the Beda College in Rome:

> I was taken aback by his delight to shock and I did not know what to make of him. It was only when I subsequently went on pilgrimage to Walsingham and heard his superb little homilies in the Slipper Chapel that I saw him in a different light. Here was somebody who communicated with God and had a charisma of communication with his fellow men. For despite the outrageous things he sometimes said and the mad practical jokes which he constantly perpetrated, he was consumed with a love for God which was contagious. And in fact he taught me more about prayer than anyone else had ever done ... I can see him now crouched on the steps of the Slipper Chapel Altar, often with a Siamese cat on his shoulder, in a great black cloak, pouring out sonorous and profound patristic spirituality ... The chief thing I remember about my quite long visits were the pangs of hunger. We would often have rusks for breakfast and then a cereal with milk for lunch. Usually once a week, Fr Bruno began to feel hungry himself and drove us many miles to the Old Swan at Lavenham where we could have a gargantuan meal which I, for one, would have preferred to be spread over the week.[15]

Many years later, the life of another Walsingham priest was to take a not dissimilar course. Fr Peter Walters came as assistant priest to the Anglican Shrine, having been involved, since a first visit in 1982, with the work of Salesians among street children in Medellín, Colombia, in South America. As a student he had visited Colombia and run out of money, when a group of street children 'adopted' him, and fed him with scraps of bread they had kneaded in their grubby hands. Each year after this he saved up his stipend, begged for money, and went out to return their kindness. At Walsingham he was allowed to advertise his work, and to this end founded the Charity *Let The Children Live!* Upon leaving Walsingham in January 1994 he went to devote the rest of his life to the street children as a Catholic priest, opening a home, *Casa Walsingham*, in Medellín. A shop in Walsingham raises funds for this home, and village people and pilgrims generously support him.

This concern for street children is not surprising, for after praying in the Holy House at Loreto on 8 September, 1979, where he must have been reflecting on the child Mary running around in it, Pope John Paul II came out and said, 'Children of the human family must have a roof over their head: they must have a home.'[16]

As early as 1928 Fr Patten was writing about the possibility of opening a boys' home in Walsingham, and the opportunity came in 1939. Fr Bernard Walke was Vicar of St Hilary in Cornwall. Like Fr Patten he was a signatory of the *Centenary Manifesto* and made his parish uncompromisingly Papalist. The BBC broadcast the church's hugely successful Nativity Play, except that Church of England Cornish people using words like 'Mass' and 'Our Lady' attracted the attention of militant Protestants. This was a most terrible example of the fragility of the Anglo-Catholic position of which Fr Patten was so aware. The Diocesan Consistory court ordered Fr Walke to remove all Catholic ornaments and statues, and to ensure he did so coach loads of protestors moved in, and wrecked the interior of the church. His health broken, Fr Walke resigned, and even his successor did not last long. One of Fr Walke's works was a home for orphans, and its position was now precarious. A Guardian, Fr Whitby, suggested that it should move to Walsingham, and Fr Patten was delighted. In *Our Lady's Mirror*, Spring 1939, he wrote:

> As we all know the church (at St Hilary) has suffered grave persecution and the impossible conditions of church life which have been intro-duced since the resignation of the last incumbent have made it out of the question for the children of the home to remain. We hope Walsingham will take them to its heart and that they will be real children of Our Lady. Two cottages have been bought for this home by Fr Walke's committee.

In fact they never occupied the cottages and lived at first with Miss Struggles, who has already been mentioned, and for a short while in the vicarage. But in 1944 a relatively modern house was obtained in Wells Road (above what later became Cleaves Drive), and there the home remained, most successfully, until it closed in 1977, when the demand for orphanages came to an end.

In 1953 a Hostel for working boys was opened in the house now called Shields by Fred and Pearl Shepherd, the parents of John, who became a member of the College and a priest. Fr Patten wrote: 'The new Hostel for those at work from S Hilary's is in occupation. The house is situated in the High Street and several years ago belonged to us, and was known as SS Michael and George. Before that in pre-Reformation days it was part of a pilgrim hostel and known as the Dower.'[17]

The fertile imagination of Fr Patten had always envisaged a choir school for the Shrine along the lines of the famous choir at the Shrine of Our Lady of Montserrat. The opportunity came when a long-established School, Quainton Hall in Harrow, had to be evacuated during the war and was moved to Long Marston Vicarage, near Tring. In 1944 the buildings they used were requisitioned, and its headmaster, Fr Eyden, suggested they move to Walsingham and become the choir school.

Sixteen boys arrived at the beginning of June 1944, and were boarded out around the village. The barn next to the Shrine, which had been the pilgrims' refectory before the war, became their classroom, dining room and recreation area. Soon a dormitory was rigged out in the cottages close to the Shrine and on the Feast of St Michael's and All Angels, 1944, they sang their first Mass. The Guardians became owners of the school; some of them became Governors, with Fr Patten their Chairman. It was soon renamed *The Sanctuary School* and under that name reopened in September 1945 in the vicarage (Fr Patten by this time being in the College). As with many private schools there were often financial problems, but it continued until 1956, when to everyone's sorrow the Guardians could not afford to go on subsidising it, and reluctantly decided to close it. Many former boys had very happy memories of their time in Walsingham. Not a few of them were the sons of Anglo-Catholic clergy and others eager for an Anglo-Catholic upbringing for their children. Meanwhile, after the war Quainton Hall was re-founded in Harrow, where it has continued to flourish, and sometimes comes up to sing Mass in the Shrine.

At the Catholic Shrine, too, there was a private attempt to start a preparatory school, to act as a choir school, in the old Grammar School in Friday Market in 1951, which lasted but a very short time. This foundation may suggest a certain rivalry and competition between the two Shrines, and this was true, for these were days long before the Vatican Council and the ecumenical movement, which were to transform the relationship between the two.

Much later and one of the fruits of the ecumenical spirit was a committee of Catholics and Anglicans who got together in 1984 to help the Sons of Divine Providence open a house in Egmere Road, near the Little Sisters, for young people with learning difficulties. The youngsters from *Southwell House* became very well known and popular in the village, helping to serve both at St Mary's and at the Chapel of Reconciliation. In 2002 the Sons handed over the running of the house to Walsingham Community Homes (now called 'Walsingham'), who looked after it for about five years, while gradually enabling the residents to move on to more independent accommodation locally.

The Anglican National Pilgrimage in the grounds of the Priory.

88.

In 2009 the Bishop of Tarbes and Lourdes attended, and a statue of Our Lady of Lourdes was carried in procession.

89.

The Dowry of Mary Pilgrimage brings together more than 20 nationalities, with many pilgrims in national costumes, carrying their own flags, accompanied by Knights of Catholic noble orders.

90.

Many Catholic Dioceses come on pilgrimage. Franciscan Friars of the Renewal on the Leeds Diocesan Pilgrimage.

91.

The Bishop of East Anglia, carrying the Blessed Sacrament, leads his diocese on the annual Diocesan Pilgrimage. Some people walk there.

92.

93.

Knights of Malta, among other groups, bring handicapped pilgrims to pray at the Shrine.

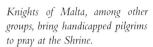

94.

The Ministry of Healing. Bishop Michael Evans of East Anglia, attended by Deacon Paul Hirons, anointing sick people at the Pilgrimage of the Society of St Vincent de Paul.

95.

96.

97.

A Pilgrim drinking water from the Anglican Holy Well. Sister Teresa praying for a pilgrim. The Pilgrimage of Healing and Renewal at the outdoor altar in the Anglican Shrine gardens.

98.

The Union of Catholic Mothers has been making an annual pilgrimage since 1946.

99.

Student Cross Pilgrimage with Catholics and Anglicans from Universities all over the country walk to Walsingham to celebrate Holy Week and Easter.

100.

New Dawn Catholic Charismatic Conference brings huge crowds of all ages to the Shrine to engage in a week of teaching, healing ministry, prayer and celebration.

101.

102.

The Anglican Children's Pilgrimage with Bishop Lindsay Urwin.

103.

The East Anglican Diocesan Children's Pilgrimage with their Bishop, Michael Evans.

104.

105.

Pilgrimages combine devotion and fun, especially on 105. the Anglican Children's Pilgrimage, and 106. the Pilgrimage of Children, Parents and Grandchildren at the Catholic Shrine.

106.

107.

Young people in silent prayer before the Blessed Sacrament on the annual Catholic Youth 2000 pilgrimage.
Anglican young people in a Dance of Thanksgiving at the end of Mass on their annual pilgrimage.

108.

109.

Aid to the Church in Need Pilgrimage in the new Church of the Annunciation.

110.

Dominicans on their annual Pilgrimage.

111.

A large pilgrimage of Chinese pilgrims with many Catholic priests at Walsingham in 2006.

112.

In 2009 the relics of St Thérèse of Lisieux visited England and came to Walsingham, where thousands venerated her. Before going to the Chapel of Reconciliation they were taken to the Anglican Shrine.

113.

Many major Catholic Pilgrimages process between the site of the original Shrine in the Priory Grounds and the Slipper Chapel and Chapel of Reconciliation. The annual Day with Mary, and the Divine Mercy Pilgrimage.

114.

115.

116.

The Tamil Pilgrimage numbers more than 7000, often the largest Catholic Pilgrimage of the year, and there are always Hindu worshippers with them.

117.

Father Eugene Francis, Father Nole Wynn, the Director of the Catholic Shrine, and Father Philip North, the Administrator of the Anglican Shrine, release doves of peace.

118.

119.

120.

121.

Devotion at the Shrines is found in quiet prayer and lighting candles, in 32. the Chapel of the Holy Spirit beside the Slipper Chapel, in 120. the Anglican Holy House, and a friar, Brother Paschal S.S.F kneeling before the Blessed Sacrament in the Anglican Pilgrimage Church.

The Mission of Our Lady of Walsingham. 'It is extremely important that a shrine be associated with the persistent and receptive hearing of the Word of God.' (The Pontifical Council for the Pastoral Care of Migrants and Itinerant People, which is responsible for pilgrimages in the Roman Catholic Church.) The Franciscan, Fr Stan Fortuna C.F.R is a popular preacher in Walsingham.

122.

123.

Pope John Paul II blessing the Pilgrim Statue of Our Lady of Walsingham, under her title, Our Lady of Reconciliation, on 24 September 1997, before this day became her feast in 2001. Ever since, the statue has been travelling around parishes and communities all over England, Wales, Ireland and Scotland, facilitating prayer and devotion. It was in Ireland during the signing of the Good Friday Agreement in 1998. The Anglican statue of Our Lady of Walsingham at the Barracks, Aldershot, which it visited as part of a tour of several venues in 2004, including a hospital, a prison, an airport, an Oxford college, a school, and York Minster, in an outreach called Magnificat.

124.

125.

There are Catholic and Anglican Shrines in several countries, especially in the USA. 125. The National Catholic Shrine of Our Lady of Walsingham is in Williamsburg, Virginia. In the Catholic parish of Our Lady of Walsingham, Houston, Texas, 126. a new Shrine is being erected, with an 'Abbey Arch' 35ft high. 127. The Shrine in St Paul's Anglican Church, Washington D.C.

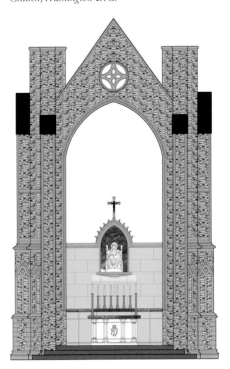

126.

127.

128.

129.

The medieval Church of St Mary's, Walsingham, originally dedicated to All Saints. The interior, restored after the 1961 fire.

The Orthodox Chapel inside the Anglican Shrine Church was blessed in 1944 by Archbishop Sava of Grodno.

130.

The old railway station was converted into an Orthodox Church in 1966 by the Brotherhood of St. Seraphim of Sarov.

131.

In 1781 John Wesley preached in Walsingham, and in 1794 the present Methodist Church was built. It is the oldest still in use in Norfolk.

132.

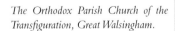

The Orthodox Parish Church of the Transfiguration, Great Walsingham.

133.

The Catholic Shrine looking across the grounds with the Stations of the Cross to the cloisters, shop and amenity buildings.

134.

The holy water fountain in the cloisters, with sculptures by Jane Quail.

135.

136.

Looking across the grounds towards the Chapel of Reconciliation, with its engraved glass panels designed by Sally Scott.

137.

138.

An aerial view of the Anglican Shrine Church, with the octagonal Guild of All Souls' Chapel in the foreground.

Calvary in the Shrine grounds.

The Welcome Centre at the Anglican Shrine.

139.　140.

141.

CHAPTER 13

UNITY IN WALSINGHAM

Many people today have no recollection of how strained relations used to be amongst Christians in England. As Michael Yelton wrote, 'it is easy to forget that at that time there was effectively a system of ecclesiastical apartheid in England, in which there were few if any contacts between the Church of England and that of Rome.'[1] Members of the *Catholic League*, like Fr Patten, were decades ahead of their time in their prayer and work for unity, and by the contacts they were making.

Just how difficult it was for Fr Patten is clear. In 1925 a Mary Howell reported to the Abbot of Downside that Fr Patten had brought a large group of pilgrims into the Slipper Chapel for prayers. The Abbot wrote to ask Fr Patten about it, who then requested permission, saying that had it been consecrated and in use he 'would not have for one moment ventured to do so.'[2] The Abbot replied,

> It is with deep regret that I feel obliged to refuse permission for public prayers in the Slipper Chapel. There is no need for me to say that I am much interested in your efforts to revive devotion to Our Lady of Walsingham and, if it were only for reasons of courtesy, I should have liked to be in a position to accede to your request. But in these matters we have to be governed by our clearly defined principles, and therefore I am obliged to say "No" when it would have been more congenial to say "Yes". Of course your pilgrims have permission to enter the Chapel – and there is nothing to prevent them from saying whatever private prayers they like. But anything in the way of public prayers e.g. the Rosary must take place outside the Chapel, as you suggest.[3]

In those days Roman Catholics were not permitted to pray with Anglicans, still less were Anglicans allowed to pray publicly inside a Catholic Church.

Undismayed, in the first Pilgrims' Manual (1928), Fr Patten prescribed the following prayers to be said outside the Slipper Chapel 'for the reunion of these provinces and the whole of Christendom, with the See of Peter':

> *Antiphon.* That they may all be one, as Thou, Father, art in me and I in Thee; that they also may be one in us; that the world may believe that Thou hast sent Me.

> V.   I say unto thee that thou art Peter.
> R.   And upon this rock I will build my Church.

LET US PRAY

> O Lord Jesus Christ, Who saidst to Thine Apostles: 'Peace I leave with you, my peace I give unto you'; regard not our sins, but the faith of Thy Church, and vouchsafe to grant her peace and unity according to Thy holy Will; Who livest … Amen.

In 1932 Fr Patten wrote to ask Prinknash Abbey to print some prayer cards for the Shrine. In his refusal, the Prior revealed the real attitude of some Roman Catholics to what Fr Patten was doing:

> You see, dear Sir, we Catholics naturally feel that the Pre-Reformation Shrine should be in *our* (sic) hands – from which it was torn at the Reformation. While we rejoice *sincerely* – at the revival of devotion to the Blessed Mother of God among Anglicans, we feel that her official cultus belongs to us.[4]

Not all Roman Catholics saw it that way, and many admired him. Fr Bruno Scott James, who was working at the Slipper Chapel, knew him well and spoke of him warmly:

> Within a few years he had galvanized the whole village into deep devotion to Our Lady, and had built within the village of Walsingham, if not on the original site of her old sanctuary, a new shrine in her honour to which Anglo-Catholic pilgrims from all parts of England began to flock in their hundreds … his achievement remains a wonderful act of faith and devotion, which it would ill become Catholics, of all people, to belittle. I would go further and say that our own return to Walsingham would hardly have been so easy had not this young Anglo-Catholic clergyman prepared the way; nor does it

258

seem inappropriate that it should have been the spiritual heirs of the reformers who first tried to restore what their forefathers had destroyed … I took to Father Hope Patten on our very first meeting, and I like to think that the attraction was mutual … he had a striking personality and an enchanting sense of humour … He could make the most devastatingly witty remark without moving a muscle on his face … but the important thing was, than one felt that behind all this he was a deeply serious and spiritual man.[5]

The accession of Pope John XXIII had an immediate impact on Walsingham. He invited Fr Patten's successor, Canon Colin Stephenson, to a private audience in 1961 to ask him about the Anglican Shrine, about which he was very interested.[6] Fr Alan Roe, the Vicar of Walsingham, was asked to address a large conference of the Focolare Movement in Trent, and also met the Pope. The fruits of the Second Vatican Council, which committed all Catholics to pray and work for Christian Unity, were changing everything in Walsingham. Fr Roe attended a Catholic Mass in Walsingham, at the end of the Week of Prayer for Christian Unity in 1963. In 1966 one hundred and twenty Methodist, Anglican and Catholic clergy and laity met in Walsingham for the first time, and in the following year Fr Roe, Canon Stephenson, Revd Morley-Waite, the Methodist minister, Mr. Mace of the Brethren, and Fr David, the Russian Orthodox priest, with about a hundred people, including the Anglican Sisters, attended a Catholic Mass. All such celebrations of unity are now commonplace in Walsingham and everywhere, but at the time they were groundbreaking.

In 1967, Martin Gillett, a writer, closely associated with Walsingham, who did much to draw both Catholics and Anglicans together, founded the Ecumenical Society of the Blessed Virgin Mary. On the celebration of its fortieth anniversary, Cardinal Kasper, the President of the Pontifical Council for Promoting Christian Unity, and a patron, wrote:

> You have helped to bring about an important transition, such that Mary is seen less and less as a source of division, and increasingly as one who we jointly understand to be the Mother of God, one who received the Eternal Word of God in her heart and in her body, one whose fiat is the supreme instance of a believer's embrace of God's will, a 'free and unqualified consent in utter self-giving and trust.'[7]

It was the Ecumenical Society of the Blessed Virgin Mary that convened a historic meeting in London on 14 March 1968, attended by over sixty people half Catholic and half Anglican, among them the Bishop of Elmham, Alan Clark, Fr Connelly S.M., Director of the Catholic Shrine, Fr Colin Stephenson, Administrator of the Anglican, and Fr Alan Roe, the Vicar. Agreements were made that were remarkable for the time. It was agreed that parishes coming on pilgrimage should be encouraged to come with their neighbours, Anglican or Catholic. Catholics could join in any worship with their Anglican brethren apart from for Eucharistic services, but the Bishop said permission for this could be given on special occasions, though all understood that Holy Communion could not be received. Fr Stephenson said Anglicans desired to share whatever they had with their Roman brethren, and Fr Roe said that subject to the approval of the Bishop of Norwich St Mary's was always available also. The Bishop said that if ever it became possible to acquire the Abbey Grounds, 'Roman Catholics would not wish to keep it for themselves alone, but only in conjunction with Anglican brethren.'[8] And literature about the Shrines would obliterate any sense of rivalry and include the other.

The first official Ecumenical Pilgrimage came in July 1970 (though there had been several ecumenical pilgrimages from parishes in the 1960s) led by the Bishop of Lynn and the Bishop of Elmham (before the Catholic diocese of East Anglia had been formed).[9]

1980 was an especially significant year in the ecumenical life of Walsingham. On 11 May, Cardinal Basil Hume O.S.B., led over 10,000 men, women, and children in a families' pilgrimage from his Archdiocese of Westminster, and after celebrating Mass in the Abbey grounds went to the Anglican Shrine to pray. Two weeks later, Archbishop Robert Runcie, the Archbishop of Canterbury, gathered a crowd of 15,000 for the National Pilgrimage, after which he went to pray in the Slipper Chapel. In 1981 the Bishops of Chichester and Arundel and Brighton led the first inter-diocesan pilgrimage.

Celebrations of anniversaries were irrevocably changed by those symbolic visits. In 1981 Anglicans celebrated the Golden Jubilee of the Holy House, and congratulations were sent from Pope John Paul II, the Archbishop of Canterbury, Cardinal Hume, the Bishop of Norwich, the Bishop of East Anglia, and a royal pilgrim, the Duchess of Kent. The Orthodox community sang devotions, and Fr Clive Birch S.M., the Director of the Catholic Shrine, preached at Benediction in the Anglican Shrine, a sermon constantly interrupted by applause. He said:

> Fr Patten was a prophet … a man chosen to speak on behalf of God, a man often rejected by the official authorities. Like the prophets of old he was an instrument in God's hands … When (Our Lady) came to Walsingam she left a promise. She said, 'Anyone who comes to my shrine will find succour – comfort and help.' And what sort of help is this Mother giving us today? She is here to heal those wounds of sin and divisions. She has used Fr Patten and indeed many other faithful workers. She has taught us to listen, to understand, to tolerate and to grow in love … that is why our new chapel has been named the Chapel of 'Our Lady of Reconciliation.' Our future seems to point towards ever-closer unity. We must learn, not only to pray together, which we do regularly … but to accept each other's differences and work together for a united future. We pray that we may be instruments in Mary's hands.[10]

In the same year some Polish pilgrims presented a lamp to burn before the icon of Our Lady of Czestochowa in the Anglican Shrine, and Fr Birch took part in its dedication.

Pope John Paul II made his pastoral visit to Britain in May 1982, and since he generally visited a Shrine of Our Lady on his travels, hopes were entertained that he might come to Walsingham. In the event the impossibility of finding a large enough venue, and the narrow Norfolk lanes, made it impractical, so Our Lady of Walsingham went instead to meet the Pope in Wembley. Born aloft by Fr Birch S.M. and Fr Christopher Colven, Administrator of the Anglican Shrine, the image received a tumultuous welcome. It was placed on a low pedestal, but the Pope insisted it should be placed on the altar. Speaking to the congregation of 80,000, and millions on television and radio, the Pope preached:

> People for centuries have made pilgrimage to Walsingham. The statue of Our Lady from Walsingham here reminds us it is Mary who will teach us how to be silent, how to listen to the voice of God in the midst of the busy and noisy world. We need to live as Mary did, in the presence of God, raising our minds and hearts to him in our daily activities and worries.[11]

*Fr Clive Birch S.M. (left) and
Fr Christopher Colven carry
the statue of Our Lady of
Walsingham out of the Slipper
Chapel on its way to Wembley.*

After the Mass, they bore the image on a 'lap of honour' around the stadium
as the people sang hymns to Our Lady, and cheered as they made their exit
through the royal tunnel. On returning to Walsingham the statue was first
taken to the Anglican Shrine where it was placed on the altar of the Holy
House, before being carried back to the Slipper Chapel along the Holy Mile.

Fr Peter Rollings, who was present, revealed what a disaster Wembley
nearly turned out to be.[12] Fr Birch decided to give the statue a bath and
spruce up the paintwork. He did the painting by electric light, but in daylight
the faces were puce, and on the morning of the great day he hurriedly
repainted it. On reaching Wembley it was found that the bath had swollen the
statue and now wouldn't fit the sedilia. A carpenter was summoned just in
time. After his homily the Pope beckoned for the statue to be brought to him,
and to Fr Rollings' horror he bent to kiss the figures of Jesus and Mary, which
were still wet in the morning. Fortunately the baking sun had dried the paint.

1984 was the Golden Jubilee of the restoration of the Shrine in the
Slipper Chapel and it began with the gift by the Orthodox faithful of a
beautiful icon of the Mother of God of Walsingham, written by Archimandrite
David. After the Liturgy in the Chapel of St Seraphim the icon was carried to
the Slipper Chapel, shielded from the sun by an ombrellino and preceded
by three deacons with censers. At the Slipper Chapel the Akathist was sung
and the icon was enthroned. The Orthodox are a much-loved presence in
Walsingham, and the small Chapel in the Anglican Shrine is regularly used.

On the Feast of the Assumption that year Delia Smith opened a 'Festival of Flowers', and a Solemn Mass was celebrated by Bishop Kevin O'Connor, Auxiliary Bishop of Liverpool, at which the preacher was Fr Christopher Colven, the Administrator of the Anglican Shrine. The following day, the actual Jubilee Day, the link with Downside was recalled by the Abbot who celebrated Mass and preached. Walkers of the Guild of Our Lady of Ransom arrived for the Mass, bearing a replica of the statue in King's Lynn, which was presented to the Church of the Annunciation. Then there came an Ecumenical Youth Pilgrimage, and the celebrations concluded with the National Pilgrimage on 9 September led by Cardinal Hume, for which Fr Connelly came back to preach. He ended by saying:

> I believe that if we have the courage to listen for the voice of Mary in this land, then she will use us for the salvation and sanctification of this world, the work of reconciliation between God and man and the work of reconciliation between man and man, and that is the grace which is daily shown to men of every age, here in England's Nazareth by Our Lady of Walsingham.[13]

In 1997 a year-long festival celebrated the centenary of the first pilgrimage to Walsingham since the Reformation, in 1897.[14] The Guild of Our Lady of Ransom marked the centenary by the gift of a magnificent modern window of the Annunciation designed by Alfred Fisher, for the Slipper Chapel. The festivities opened with an outdoor Mass beside the Red Mount Chapel in King's Lynn celebrated by Bishop Peter Smith of East Anglia, on 19 August, the actual anniversary, in the presence of Cardinal Cahal Daly, and next day the Cardinal presided and preached, in the Chapel of Reconciliation, each of them paying tribute to the work of Fr Patten, as well as the early Roman Catholic pioneers. The Guardians of the Anglican Shrine in their blue mantles joined the celebrations.

The year included a Historical Conference of lectures,[15] masterminded by Tim McDonald the Centenary Co-ordinator and Anne Milton the Shrine archivist. There were music festivals arranged by Nigel Kerry, in which more than 650 musicians, many highly distinguished, performed in the acoustically brilliant Chapel of Reconciliation, a flower festival in which all the churches in Walsingham took part, and a broadcast for the BBC World of Faith Week. In his message at the close of the Year, Pope John Paul II said:

> More and more people of goodwill, and of various Christian denominations are now making their way to 'England's Nazareth' in their search for God under the patronage of Our Lady of Walsingham. It is my prayer that God's work in Walsingham over the next 1000 years will once again surpass our greatest hopes and desires.[16]

The 75th anniversary of the building of the Anglican Shrine in 1931 was celebrated in 2006 with an evening Service of Thanksgiving in St Mary's at which there were uniquely two sermons one by the Anglican Bishop of Norwich, the other by the Catholic Bishop of East Anglia. And on the following day after Mass a long procession made its way to the Shrine. Part of the celebration included a series of lectures held at various venues around the country on the subject of 'Sacred Space.'[17]

As the years have gone there have been many joint Anglican-Catholic Pilgrimages. The Catholic Diocese of Nottingham begins its pilgrimage in the garden of the Anglican Shrine, while the Diocese of Northampton starts in St Mary's. The Anglican Diocese of Llandaff usually attends Evening Prayer and Benediction in the Chapel of Reconciliation, and the Diocese of Monmouth often arranges a 'Service of Light' in the Slipper Chapel. The Diocese of Chichester generally begins its pilgrimage in the Chapel of Reconciliation.

As in Fr Patten's day, Anglican pilgrims are encouraged to visit the Slipper Chapel but now, of course, they go inside to pray, while Catholic pilgrims are encouraged to pray in the Anglican Holy House, and take part in the Sprinkling at the Holy Well. For a time both Catholics and Anglicans celebrated the Saturday evening Pilgrim Service together in the Anglican Shrine Church, but because of the well-understood difficulty in attending Benediction, the Catholics withdrew after the procession of Our Lady, and the numbers involved made it too uncomfortable to continue. Even for Anglicans alone the Church is not really as big as it needs to be.

All the churches in Walsingham have continued to draw closer together in work and prayer. Each Advent in the Chapel of Reconciliation a Service of Readings and Advent Carols is shared by Anglicans, Methodists and Catholics, and the Week of Prayer for Christian Unity is faithfully observed. In Lent Stations of the Cross are celebrated in the different churches and a Lent course is attended by all. On Palm Sunday the Anglican and Catholic parishes start their Liturgy together in the Abbey grounds. The principal Ecumenical event of the year is on the Eve of the Assumption when a thousand or more pilgrims cram into St Mary's for the Rosary and a meditation, before walking in a torchlight procession singing hymns into Friday Market for another decade of the Rosary and meditation, before concluding at the outdoor altar in the Anglican Shrine gardens for a final decade of the Rosary and meditation. It all concludes with a firework display and drinks provided by the Shrines.

A long time has passed since the Shrines were rivals, and their closeness today is surely a fruit of the hopes and prayers of Fr Patten, Charlotte Boyd and all those whom God raised up to bring devotion and pilgrimage back to Walsingham. Pope Leo XIII told Fr Fletcher, 'When Mary comes back to Walsingham, England will come back to Mary.' He did not say 'when Catholics come back to Walsingham,' but 'when England comes back,' and though he could never have known it at the time, he was speaking of Anglicans, Orthodox and all Christians too.

Fr Patten saw clearly the connection between devotion to Our Lady, mission and unity:

> If England is ever to be reconverted: if these Provinces are ever to be reunited to their parent stock, devotion to Mary must become widely accepted among us, for it is impossible to hold the true Faith apart from Our Lady. She is the instrument of the divine plan of redemption ... Walsingham, therefore has a real place in the scheme not only of restoring the fundamental principles of the faith, but in preparing for the outward reunion of Christendom.[18]

CHAPTER 14

THE GLORIOUS VISION

Vessel of Devotion Wondrous

One of the popular devotions at both Shrines in Walsingham is the Litany of Our Lady, known as the *Litany of Loreto*, with its cascading epithets in honour of Mary. In particular she is addressed repetitively as a Vessel of the Spirit, a Vessel of Honour, a Vessel of Devotion Wondrous, Tower of Ivory, House of Gold, and Ark of the Covenant.

The meaning is clear, of course. Mary is the chosen vessel, the sacred vessel, who carried the Son of God. But there is now a problem with this idea, for as Sarah Boss has pointed out, in contemporary Europe it is common to regard a vessel as something which is purely functional. 'For example, people buy milk in cartons, and when the milk is finished, the carton is thrown away.'[1] Before this was a long tradition of the idea that the more precious the content the more beautiful should be the vessel to contain it. There are still cultures where the wrapping of a gift is intricate and artistic, where the more valuable the gift the more it is reflected by its container. The receptacles for the Blessed Sacrament illustrate this principal. The Blessed Sacrament is placed in a beautiful ciborium, which no one sees because it is covered by a silk veil. This is placed inside a tabernacle that is itself lined in silk and cedar. The tabernacle may be magnificent, though it is not seen because it too is covered with a fine embroidered veil. There may even be a baldachino above it all, and still higher a dome in the roof. These gradual epiphanies, as one by one the coverings are removed, until the Blessed Sacrament is reached, are not for art's sake, because they are not all visible, yet each precious layer indicates that what is eventually found within is of inestimable value. In medieval churches the Chapel of the Blessed Sacrament often had a fresco of the Annunciation, for the worshipper understood the symbolism of Our Lady as the tabernacle of Jesus.

Our Lady, then, is not 'just a vessel', not just the necessary instrument for the Son of God to be made man. She is a vessel beyond compare. She is God's work of art. She is fashioned to perfection for what her womb is to contain. That is why we treat her with love and awe, as we would anything of beauty. Yet, there has been a decline in devotion to Our Lady, one of the unforeseen consequences of the Second Vatican Council's reforms. It was not intentional, for the Council stressed that the cult of the Blessed Virgin is to 'be generously fostered, and that the practices and exercises of devotion towards her, recommended by the teaching authority of the Church in the course of centuries … be religiously observed,'[2] although the warning to refrain from 'false exaggeration' perhaps led to a certain caution.

Devotion to Our Lady, and the significance of the vessel, have implications in the idea of sacred space and sacred place, and consequentially in the architecture of churches as well as the construction of sacred vessels. Sarah Boss again:

> The awareness that vessels have the capacity to be infused with holiness has permeated Catholic consciousness for many centuries … all these things are holy objects in themselves, because of the precious contents they may bear. Mary's body, therefore, which carried God incarnate, and part of whose very substance became God's flesh is necessarily the most sacred of all vessels.[3]

Canon Michael Tavinor, in a thoughtful contribution to a series of lectures celebrating the 75th anniversary of the restoration of the Anglican Shrine, explains how in medieval days sacred spaces were created and built. Worshippers and pilgrims did not see the full sacredness of the place all at once. The mystery was gradually revealed, like an unveiling.[4] This is in marked contrast to the notion that since the people are the Church, a church building merely serves the function of a place where Christians can gather around the altar. No one denies the people are the Church, no one denies the Church is a community. But churches are far more than this. Speaking of the incomparable architecture of Prague's churches on his visit there in October 2009, Pope Benedict commented:

Their beauty expresses faith; they are epiphanies of God that rightly leave us pondering the glorious marvels to which we creatures can aspire when we give expression to the aesthetic and cognitive aspects of our innermost being … The creative encounter of the classical tradition and the Gospel gave birth to a vision of man and society attentive to God's presence among us.[5]

This is not to say that Church architecture and furnishings have to be elaborate. The Second Vatican Council notes that the Church has always admitted different artistic styles at different times, and now recommends 'noble beauty rather than sumptuous display', but all things set apart for divine worship should be 'worthy, becoming, and beautiful signs and symbols of things supernatural.'[6] This is a far cry from the 'functional' Catholic and Anglican churches erected since the 1950s, which break the continuity of the Church's tradition of art and architecture, and neglect its ability to inspire and elevate the human spirit. It has also been true of schools and other public buildings. Drab architecture, like bad art and poor music, depresses the spirit, devalues humanity, affects behaviour, and eliminates the sense of awe that is at the heart of worship. Churches are not 'merely functional' any more than Our Lady was 'merely functional.' Many laity were acutely sensitive to this, and made comments like 'it doesn't seem like a church.' But the *sensus fidelium* was strangely unheeded in the days of the People of God, when the ministry of the laity was supposedly encouraged. Had devotion and appreciation of Our Lady as the House of Gold and the Vessel of the Spirit not been neglected, and the understanding of the church building as a sacred vessel, a sacred space, not been forgotten, many mistakes might have been avoided.

A tradition from early days,[7] unbroken until the end of the twentieth century, is the belief that God deserves beauty, and only the best. Beauty is one of the ways to discover and love God.

Pope Benedict quotes St Augustine:

'Ask the beauty of the earth, ask the beauty of the sea, ask the beauty of the ample and diffused air. Ask the beauty of heaven, ask the order of the stars, ask the sun, which with its splendour brightens the day; ask the moon, which with its clarity moderates the darkness of night. Ask the beasts that move in the water, that walk on the earth, that fly in the air: souls that hide, bodies that show themselves; the visible that lets itself be guided, the invisible that guides. Ask them! All will answer you:

Look at us, we are beautiful! Their beauty makes them known. This mutable beauty, who has created it if not Immutable Beauty?'

Dear brothers and sisters, may the Lord help us to rediscover the way of beauty as one of the ways, perhaps the most attractive and fascinating, to be able to find and love God … When faith, celebrated in a particular way in the liturgy, encounters art, a profound synchrony is created, because both can and want to praise God, making the Invisible visible.[8]

Pope John Paul II similarly reminded us that the contemplation of natural beauty, art and culture is a source of spirituality, and he related it to shrines:

In shrines or in places adjacent to them, votive offerings of popular art and devotion are to be displayed and carefully safeguarded. Pilgrims must be shown these treasures; through art they may find serenity again in the contemplation of marvellous things and through the grandeur and beauty of the creatures … by analogy, contemplate their author.[9]

While persons are on pilgrimage, they also have the chance to enter the tent of cosmic meeting with God. Shrines are often located in places with an extraordinary panorama; they manifest greatly fascinating artistic forms; they concentrate on themselves ancient historical memories; they are expressions of popular and refined culture.[10]

We are most fortunate in England that our greatest Shrine is set in beautiful countryside and in a beautiful village, for the 'contemplation of marvellous things … and by analogy their creator.' Many pilgrims arrive in Walsingham from cities, some made ugly with vandalism, poverty and fear, and Walsingham speaks to them literally of another world. It is incredibly fortunate to have treasures of art and beauty in its ancient streets and in its churches, from the majestic medieval St Mary's with its light interior, the quietly lit and devotional Anglican shrine, the well-appointed eighteenth-century Methodist Church prayerful little Orthodox Chapel, and modern Church of the Annunciation, to the fine perpendicular Slipper Chapel beside the wide and spacious Chapel of Reconciliation. Pilgrims may also visit Great Walsingham and pray in the old St Peter's, with its fifteenth-century carved poppy head pews, and the exquisite Orthodox Church of the Transfiguration, as well as St Giles' Houghton, with its medieval screen before which medieval pilgrims used to pray.

Walking from one church or shrine to another, perhaps praying the rosary, was part of the old pilgrimage way, and Walsingham like other shrines had many relics, images and objects within the domain, to draw the pilgrim's devotion. Both Anglicans and Catholics recognise this need to have several centres of devotion at Walsingham. There are holy places all over Walsingham for personal prayer and where small groups of pilgrims can pause and pray together. In early Anglican Pilgrim Manuals from 1928 Fr Patten prescribed prayers to be said around the fifteen altars of the Shrine Church in honour of the rosary, and outside before the Hatcham Crucifix and at the Altar of Our Lady of Sorrows. Visits around Walsingham included St Giles, and prayers for unity at the Slipper Chapel, and on the site of the Priory and the Holy House prayers of reparation for their destruction, as well as sprinkling at the twin wells (before the holy well was discovered close to the Anglican Holy House). Pilgrims later venerated relics of the True Cross and St Vincent. The Catholic Pilgrim Handbook similarly prescribes prayers at the site of the original Holy House, and prayers to be offered in the Holy Ghost Chapel, the Church of the Annunciation, at the Anglican Shrine, St Mary's Anglican parish church, the Methodist Church and the two Orthodox churches.

Stations of the Cross, Adoration, Processions of Our Lady, the daily rosary, sprinkling with holy water, the Sacrament of Reconciliation, the Sacrament of the Sick, and of course the centrality of the Eucharist are all common elements of Catholic and Anglican pilgrimages today, nothing very different from medieval days. Prayers on the Martyrs' Field where Fr Nicholas Mileham and George Guisborough, and perhaps William Allen, were put to death, are sometimes part of the pilgrimage too.

There should be no need for pilgrims to spend a day away from the spiritual treasures and beauty Walsingham, unless perhaps to make a pilgrimage to other shrines nearby, as medieval pilgrims often did, maybe to the Pontifical Shrine in King's Lynn, or St Julian's in Norwich, or maybe for Mass in the church beside Oxburgh Hall, with its priest's hole and recusant history.

Recovering the Joy of Devotion

There has been a decline of devotion in many parishes which means that pilgrims to Walsingham encounter devotions and prayer that some have never known before. Many Anglicans have never before sung the *Salve Regina* or the *Litany of Loreto*. Roman Catholics come out of Benediction at the Shrine and say they no longer have it in their parish. Never intended by the Vatican Council, it has been a consequence of reforming the Liturgy, and replacing Rosary and Benediction and other devotions with evening Masses. Yet the Church has a rich heritage of devotions to suit everyone. Silence, adoration of the Blessed Sacrament, personal visits to the Blessed Sacrament, lighting a candle, Stations of the Cross, devotions for different months, the meditative Rosary with its pictures of Gospel mysteries, devotion to the Sacred Heart and Divine Mercy centring on the love of Jesus, the *Lectio Divina*, that contemplative meditation on the Scriptures; devotions to the Blessed Trinity, the Holy Spirit, Jesus, his mother, and the heavenly kingdom of saints, and many more. The loss of them means that attending Mass is the only prayer that many know. The tendency to talk before Mass means that many no longer experience silence, except in the often brief moments after Holy Communion, and it is a huge loss when preparation for Holy Communion is fleeting. Devotional books of prayers and litanies, once so popular, have all but disappeared. And in some circles the 'reading of prayers' was discouraged, and the treasury of wonderful prayers composed by holy men and women was forgotten, in the unrealistic idea that everyone should make up their own.

A regrettable consequence of letting go the Church's treasury of devotions has been, as Professor Saglio has pointed out, that we are asking people 'to develop their own sense of piety and spirituality, rather than incorporating them into a Church that practises spirituality and determines what pious behaviour is.'[11] Spirituality has consequently become a personal affair, rather than a communal one, which is the opposite of what the Second Vatican Council intended. Not only that, but public devotions learned in church often formed the basis of personal prayer at home and family prayers, a loss now keenly felt.

Bishop Martin Warner, formerly an Administrator of the Anglican Shrine, writes beautifully of devotion in his preface to a book of prayers:

> Devotion is the offering of your love to God. Christian life without devotion is like a relationship of unrequited love.[12]

The Christian who enters the joyful world of devotional prayer is responding to a personal relationship with Jesus and his holy Mother and the saints.

Devotional prayer is not unrelated to the idea of a precious vessel containing the most holy within. The Mass is the treasure, but devotion enfolds it. Shrines are places where devotion can be discovered, and the Anglican Shrine Church is especially conducive to it. Walsingham has many religious and lay people who can teach and lead different ways of prayer, Scripture study, conducted Holy Hours, rosary, fiat rosary, meditation in its various methods, a whole programme of possibilities; for those who have no experience of these things often need a gentle guide to show them the way.

Our Lady's Shrine at Walsingham is a most suitable place for this, for Mary is a teacher of prayer; she after all taught Jesus to pray. And when he was in the depths of his agony in the Garden of Gethsemane it was the prayer his Mother taught him that came to his lips. 'Father, let this cup pass from me; nevertheless, not my will but yours be done.' Just as Mary had prayed before the angel, 'Let it be done to me according to your word.'

Our Lady's Powerful Intercession

The great devotion at Walsingham is, of course, to the Mother of God, in particular the Annunciation, that moment when God became incarnate and when Mary, the maiden of Nazareth, was glorified though her consent to be the Mother of the Lord. Her soul magnified the Lord, and he that is mighty magnified her.[13] Mary is now, as recalled in the Ballad, the heavenly Empress, and the image of Our Lady of Walsingham is the powerful Virgin crowned in majesty. The prayers in the Pilgrim Manuals of both the Catholic and Anglican Shrines emphasise her power:

> O gracious mother by your powerful intercession you keep and protect from all harm those who lovingly celebrate your glorious memory and call to you in prayer. You are our strength and support, and your Son and our God is alone our divine joy.[14]

> You are our Mother, we desire ever to remain your devout children. Let us feel the effect of your powerful intercession with Jesus Christ. Make your name again glorious in this place, once renowned throughout our land by your visits, favours and many miracles.[15]

272

Walsingham in the Middle Ages was like the Pool of Bethesda in New Testament days, thronged with sick people lying around, hoping for a cure. The crowds today are found in the waiting rooms of hospitals. There has thus been a major shift of emphasis, but the ministry of healing still occupies an important place through the Sacrament of the Sick, which is always available, and in the pilgrimages of the sick at both Shrines, and the Catholic Charismatic Pilgrimage Conference of New Dawn, which lays great expectation on healing both of body and soul. Unlike Lourdes, Walsingham has no medical bureau, no way of confirming miracles, but anecdotal evidence is strong.

'Do miracles still happen in Walsingham?' the writer was asked one day while he was browsing in the *Let The Children Live!* shop in Walsingham. I related the most remarkable miracle I had ever heard of. An eight-year-old girl some years earlier had sustained grave head injuries in a road accident, with one side of her skull badly crushed and shattered. The surgeon warned her parents that her brain was severely damaged. Next day the hospital chaplain anointed her and also sprinkled water on her from the Holy Well at Walsingham. A few days later she regained consciousness, opened her eyes, reached out to a crucifix on her bedside table, and spoke. Her first words were, 'I have been to Walsingham.' Then I added, 'I understand she made a complete recovery.' A woman in the shop, who had been listening-in, said, 'I know that story is true because I was that girl.' And she filled in the details. A wooden plaque in thanksgiving for her healing hangs in the Anglican Shrine above the main door, in a collection started by Fr Patten.

There was another little girl with a nasty verruca on her foot that no treatments had cured, and she was due to have it surgically removed in hospital when she got home from Walsingham on pilgrimage. She asked me to pour Holy Water on it during a healing service. Verrucae do mysteriously disappear, but she had had this one for several months, and the fact is that there was no trace of it an hour later. Only a little miracle, but a big one for a fearful little child, full of faith.

Another concerned a woman with a high powered job who was drinking heavily, and rapidly going downhill. Each evening she consumed a whole bottle of red wine, and after work before going home frequently went with colleagues for a drink. She came to Walsingham quite often, and I would listen to her and offer useless advice about trying only to drink with colleagues and not at home alone. Or to make a bottle last two days. On one visit I felt impelled to ask if I might give her the Sacrament of the Sick, and while doing so pleaded with Our Lady of Walsingham to heal her. Months went by and I didn't see her again, fearing, in a faithless way, the worst. Then one day she arrived, looking ten years younger. She told me she hadn't had a single drink since being at Walsingham. 'That's marvellous,' I responded. 'No', she answered, 'it's a miracle because I haven't even wanted a drink, the need has gone. I can even go out with my colleagues and be quite happy with an orange juice.' Anyone who knows anything about alcoholism will agree with her.

Some answers to prayer are more mundane. Parishioners of mine had been trying for months to sell their home because they were emigrating to Australia. There was no interest at all, there was a housing slump, and hardly anyone came to see it. They went to Walsingham on pilgrimage, prayed they would sell it, and on the day they got back the estate agent rang to say there had been two enquiries. The first couple came and immediately said they wished to buy it. Same day the other couple came, and they said, 'If it falls through please let us know because we definitely would like it.' The first couple bought it.

These are remarkable answers to prayer from my personal experience, but many pilgrims have their own stories to tell, and some have been recorded in letters to both Shrines. In an interview for Church Times, a former Administrator of the Anglican Shrine, Fr Philip North said,

> Walsingham is a place of healing, where one can encounter the living God and where miracles happen. A lot of people come to Walsingham looking for the gift of a child, as they have been unable to conceive; and the gift has often been given.[16]

In the Gospels, the ministry of Jesus to those who are sick always involves more than what we would call 'physical healing.' When he heals blind people, they now 'see' what they couldn't 'see' before, and begin to praise God. Jesus often linked healing with the forgiveness of sins, for there is a healing of the soul, a healing from sin and its consequences, a healing of relationships, and of emotions, healing from past hurts and present patterns of behaviour, and from addictions. Healing is to be found in reconciliation and a renewal of life. All of this is rightly emphasised at Walsingham, where such healings are often experienced. Some Shrines around the world, finding an increasing need for this, offer counselling services alongside the healing ministry of prayer, the Sacrament of Reconciliation and the Sacrament of the Sick, while Communities like the Cenacolo Community specialise in releasing people from addiction, and it is likely that Walsingham, too, should increasingly reach out in this way.

Pilgrims Today and Tomorrow

Eamon Duffy has pointed out the principal purpose of pilgrimage in the Middle Ages was not the journey itself but the spiritual value of the image or relic, the hope of healing, or the gaining of an indulgence.[17] The Reformers, who attacked pilgrimages and destroyed the shrines of England, would be astonished at the popularity of pilgrimage today. What has come to the fore in recent times is the value of the journey, symbolic of the journey through life. 'Journey in Faith' is the popular name for a course of exploration, instruction, and discussion, for adults in the Christian Faith. Going on pilgrimage, especially on foot, is increasingly popular.

Ian Bradley[18] has described the modern phenomenon of pilgrimage, which is not confined to Roman Catholics or Anglicans, but is attracting the attention of all Christians, and those who would not profess any faith at all, not least younger people. Taizé is a magnet for thousands of young Christians, Catholic and Protestant, and Iona off the West Coast of Scotland attracts crowds of pilgrims, young and old, every year. He points out that across Scandinavia dedicated pilgrim pastors appointed by the Lutheran churches welcome people to shrines and lead pilgrimages. The old Pilgrim Routes to Compostela are busy with pilgrims walking to the Shrine of St James, and European money has been spent researching and renovating the old roads, and providing accommodation on the route. A resident of Walsingham, John Clark, walked all the way from Walsingham to Compostela. Young adults from the Diocese of Arundel and Brighton have been arranging ecumenical walking pilgrimages every year since 1975. The Student Cross walking pilgrimage to Walsingham has already been described. The modern phenomenon of Medjugorge, with or without official approval, draws vast numbers, as does the Shrine of St Pio Pietrelcina, Padre Pio, while longer established

Shrines like Lourdes and Fatima, to mention no more, show no signs of losing favour. Nor does Walsingham; and the attractive new facilities at the Anglican Shrine for greeting visitors and pilgrims is a response to growing need, a need recognised by Pope Benedict in his message to the 2nd World Conference on the Pastoral Care of Pilgrimages and Shrines held in Santiago de Compostela, Spain, in September 2010: 'Very careful attention should also be given to welcoming the pilgrims, by highlighting, among other elements, the dignity and beauty of the shrine, the image of "God's dwelling... with the human race", the moments and spaces for both personal and community prayer, and attention to devotional practices.'

As well as the fostering of devotion, the vocation of a shrine is to evangelise. Archbishop Antonio Maria Vegliò, the president of the Pontifical Council for Migrants and Travellers, in his address to the Conference, goes so far as to affirm that over the past decades the Church has come to realise 'that the main objective of pilgrimages to a shrine is now evangelisation.' 'Moments of pilgrimage, because of the circumstances that motivate them, the places to which they go and their closeness to daily needs and joys, are a fertile field for the word of God to take root in hearts … discovering, this moment becomes an occasion for the renewal of faith and also for a first evangelisation.' He added that 'in Christ all our searching finds its answer.' Pope Benedict also underlined the opportunity of evangelisation:

> In these historic moments in which we are called, with greater force if possible, to evangelise our world, the riches offered to us by the pilgrimage to shrines should be highlighted. First of all, for its great ability to summon and bring together a growing number of pilgrims and religious tourists, some of whom are in complicated human and spiritual situations, somewhat distant from living the faith and with a weak ecclesial affiliation. Christ speaks to all of them with love and hope. The desire for happiness that is imbedded in the soul finds its answer in Him, and human suffering together with Him has a meaning.[19]

Many people today describe themselves as 'spiritual' rather than 'religious', which they regard as a pejorative word, over-connected with institutions, power, authority, conflict, and even corruption. It would be a mistake to dismiss their reaction, and some parallel might be found in the New Testament where Jesus seems to rub up against the religious authorities and to be sympathetic to those who are open and searching, recommending they worship in spirit and in truth, an expression that would not be alien to many 'spiritual' people today who have never been seen in a church. Paganism has asserted itself again in our country. Religious indifference may be giving way to the 'new atheism' in some circles, but in others is leading to spiritual searching, to pagan rituals, to yoga and ways of meditation, to dissatisfaction with material things alone, and to a questioning about the meaning of life. Often the motive is a desire to 'feel good' or to have an inner tranquillity, the fullness of which Christians recognise in Jesus as the Way the Truth and the Life. The conversation of Jesus with the Samaritan woman at the well, whose life lacked real fulfilment, when he told her 'anyone who drinks the water that I shall give will never be thirsty again'[20] is surely one that can be repeated at the Holy Wells in Walsingham. Jesus said, 'If anyone is thirsty, let him come to me! Let the one come and drink who believes in me.'[21] The Incarnation enables a rather vague spirituality to be earthed by living a human life in Christ. It provides a pathway for a person to journey from a perceived spiritual need into faith in the One who said, 'I have come that they may have life and have it to the full.'[22] At least there is a possible meeting point, which has not been fully explored. The Pontifical Council for the Pastoral Care of Migrants and Itinerant People, which is responsible for pilgrimages in the Roman Catholic Church, published an illuminating document in 1999 entitled *The Shrine*.

> It is extremely important that a shrine be associated with the persistent and receptive hearing of the Word of God, which is no mere human word, but the living God himself present in his Word. The shrine, in which the Word of God resounds, is a place of covenant, where God reminds his people of his faithfulness, in order to shed light on their journey and to offer them consolation and strength.[23]

The woman at the well was searching and Jesus approached her where she was. A holy place, like Walsingham, surely can be a gentle and encouraging place to meet Jesus, not least because he is found with his mother, for many 'spiritual' people have a natural empathy with a mother-figure. While the regular pilgrim wishes to have a certain programme, centred on the Mass and other pilgrimage devotions, the seeker, the one who finds his way there because someone has told him, or he has read somewhere that it is a sacred place, a spiritual location, is looking for something informal. *The Shrine* takes this up this need for sensitivity. Shrines

> should take into consideration the specific characteristics of each group and each individual, the yearnings of their hearts and their authentic spiritual needs. In the shrine, we learn to open our heart to everyone, in particular to those who are different from us: the guest, the stranger, the immigrant, the refugee, those of other religions, non-believers. In this way the shrine does not only exist as the setting for an experience of Church, but also becomes a gathering-place open to all humanity.[24]

Sarah Boss makes the point that many of Our Lady's shrines in which Virgin in Majesty figures are housed are built far away from human habitation, in places that are wild or semi-wild. 'It is as though the meeting of God and humanity occurs most powerfully in separation from civilisation – that God is met most surely amongst plants, animals, rocks and springs.'[25] It is not surprising that pagan wells and shrines of goddesses and earth mothers were converted to shrines in honour of Our Lady. It may be that the loss of devotion to Our Lady has contributed to the resurgent pagan homage to goddesses. While different from pantheism, the Incarnation nonetheless means God is part of creation as well as its creator. Shrines of Our Lady proclaim that a sacred presence is immanent in the material creation, while leading pilgrims to the transcendent.

Recovering a sense of the unity between mankind and creation is closely related to our devotion to Our Lady and the Incarnation. Sarah Boss enlarges on this:

> Mary as the God-bearer brings her devotees not only hope for a world transformed, but also the God who is the source and dwelling-place of that hope. Against a culture which is set against nature, and in which all flesh is meaningless, the Mother of God is still able to proclaim God's presence within the blood and the milk, the cells and the atoms, of the material creation, and in this too she constitutes a potential point of subversion of the present social order.[26]

Successive popes and Christian leaders have called attention to an understanding of human beings as stewards of creation, and this is something that pilgrims, especially searching pilgrims, should be made very aware of, for they often have a great concern for the environment. Bishop Martin Warner writes, Walsingham 'has to be a place where we recover a vision of creation as more than a commodity to be plundered for our pleasure'.[27] Pope Benedict XVI, in his encyclical *Caritas in Veritate*, while warning against the 'attitudes of neo-paganism or a new pantheism – human salvation cannot come from nature alone, understood in a purely naturalistic sense', continues, 'this having been said, it is also necessary to reject the opposite position, which aims at total technical dominion over nature, because the natural environment is more than raw material to be manipulated at our pleasure; it is a wondrous work of the Creator containing a "grammar" which sets forth ends and criteria for its wise use, not its reckless exploitation.'[28] Concern for the environment, deriving from the Incarnation, is a meeting point with those who seek what is spiritual in the mysteriousness of nature. According to Pope John Paul II,

> a greater inclination to appreciate nature reveals a precious spiritual dimension of the modern person. This contemplation could become the theme of moments of reflection and prayer, so that the pilgrim may praise the Lord for the heavens that declare his glory.[29]

Gerard Manley Hopkins addressed Mary as 'world-mothering air', likening her to the all-embracing and life-giving air we breathe.[30] There is a huge library of 'spiritual' books on the shelves of booksellers, often labelled, 'Spirituality, Angels, Body, Mind and Soul,' which are not particularly Christian. The popular paraphernalia in New Age shops, of candles, incense, water, medals and rosaries, originate in the Church, where after being blessed they are known as sacramentals, because they 'prepare us to receive grace', and 'signify effects, particularly of a spiritual nature', which may include a person or object being 'protected against the power of the Evil One and withdrawn from his dominion.'[31] Surely we need to emphasise these things and advertise them beyond the confines of a repository shop in church, along with simple explanations of our teaching as is done at shrines including Walsingham? The Church has an immense resource in ways of meditation, spirituality, spiritual experience, healing, and of music, including Gregorian chant, that is marketed even in the secular world as spiritual and relaxing. It seems unnecessary for people to seek for these things in pagan or Eastern religions, yet that is where they tend to look because they do not know we have them. In 2003 a document entitled, *Jesus Christ, The Bearer of the Water of Life,* published by the Pontifical Council for Culture acknowledges that

> The success of *New Age* offers the Church a challenge. People feel the Christian religion no longer offers them – or perhaps never gave them – something they really need. The search which often leads people to the *New Age* is a genuine yearning: for a deeper spirituality, for something that will touch their hearts, and for a way of making sense of a confusing and alienating world. There is a positive tone in *New Age* criticisms of 'the materialism of daily life, of philosophy and even of medicine and psychiatry; reductionism, which refuses to take into consideration religious and supernatural experiences; the industrial culture of unrestrained individualism, which teaches egoism and pays no attention to other people, the future and the environment.'[32]

A 'Seekers' Centre' has been established at Pantasaph Friary to meet the need. Worth Abbey is pioneering ways of allowing people to experience something of the depths of monastic life, meditation and silence. At Glastonbury the churches have developed a ministry to engage with people of other Faiths, with pagans, with the New Age, and other 'alternative cultures'. Ignatian meditation is provided at Abbey House. The Catholic Parish has a team of people trained in Healing Ministry and Counselling. Healing Masses and Healing Services are held frequently and regularly as well as private healing prayer in the context of Exposition of the Blessed Sacrament. The church is always open and is attended by sensitive people on the look-out for individuals who wish to talk or who are in need of prayer or seeking deliverance. Food packs are provided for pilgrims of any kind who arrive with few resources. Hostility is sometimes encountered from those involved in the occult or witchcraft, a spiritual warfare, but many others welcome the opportunity to talk about spirituality and are open and gentle. Some come in to the churches to be alone, to pray or be still, finding in them an oasis of peace. Some sense what they call 'energy' which Catholics recognise as the Real Presence. Devotees of the Glastonbury Goddess Temple sometimes find their way to the Shrine of Our Lady of Glastonbury.

Our Lady's Shrine at Walsingham is well placed to respond to the growing pilgrimage movement today, especially among young people, searching and eager to walk and connect with holy places. In Walsingham people do often find what they are looking for, as Anglican Bishop Mervyn

Stockwood did: 'No matter how we explain Walsingham we cannot explain it away. And I am one of those thousands to whom it has been a Jacob's ladder, a meeting point between heaven and earth. May thousands more make the pilgrimage and discover the ladder for themselves.'[33] Pope John Paul II said that within 'the holy tent of a Shrine' pilgrimages

> have as their goal the tent of personal meeting with God and with oneself. Lost in the multiplicity of daily anxieties and realities, people need to discover themselves through reflection, meditation, prayer, an examination of conscience, silence. The great questions on the meaning of existence, on life, on death, on the ultimate destiny of the human person must resound in the heart of the pilgrim such that the journey would not only be a movement of the body but also an itinerary of the soul. In interior silence, God will reveal himself exactly as a 'sound of a gentle breeze' that transforms the heart and existence. [34]

Fr Jeremy Sheehy, in a valuable contribution to the lecture series already mentioned, points out that there has been opposition to the idea of 'sanctified place.' He quotes the Reformed theologian, Joan Taylor: 'The concept of the intrinsically holy place was basically pagan…it would appear that the idea of the holy place is dangerously close to idolatry.'[35] Fr Sheehy argues on the other hand that the idea of a holy place is closely connected to the Incarnation. This is why 'at its best the Christian faith has been able to overcome the polarity between the material and the spiritual, the profane and the sacred, the natural and the supernatural.'[36] As we saw in Chapter 1, the missionary Church required pagans to make a clean break with idolatry, but had a surprisingly flexible attitude to paganism, adopting myths and motifs that were not contrary to Christianity, Christianising them and building on a *tradition of sanctity*. Pagan holy places were blessed with holy water and prayer to become Christian holy places. While St Paul was revolted by the idolatry he found in Athens, he nonetheless admired their 'sacred monuments' and offered a pattern for evangelism by using the altar to an Unknown God as a focus for preaching the God 'whom you already worship without knowing it.'[37] If Christians denigrate the idea of holy places they destroy possible meeting points between the Church and today's pilgrim on a spiritual search.

The Church is often called a 'Pilgrim Church', and so it is not a case of confronting the searching pilgrim, however sensitively, but rather conveying the awareness that we are all pilgrims, learning together, and walking side by side. *The Shrine*, again:

> To this end, a shrine needs the presence of pastoral workers capable of helping people to enter into dialogue with God and to contemplate the immense mystery that enfolds and attracts us. The significance of the ministry of the priests, religious and communities in charge of shrines must be stressed, and consequently the urgent need for them to receive proper training for the service they are called to provide. At the same time, encouragement should be given to lay people trained to carry out the work of catechesis and evangelisation associated with the life of the shrine.[38]

There is always the danger that when the Church moves towards people who are on a spiritual search or journey that they slide away because they have no thought that the Church has something to offer. Therefore, the pastoral worker needs to convey the sense that we are journeying together, with riches and experiences to share with one other. A Marist Father, Francis Marc, explains the meaning of a Marian Church:

> The Marian Church does not know the answers before the questions are posed. Her path is not traced out in advance. She knows doubt and unease, night and loneliness. That is the price of trust. She takes her part in the conversation, but makes no claim to know everything. She accepts that she must search.[39]

It can hardly be a coincidence, more the working of the Holy Spirit, that the rise of spiritual searching outside the Church has been accompanied by the emergence of New Movements[40] within the Catholic Church, communities well-placed for such a ministry as this. Among them are the Friars of the Renewal, the Community of St John, the contemplative Community of the Beatitudes, the Sant'Egidio Community, which works alongside seekers and people of other Faiths, and the evangelistic Community of Sion, who minister in England on the interface between searching and finding. God will send searching walkers and pilgrims when Walsingham is ready. Addressing 400,000 members of New Movements Pope Benedict told them

> The pasture where the sources of life flow is the Word of God as we find it in Scripture, in the faith of the Church. The pasture is God

himself whom we learn to recognise in the communion of faith through the power of the Holy Spirit. Dear friends, the Movements were born precisely of the thirst for true life; they are Movements for life in every sense.[41]

The raising up of New Movements in the Church is a sign that evangelism and renewal is the work of God. It is God's work, and not man's; not the undertaking of committees, organisation or human effort. God raises up men and women, who renew the Church by their holiness. The veneration of Our Lady and the saints ensures that Christians never forget that it is God who renews the Church and brings it to life. The working of miracles conveys the same message, as does the consecration of a country to Our Lady, for these are acts of Faith in the power of God rather than in the resources of man. From age to age men and women are called by God, and form new movements with their followers. Throughout Europe, and most of the world, and throughout history, it has been new movements of Religious communities that have spread the Gospel. Sometimes, as we have seen in the Gregorian Reform, inspired individuals have reformed old orders, so they have in effect been 'reinvented' as new movements. One of the Prefaces in the Roman Rite of Mass speaks to the Father:

> You renew the Church in every age
> By raising up men and women outstanding in holiness,
> Living witnesses of your unchanging love.[42]

An example of this would be St Philip Neri, who lived in Rome in the sixteenth century when church life was at a low ebb. He was raised up to renew the Church, and he started to do this by looking after pilgrims to Rome and the poor, and combining this with gathering followers to make the traditional pilgrimage around the seven basilicas of Rome, and by informal services, comprising evening prayer and compline, Scripture studies, and many devotions, especially the Forty Hours, along with conferences and discussions. He reached people's souls in his oratory by the beauty of music, consequently called 'oratorios.' So remarkable was his life and work that he became popularly known as the 'apostle of Rome,' but his influence spread all over the world. He is an example of how God chooses a saint to renew the Church, and his method of using the pilgrimage opportunities of Rome, devotions, discussions, and music seems to have a contemporary attraction.

Our Two Shrines

The Catholic Shrine is part of the *Association of European Shrines of Our Lady*, which holds an annual *Reseau* at the different shrines in turn, where the Rectors and Directors meet for a few days to pray together and share ideas. The Adminstrator of the Anglican Shrine also attends. It is clear that even in former communist countries Marian Shrines occupy a central and influential place, and civic as well as religious representatives normally attend important events. One of the bi-annual Bishops' Conferences is held in many of them. Most European shrines have well-used conference facilities, permanent youth programmes, media and publishing agencies, and some have counselling services. They see renewal, evangelism, and catechesis at the heart of their ministry. Some shrines have a rota of chaplains, priests who spend a few days in the season each year to meet, greet and talk to pilgrims, and hear confessions. Several shrines have communities of the New Movements.

As they did before the Reformation, pilgrimages bridge cultural and national divides. Far from being an experience of individualism, the pilgrim, whether beginning by travelling alone or as part of a parish or other group, is soon enriched by all the others he meets, so that pilgrimage creates community. The European ministers of culture recognised this when they met in Santiago in 1987:

> May the faith which has inspired pilgrims throughout history, uniting them in a common aspiration and transcending national differences and interests, inspire us today, and young people in particular, to travel along these (pilgrim) routes in order to build a society founded on tolerance, respect for others, freedom and solidarity.[43]

Many European Shrines welcome people from other religions, Moslems, Sikhs, Hindus and others. Hindus gather in considerable numbers at the Catholic Shrine in Walsingham. But this, like other potential developments, is held back for the want of facilities. Pope John Paul II addressed its importance:

> Worthy of special attention on the part of pastoral care is the fact that numerous Christian shrines are goals of pilgrimages of believers of other religions, due to secular tradition and to recent immigration as well. This solicits the pastoral action of the Church to respond with

initiatives of hospitality, dialogue, assistance and genuine fraternity. The hospitality reserved to pilgrims will surely help them discover the profound meaning of pilgrimages.[44]

It has to be admitted that Walsingham, popular as it undoubtedly is, has not developed to the extent that other European shrines have done, and for this reason. Walsingham has two Shrines. An article in the (Anglican) *Our Lady's Mirror* as long ago as 1953, either written or approved by Fr Patten, deplored this:

> There is a close connection between Walsingham and prayer for Christian unity…Every Anglican pilgrim to Walsingham prays for unity among Christians, either in the Pilgrimage Church or when Pope Benedict XV's prayers are said in the roadway outside the Slipper Chapel. For Our Lady originally had, and still wills to have, but one shrine at Walsingham. Yet she has two; and the two do not do her a double honour, but rather diminish her glory, because they are really the one shrine of other ages now split in two by the Christians who ought to be joining together in propagating its honour.[45]

They have turned out to be prophetic words. Disunity hinders Walsingham's mission. The Souvenir Programme published in 1984 for the Golden Jubilee of the Catholic Shrine in the Slipper Chapel, also looks to a future of one united Shrine:

> It is clear that Walsingham is becoming a centre of ecumenical prayer. Mary is bringing her family together in this Holy Place … We see people from all walks of life and many Christian denominations finding in Walsingham a place of peace and of spiritual strength. Our hope and prayer is that in the future – when and how the Lord himself wills it – there will be one united Shrine.'[46]

Unity belongs to the very nature of the Church, which is why Fr Patten put such emphasis on 'reuniting these two Provinces' with the Roman Catholic Church. The influence of Walsingham would be immensely enriched and facilitated by 'one united shrine.' Now that competition is in the past it is easier to be more honest about our mutual weaknesses and difficulties, for there are sensitive matters, which both Shrines could address together. They could map a glorious vision for the future if unity is to be taken seriously. The Catholic Shrine has all the problems of a split site between the Slipper

Chapel complex and the village. It has no land on which to expand around the Slipper Chapel, and is entirely dependant on the goodwill (which has never been lacking) of the Walsingham Estate Company and local farmers, for the hire of fields for parking and tents in the summer. In the village it is impossible to upgrade the bedrooms without reducing their number. Amenities for conferences or retreats are very limited; there is nowhere to develop special ministries, no permanent youth facilities, and no welcome centre. There are no rooms or areas where priests or others can easily meet and be available to pilgrims. Substantial properties in Friday Market and the High Street, formerly owned by the Shrine, that had the potential of being 'shop windows' for the Shrine have been sold, which may have been a huge mistake. On the other hand, the Catholic Shrine has immeasurable resources in terms of people, in the New Movements, which often come on pilgrimage, and some older Religious Orders experiencing renewal and growth, and in the sheer numbers of people, particular groups and associations, communities of different kinds, as well as all the bishops and dioceses and parishes of England and Wales, who look to Walsingham as the National Shrine of Our Lady. It ministers on a vast scale, with huge day pilgrimages on Saturdays and Sundays, as well as residential parish groups throughout the week. It struggles to do so, and has the potential for much more.

The Anglican Shrine, on the other hand, has all the advantages of a pilgrimage centre on one large site, comprising a beautiful open garden and altar with excellent facilities all around it, including modern bedrooms for residential groups, a splendid refectory, a large coffee bar where people can meet and talk, conference rooms, the Education Centre, and its Welcome and Visitors' Reception complex. The priests and sisters, too, live on the campus. But it too has problems, which unlike the Roman Catholic Shrine's are more theological than practical. In Fr Patten's day most pilgrims were Anglo-Catholics, but in these last decades the Shrine has been much more integrated into the wider stream of Anglicanism, an integration now imperilled by the ordination of women. This development has caused grave problems for the Anglo-Catholic Movement in the Church of England even, some have suggested, threatening its long-term survival. This would be a terrible disaster, for Anglo-Catholicism is a movement, and like the New Movements in the Catholic Church, and all movements, at its best, it was and is fired by vision and enthusiasm, undergirded by a strong spirituality. This is evident in

Walsingham not only in the remarkable life and legacy of Fr Patten and his supportive friends, but also right up to the present day with the Anglican Shrine's imaginative growth in ministry and facilities. What is not always acknowledged is the contribution Anglo-Catholicism has made to the restoration of the Roman Catholic Shrine. Not only is the origin of both Shrines to be located, as we have seen, in the Walsingham Chapel of St Mary's Buxted, built by the Anglo-Catholic Fr Wagner, but it is very striking, as Fr Peter Cobb, a former Master of the Guardians, pointed out, how many of those who were instrumental in restoring the Catholic Shrine received their formation as Anglo-Catholics.[47] Fr Philip Fletcher, Charlotte Boyd, Dom Philibert Feasey, Dudley Baxter, Fr Bruno Scott James, Claude Fisher and Arthur Bond were all converts. Anglo-Catholics from the time of Newman have brought a welcomed enrichment to the Catholic Church in England, and the Ordinariate of Our Lady of Walsingham seems to be an acknowledgement by Pope Benedict XVI of the value of maintaining this Anglo-Catholic patrimony. It certainly would be a huge loss if the vision, life, gifts and mission of Anglo-Catholics were no longer able to flourish, when they still have so much to bring to the wider Church.

Everyone acknowledges that the ordination of women has not only caused difficulties for Anglo-Catholics but is an insuperable obstacle to unity between the Anglican and Roman Catholic and Orthodox Churches. Despite this, the desire for unity continues to be expressed in Walsingham. The Archbishop of York, Dr David Hope, a Guardian of the Shrine, in his sermon at the National Pilgrimage in 1996, reiterated the theme of unity and spoke of Walsingham's prophetic calling:

> Here in Walsingham the paradox of the one domain, which encompasses the two Shrines, is perhaps already a sign and foretaste of that day when the now imperfect communion which we share will be brought to the fullness of perfection through the Lord and Saviour of us all.

In the service sheets distributed in the Anglican Shrine:

> We have chosen to use Morning and Evening Prayer of the Catholic Church to express the imperfect but real unity and love we share with Roman Catholics and our longing for the day when we will be together at the Eucharist.[48]

And in the new Anglican Visitor Centre:

> At both Shrines we pray for the unity of the Church and for the day
> when there need only be one church in this holy domain.

In 2061 it will be a thousand years since the foundation of the Shrine.
Will there still be the need then for two shrines? Or is there sufficient trust
between the Guardians of the Anglican Shrine, and the Bishop and Council
of the Catholic Shrine, to begin to plot a course together towards this great
Millennium in which vision and gifts can be shared?

Fr John Mason Neale, the founder of the Society of St Margaret, the
sisters at the Anglican Shrine, is credited with the saying,

> Possible things *may* be done, impossible things *must* be done.

At the Annunciation, Walsingham's fundamental mystery, the Angel told Our
Lady, in her perplexity and anxious questioning,

> Nothing is impossible for God.[49]

The impossible does happen. One place of pilgrimage where it has is Taizé. It
may not provide an exact model for Walsingham, but it shows that the
impossible is possible. At its heart is a Religious Community, founded in 1940
by a Reformed Church Pastor, Brother Roger Schutz, who remained its prior
for sixty-five years until his untimely death in 2005. Yet the Community is
completely ecumenical, with Catholic, Anglican, Orthodox and Reformed
members, who elected, as it happens, a Catholic, Brother Alois, to succeed
Brother Roger. There is a Roman Catholic community of women too, and
they minister to everyone. Thousands of pilgrims, especially young people,
belonging to different Churches, gather in Taizé every week, and they worship
together in the Eucharist, Morning Prayer, Evening Prayer, and Night Prayer,
with other devotions, silence, and night vigils; they fast together, and spend
the week in prayer groups, Bible study, work, recreation, and workshops of
various kinds. And some come for a week's totally silent retreat.

Pope John XXIII called Taizé a 'little springtime,' and it has enjoyed the
support and visits of successive popes. Pope Paul VI invited Brother Roger to
accompany him to South America in 1968, for the inauguration of the Latin
American Episcopal Conference meeting at Medellín. Pope John Paul II
stayed at Taizé twice when he was Archbishop of Krakow, and every year after

his election as pope received Brother Roger in private audience. In 1986 he visited Taizé as pope, and addressed the young people:

> Like you, pilgrims and friends of the community, the pope is only passing through. But one passes through Taizé as one passes close to a spring of water. The traveller stops, quenches his thirst and continues on his way. The brothers of the community, you know, do not want to keep you. They want, in prayer and silence, to enable you to drink the living water promised by Christ, to know his joy, to discern his presence, to respond to his call, then to set out again to witness to his love and to serve your brothers and sisters in your parishes, your schools, your universities, and in all your places of work.
>
> Dear young people, to bring to the world the joyful news of the Gospel, the Church needs your enthusiasm and your generosity. You know, it can happen that your elders, after the difficult journey and the trials they have undergone, fall prey to fear or weariness and let the dynamism which is a mark of every Christian vocation grow weak. It can also happen that institutions, because of routine or the deficiencies of their members, are not sufficiently at the service of the Gospel message. Because of this, the Church needs the witness of your hope and your zeal in order to fulfil her mission better.

To the brothers of the Community he revealed his mind concerning their vocation in ecumenism:

> I do not forget that in its unique, original and in a certain sense provisional vocation, your community can awaken astonishment and encounter incomprehension and suspicion. But because of your passion for the reconciliation of all Christians in a full communion, because of your love for the Church, you will be able to continue, I am sure, to be open to the will of the Lord. By listening to the criticisms or suggestions of Christians of different Churches and Christian communities and keeping what is good, by remaining in dialogue with all but not hesitating to express your expectations and your projects, you will not disappoint the young, and you will be instrumental in making sure that the effort desired by Christ to recover the visible unity of his Body in the full communion of one same faith never slackens.

And he continued in words that may surprise:

> You know how much I personally consider ecumenism a necessity incumbent upon me, a pastoral priority in my ministry for which I count on your prayer. By desiring to be yourselves a 'parable of community', you will help all whom you meet to be faithful to their denominational ties, the fruit of their education and their choice in conscience, but also to enter more and more deeply into the mystery of communion that the Church is in God's plan.

In a talk he gave in the presence of Pope John Paul II in Saint Peter's Basilica during the young adult European meeting in Rome in 1980, Brother Roger described his own personal journey in words that many Anglo-Catholics may echo: 'I have found my own Christian identity by reconciling within myself the faith of my origins with the Mystery of the Catholic faith, without breaking fellowship with anyone.'

Pope Benedict XVI was a good friend of Brother Roger, and on Wednesday 17 August 2005, at the end of the general audience at Castelgandolfo, spoke of his distress at Brother Roger's death:

> This morning I received very sad, tragic news. During vespers yesterday evening, our beloved Brother Roger Schutz, founder of the Taizé Community, was stabbed and killed, probably by a mentally disturbed woman. This news has affected me even more because precisely yesterday I received a very moving, affectionate letter from Frère Roger. In it he wrote that from the depth of his heart he wanted to tell me that 'we are in communion with you and with those who have gathered in Cologne (for the World Youth Day).'

Two days later, the Pope spoke of him again to representatives of various Christian confessions in Cologne:

> I would also like in this context to remember the great pioneer of unity, Brother Roger Schutz, who was so tragically snatched from life. I had known him personally for a long time and had a cordial friendship with him. He often came to visit me and, as I already said in Rome on the day of his assassination, I received a letter from him that moved my heart, because in it he underlined his adherence to my path and announced to me that he wanted to come and see me. He is now visiting us and speaking to us from on high. I think that we must listen

to him, from within we must listen to his spiritually lived ecumenism and allow ourselves to be led by his witness towards an interiorised and spiritualised ecumenism.

It is because of this deep love and its sincere ecumenism that Taizé draws Christians together from all the Churches, as well as other young people seeking faith or meaning in life. Everyone goes there, Anglicans of all persuasions, Roman Catholics, Evangelicals, searchers. It has found a way to welcome everyone, and no theological argument or disagreement spoils its peace. It may not be an exact model for Walsingham, a better one may present itself, but it shows what can be done. No one even thinks of asking, 'is Taizé Catholic?' or 'is it Anglican?' or 'is it a Protestant community?' It is just – Taizé. Please God before Our Lady's Shrine at Walsingham celebrates, in 2061, the thousandth anniversary of its founding by Richeldis, it will be just – Walsingham.

1061 AND ALL THAT

It was in 1061, during the reign of King Edward the Confessor, according to the Ballad, that the noble widow, Rychold (or Richeldis), built her Chapel. Richeldis was the mother of Geoffrey de Favarches. The date is confirmed by a Book of Hours now in Cambridge University Library.[1] But these are fifteenth-century sources, and John Dickinson considered that the foundation date would have been 1130-1.[2] Many historians have followed him, including Professor Harper-Bill, who considers it could be as late as the 1140s or 1150s.[3]

They suggest that religious communities had a tendency to exaggerate the antiquity of their origins, citing the example of Glastonbury Abbey and its legendary foundation by Joseph of Arimathea. This story is so extraordinary as to hardly bear comparison with Walsingham's modest claim. A better example might be the foundation-traditions of Abingdon Abbey, which at the time Dickinson was writing were generally rejected as incoherent invention, but which have been reassessed in the light of new evidence, particularly through archaeology.[4] It is not impossible that the canons of Walsingham found some tax advantage in claiming a pre-conquest foundation, but the Ballad tradition should not be dismissed too lightly, and needs to be re-examined.

We know that the Augustinian Priory in Walsingham was founded in 1153, for the Cartulary lists its Priors beginning with Ralph in that year. Dickinson and others assume Geoffrey Favarches founded it, and so could not have been born as early as 1061. His mother could not therefore have been a widow at that date. Consequently they suggest Richeldis built the Holy House only a decade or two before the Priory's foundation.

References to the de Favarches family are scanty. There is no mention of them in the Domesday Book, no reference to any manor held by the de

Favarches either before the Norman Conquest of 1066, or after. But this is not surprising. Under the feudal system the monarch owned all land. Apart from the demesne he kept for himself, the monarch apportioned vast estates to tenants-in-chief, powerful men like barons, bishops, and abbots, in return for service, generally the supply of knights for military service. It is mainly the tenants-in-chief who are listed in the Domesday Book, and the de Favarches were never tenants-in-chief. These major landowners in turn parcelled out some of their land to under-tenants for service, and so on in successive steps, right down to peasant farmers, who held a few acres in return for working on the land of their local lord.

The pre-conquest landowner, or thegn, of Walsingham was Ketel, then Wihenoc (apparently a Breton), who was dispossessed by William the Conqueror, in favour of one of his conquest companions, Ranulf (Rainald FitzIvo) as tenant-in-chief. Both Ketel and Ranulf held lands and manors across many counties and there is no reason to assume either of them lived in Walsingham. Blomefield confirms that Rainald 'obtained two of the principal manors in these towns,'[5] Great Walsingham and Little Walsingham. The de Favarches are not listed, but this does not mean they had no manor in Walsingham, for manors are elusive both before and after the conquest, and varied greatly in size. The Domesday Survey was about service, and large tracts of land were unassessed. In addition to the main Domesday Book entry for Walsingham there was, for instance, in Great Walsingham, some land delivered to make up a manor, but it was not known which one.[6]

Interestingly, there was a manor in Walsingham, assessed in Fakenham, held by Harold, Earl of East Anglia, the future king.[7] Earl Harold was a landowner, second only to King Edward the Confessor himself. It is not known how he managed to administer these vast estates, but during the 1050s he travelled in Normandy, seeking advice on management,[8] and it is not impossible that he brought the de Favarches family to Walsingham. Edward the Confessor had lived in exile in Normandy from 1016 until 1041, and as King of England welcomed some Normans into the country for support and advice in the face of threats from Scandinavia and powerful earldoms in England. This particular King's manor in Walsingham was seized by William the Conqueror as his own demesne on the death of King Harold at Hastings, and according to Blomefield, was held by William de Brencourt (Brucourt), eventually passing into the hands of Richard, Earl of Clare. Both the de Clare family and the de Brucourt featured very prominently in the history of the shrine, and it is therefore most likely that the de Favarches' manor was on this land.

No church is mentioned in Walsingham, but it certainly existed. The Domesday Book mentions just over three hundred churches in Norfolk, but evidence suggests there were over six hundred. In 1086 East Anglia was documented as one of the richest regions in England with one of the densest concentrations of churches in the emerging parish system.[9]

To cast more light on the foundation of the Holy House we need to examine the first of three charters from the Walsingham Cartulary.

Charter of Geoffrey de Favarches about the Foundation of a Church

Gaufre de Fauarches to all the faithful of Holy Church which is in Christ, Greeting. Be it known to you that I have conceded to God and to St Mary and to Edwy my clerk, for instituting a religious order which he himself will have provided, for the salvation of my soul and that of my parents and friends as a perpetual alms, the chapel which my mother founded in Walsingham in honour of the ever-virgin Mary, together with possession of the church of All Saints of the same village and all that appertains to it both by way of lands and also of tithes and rents and homages and everything that the aforesaid Edwy possessed on the day when I undertook the journey to Jerusalem; and in particular twenty shillings annually received as rent from my demesne, for two parts of the tithes of my money. Also the land of Snoring which Hawis gave to God and to the aforesaid chapel, that is to say the half acre in the village of Snoring which lies next to the land and house of Thony, and eight acres in the fields of the same village with the parts of the meadow which pertains to the same land. Therefore I corroborate and confirm this donation and concession of mine, that the aforesaid Edwy and his successors having professed regular life should by undisturbed perpetual right hold it in ecclesiastical possession: by attestation of my charter and of my seal, to the honour of God and of Blessed Mary ever virgin. The witnesses of this donation and concession are Alan priest of Thursford etcetera.[10]

Agreements like this were first made on an altar, and then confirmed in writing by the charter, signed, witnessed, and sealed, which is why charters are written in the past tense. Until into the twelfth century they were often undated. This undated Charter makes it absolutely certain that Geoffrey held a manor in Walsingham.

Whatever date this first Charter was made it is clear that the Holy House was by then important enough to warrant a considerable endowment, including the income from All Saints (now St Mary's), various rents and tithes. Edwy, an Anglo-Saxon priest, was to provide a religious order (*ordinem religionis*) in professed regular life (*regularem uitam professi*), to serve it, but no particular religious order is specified. Most parish priests were married, but under the influence of the Monastic Reform many priests began to live a celibate life in communities and minsters.

Then we note that Geoffrey undertook a journey to Jerusalem. It has been questioned whether he went on a pilgrimage or a crusade, for the Latin word *iter* he uses for 'journey' can mean either. But Professor Jonathan Riley-Smith is clear that in a charter, when preceded by the record of a gift and the words 'on the day when I have undertaken the journey to Jerusalem,' and especially when it involves the foundation of a religious order, the donor is almost certainly a crusader.[11] The crusade was so dangerous that the knight wished to secure from God his blessing and safety, and the gift gave the donor some share in the spiritual benefits enjoyed by the religious community.

But which crusade? If Dickinson is right about a later date then it must have been the Second in 1144, but if the earlier date is preferred he went on the First Crusade in 1096. Not many knights from England went on the First Crusade unless they had relatives in Normandy who did. And Geoffrey was one who had, for we know that a son of Robert de Brucourt went on the First Crusade.[12] The lordship of Fervaques (Favarches), Calvados, in the arrondissement of Lisieux, was held by the immensely powerful de Brucourt family, who were under the barony of the d'Auquainville. Also connected to Fervaques, according to Lloyd, was Richard FitzGilbert, lord of Clare.[13] Robert de Brucourt had come over to England with the Conqueror; indeed, Wace, in his *Roman de Rou*, although not always reliable, tells us that in the actual Battle of Hastings 'the lords of Crèvecoeur and Drucourt and the lord of Brucourt followed the Duke (William) whichever way he went.'[14] He confirms that 'Robert, son of Ralph de Brucourt, and his brother Gilbert occur in the time of William I.'[15] The de Brucourt name lives on in Walsingham as Brooker's Dock, the land to the east of Knight Street by the Stiffkey, where stone was unloaded for the building of the Priory.

Geoffrey survived the Crusade, for we next find him in 1108 witnessing the Charter of Binham Priory between Herbert, Bishop of Norwich and its founder, Peter de Valognes. Another witness was William de Hocton,[16] whose name appears next to Geoffrey's. An earlier and undated foundation Charter of Binham was witnessed by *'Asketel, Alwold, and Wimundo presbyteris de Walsingham.'*[17] It is possible that they were the priests of St Peter's and All Saints, Great Walsingham, and All Saints, Little Walsingham, but listed as they are together it is not impossible that they were three members of the order, which Edwy had formed. That Edwy did not sign suggests he was no longer alive, and it is worth noting that none of the three priests had a Norman name.

In 1108 Geoffrey grants lands in Massingham to Castle Acre Priory, a gift confirmed by Adelicia de Clermont, wife of Gilbert FitzRichard, Lord of Clare.[18] This establishes a connection between Geoffrey and the de Clare family, and what is interesting is that the land of Ranulf (Rainald) in Walsingham was escheated (forfeited to the King) soon after 1086 and was then granted to Roger de Clare. By 1166 he was dead and his land had passed to Robert de Brucourt.[19] He was probably the son of the de Brucourt who went on the first crusade, and grandson of the earlier Robert. Subsequently the de Clare family held it into the thirteenth century, making a major contribution to the Shrine at Walsingham. Harold's land, deemed by William the Conqueror, passed into the hands of William de Briencurt (Brucourt), as we have seen, and eventually to Richard, Earl of Clare. The de Brucourt (or Briencurt), de Clare, and de Favarches families were closely linked both in Normandy and Walsingham. This introduces us to the second Walsingham Charter, which was made by Robert de Brucourt to William de Turbe, who was Bishop of Norwich from 1146 to 1174. Clearly, his dates fit the foundation of the Priory, so we may assume that this Charter was made shortly before 1153.

Confirmation of Robert de Brucurt

To William by the grace of God Bishop of Norwich and to all the faithful of Holy Church, both present and future, Robert de Brucurt: Greeting. Be it known to you that I have given and conceded to God and to St Mary and to the canons of Walsingham all the possessions which the church possessed on the day when Geoffrey de Favarches undertook the journey to Jerusalem for the salvation of my soul and of my parents as a perpetual alms, together with all that pertains to it of lands, of tithes, and of rents. And particularly the land which the aforesaid Geoffrey gave to Robert de Sprotel, just as Robert himself gave [it] to them. And the land of Snoring which Hawis gave to God and to the church of the blessed Mary, with the assent of lord Geoffrey. I also concede to them twenty shillings for my mill in Walsingham until I provide other [lands] for them. Therefore I confirm this donation by attestation of my charter and my seal, in order that the canons themselves should hold [it] in ecclesiastical possession by perpetual right. Of this grant the witnesses are: Peter the Deacon etc.

Charters were made in perpetuity, but to give assurance were often confirmed by a new landlord. In the second Charter Lord Geoffrey's grant is confirmed to the Bishop by Robert de Brucourt and it may well be that Geoffrey had died. This is evident in the third Charter. It is possible that the Hawis in the Charters was Geoffrey's wife. She seems to have been younger than he was; for we learn that William de Hocton (Houghton) was given leave in 1130 to marry Geoffrey's widow. William had to pay 30 shillings for the Manor of Wighton belonging to the King, and 10 marks to marry her and have custody of her son until he was a knight and hold lands of him.[20] William was well known to Geoffrey, for like Geoffrey he too had been a witness to the Charter of Binham Priory. To fit his dating Dickinson had to assume that this widow was Geoffrey's mother, Richeldis, rather than his wife.

The young son left by Geoffrey may have been named after his father, because a Geoffrey de Favarches held land in 1166 from his tenant-in-chief, the Abbot of Abingdon, in return for which Geoffrey had to render the service of a knight and a half. The land held from Abingdon may have been marginal to Geoffrey's holdings, who could have had more extensive lands elsewhere, including Walsingham. The Abbot himself had to render to King Henry II a total of thirty-three knight's service.[21]

We should also notice that this second Charter is now specific about the community being a Community of Canons, but the third Charter, which must be close in date to the second, is even more informative.

Charter of Roger Count of Clare
about the Church of All Saints in Little Walsingham

To William by the grace of God Bishop of Norwich and to all the faithful of Holy Church, both present and future: Roger count of Clare: Greeting. Be it known to you that I have given and granted to God and St Mary and to my clerks of Walsingham Ralph and Geoffrey, for instituting a regular canonical order for the salvation of my soul and of my parents as a perpetual alms, the chapel which Richeldis the mother of Geoffrey de Favarches founded in Walsingham with all that pertains to it in lands, in tithes and in rents, and with all the possessions which the chapel itself owned on the day when the aforesaid Geoffrey de Favarches undertook the journey to Jerusalem; together with possession of the church of All Saints of the same village; and whatever they can obtain justly and canonically, the lord [of the manor] being surety. I also grant them the mill whence Geoffrey de Favarches used regularly to acquire two garb[22] of his tithe, also by transferring in one year twenty shillings to the monks of Clare; and that the men of that same village and those who wish should mill at the aforesaid mill freely and without any hindrance, as they were used to do in the time of Geoffrey. Therefore, that the aforesaid Ralph and Geoffrey, with those whom they themselves choose and their successors, having professed regular life, should by undisturbed perpetual right hold this donation and grant in ecclesiastical possession, I corroborate and confirm this donation by attestation of my charter and of my seal. These are the witnesses: Walter son of Robert, Robert son of Baldwin etc.

First, we should note the words *as they were used to do in the time of Geoffrey*, puts it beyond doubt that Geoffrey de Favarches had died. It is, incidentally, from this Charter that we learn the name of Geoffrey's mother, Richeldis. According to Blomefield it is a Norfolk name,[23] but almost certainly it originated in Normandy, where it was not uncommon. It appears, for example, many times in the foundation documents of St Josaphat's monastery at Lèves, near Chartres.[24]

Moreover, Roger speaks of *his* clerks, Ralph and Geoffrey who are charged with instituting a regular canonical order (*ad ordinem canonicalem regularem instituendum*). This can only mean that Robert de Brucourt and Roger de Clare founded the Priory of Augustinian Canons. Ralph, it may be assumed, is the Ralph who is listed in the Cartulary as the first Prior in 1153. Many existing communities at the time were encouraged to adopt the Augustinian rule, and it appears that this is what happened to the original community of Geoffrey de Favarches instituted by Edwy. Dr Pestell has shown that Norfolk Anglo-Saxon monasteries in Mendham, Thetford St George's, and possibly Butley and Coxford replaced extant communities in the years following the Conquest.[25] It seems this was true of Walsingham also.

Dickinson may have relied on an abbreviated text of the Charters or else he would have spotted this. We can only conclude he was mistaken in his assumption that Geoffrey, the son of Richeldis, founded the Augustinian Priory, from which followed his conclusion that Richeldis could not have built the Holy House as early as 1061. Although there are no clear indications when the de Favarches family arrived in England, the Ballad may well relate a reliable tradition, when it tells us that in 1061 Richeldis built her Chapel in Walsingham.

APPENDIX 2
THE PYNSON BALLAD

1 Of this chapell se here the fundacyon,
Bylded the yere of Crystes incarnacyon,
A thousande complete syxty and one,
The tyme of sent Edward kyng of this region.

2 Beholde and se, ye goostly folkes all,
Which to this place haue deuocyon
Whan ye to Our Lady askynge socoure call
Desyrynge here hir helpe in your trybulacyon;
Of this hir chapell ye may se the fundacyon,
If ye wyll this table ouerse and rede
Howe by myracle it was founded in dede.

3 A noble wydowe, somtyme lady of this towne,
Called Rychold, in lyuynge full vertuous,
Desyred of Oure Lady a petycyowne
Hir to honoure with some werke bountyous,
This blyssed Virgin and Lady most gracyous
Graunted hir petycyon, as I shall after tell,
Unto hir worshyp to edefye this chapell.

4 In spyryte Our Lady to Nazareth hir led
And shewed hir the place where Gabryel hir
   grette:
'Lo doughter, consyder' to hir Oure Lady sayde,
'Of thys place take thou suerly the mette,
Another lyke thys at Walsyngham thou sette
Unto my laude and synguler honoure;
All that me seche there shall fynde socoure,

1 Of this chapel see here the foundation,
Built in the year of Christ's incarnation,
A thousand complete sixty and one,
The time of Saint Edward king of this region.

2 Behold and see ye spiritual folks all,
Which to this place have devotion
When ye to our Lady asking succour call
Desiring here her help in your tribulation;
Of this her chapel ye may see the foundation;
If ye will this tablet turn over and read
How by miracle it was founded indeed.

3 A noble widow, sometime lady of this town,
Called Rychold, of full virtuous life,
Desired of Our Lady a petition
To honour her with some work bounteous,
This blessed virgin and lady most gracious
Granted her petition, as I shall after tell,
Unto her worship to edify this chapel.

4 In spirit our Lady to Nazareth led her
And showed her the place where Gabriel greeted
   her:
'Lo daughter consider' Our Lady said to her,
'Of this place take accurately the measurement
And another like this at Walsingham set
To my praise and singular honour;
All that beseech me there shall find help.

5 Where shall be hadde in a memoryall
The great ioy of my salutacyon,
Fyrste of my ioyes grounde and orygynall
Rote of mankyndes gracyous redempcyon,
Whan Gabryell gaue to me relacyon
To be a moder through humylyte,
And goddys sonne conceyue in virgynyte.'

6 This visyon shewed thryse to this deuout
 woman,
In mynde well she marked both length and
 brede;
She was full gladde and thanked Oure Lady than
Of hir great grace neuer destytute in nede.
This forsayd hous in haste she thought to spede,
Called to hir artyfycers full wyse,
This chapell to forge as Our Lady dyd deuyse.

7 All this, a medewed wete with dropes celestyall
And with syluer dewe sent from hye adowne
Excepte tho tweyne places chosen aboue all
Where neyther moysterf ne dewe myght be
 fowne,
This was the fyrste pronostycacyowne
Howe this our newe Nazareth here shold stande,
Bylded lyke the fyrste in the Holy Lande.

8 Whan it was al fourmed, than had she great
 doute
Where it shold be sette and in what maner place,
In as moche as tweyne places were founde oute
Tokened with myracle of Our Ladyes grace;
That is to say, tweyne quadrates of egall space
As the flees of Gedeon in the wete beynge drye,
Assygned by myracle of holy mayde Marye.

9 The wydowe thought it most lykly of
 congruence
This house on the fyrste soyle to bylde and arere.
Of this who lyste to have experyence,
A chapell of saynt Laurence standeth nowe there
Faste by tweyne wells, experyence doth thus lere,
There she thought to have set this chapell
Which was begonne by Our Ladyes counsell.

---

5 Where shall be held in memory
The great joy of my annunciation,
The first of my joys ground and original
Cause of mankind's gracious redemption,
When Gabriel announced to me
To be a mother through humility,
And God's son conceive in virginity.'

6 This vision showed thrice to this devout
 woman,
In her mind marking well the length and breadth;
She was full of gladness and thanked our Lady then
Of her great grace never destitute in need.
This foresaid house she thought to accomplish
 successfully,
She called her experienced workmen,
This chapel to forge as our Lady did devise.

7 All this a meadow wet with drops celestial
And with silver dew sent down from on high
Except the two places chosen above all
Where neither moisture nor dew might be
 found,
This was the first indication
Of how this our new Nazareth here should stand,
Built like the first in the Holy Land.

8 When it was all formed then had she great
 doubt
Where it should be set and in what kind of place,
Inasmuch two places were found out
Tokened with miracle of our Lady's grace;
That is to say two surfaces of equal space
Like Gideon's fleece being dry in the wet,
Assigned by miracle of holy maid Mary.

9 The widow thought it most consistent
To build and erect this house on the first soil.
For those who wish to observe it,
A chapel of Saint Lawrence stands there now
Close to twin wells experience doth teach,
There she thought to have set this chapel
Which was begun by our Lady's counsel.

10 The carpenters began to set the fundamente
This heuenly house to arere up on hye,
But sone their werkes shewed inconuenyente,
For no pece with oder wolde agre with
   geometrye;
Than were they all sory and full of agonye
That they could nat kenfneyther mesure ne
   marke
To ioyne togyder their owne proper werke.

11 They went to reste and layde all thynge on
   syde,
As they on their maystresse had a
   commaundement;
She thought Our Lady, that fyrste was hir gyde,
Wold conuey this worke aftyr hir owne en tent;
Hir meyny to reste as for that nyght she sente
And prayed Our Lady with deuoute
   exclamacyon,
As she had begonne, to perfourme that
   habytacion.

12 All nyghte the wydowe permayninge in this
   prayer,
Oure blyssed Lady with heuenly mynystrys,
Hirsylfe beynge here chyef artyfycer,
Areryd this sayd house with aungellys haudys,
And not only reyrd it but set it there it is,
That is, two hundred fote and more in dystaunce
From the fyrste place bokes make remembraunce.

13 Erly whan the artyfycers earn to their trauayle
Of this sayd chapell to have made an ende,
They founde eche parte conioyned sauns fayle
Better than they coude conceyue it in mynde;
Thus eche man home agayne dyd wynde,
And this holy matrone thanked Oure Lady
Of hir great grace shewyd here specyally.

10 The carpenters began to set the foundations
This heavenly house to build up on high,
But soon their work became troublesome,
For no piece would agree with another in
   geometry;
Then were they all sorry and full of agony
That they could not understand nor measure nor
   mark
To join together their own proper work.

11 They went to rest and laid everything aside,
As they from their mistress had a commandment;
She thought that our Lady who first was her
   guide,
Would manage this work after her own
   intention;.
She sent her household to rest for that night
And prayed our Lady with devout exclamation,
As she had when she began to build the house.

12 All night the widow persisting in this prayer,
Our blessed Lady with heavenly aid,
Herself being here chief worker,
Built up this said house with angels' hands,
And not only built it but set it where it is,
That is two hundred foot and more in distance
From the first place mentioned in the books.

13 When the workmen arrrived early for their
   work
This said chapel to complete,
They found each part joined up without mistake
Better than they could have imagined it;
Thus each man went home again.
And this holy matron thanked our Lady
For her great grace showed here specially.

14 And syth here Our Lady hath shewyd many
  myracle
Innumerable, nowe here for to expresse
To suche as visyte thys hir habytacle,
Euer lyke newe to them that call hir in dystresse;
Four hundreth yere and more, the cronacle to
  witnes,
Hath endured this notable pylgrymage,
Where grace is dayly shewyd to men of euery
  age.

14 And since here our Lady hath shewed many
  miracles
Too many here and now to express
To such as visit this her abode,
She is ever like new to those who call on her in
  distress;
Four hundred years and more as the chronicle
  witnesses,
Hath undergone this notable pilgrimage,
Where grace is daily showed to men of every age.

15 Many seke ben here cured by Our Ladyes
  myghte,
Dede agayne reuyued, of this is no dought,
Lame made hole and blynde restored to syghte,
Maryners vexed with tempest safe to porte
  brought,
Defe, wounded and lunatyke that hyder haue
  sought,
And also lepers here recouered haue be
By Oure Ladyes grace of their infyrmyte.

15 Many sick have been cured here by Our
  Lady's might,
Dead again revived, of this is no doubt,
Lame made whole, and blind restored to sight,
Mariners vexed with tempest safe to port
  brought,
Deaf, wounded and lunatics that hither have
  sought,
And also lepers have recovered here,
By our Lady's grace from their infirmity.

16 Folke that of fendys haue had acombraunce
And of wycked spyrytes also moche vexacyon
Have here be delyuered from euery such
  chaunce,
And soules greatly vexed with gostely
  temptacion,
Lo, here the chyef solace agaynst all tribulacyon
To all that be seke, bodely or goostly,
Callynge to Oure Lady deuoutly.

16 Folk that of fiends have been oppressed
And much vexed by wicked spirits also
Here be delivered from every such chance,
And souls greatly vexed with spiritual temptation,
Lo here the chief solace against all tribulation
To all that be sick bodily or spiritually,
Calling to Our Lady devoutly.

17 Therfore euery pylgryme gyue your
  attendaunce
Our Lady here to serue with humble affeccyon,
Your sylfe ye applye to do hir plesaunce,
Remembrynge the great ioye of hir
  Annunciacion,
Therwyth conceyuynge this bryef compylacyon,
Though it halte in meter and eloquence,
It is here wryten to do hyr reuerence.

17 Therefore every pilgrim, give your attention
To serve Our Lady here with humble affection,
Apply ye to do her pleasure,
Remembering the great joy of her annunciation,
Taking notice of this brief compilation,
Though it lacks metre and eloquence,
It is here written to do her reverence.

18 All lettred that wyll have more intellygence
Of the fundacyon of this chapell here,
If you wyll aske bokes shall you encence
More clerely to understande this forsayd matere;
To you shall declare the cronyclere
All cyrcumstaunce by a noble processe
Howe olde cronyclers of thys bere wytnesse.

19 O Englonde, great cause thou haste glad for
     to be,
Compared to the londe of promys yon,
Thou atteynest my grace to stande in that degre
Through this gloryous Ladyes supportacyon,
To be called in euery realme and regyon
The holy lande, Oure Ladyes dowre;
Thus arte thou named of olde antyquyte.

20 And this is the cause, as it apereth by
     lyklynesse,
In the is belded newe Nazareth, a mancyon
To the honoure of the heuenly empresse
And of hir moste gloryous salutacyon,
Chyef pryncypyll and grounde of oure saluacyon,
Whan Gabryell sayd at olde Nazereth 'Aue',
This ioy here dayly remembred for to be.

21 O gracyous Lady, glory of Jerusalem,
Cypresse of Syon and Ioye of Israel,
Rose of Jeryco and Sterre of Bethleem,
O gloryous Lady, our askynge nat repell,
In mercy all wymen euer thou doste excell,
Therfore, blissed Lady, graunt thou thy great
     grace
To all that the deuoutly visyte in this place.
Amen.

18 All literate persons who wish to understand more
About the foundation of this chapel here,
If ye will ask, books shall enlighten you
To understand more clearly this foresaid matter;
The chronicler will declare to you
All the circumstancs by a noble narrative
And how old chroniclers bear witness to this.

19 O England great cause hast thou to be glad
     to be
Compared to the land of promise, Sion,
Thou attainest by grace to stand in that degree
Through this glorious Lady's support,
To be called in every realm and region
The Holy Land, Our Lady's Dowry;
Thus art thou named in old antiquity.

20 And this is the reason as it appears by a
     likeness,
For in thee is built new Nazareth, a mansion,
To the honour of the heavenly empress
And of her most glorious annunciation,
Chief principal and ground of our salvation,
When Gabriel said at old Nazareth 'Ave',
This joy to be daily remembered here.

21 O gracious Lady, glory of Jerusalem,
Cypress of Sion, and joy of Israel,
Rose of Jericho, and star of Bethlehem,
O glorious lady our asking do not repel,
In mercy all women thou dost ever excel,
Therefore blessed Lady, grant thou thy great
     grace
To all that thee devoutly visit in this place.
Amen.

The Ballad is in book 1254 of the Pepys Library, Magdalene College, Cambridge.

WALSINGHAM BALLADS

GENTLE HERDSMAN

"Gentle herdsman, tell to me,
Of courtesy I thee pray,
Unto the town of Walsingham
Which is the right and ready way?

Unto the town of Walsingham
The way is hard for to be gone;
And very crooked are those paths
For you to find out all alone.

Were the miles doubled thrice
And the way never so ill,
It were not enough for mine offence,
It is so grievous and so ill!

Thy years are young, thy face is fair,
Thy wits are weak, thy thoughts are green;
Time hath not given thee leave as yet
For to commit so great a crime.

I am not what I seem to be,
My clothes and sex do differ far;
I am a woman, woe is me!
(Born) to grief and irksome care.

(For my) beloved and well beloved
(My wayward cruelty could kill,
And though my tears will nought avail
Most dearly I bewail him) still.

(He was) the flower of noble wights,
(None ever more sincere could) be;
(Of comely mien and shape) he was
(And tenderly he) loved me.

(When thus I saw he) loved me well,
(I grew so proud his pain to see
(That I who did not) know myself
(Thought scorn) of (such a youth) as he.

And grew so coy and nice to please
As womens' looks are often so,
He might not kiss, nor hand forsooth
Unless I willed him so to do.

Thus being wearied with delay
To see I pitied not his grief,
He got him to a secret place
And there he died without relief

And for his sake these weeds I wear
And sacrifice my tender age;
And every day I'll beg my bread
To undergo this pilgrimage.

Thus every day I fast and pray
And ever will do till I die;
And get me to some secret place,
For so he did, and so will I.

Now gentle herdsman, ask no more,
But keep my secrets I thee pray;
Unto the town of Walsingham
Shew me the right and ready way.

Now go thy ways, and God before!
For He must ever guide thee still:
Turn down that dale, the right hand path
And so, fair pilgrim, fare thee well!"

Words in brackets are supplied by Thomas Percy where the original is missing.

AS YE CAME FROM THE HOLY LAND

As you came from the holy land
Of blessed Walsingham,
Met you not with my true love
By the way as you came?

How shall I know your true love,
That have met many one,
As I went to the holy land,
That have come, that have gone?

My love is neither white nor brown
But as the heavens fair;
There is none hath her form divine
Either in earth or air.

Such a one did I meet, good sir,
With an angelic face,
Who, like a nymph, a queen, appeared
Both in her gait, her grace.

Yes, she hath clean forsaken me
And left me all alone,
Who some time loved me as her life,
And called me her own.

What is the cause she leave thee thus
And a new way doth take,
That some times loved thee as her life
And thee her joy did make?

I that loved thee all my youth,
Grow old now as you see
Love liketh not the falling fruit
Nor yet the withered tree.

For love is like a careless child,
Forgetting promise past;
He is blind, he is deaf whene'er he list;
His faith is never fast.

His fond desire is fickle found
And yields a trustless joy,
Won with a world of toil and care
And lost with a toy.

Such is the love of womankind
Of love's name abused,
Beneath which many vain desires
And follies are excused.

But true love is a lasting fire
Which viewless vestals (virgins) tend,
That burns for ever in the soul
And knows no change nor end.

Ballads from *Reliques of Ancient English Poetry*, ed. Thomas Percy, London, 1839.

NOTES

1. FROM MERCURY TO MARY [pages 17–30]

1 David Gurney (ed.), *Small Towns and Villages of Roman Norfolk*, in *Roman Small Towns in Eastern England and Beyond*, A.E. Brown, Oxbow Monograph 52, 1995, p.59.

2 See K.S. Painter, *The Water Newton Early Christian Silver*, British Museum Publications, 1977.

3 Jean Bagnall Smith, *Votive Objects and Objects of Votive Significance from Great Walsingham*, Britannia, vol. XXX, Society for the Promotion of Roman Studies, 1999, p.48.

4 Martin Henig, *Religion in Roman Britain*, Routledge, 1992, pp.144 ff.

5 Bagnall Smith, *Votive Objects,* p.52.

6 Graham Webster, *The British Celts and their Gods under Rome*, Batsford, 1986, p.111.

7 Webster, *The British Celts*, p.113.

8 Dorothy Watts, *Christians and Pagans in Roman Britain*, Routledge, 1991, p.107.

9 Henig, *Religion in Roman Britain*, p.226.

10 Acts 15:29.

11 Acts 17:16-31.

12 Justin Martyr, *Apology*, lxv-lxvii, in Henry Bettenson (ed.), *Documents of the Christian Church*, Oxford University Press, 1965, p.95.

13 Luke Timothy Johnson, *Among the Gentiles,* Yale University Press, 2009, p.157.

14 Bede, *The Ecclesiastical History of the English People*, Oxford University Press, 2008, I: 4, p.14.

15 James Rattue, *The Living Stream*, Bodywell, 1995.

16 Henig, *Religion in Roman Britain*, p.225.

17 K.R. Dark, *Civitas to Kingdom: British Political Continuity 300-800*, Leicester University Press, 1994, p.32.

18 Henig, *Religion in Roman Britain*, p.224.

19 Bede, *The Ecclesiastical History of the English People*, I.15, p.28. See also Henry Mayr-Harting, *The Coming of Christianity to Anglo-Saxon England*, Batsford, 1972.

20 Nicholas Higham, *Rome, Britain and the Anglo-Saxons*, Seaby, 1992, p.4.

21 Bede, *The Ecclesiastical History* I: 22, p.36.

22 Bede, *The Ecclesiastical History* I: 23, p.37.

23 Watts, *Christians and Pagans*, p.226.

24 Dark, *Civitas to Kingdom*, pp.64-70.

25 Miranda J Aldhouse-Green, *The Gods of Roman Britain*, Shire Publications, 2003, p.70

26 *Letters of Boniface*, 16:85.

27 Bede, *The Ecclesiastical History* I:30-31, p.57

28 Watts, *Christians and Pagans* pp.107 ff.

29 Miranda J. Aldhouse-Green, *Pilgrims in Stone. Stone images from the Gallo-Roman Healing Sanctuary of Fontes Sequanae*, Oxford, 1999, p.79.

30 Henig, *Religion in Roman Britain*, p.227.

31 Bede, *The Ecclesiastical History* II:15, p.98.

32 Bede, *The Ecclesiastical History* II:15, p.99.

33 Dorothy Whitelock, *The pre-Viking Age Church in East Anglia*, in *Anglo-Saxon England, Vol* I, P. Clemoes (ed.), Cambridge University Press, 2007, p.1.

34 Tim Pestell, *Landscapes of Monastic Foundation. The Establishment of Religious Houses in East Anglia, c 650 – 1200*, Boydell Press, 2004, p.57.

35 Flavell Edmunds, *Traces of History in the Names of Places,* London, 1872, p.81.

36 John McNeal Dodgson, *The Significance of the Distribution of the English Place-name in -ingas, -inga- in South-East England*, Medieval Archaeology X, p.3.

37 Gavin Smith, *Recovering the Lost Religious Place-names of England*, in At the Edge, Heart of Albion Press, September 1996, Issue 3, p.14.

38 Gavin Smith, *Ingas and the Mid-Seventh Century Diocese*, Nomina, Vol. 31, 2008, p.76.

39 Smith, *Recovering the Lost Religious Place-names of England*, p.15. See also, Whitelock, *The Pre-Viking Age Church in East Anglia*, in *Anglo-Saxon England, Vol*.I, p.10.

40 David Knowles, *The Monastic Order in England*, Cambridge University Press, 1963, p.33.

41 Pestell, *Landscapes of Monastic Foundation*, pp.72ff.

42 Sue Margeson, *Vikings in Norfolk*, Norfolk Museums Service, 1997, pp.4–5.

43 Diana Webb, *Pilgrimage in Medieval England*, Hambledon, 2000, p.1.

44 Nick Corcos, *Churches as Pre-Historic Ritual Monuments*, The Sheffield Graduate Journal of Archaeology, Issue 6, August 2001.

2. FROM WALSINGHAM TO NAZARETH [pages 31-45]

1 Eamon Duffy, *Dynamics of Pilgrimage in Late Medieval England*, in C. Morris and P. Roberts, *Pilgrimage, The English Experience from Becket to Bunyan*, Cambridge University Press, 2002, p.168.

2 Diana Webb, *Pilgrimage in Medieval England*, Hambledon, 2000, p.86.

3 John 1:46.

4 Sean Freyne, *Galilee, Jesus and the Contribution of Archeology*, Expository Times, Vol. 119, No. 12, p.577.

5 Richard Batey, *Sepphoris and the Jesus Movement*, New Testament Studies, Cambridge University Press, 2001, p.404.

6 Luke 4:29.

7 *Bulletin of the Anglo-Israel Archeological Society*, 2007, Vol. 25, p.20.

8 *Bulletin of the Anglo-Israel Archeological Society*, p.69.

9 News International Report, December 21, 2009.

10 Cited in Jerome Murphy O'Connor, *The Holy Land, an Oxford Archaeological Guide from Earliest Times to 1700*, Oxford University Press, 2005, p.375.

11 Mark 6:1-6.

12 Matthew 13:55.

13 Matthew 12:46–47; Mark 3:31.

14 Luke 8:19.
15 Mark 3:20-21.
16 Acts 1:12-14.
17 1 Corinthians 9:5.
18 Max Thurian, *Mary, Mother of the Lord*, Faith Press, 1963, pp.38-39.
19 Richard Bauckham, *Jude and the Relatives of Jesus in the Early Church*, T & T Clark, 1990, pp.16-17.
20 John 19:25.
21 Luke 24:18.
22 John P. Meier, *A Marginal Jew, Rethinking the Historical Jesus*, Doubleday, 1991, p.317.
23 Eusebius, *The History of the Church*, Penguin, 2004, 3:32, p.95.
24 Josephus, *Jerusalem and Rome*, Fontana, 1966, p.162.
25 Eusebius, 4:22; p.129.
26 Eusebius 23:20, pp.81-82.
27 Eusebius 1:7, p.22.
28 1 Thessalonians 2:9.
29 Matthew 1:1-17; Luke 3:23-38.
30 Bauckham, *Jude and the Relatives of Jesus,* pp.315ff.
31 Bauckham, *Jude and the Relatives of Jesus,* pp.68-69.
32 Mart. Conon 4:2. Cited in Bauckham, *Jude and the Relatives of Jesus,* p.122.
33 Bellarmino Bagatti, *Excavations in Nazareth, Vol. I*, Jerusalem Franciscan Printing Press, 1969, p.197.
34 Eusebius, 7:19, p.234.
35 Bagatti, *Excavations in Nazareth, Vol. I,* p.151.
36 Acts 24:5.
37 Acts 11:26.
38 Luke 4:16.
39 Acts 2:42-47. Cf. Justin Martyr, *First Apology*, 67, in Herbert A. Musurillo, *The Fathers of the Primitive Church*, Mentor-Omega, 1966, p.134.
40 Epiphanius, Pan. 30:11:9-10. Cited in Bagatti, *Excavations in Nazareth, Vol. I*, p.17.

3. THE CONQUESTS OF ISLAM [pages 46-61]

1 *Declaration on the Relation of the Church to Non-Christian Religions*, para. 3, in A. Flannery (ed.), *Vatican Council II*, Dominican Publications, 1992, p.740.
2 *The Koran* III 42ff. Mohammad M Pickthall (trnsl.), Star, 1930 p.66.
3 *Walsingham Review*, No 27, April 1968.
4 Evangelos Papaioannou, *The Monastery of St Catherine Sinai*, St Catherine's Monastery Press, p.10.
5 Kenneth Scott Latourette, *A History of Christianity*, Eyre and Spottiswoode, 1955, p.270.

6 Bellarmino Bagatti, *Excavations in Nazareth Vol. I*, Franciscan Printing Press, Jerusalem, 1969, p.24.

7 Steven Runciman, A *History of the Crusades, Vol. 1*, Penguin, 1952, p.27.

8 His biographer, Ralph of Caen, cited in Jonathan Riley-Smith, The *First Crusade and the Idea of Crusading*, University of Pennsylvania Press, 1986, p.36.

9 Riley-Smith, The *First Crusade and the Idea of Crusading*, p.17.

10 See Appendix 1.

11 *Translations and Reprints from the Original Sources of European History*, Vol. 1, No. 2, Philadelphia: University of Pennsylvania, 1895, in Dana C. Munro, *Urban and the Crusaders*, BiblioBazaar, LLC, 2009, p.5.

12 From the official Vatican website, *Speeches of Pope John Paul II, Welcome Address of John Paul II to the Ecumenical Patriarch Bartholomew I*, Solemnity of SS Peter and Paul, Tuesday, 29 June 2004.

13 Jonathan Riley-Smith, *Religious warriors. Reinterpreting the Crusades*, in The Economist, 23 December 1995, p.37.

14 Thomas F. Madden, *Crusade Propaganda, the Abuse of Christianity's Holy Wars*, online National Review, November 2, 2001.

15 Bellarmino Bagatti, *Excavations in Nazareth Vol. II*, Franciscan Printing Press, Jerusalem, 2001, p.15.

16 Bagatti, *Excavations in Nazareth Vol. II*, p.16.

17 Bagatti, *Excavations in Nazareth Vol. II*, p.24.

18 Bagatti, *Excavations in Nazareth Vol. II*, p.24.

19 Cited in Denys Pringle, *The Churches of the Crusader Kingdom of Jerusalem Vol. II*, Cambridge University Press, 1998, p.119.

20 Bagatti, *Excavations in Nazareth Vol. II*, p.26

21 as above. See also Giuseppe Santorelli, *La Santa Casa di Loreto*, Loreto, 2003, p.94.

22 Santarelli, *La Santa Casa*, pp.225-226.

23 Santarelli, *La Santa Casa*, pp.235-248.

24 Nanni Monelli, *Gleanings on the Altar of the Apostles*, Loreto, vol. 40, May/August 2006, p.55.

25 Gregory of Nyssa, O*n the Baptism of Christ: a Sermon for the Day of the Lights*, in Wilson Austin Henry (ed.), *The Early Church Fathers and Other Works*, Eerdmans, 1867.

4. THE MEDIEVAL CHURCH [pages 62-74]

1 Eamon Duffy, *Saints and Sinners, A History of the Popes*, Yale University Press, 2006, p.135.

2 Richard Rex, *Henry VIII and the English Reformation*, Macmillan, 1993, pp.87ff.

3 W. Butler-Bowden, *The Book of Margery Kempe*, Jonathan Cape, 1936, pp.222-223.

4 *English Hymnal* 115.

5 Colossians 1:24.

6 Eamon Duffy, *The Stripping of the Altars*, Yale University Press, 1992, p.259.

7　Jerome, *De nominibus hebraicis*. Cited in Luigi Gambero, *Mary in the Middle Ages*, Ignatius, 2000, p.84.

8　Maurus, *Homiliae in Evangelia et Epistolas 163*. Cited in Gambero, *Mary in the Middle Ages*, p.68.

9　Gambero, *Mary in the Middle Ages*, p.105.

10　Sarah Boss, *Mary*, Continuum, 2003, pp.3-4.

11　Luke 1:38.

12　Augustine, Sermon 196 (1).

13　Sarah Boss, *Empress and Handmaid*, Cassell, 2000, p.31.

14　St Bernard of Clairvaux, *In Praise of the Virgin Mother*, Sermon 4: 8-9.

15　See Edward Sri and Scott Hahn, *Queen Mother: a Biblical Theology of Mary's Queenship*, Emmaus, 2005, pp.50-53.

16　Cited in Boss, *Empress and Handmaid*, p.48.

17　as above.

18　Both the original version and a modernised version of the Ballad are found in Appendix 2.

19　Cited in Boss, *Mary*, p.118.

20　Harleian MSS No 360, *Relation of the Apprehension of Henrie Garnett*, fol. 98, 6. Cited in T. E. Bridgett, *Our Lady's Dowry*, Burns & Oates, 1875, p.vi.

21　Nigel Saul, *Richard II*, Yale University Press, 1999, pp.304-307.

22　Froissart, *Chronicles*, Penguin, 1978, p.224.

23　Luke 1:52-53.

5. THE GROWTH OF THE SHRINE [pages 75-93]

1　J.C. Dickinson, *The Shrine of Our Lady of Walsingham*, Cambridge University Press, 1956, p.9.

2　Charles Green and A.B. Whittingham, *Excavations at Walsingham Priory, Norfolk, 1962*, The Archaeological Journal, CXXV, The Royal Archaeological Institute, p.269.

3　Sarah Salih, *Two Travellers' Tales*, in Christopher Harper-Bill (ed.), *Medieval East Anglia*, Woodbridge: Boydell, 2005, p.330.

4　M.F. Hearn and Lee Willis, *The Iconography of the Lady Chapel of Salisbury Cathedral*, in Laurence Keen and Thomas Cocke (eds.), *Medieval Art and Architecture at Salisbury Cathedral*, The British Archaeological Association Conference Transactions XVII, 1996, pp.40-45.

5　Desiderius Erasmus, *Pilgrimages to Saint Mary of Walsingham and Saint Thomas of Canterbury*, J.G. Nichols (trans.), Westminster, 1849, p.14.

6　Erasmus, *Pilgrimages*, p.14.

7　Dickinson, *The Shrine*, p.44.

8　Charles Green and A.B. Whittingham, *Excavations* pp.263 and 268.

9　Erasmus, *Pilgrimages*, pp.14-15.

10　Erasmus, *Pilgrimages*, p.37.

11 Dickinson, *The Shrine*, p.8.

12 Christopher Harper-Bill, *The Foundation and Later History of the Medieval Shrine*, in *Walsingham: Pilgrimage and History*, R.C. National Shrine, 1999, p.71.

13 I am grateful to Jon Cannon for pointing this out to me.

14 Green and Whittingham, *Excavations*, p.270.

15 Harper-Bill, *The Foundation*, p.73.

16 Dickinson, *The Shrine*, p.18.

17 Dickinson, *The Shrine*, pp.15-16.

18 Howard Fears, *An Intimate History of Little Walsingham, during 1,000 Years*, Walsingham, 2007, p.18.

19 Howard Fears, *An Approach to a History of Little Walsingham, Early days, Vol. I,* Walsingham, 2004, p.89.

20 Fears *An Intimate History* p.15.

21 See Dickinson, *The Shrine*, pp.28ff.

22 See Appendix 1.

23 Fears, *An Intimate History of Little Walsingham*, p.13.

24 Erasmus, *Pilgrimages*, p.20.

25 Dickinson, *The Shrine*, p.94.

26 Erasmus, *Pilgrimages*, p.13.

27 A.R. Martin, *The Greyfriars of Walsingham*, in Norfolk Archaeology, vol. xxv, 1935.

28 Cited in Fears, *An Approach to a History of Little Walsingham, Early days, Vol. I*, p.120.

29 Fears, *An Approach to a History of Little Walsingham, Early days, Vol. I,* p.84.

30 Norfolk and Norwich Archeological Society, Vol. 25.

31 L.E. Whatmore, *Highway to Walsingham*, The Pilgrim Bureau, 1973, p.63.

32 Peter Rollings, *Walsingham, England's Nazareth*, R.C. National Shrine, 1998, p.18.

33 Whatmore, *Highway*, p.63.

34 Whatmore, *Highway*, p.82.

6. THE IMAGE OF OUR LADY OF WALSINGHAM [pages 94-106]

1 Exodus 20:4.

2 Exodus 33:20.

3 Colossians 1:15.

4 Now set in a window in the Guilds Chapel in St Mary's.

5 Hebrews 9.

6 1 Corinthians 10:1-5.

7 1 Corinthians 15:45.

8 Proverbs 8: 22-23.

9 1 Corinthians 1:24.

10 II Chronicles 9:17-18.

11 Sarah Boss, *Mary*, Continuum, 2003, p.109.

12 Jaroslav Pelikan, *Mary Through the Centuries*, Yale University Press, 1996, p.55.

13 John 1:14.

14 Theodore the Studite, *On the Images I*, (PG 99:489) quoted in Pelikan, *Mary*, p.57.

15 Luke 1:49.

16 Boss, *Mary*, p.107.

17 Bernard Leeming, S.J., *Principles of Sacramental Theology*, Longmans, 1956, p.568.

18 Sermo. 45. Cited in Gambero Luigi, *Mary in the Middle Ages*, Ignatius Press, 2005, p.96.

19 Matthew 27:51.

20 Hebrews 10:19-20.

21 2 Samuel 6:9-11, 16.

22 1 Kings 8:10.

23 Luke 1:39-45.

24 2 Maccabees 2:4-9.

25 Revelation 11:19 - 12:17.

26 Athanasius, *Homily of the Papyrus of Turin, 71: 216.*

27 *Catechism of the Catholic Church*, 2676, Geoffrey Chapman, 1994, p.570.

28 Rowan Williams, *Ponder These Things, Praying with Ikons of the Virgin*, Canterbury Press, 2002, pp.63, 67.

29 Desiderius Erasmus, *Pilgrimages to Saint Mary of Walsingham and Saint Thomas of Canterbury*, J.G. Nichols (trans.) Westminster, 1849, pp.37, 41.

30 Sarah Boss, *Empress and Handmaid*, Cassell, 2000, p.142.

31 Boss, *Empress*, p.145.

32 Cited in Mary Clayton, *The Cult of the Virgin Mary in Anglo-Saxon England*, Cambridge University Press, 1990, pp.48–9.

33 Boss, *Empress*, pp.1-2.

34 Boss, *Empress*, p.4.

35 2 Peter 1:4.

36 Prayer in the Roman Mass, at the mingling of water and wine in the chalice.

7. PILGRIMAGE AND PILGRIMS [pages 107-126]

1 Diana Webb, *Pilgrimage in Medieval England*, Hambledon, 2000, p.27.

2 Eamon Duffy, *The Stripping of the Altars*, Yale University Press, 1992, pp.198-199.

3 Webb, *Pilgrimage*, p.40.

4 Appendix 2, v. 15.

5 Webb, *Pilgrimage*, p.37.

6 Webb, *Pilgrimage*, p.32.

7 Webb, *Pilgrimage* p.182.

8 Nigel Saul, *Richard II*, Yale University Press, 1999, p.309.

9 Duffy, *The Stripping of the Altars*, p.197.

10 L.E. Whatmore, *Highway to Walsingham*, The Pilgrim Bureau, 1973, p.38.

11 Eamon Duffy, *Dynamics of Pilgrimage in Late Medieval England,* in Colin Morris and Peter Roberts (eds.), *Pilgrimage: The English Experience from Becket to Bunyan*, Cambridge University Press, 2002, p.166.

12 Susan Signe Morrison, *Women Pilgrims in Late Medieval England*, Routledge, 2000, p.2.

13 Morrison, *Women Pilgrims,* p.57.

14 Appendix 3. See Leonard Whatmore, *Highway to Walsingham*, The Pilgrim Bureau, 1973, pp.8-9.

15 Morrison, *Women Pilgrims*, pp.27ff.

16 1 Peter 4:8.

17 Webb, *Pilgrimage*, p.217.

18 Morrison, *Women Pilgrims*, pp.54–55.

19 Webb, *Pilgrimage*, p.49.

20 Webb, *Pilgrimage*, pp.195ff.

21 Brian Spencer, *Pilgrim Souvenirs and Secular Badges*, Boydell Press, 2010, p.135.

22 Webb, *Pilgrimage*, p.236.

23 J.C. Dickinson, *The Shrine of Our Lady of Walsingham*, Cambridge University Press, 1956, p.26.

24 Webb, *Pilgrimage*, p.231.

25 Webb, *Pilgrimage*, p.200.

26 Sarah Salih, *Two Travellers' Tales*, in Christopher Harper-Bill, (ed.), *Medieval East Anglia*, Woodbridge: Boydell, 2005, p.319.

27 Howard Fears, *An Approach to a History of Little Walsingham: Vol. I, Early Days*, Walsingham, 2004, p.90.

28 Dickinson, *The Shrine*, p.46.

29 S. Rosso, *Pellegrinaggi*, cited in Luigi Gambero, *Mary in the Middle Ages*, Ignatius, 2000, p.106.

30 Whatmore, *Highway*, p.2.

31 Webb, *Pilgrimage,* p.189.

32 Crucified Christ in a Colobium, WA1908.233, The Ashmolean Museum, Oxford.

33 Webb, *Pilgrimage*, p.224.

34 Whatmore, *Highway*, p.51.

35 Whatmore, *Highway*, p.2.

36 Whatmore, *Highway*, p.72.

37 E. Waterton, *Pietas Mariana Britannica: A History of English Devotion to the Most Blessed Virgin Mary, Mother of God* (1879), Kessinger Publishing, 2007, p.97.

38 P. Richards, *The Red Mount Chapel, King's Lynn*, in *Walsingham: Pilgrimage and History*, R.C. National Shrine, 1999, p.133.

39 See Howard Fears and Peter Rollings, *The Medieval Inns of Walsingham*, Walsingham, 2000.

40 Webb, *Pilgrimage*, p.225.

41 Spencer, *Pilgrim Souvenirs and Secular Badges*, p.135.

42 Brian Spencer, *Pilgrim Souvenirs* and *Medieval Pilgrim Badges from Norfolk*, Norfolk Museums Service, 1980.

43 Spencer, *Pilgrim Souvenirs and Secular Badges*, p.136.

44 S. Margeson, *Norwich Households: Medieval and Post Medieval Finds,* East Anglian Archeol. Rep. 58, 1993, pp.6-8.

45 Spencer, *Pilgrim Souvenirs and Secular Badges*, p.137.

46 Spencer, *Pilgrim Souvenirs* and *Medieval Pilgrim Badges from Norfolk*, p.14.

47 Spencer, *Pilgrim Souvenirs* and *Medieval Pilgrim Badges from Norfolk*, p.11.

48 Dickinson, *The Shrine*, p.107.

49 Desiderius Erasmus, *Pilgrimages to Saint Mary of Walsingham and Saint Thomas of Canterbury*, J.G. Nichols (trans.), Westminster, 1849, pp.17-18.

50 Spencer, *Pilgrim Souvenirs and Secular Badges*, p.148.

51 Spencer, *Pilgrim Souvenirs* and *Medieval Pilgrim Badges from Norfolk*, p.16.

52 Spencer, *Pilgrim Souvenirs* and *Medieval Pilgrim Badges from Norfolk*, p.16.

53 Fears, *Early Days*, p.91.

54 Christopher Harper-Bill, *The Foundation and Later History of the Medieval Shrine*, in *Walsingham: Pilgrimage and History*, Centenary Historical Conference, R.C. National Shrine, 1999, p.74.

55 Fears *Early Days*, p.91.

56 Dickinson, *The Shrine*, pp.46-47.

8. ROYAL PATRONAGE [pages 127-138]

1 See 1 Timothy 2:1-2 and Romans 13:1-7.

2 Gregory the Great, *Homilies on the Book of Ezekiel, I, II.* Cited in *The Divine Office*, Office of Readings, September 3.

3 N. Vincent, *The Court of Henry II*, in Christopher Harper-Bill & Nicholas Vincent (eds.), *Henry II: New Interpretations*, 2007, The Boydell Press, p.328.

4 Diana Webb, *Pilgrimage in Medieval England*, Hambledon, 2000, p.114.

5 Webb, *Pilgrimage*, p.25.

6 Vincent, *The Court of Henry II*, p.307.

7 J.C. Dickinson *The Shrine of Our Lady of Walsingham*, Cambridge University Press, 1956, p.19.

8 Webb, *Pilgrimage*, pp.89-90.

9 Vincent, *The Court of Henry II*, p.328.

10 Webb, *Pilgrimage*, p.119.

11 Webb, *Pilgrimage*, p.121.

12 Dickinson, *The Shrine*, p.20.

13 Howard Fears, *An Approach to a History of Little Walsingham: Vol. I, Early Days*, Walsingham, 2004, p.89.

14 Dickinson, *The Shrine*, pp.39-40.

15 Webb, *Pilgrimage*, p.131.

16 Webb, *Pilgrimage*, p.133.

17 Nigel Saul, *Richard II*, Yale University Press, 1999, p.309.

18 Saul, *Richard II*, p.308.

19 Saul, *Richard II*, p.312.

20 Kate Parker, *A Little Local Difficulty: Lynn and the Lancastrian Usurpation*, in Christopher Harper-Bill (ed.), *Medieval East Anglia*, The Boydell Press, 2005, p.125.

21 Cited in Antonia Fraser (ed.), *The Lives of the Kings and Queens of England*, Weidenfield and Nicholson, 1975, p.124

22 Webb, *Pilgrimage*, pp.136-137.

23 Howard Fears, *An Intimate History of Little Walsingham during 1,000 Years*, Walsingham, 2007, p.30.

24 Carole Hill, *Leave My Virginity Alone,* in Christopher Harper-Bill (ed.), *Medieval East Anglia*, Boydell Press, 2005, p.240.

25 M.R. James, *Henry VI, a reprint of John Blacman's Memoir*, Cambridge University Press, 1919, p.34.

26 James, *Henry VI*, p.50.

27 Webb, *Pilgrimage*, p.138.

28 Dickinson, *The Shrine*, pp.34-35.

29 Brian Spencer, *Pilgrim Souvenirs and Secular Badges*, The Stationery Office, 1998, p.135.

30 *Anglica Historia*, ed. D. Hay, Camden Society LXXIV (1950), 21. Cited in Dickinson, *The Shrine*, pp.41-42.

31 Webb, *Pilgrimage*, p.139.

32 Spelman, *English Works*, 2nd edn., 1727, ii, 149.

33 Cited in Dickinson, *The Shrine*, p.44.

34 Dickinson, *The Shrine*, p.43.

35 James Gairdner (ed.), *Letters and Papers, Foreign and Domestic, Henry VIII,* Vol. 13, Part 2, (August-December 1538), 1893.

9. DESTRUCTION [pages 139-165]

1 Diana Webb, *Pilgrimage in Medieval England*, Hambledon, 2000, p.239.

2 Thomas à Kempis, *The Imitation of Christ*, Bk. IV, 1, 9, Ronald Knox and Michael Oakley (transl.), Burns & Oates, 1960, p.184.

3 Webb, *Pilgrimage,* p.234.

4 William Langland, *Piers Plowman: A New Translation of the B-text,* A.V. C. Schmidt, Oxford University Press, 2001, p.2.

5 Langland, *Piers Plowman*, p.50.

6 Susan Signe Morrison, *Women Pilgrims in Late Medieval England*, Routledge, 2000, p.112.

7 Cited in Morrison, *Women Pilgrims*, p.32.

8 Cited in Miri Rubin, *Mother of God, A History of the Virgin Mary*, Allen Lane, 2009, p.300.

9 Erasmus, *Pilgrimages to Saint Mary*, pp.21-22.

10 Eamon Duffy, *Saints and Sinners*, Yale University Press, 2006, p.198.

11 Richard Rex, *The Lollards*, Palgrave, 2002, p.148.

12 Cited Desiderius Erasmus, *Pilgrimages to Saint Mary of Walsingham and Saint Thomas of Canterbury*, J.G. Nichols (trans.), Westminster, 1849, pp.188-189.

13 Cited in Whatmore, *Highway to Walsingham*, p.13.

14 Cited in Webb, *Pilgrimage*, p.248.

15 J.C. Dickinson, *The Shrine of Our Lady of Walsingham*, Cambridge University Press, 1956, p.27.

16 Margaret Aston, *Lollards and Reformers*, Continuum, 1984, p.152.

17 Webb, *Pilgrimage*, p.141.

18 Rex, *The Lollards*, p.143.

19 Webb, *Pilgrimage*, p.245.

20 Webb, *Pilgrimage*, p.254.

21 Webb, *Pilgrimage*, pp.244-245.

22 Richard Rex, *Henry VIII and the English Reformation*, Macmillan, 1993, p.85.

23 Eamon Duffy, *The Stripping of the Altars, Traditional Religion in England c.1400-c.1580*, Yale University Press, *1992,* p.191.

24 Dickinson, *The Shrine of Our Lady of Walsingham*, p.59.

25 At the Wednesday Audience in St Peter's Square, 19 November 2008.

26 See James D. G. Dunn, *The New Perspective on Paul*, Eerdmans, 2007.

27 Peter Ackroyd, *The Life of Thomas More*, Chatto & Windus, 1998, p.222.

28 Henry VIII, *Defence of the Seven Sacraments*, Raymond de Souza (ed.), St Gabriel Communications, 2007, p.22.

29 Ackroyd, *The Life of Thomas More*, p.223.

30 Nigel Saul, *Richard II*, Yale University Press, 1999, p.301.

31 Leviticus 20:21 cf. Deuteronomy 25:5.

32 Duffy, *Saints and Sinners*, p.208.

33 Duffy, *Saints and Sinners*, p.211.

34 Dickinson, *The Shrine of Our Lady of Walsingham*, pp.49-50.

35 Philip Hughes, *The Reformation*, Burns & Oates, 1960, p.178.

36 Rex, *Henry and the English Reformation*, p.58.

37 Cited in Martin Gillett, *Walsingham, The History of a Famous Shrine*, Burns Oates & Washbourne, 1946, p.59.

38 T. H. Swales, *Opposition to the Suppression of the Norfolk Monasteries; Expressions of Discontent; The Walsingham Conspiracy*, Norfolk Archeology, vol. 34, 1965, p.254.

39 Swales, *Opposition to the Suppression of the Norfolk Monasteries*, p.255.

40 Dickinson, *The Shrine of Our Lady of Walsingham*, p.63.

41 C.E. Moreton, *The Walsingham Conspiracy of 1537*, Institute of Historical Research, Vol. 63, Feb. 1990, p.29.

42 Swales, *Opposition to the Suppression of the Norfolk Monasteries*, p.255.

43 Dickinson, *The Shrine of Our Lady of Walsingham*, p.63.

44 Swales, *Opposition to the Suppression of the Norfolk Monasteries*, p.258.

45 Fears, *An Intimate History of Little Walsingham*, Walsingham, 2007, p.55.

46 Swales, *Opposition to the Suppression of the Norfolk Monasteries*, p.258.

47 Swales, *Opposition to the Suppression of the Norfolk Monasteries*, p.261.

48 Swales, *Opposition to the Suppression of the Norfolk Monasteries*, p.260.

49 Eamon Duffy, *The Stripping of the Altars*, 1992, pp.385–386.

50 Gillett, *Walsingham, The History of a Famous Shrine*, p.63.

51 Swales, *Opposition to the Suppression of the Norfolk Monasteries*, p.259.

52 Webb, *Pilgrimage*, p.257.

53 Webb *Pilgrimage*, p.258.

54 Gillett, *Walsingham, The History of a Famous Shrine*, p.65.

55 Cited in Duffy, *The Stripping of the Altars*, p.387.

56 Cited in Duffy, *The Stripping of the Altars*, p.407.

57 Cited in Duffy, *The Stripping of the Altars*, pp.409–410.

58 Dickinson, *The Shrine of Our Lady of Walsingham*, p.65.

59 Cited in Morrison, *Women Pilgrims*, p.6.

60 Dickinson, *The Shrine of Our Lady of Walsingham*, p.66.

61 Rex *Henry VIII*, pp.66-67.

62 Baskerville G., *Married Clergy and Pensioned Religious in Norwich Diocese, 1555*, Part II, The English Historical Review, 1933, p.119.

63 Howard Fears, *An Approach to a History of Little Walsingham: Vol I, Early Days*, Walsingham, 2004, p.71.

64 Henry Spelman, *History and Fate of Sacrilege*, London, 1698, p.247.

65 Rex *Henry VIII*, p.101.

66 Cited in Rubin, *Mother of God*, p.373.

67 Rex, *Henry VIII*, pp.173-175.

68 2 Kings 23:1-20.

69 1 Kings 22:47.

70 2 Kings 12:18.

71 See Rex, *Henry VIII*, p.174. And Morison, *An Invective against the great and detestable vice, treason*, London 1539. And Tunstall C., *A Letter to Reginald Pole*, London, 1560.

72 The Psalter of Henry VIII, Royal MS 2 A XVI, f. 63v, in the British Library.

73 *The Parliamentary History of England*, Vol. I, Hansard, 1806, p.644.

74 Cited in A. & J. Gurney, *Walsingham A Place of Pilgrimage for 700 years*, Walsingham Estate Company, 1965, p.3.

75 The original is in the PRO, Royal Wills, E.23, Vol. IV, Pt. 1, 1-17. The most available printed version is in Thomas Rymer, *Foedera*, London, 1726-35, XV, pp.110-17.

10. REMEMBERED WITH DEVOTION [pages 166-186]

1 William Richards, *The History of Lynn, Vol. II*, Baldwin, Paternoster Row, 1812, p.690.

2 Zillah Dovey, *An Elizabethan Progress, The Queen's Journey into East Anglia, 1578*, Sutton Publishing, 1999, pp.99–101.

3 James Gairdner and R. H. Brodie (ed.), *Letters and Papers, Foreign and Domestic, Henry VIII*, Volume 15, No. 86, (20 January 1540), 1896.

4   G. Baskerville, *Married Clergy and Pensioned Religious in Norwich Diocese, 1555*, Part II, The English Historical Review, 1933, p.13.

5   Howard Fears, *An Intimate History of Little Walsingham during 1,000 Years*, Walsingham, 2007, p.65.

6   Eamon Duffy, *The Stripping of the Altars*, Yale University Press, 1992, p.526.

7   Fears, *An Intimate History*, pp.65-66.

8   Duffy, *The Stripping of the Altars*, p.566.

9   Fears, *An Intimate History*, p.71.

10 Fears, *An Intimate History*, p.70.

11 Frank Devany, unpublished *Thesis on Recusancy*, in Walsingham R.C. Archives, p.155.

12 Dovey, *An Elizabethan Progress*, p.91.

13 Tim Matthews, *Catholic Norfolk*, Wells-next-the-Sea, 2005, p.59.

14 Dovey, *An Elizabethan Progress* pp.54 and 89.

15 F. Blomefield and C. Parkin, *An Essay Towards a Topographical History of the County of Norfolk*, Vol. IX, London, 1808, pp.274 and 281.

16 Leonard Whatmore, *Highway to Walsingham*, The Pilgrim Bureau, 1973, pp.108-109.

17 Modernised version in Peter Rollings, *Walsingham England's Nazareth*, R.C. National Shrine, 1998, pp.48-49.

18 William M. McLoughlin, *Remembrance of the Shrine 1538-1897*, in *Walsingham: Pilgrimage and History*, 1998, R.C. National Shrine, p.88.

19 McLoughlin, *Remembrance of the Shrine*, p.88.

20 Catholic Record Society, III, pp.105ff.

21 In an email to the author.

22 Michael Rear, *One Step More*, Catholic League and Church Literature Association, 1987, p.23.

23 *English Hymnal* No. 217.

24 See A.M. Allchin, Our *Lady in Seventeenth-century Anglican Devotion and Theology*, in E.L. Mascall and H.S. Box, *The Blessed Virgin Mary: Essays by Anglican Writers*, Darton, Longman & Todd, 1963, p.53.

25 Horace Keast, *Our Lady in England*, Society of Mary, 1984, p.36.

26 Zinnia Knapman, *A Reappraisal of Percy's Editing*, Folk Music Journal, Vol. 5, No. 2, 1986, p.202.

27 See Philip Edwards, *Pilgrimage and Literary Tradition*, Cambridge University Press, 2005, p.36.

28 Thomas Percy, *Reliques of Ancient English Poetry, Vol. 1*, BiblioLife, 2009, p.346.

29 Percy, *Reliques of Ancient English Poetry*, p.112.

30 Cited in Whatmore, *Highway to Walsingham*, pp.12-13.

31 in the collection of keyboard pieces known as *The Fitzwilliam Virginal Book*, Vol. I, Fuller Maitland/Barclay Squire edition.

32 Cited in Whatmore, *Highway to Walsingham*, p.17.

33 *Letter to a Roman Catholic*, July 18, 1749, in *The Works of the Rev. John Wesley*, Volume 15, Joseph Benson, London, 1812, p.112.

34 The Rosary is preserved amongst artefacts of John Wesley at The Leys School, Cambridge.

35 J. Lee Warner, *Walsingham Priory*, Archeological Journal, XIII, 1856, pp.115-34.

36 Blomefield, *An Essay towards a Topographical History*, Vol. VIII, Kings Lynn, 1775, p.839.

37 Frederick Hibgame, *A Great Gothic Fane: a Retrospective of Catholicity in Norwich*, 1913,

38 Cited in McLoughlin, *Remembrance of the Shrine,* pp.92-93.

39 Mary Heimann, *Catholic Devotion in Victorian England*, Oxford University Press, 1995, p.9.

40 Heimann, *Catholic Devotion in Victorian England*, pp.170-171.

41 Edmund Waterton, *Pietas Mariana Britannica: A History of English Devotion to the Most Blessed Virgin Mary, Mother of God*, Kessinger Publishing, 2007.

42 T.E. Bridgett, *Our Lady's Dowry, How England gained that Title*, 3rd edn., Burns & Oates, p.iii.

43 John Henry Newman, *Apologia Pro Vita Sua*, Fontana, 1959, p.114.

44 Newman, *Apologia*, p.222.

45 Newman, *The Reverence Due to the Virgin Mary*, in P. Boyce (ed.), *Mary, The Virgin Mary in the Life and Writings of John Henry Newman*, Gracewing, 2001, p.120.

46 Pope Paul VI, *Marialis Cultus*, para. 32.

47 Peter Cobb, *The Development of Modern Day Pilgrimage*, in *Walsingham: Pilgrimage and History*, R.C. National Shrine, 1999, p.157.

48 Kate Summerscale, *The Suspicions of Mr Whicher*, Bloomsbury, 2009.

49 *The Mariological Lectures of Fr John Milburn*, The Society of Mary, 1998, p.2.

11. RESTORATION [pages 187-242]

1 *King's Lynn*, Archives in the Church of the Annunciation, King's Lynn, p.88.

2 *King's Lynn*, p.91.

3 Philip Fletcher, *Recollections of a Ransomer*, Sands & Co., 1928, p.161.

4 Michael Yelton, *Alfred Hope Patten and the Shrine of Our Lady of Walsingham*, Canterbury Press, 2006, p.232.

5 Fletcher, *Recollections of a Ransomer*, p.85.

6 The Tablet, 12 June 1897.

7 Letter from Fr Wrigglesworth to Bishop Riddell, 11 December 1896, R.C. Archives Document 5.

8 Robin Gard, *The 1897 Walsingham Revival as Reported in the Catholic Press*, in *Walsingham 1062-1538, 1897-1997 A Centenary Celebration*, Guild of Our Lady of Ransom, 1998, p.77.

9 Gard, *The 1897 Walsingham Revival*, pp.80-81.

10 Cited in Martin Gillett, *Shrines of Our Lady in England and Wales*, London, 1956, p.174.

11 William Strange, *The Shrine of Our Lady of Walsingham*, Lown and Capps of King's Lynn, 1925, pp.16-17.

12 Ethel M. Hostler, *Charlotte Boyd, Some Notes on Her Life*, The Catholic League, 1996, p.2.

13 R.C. Shrine Archives, Documents (Early Letters) 1890-1911, 1.

14 R.C. Shrine Archives, Document 2.

15 R.C. Shrine Archives, Document 3.

16 Letter from Bishop Riddell to Miss Boyd, 13 August 1895, Downside Abbey Archives.

17 R.C. Shrine Archives, Document 9.

18 R.C. Shrine Archives, Document 11.

19 R.C. Shrine Archives, Document 12.

20 R.C. Shrine Archives, Document 17.

21 Letter from Launcelot Lee-Warner to Mr Baxter, 2 February 1907, R.C. Shrine Archives, Document 48c.

22 Letter from Launcelot Lee-Warner to Mr Baxter, 11 October 1907, R.C. Shrine Archives, Document 48e.

23 Letter from Miss Boyd to Abbot Ford, 2 June 1903, R.C. Archives, Document C (17).

24 Dom Aidan Bellenger OSB, *Walsingham: Downside and the Benedictines,* in *Walsingham: Pilgrimage and History*, p.125.

25 R.C. Shrine Archives, Document 18.

26 Letter from Bishop Riddell to Mr Baxter, 20 September 1903, R.C. Archives, Document 21.

27 Letter from Bishop Riddell to Mr Baxter, 22 October 1904, R.C. Archives, Document 42.

28 Letter from Abbot Chapman to Fr Russell, 4 August 1929, R.C. Archives, Document 64.

29 Hostler, *Charlotte Boyd*, p.11.

30 Hostler, *Charlotte Boyd*, p.11.

31 Letter from Cardinal Bourne to Fr Russell, 29 November 1928, R.C. Archives, Document 62.

32 The Ransomer, Vol. VI, January 1935.

33 Letter from Canon Squirrel to the Bishop of Northampton, 23 May 1947, R.C. Archives.

34 Claude Fisher, *Walsingham Lives On*, Catholic Truth Society, 1979, p.64.

35 Claude Fisher, *Walsingham, A Place of Pilgrimage for All People*, The Salutation Press, 1983, p.89. See also, Claude Fisher, *Walsingham Lives On*, p.37.

36 Dom Aidan Bellenger OSB, *Downside*, p.125.

37 Bruno Scott James, *Asking for Trouble*, London, 1962, p.54.

38 Page 252.

39 James, *Asking for Trouble*, p.122.

40 James, *Asking for Trouble*, p.124.

41 James, *Asking for Trouble*, p.123.

42 Yelton, *Alfred Hope Patten and the Shrine of Our Lady of Walsingham*, back cover.

43 See page 241.

44 Yelton, *Alfred Hope Patten and the Shrine of Our Lady of Walsingham*, p.17.

45 The Manifesto is obtainable from The Anglo-Catholic History Society.

46 Cited in Yelton, *Alfred Hope Patten and the Shrine of Our Lady of Walsingham*, p.84.

47 *Our Lady's Mirror*, Spring 1943.

48 Geoffrey Curtis, *Paul Couturier and Unity in Christ*, SCM, 1964, p.163.

49 Anglican-Roman Catholic International Commission, *The Final Report*, CTS/SPCK, 1982, p.113.

50 The Anglican-Roman Catholic International Commission, *Mary, Grace and Hope in Christ*, Morehouse, 2005.

51 Papers of Peter Cobb, Anglican Shrine Archives.

52 *Our Lady's Mirror*, Autumn 1958 – Winter 1959, p.16.

53 Michael Yelton, *Anglican Papalism*, Canterbury Press, 2008, p.33.

54 Letter from the Bishop of Norwich to Hope Patten, 24 February 1928, Anglican Shrine Archives.

55 Cited in Yelton, *Alfred Hope Patten and the Shrine of Our Lady of Walsingham*, p.74.

56 Colin Stephenson, *Walsingham Way*, Darton, Longman & Todd, 1970, p.153.

57 Letter from the Bishop of Norwich to Hope Patten, 28 May 1931, Anglican Shrine Archives.

58 Cited in Yelton, *Alfred Hope Patten and the Shrine of Our Lady of Walsingham*, pp.87-88.

59 Hope Patten, *An Account of Some Recent Discoveries at the Shrine of Our Lady of Walsingham, Norfolk.*

60 See Howard Fears, *An Approach to a History of Walsingham, Vol. I, Early Days,* Walsingham, 2004, pp.66-67.

61 John Elsner, *Replicating Palestine and Reversing the Reformation*, Journal of the History of Collections, 1997, Oxford University Press, p.126.

62 Holy House Leaflet No. 1.

63 The Latin and English translation is found on the Walsingham Anglican Archives website: http://www.walsinghamanglicanarchives.org.uk/1931stoneinscription.htm

64 Yelton, *Alfred Hope Patten and the Shrine of Our Lady of Walsingham*, p.97.

65 Letter from the Bishop of Norwich to Hope Patten, 5 August 1931, in the Anglican Shrine Archives.

66 Letter from Hope Patten to the Bishop of Norwich, 7 August 1931, in the Anglican Shrine Archives.

67 Letter from Hope Patten to the Bishop of Norwich, 12 October 1931, in the Anglican Shrine Archives.

68 Letter from the Bishop of Norwich to Hope Patten, 13 October 1931, in the Anglican Shrine Archives.

69 Letter from the Bishop of Norwich to Hope Patten, 16 May 1938, in the Anglican Shrine Archives.

70 Yelton, *Anglican Papalism*, p.27.

71 William Garratt, *Loreto the New Nazareth and its Centenary Jubilee*, Art and Book Company, 1895.

72 The Pilgrim's Manual, 1949, pp.65-66.

73 Garratt, *Loreto, the New Nazareth and its Centenary Jubilee*, p.279.

74 *Our Lady's Mirror*, Autumn 1958 – Winter 1959, p.16.

75 Peter Cobb, *The Development of Modern-Day Pilgrimage*, in *Walsingham: Pilgrimage and History*, R.C. Shrine, 1999, p.161.

76 James, *Asking for Trouble*, p.121.

77 *Logbook*, R.C. Archives, p.4.

78 Fisher, *Walsingham Lives On*, p.62.

79 Ian Bradley, *Pilgrimage, A Spiritual and Cultural Journey*, Lion, 2009, p.19.

80 Luke 2:19.

12. ANNUNCIATION AND INCARNATION [pages 243-256]

1 Luke 11:27-28.
2 Luke 8:21.
3 Luke 18:29.
4 Letter from the Bishop of Norwich to Hope Patten, 25 November 1952, in the Anglican Shrine Archives.
5 Colin Stephenson, *Walsingham Way*, Darton, Longman & Todd, 1970, pp.176-177.
6 Cited in Claude Fisher, *Walsingham Lives On*, Catholic Truth Society, 1979, p.43.
7 Cited in Claude Fisher, *Walsingham, A Place of Pilgrimage for All People*, The Salutation Press, 1983, p.133.
8 Craig Larkin S.M., *A Certain Way*, Center for Marist Studies, 1995, p.41.
9 Larkin, A Certain Way, p.50.
10 Elizabeth Ruth Obbard, *The History and Spirituality of Walsingham*, Canterbury Press, 1997, p.57.
11 Peter Anson, *The Call of the Cloister*, SPCK, 1964, p.203.
12 Bruno Scott James, *Asking for Trouble*, William Clowes, 1962, p.141.
13 Letter from the Fr Bruno Scott James to Bishop Parker, 14 December 1942, in the R.C. Shrine Archives, Document 398.
14 James, *Asking for Trouble*, p.156.
15 *The Times*, 20 March 1984.
16 *Loreto, The Shrine of the Holy House*, September/November 1979, p.73.
17 *Our Lady's Mirror*, Autumn Number 1953.

13. UNITY IN WALSINGHAM [PAGES 257-265]

1 Michael Yelton, *Anglican Papalism*, Canterbury Press, 2008, p.4.
2 Letter from Hope Patten to Abbot Butler, 8 August 1925, in Downside Abbey Archives (Walsingham Files).
3 Letter from the Abbot of Downside to Hope Patten, 12 August 1925, in the Anglican Shrine Archives.
4 Letter from Dom Benedict Steuart to Hope Patten, 20 December 1932, in the Anglican Shrine Archives.
5 James, Bruno Scott, *Asking for Trouble*, William Clowes, 1962, pp.50-51, 53.
6 Colin Stephenson, *Walsingham* Way, Darton, Longman & Todd, 1979, p.245.
7 *Ecumenical Society of the Blessed Virgin Mary*, online.
8 Peter Cobb (ed.), *Walsingham*, White Tree Books, 1990, pp.154-155.
9 Peter Cobb (ed.), *Walsingham*, p.85.
10 Cited in Claude Fisher, *Walsingham, A Place of Pilgrimage for All People*, The Salutation Press, 1983, p.67.
11 Cited in Claude Fisher, *Walsingham, A Place of Pilgrimage for All People*, pp.16-17.

12 Peter Rollings, *Walsingham, England's Nazareth*, R.C. National Shrine, 1998, pp.67-68.

13 In the R.C. Shrine Archives.

14 See Timothy McDonald, *Walsingham: A Year of Celebration*, R.C. National Shrine Walsingham, 1999.

15 *Walsingham: Pilgrimage and History, Papers presented at the Centenary Historical Conference,* R.C. National Shrine, 1999.

16 Cited in McDonald, *Walsingham: A Year of Celebration*, p.160.

17 Philip North and J. North (eds.), *Sacred Space, House of God and Gate of Heaven*, Continuum, 2007.

18 *Our Lady's Mirror*, Spring 1945.

14. THE GLORIOUS VISION [pages 266-291]

1 Sarah Boss, *Empress and Handmaid*, Cassell, 2000, p.30.

2 Vatican Council II, *Lumen Gentium*, para 67, in The *Conciliar and Post Conciliar Documents*, Austin Flannery (ed.), Dominican Publications, 1992, p.422.

3 Boss, *Empress and Handmaid*, pp.30-31.

4 Michael Tavinor, *Sacred Space and Built Environment*, in *Sacred Space*, Philip North and John North, (eds.), Continuum, 2007, pp.29-31.

5 Reported in the Catholic Herald, 2 October 2009.

6 Vatican Council II, *Sacrosanctum Concilium*, para. 122-124, in *The Conciliar and Post Conciliar Documents*, pp.34-35.

7 Page 22.

8 Pope Benedict XVI, *Beauty Is a Privileged Way to Approach the Mystery of God*, General Audience, Wednesday 18 November 2009.

9 Pope John Paul II, *The Pilgrimage in the Great Jubilee*, April 11, 1998, para. 4.

10 Pope John Paul II, *The Pilgrimage in the Great Jubilee*, para. 41.

11 Charles Saglio, *Be Catholic by being Catholic*, The Tablet, 28 August 2010, p.16.

12 Martin Warner, *The Habit of Holiness*, Geoffrey Chapman, 2004, p.14.

13 Luke 1:46-55.

14 *Walsingham Pilgrim Handbook*, R.C. National Shrine, 1992, p.39.

15 *The Walsingham Pilgrim Manual*, Walsingham College Trust Association, 2010, p.15.

16 *Church Times* Issue 7524, 25 May, 2007.

17 Eamon Duffy, *Dynamics of Pilgrimage in Late Medieval England*, pp.174-175, in C. Morris & P. Roberts, *Pilgrimage, The English Experience from Becket to Bunyan*, Cambridge University Press, 2002.

18 Ian Bradley, *Pilgrimage: A Spiritual and Cultural History*, Lion, 2009.

19 *Papal Message for the Pilgrimages and Shrines Conference in Santiago de Compostela, Spain,* Vatican City, September 27, 2010.

20 John 4:5-26.

21 John 7:38.

22 John 10:10.

23 Pontifical Council for the Pastoral Care of Migrants and Itinerant People, *The Shrine*, Vatican City, 8 May 1999, para. 10.

24 Pontifical Council for the Pastoral Care of Migrants and Itinerant People, *The Shrine*, para. 12.

25 Boss, *Empress and Handmaid*, p.7.

26 Boss, *Empress and Handmaid*, p.23.

27 *Walsingham Review*, No 144, Assumptiontide 2009, p.3.

28 Pope Benedict XVI, *Caritas in Veritate*, para. 48.

29 Pope John Paul II, *The Pilgrimage in the Great Jubilee*, para. 41.

30 Gerard Manley Hopkins, *Poems and Praise*, W. H. Gardner (ed.), 1953, pp.54-58. Cited in Boss, *Empress and Handmaid*, p.22.

31 *Catechism of the Catholic Church* 1667 – 1679.

32 Pontifical Council for Culture, *Jesus Christ, the Bearer of the Water of Life. A Christian Reflection of the 'New Age'*, Catholic Truth Society, 2003, p.11.

33 Bishop Mervyn Stockwood, Preface to *England's Nazareth*, published by the Guardians, 1969 edition.

34 Pope John Paul II, *The Pilgrimage in the Great Jubilee*, para. 40.

35 Jeremy Sheehy, *Sacred Space and the Incarnation*, in Philip North and John North (eds.), *Sacred Space*, p.14.

36 Sheehy, *Sacred Space and the Incarnation*, p.16.

37 Acts 17: 16-31.

38 Pontifical Council for the Pastoral Care of Migrants and Itinerant People, *The Shrine*, para. 10.

39 Cited in Craig Larkin S.M., *A Certain Way, An Exploration of Marist Spirituality*, Rome Center for Marist Studies, 1995, p.81.

40 Ian Ker, *The New Movements*, Catholic Truth Society, 2001, p.4.

41 Pope Benedict XVI, *Meeting with the Ecclesial Movements and New Communities*, St Peter's Square, 3 June 2006.

42 Preface of Holy Men and Women II in the Roman Mass.

43 Cited in Bradley, *Pilgrimage*, p.14.

44 Pope John Paul II, *The Pilgrimage in the Great Jubilee*, para. 39.

45 *Our Lady's Mirror*, Summer 1953, p.13.

46 *Souvenir Programme of the Golden Jubilee of the Restoration*, R.C. Shrine, 1984, p.32.

47 Peter Cobb, *The Development of Modern Day Pilgrimage*, in *Walsingham: Pilgrimage and History*, R.C. National Shrine, 1999, p.162-163.

48 *Welcome to Evening Prayer*, Walsingham College Trust.

49 Luke 1:37.

APPENDIX 1 [pages 292-299]

1   University Library, Cambridge, MS. Ii. vi. 2, folio, 71r.

2   J.C. Dickinson, *The Shrine of Our Lady of Walsingham*, Cambridge University Press, 1956, p.7.

3   Christopher Harper-Bill, *The Foundation and Later History of the medieval Shrine*, in *Walsingham: Pilgrimage and History*, Centenary Historical Conference, R.C. National Shrine, 1999, p.64.

4   M. Biddle, H. T. Lambrick and J. N. L. Myres, *The Early History of Abingdon, Berkshire, and its Abbey* and G. Lambrick, *The Foundation-Traditions of the Abbey*, Medieval Archaeology, Vol. 12, 1968.

5   Blomefield and C. Parkin, *An Essay Towards a Topographical History of the County of Norfolk*, Vol. IX, London, 1808, pp.267-282.

6   Domesday Book, Ann Williams (ed.), Penguin Books, 1992, p.1167.

7   Domesday Book, p.1055.

8   At the height of his power he held estates in Wessex, Sussex, Berkshire, Dorset, Wiltshire, Surrey, Cornwall, Devon, Somerset Herefordshire, Gloucestershire, Lincolnshire, Hampshire, Essex East Anglia, Yorkshire, Mercia, the East Midlands and Northumberland. See, Frank Barlow, *The Godwins*, Longman, 2002, pp.55, 61.

9   Tim Pestell, *Landscapes of Monastic Foundation. The Establishment of Religious Houses in East Anglia, c.650 – 1200*, Boydell Press, 2004, p.146.

10 British Library MS Cotton Collection, Nero E vii folio 8r. I am most grateful to Keith Syed for his transcription and translation.

11 Jonathan Riley-Smith, The *First Crusade and the Idea of Crusading*, Philadelphia: University of Pennsylvania Press, 1991, pp.4 and 120.

12 Arcisse de Caumont, *Statistique monumentale de l'arrondissement de Pont-l'Évêque* (1859), Les Éditions de la Grande Fontaine, rééd, 1996, p.104.

13 L.C. Lloyd, *The Origins of some Anglo-Norman Families*, The Harleian Society, 1951, p. 41.

14 Wace's *Roman de Rou*, (ed.) Glyn Burgess, The Boydell Press, 2004, p.188.

15 Wace's *Roman de Rou*, p.lii

16 William Dugdale, *Monasticon Anglicanum*, Vol. III, 1821, Charter VI, p.348.

17 Dugdale, *Monasticon Anglicanum*, Vol. III, 1821, Charter I, p.346

18 Dugdale, *Monasticon Anglicanum*, Vol. V, 1693, p.5.

19 Keats-Rohan Katherine, COEL Database.

20 Pipe Roll 31, Henry I, 1130-1.

21 The Cartae Baronum of 1166, in *English Historical Documents*, David Douglas (ed.), Vol. II, Eyre & Spottiswoode, 1953, p.910.

22 garb: a wheat-sheaf, i.e. a garb-tithe.

23 Blomefield and C. Parkin *An Essay*, Vol V, London, 1806, p.37.

24 *Cartulaire de Notre-Dame de Josaphat* par M. L'Abbé Ch. Métais, Chartres, 1912.

25 Pestell, *Landscapes of Monastic Foundation*, pp.227-228.

BIBLIOGRAPHY

Ackroyd Peter, *The Life of Thomas More*, Chatto & Windus, 1998.

Aldhouse-Green Miranda J., *Pilgrims in Stone. Stone images from the Gallo-Roman Healing Sanctuary of Fontes Sequanae*, Oxford, 1999.

Aldhouse-Green Miranda J., *The Gods of Roman Britain*, Shire Publications, 2003.

Anglican-Roman Catholic International Commission, *The Final Report*, CTS/ SPCK, 1982.

Anson Peter, *The Call of the Cloister*, SPCK, 1964.

Arcisse de Caumont, Statistique monumentale de l'arrondissement de Pont-l'Évêque (1859), Les Éditions de la Grande Fontaine, rééd, 1996.

Aston Margaret, *Lollards and Reformers*, Continuum, 1984.

Bagatti Bellarmino, *Excavations in Nazareth, Vol. I*, Franciscan Printing Press, Jerusalem, 1969.

Bagatti Bellarmino, *Excavations in Nazareth, Vol. II*, Jerusalem Franciscan Printing Press, 2002.

Bagnall Smith Jean, *Votive Objects and Objects of Votive Significance from Great Walsingham*, Britannia, vol. XXX, Society for the Promotion of Roman Studies, 1999.

Barlow Frank, *The Godwins*, Longman, 2002.

Baskerville G., *Married Clergy and Pensioned Religious in Norwich Diocese, 1555, Part II*, The English Historical Review, 1933.

Batey Richard, *Sepphoris and the Jesus Movement*, New Testament Studies, Cambridge University Press, 2001.

Bauckham Richard, *Jude and the Relatives of Jesus in the Early Church*, T & T Clark, 1990.

Bede, *The Ecclesiastical History of the English People*, Oxford University Press, 2008.

Bellenger Dom Aidan OSB, *Walsingham: Downside and the Benedictines*, in *Walsingham: Pilgrimage and History*, R.C. National Shrine, 1999.

Bettenson Henry (ed.), *Documents of the Christian Church*, Oxford University Press, 1965.

Biddle M., Lambrick H.T. and Myres J.N.L., *The Early History of Abingdon, Berkshire, and its Abbey* and Lambrick G., *The Foundation-Traditions of the Abbey*, Medieval Archaeology, Vol. 12, 1968.

Blomefield F. and Parkin C., *An Essay Towards a Topographical History of the County of Norfolk, Vol. V*, London, 1806.

Blomefield, *An Essay towards a Topographical History, Vol. VIII*, Kings Lynn, 1775.

Blomefield, *An Essay Towards a Topographical History, Vol. IX*, London, 1808.

Boss Sarah, *Empress and Handmaid*, Cassell, 2000.

Boss Sarah, *Mary*, Continuum, 2003.

Boss Sarah, *Mary: the Complete Resource*, Oxford University Press, 2007.

Bradley Ian, *Pilgrimage: A Spiritual and Cultural History*, Lion, 2009.

Bridgett T.E., *Our Lady's Dowry*, Burns & Oates, 1875.

Bryden John, *Behold the Wood. A History of the Student Cross Pilgrimage 1948–1998*, The Student Cross Association, 1998.

Bulletin of the Anglo-Israel Archeological Society, 2007, Vol. 25.

Bush Michael, *The Pilgrimage of Grace*, Manchester University Press, 1996.

Butler-Bowden W., *The Book of Margery Kempe*, Jonathan Cape, 1936.

Cameron Kenneth, *The Meaning and Significance of Old English walh in English Place-Names*, in Journal of the English Place-Name Society, 12, 1979/80.

Cartulaire de Notre-Dame de Josaphat par M. L'Abbé Ch. Métais, Chartres, 1912.

Catechism of the Catholic Church, Geoffrey Chapman, 1994.

Clayton Mary, *The Cult of the Virgin Mary in Anglo-Saxon England*, Cambridge University Press, 1990.

Clemoes Peter (ed.) *Anglo-Saxon England I,* Cambridge University Press, 2007.

Cobb Peter (ed.), *Walsingham,* White Tree Books, 1990.

Cobb Peter, *The Development of Modern Day Pilgrimage*, in *Walsingham: Pilgrimage and History*, R.C. National Shrine, 1999.

Cobb Peter, *Papers,* Anglican Shrine Archives.

Cole Mary Hill, *The Portable Queen,* University of Massachusetts Press, 1999.

Corcos Nick, *Churches as Pre-Historic Ritual Monuments,* The Sheffield Graduate Journal of Archaeology, Issue 6, August 2001.

Craig Larkin S.M., *A Certain Way, An Exploration of Marist Spirituality*, Rome Centre for Marist Studies, 1995, p.81.

Curtis Geoffrey, *Paul Couturier and Unity in Christ*, SCM, 1964.

Dark K.R., *Civitas to Kingdom: British Political Continuity 300-800*, Leicester University Press, 1994.

Declaration on the Relation of the Church to Non-Christian Religions, in Flannery A. (ed.), *Vatican Council II*, Dominican Publications, 1992..

Devany Frank unpublished *Thesis on Recusancy*, in Walsingham R.C. Archives.

Dickinson J.C., *The Shrine of Our Lady of Walsingham*, Cambridge University Press, 1956.

Dodgson J. McNeal, *The Significance of the Distribution of the English Place-Name in -ingas, -inga- in South-east England*, Medieval Archaeology X.

Domesday Book, Ann Williams (ed.), Penguin Books, 1992.

Dovey Zillah, *An Elizabethan Progress, The Queen's Journey into East Anglia, 1578,* Sutton Publishing, 1999.

Duffy Eamon, *Dynamics of Pilgrimage in Late Medieval England*, in Morris C. and Roberts P., *Pilgrimage, The English Experience from Becket to Bunyan,* Cambridge University Press, 2002.

Duffy Eamon, *Saints and Sinners, A History of the Popes,* Yale University Press, 2006.

Duffy Eamon, *The Stripping of the Altars,* Yale University Press, 1992.

Dugdale William, *Monasticon Anglicanum,* Vol. III, 1821.

Dugdale William, *Monasticon Anglicanum,* Vol. V, 1693.

Dunn James G., *The New Perspective on Paul*, Eerdmans, 2007.

Edwards Philip, *Pilgrimage and Literary Tradition*, Cambridge University Press, 2005.

Elsner John, *Replicating Palestine and Reversing the Reformation*, Journal of the History of Collections, Oxford University Press, 1997.

Erasmus Desiderius, *Pilgrimages to Saint Mary of Walsingham and Saint Thomas of Canterbury*, J.G. Nichols (transl.), Westminster, 1849.

Eusebius, *The History of the Church*, Judith McLure and Roger Collins (ed.), Oxford University Press, 2008.

Fears Howard, *An Intimate History of Little Walsingham during 1,000 Years,* Walsingham, 2007.

Fears Howard, *An Approach to a History of Little Walsingham, Early Days, Vol. I,* Walsingham, 2007.

Fears Howard and Rollings Peter, *The Medieval Inns of Walsingham,* Walsingham, 2000.

Finegan Jack, *The Archeology of the New Testament*, Princeton University Press, 1969.

Fisher Claude, *Walsingham Lives On*, Catholic Truth Society, 1979.

Fisher Claude, *Walsingham, A Place of Pilgrimage for All People*, The Salutation Press, 1983.

Fletcher Philip, *Recollections of a Ransomer*, Sands & Co, 1928.

Fraser Antonia (ed.), *The Lives of the Kings and Queens of England*, Weidenfield and Nicholson, 1975.

Freyne Sean, *Galilee, Jesus and the Contribution of Archeology*, Expository Times, Vol. 119, No. 12.

Froissart, *Chronicles*, Penguin, 1978.

Fuller Thomas, *The Church History of Britain from the Birth of Jesus Christ until the Year MDCXLVIII*, Vol. III, Oxford, 1845.

Gambero Luigi, *Mary in the Middle Ages*, Ignatius, 2000.

Gard Robin, *The 1897 Walsingham Revival as Reported in the Catholic Press*, in *Walsingham 1062-1538 1897-1997 A Centenary Celebration*, Guild of Our Lady of Ransom, 1998.

Garratt William, *Loreto, the New Nazareth and its Centenary Jubilee*, Art and Book Company, 1895.

Gillett Martin, *Shrines of Our Lady in England and Wales*, London, 1956.

Gillett Martin, *Walsingham, The History of a Famous Shrine*, Burns Oates, 1946.

Green Charles and Whittingham A.B., *Excavations at Walsingham Priory, Norfolk, 1962*, The Archaeological Journal, CXXV, The Royal Archaeological Institute.

Green Miranda J., *The Gods of Roman Britain*, Shire Publications, 2003.

Gregory of Nyssa, On the Baptism of Christ: a Sermon for the Day of the Lights, in Wilson Austin Henry (ed.), *The Early Church Fathers and Other Works*, Eerdmans, 1867.

Gregory the Great, *Homilies* Bk. I, II.

Gurney A. & J., *Walsingham A Place of Pilgrimage for 700 years*, Walsingham Estate Company, 1965.

Gurney David (ed.), *Small Towns and villages of Roman Norfolk*, in *Roman Small Towns in Eastern England and Beyond*, A.E. Brown, Oxbow Monograph 52, 1995.

Hall D. J., *English Medieval Pilgrimage*, Routledge & Kegan Paul, 1965.

Hamilton Bernard, *The Ottomans, the humanists and the Holy House of Loreto*, in *Culture, Theory and Critique*, Routledge, 1987.

Harleian MSS No 360, *Relation of the Apprehension of Henrie Garnett*, fol. 98,6.

Harper-Bill Christopher, *The Foundation and Later History of the Medieval Shrine*, in *Walsingham: Pilgrimage and History*, R.C. National Shrine, 1999.

Harrod, *Gleanings among the Castles and Convents of Norfolk*, Norwich, 1857.

Hearn M.F. and Willis Lee, *The Iconography of the Lady Chapel of Salisbury Cathedral*, in Laurence Keen and Thomas Cocke, *Medieval Art and Architecture at Salisbury Cathedral*, The British Archeological Association Conference Transactions XVII, 1996.

Heimann Mary, *Catholic Devotion in Victorian England*, Oxford University Press, 1995.

Henig Martin, *Religion in Roman Britain*, Routledge, 1992.

Henry VIII, *Defence of the Seven Sacraments*, Raymond de Souza (ed.), St Gabriel Communications, 2007.

Hibgame Frederick, *A Great Gothic Fane: a Retrospective of Catholicity in Norwich*, 1913.

Higham Nicholas, *Rome, Britain and the Anglo-Saxons*, Seaby, 1992.

Hill Carole, *Leave my Virginity Alone*, in *Medieval East Anglia*, ed Christopher Harper-Bill, The Boydell Press, 2005.

Hostler Ethel M., *Charlotte Boyd, Some Notes on Her Life*, The Catholic League, 1996.

Hughes Philip, *The Reformation*, Burns & Oates, 1960.

Humble, Richard, *The Saxon Kings. London: Weidenfeld and Nicolson, 1980.*

James Bruno Scott, *Asking for Trouble*, William Clowes, 1962.

James M.R., *Henry VI, a reprint of John Blacman's Memoir,* Cambridge University Press, 1919.

Josephus, *Jerusalem and Rome*, Fontana, 1966.

Justin Martyr, *Apology, lxv-lxvii*, in Henry Bettenson (ed.), *Documents of the Christian Church*, Oxford University Press, 1965.

Keast Horace, *Our Lady in England*, Society of Mary, 1984.

Keats-Rohan Katherine, COEL Database.

Ker Ian, *The New Movements*, Catholic Truth Society, 2001.

Knapman Zinnia, *A Reappraisal of Percy's Editing*, Folk Music Journal, Vol. 5, No. 2, 1986.

Knowles David, *The Monastic Order in England*, Cambridge University Press, 1963.

Langland William, *Piers Plowman*: A New Translation of the B-text, A.V.C. Schmidt, Oxford University Press, 2001.

Latourette Kenneth Scott, *A History of Christianity*, Eyre and Spottiswoode, 1955

Lee James and Brodie R.H. (ed.), *Letters and Papers, Foreign and Domestic, Henry VIII,* Volume 15, No. 86, 1896.

Leeming Bernard, S.J., *Principles of Sacramental Theology*, Longmans, 1956.

Leys M.D.R., *Catholics in England 1559-1829*, Catholic Book Club, 1961.

Lloyd L.C., *The Origins of some Anglo-Norman Families*, The Harleian Society, 1951.

Loreto, The Shrine of the Holy House, September/November 1979.

Madden Thomas F, *Crusade Propaganda, The abuse of Christianity's holy wars*, online National Review, November 2, 2001.

Margeson S., *Norwich Households: Medieval and Post Medieval Finds,* E. Anglian Archeol. Rep. 58, 1993.

Margeson Sue, *Vikings in Norfolk*, Norfolk Museums Service, 1997.

Martin A.R., *The Greyfriars of Walsingham*, in Norfolk Archaeology, vol. xxv, 1935.

Mascall E.L. and Box H.S. *The Blessed Virgin Mary: Essays by Anglican Authors*, Darton, Longman & Todd, 1963.

Mayr-Harting Henry, *The Coming of Christianity to Anglo-Saxon England*, Batsford, 1972.

McDonald Timothy, *Walsingham: A Year of Celebration*, R.C. National Shrine Walsingham, 1999.

McLoughlin William and Pinnock Jill, *Mary for Heaven and Earth, Essays on Mary and Ecumenism*, Gracewing, 2002.

McLoughlin William M., *Remembrance of the Shrine 1538-1897*, in *Walsingham: Pilgrimage and History*, R.C. National Shrine, 1998.

Matthews Tim, *Catholic Norfolk*, Wells-next-the-Sea, 2005.

Meier John P., *A Marginal Jew, rethinking the historical Jesus*, Doubleday, 1991.

Milburn John, *The Mariological Lectures of Fr John Milburn*, The Society of Mary, 1998.

Miracula Sanctae Virginis Mariae,. E.F. Dexter (ed.), University of Wisconsin, Stud. in the Social Stud. and Histories 12, Madison, Wis., 1927.

Monelli Nanni, *Gleanings on the Altar of the Apostles*, in *Loreto*, vol. 40, May/August 2006.

Moorman John, *A History of the Church in England*, Black, 1954.

Moreton C.E., *The Walsingham Conspiracy of 1537*, Institute of Historical Research, Vol. 63, Feb. 1990.

Morison, *An Invective against the great and detestable vice, treason*, London 1539.

Morris C. and Roberts P., *Pilgrimage, The English Experience from Becket to Bunyan*, Cambridge University Press, 2002.

Morrison Susan Signe, *Women Pilgrims in Late Medieval England*, Routledge, 2000.

Munro Dana C., *Urban and the Crusaders*, in *Translations and Reprints from the Original Sources of European History, Vol 1:2*, Philadelphia: University of Pennsylvania, 1895.

Newman John Henry, *Apologia Pro Vita Sua*, Fontana, 1959.

Newman, *The Reverence Due to the Virgin Mary*, in Boyce P. (ed), *Mary, The Virgin Mary in the Life and Writings of John Henry Newman*, Gracewing, 2001.

Norfolk and Norwich Archeological Society, Vol. 25.

North Philip and North J. (eds.), *Sacred Space, House of God and Gate of Heaven*, Continuum, 2007.

O'Connor Jerome Murphy, *The Holy Land, an Oxford Archaeological Guide from Earliest Times to 1700*, 1998.

Obbard Elizabeth Ruth, *The History and Spirituality of Walsingham*, Canterbury Press, 1997.

On the Baptism of Christ, A Sermon for the Day of the Lights. Trans. Rev. Henry Austin Wilson, in *The Early Church Fathers and Other Works*, Edinburgh, 1867.

Painter K.S., *The Water Newton Early Christian Silver*, British Museum Publications, 1977.

Papaioannou Evangelos, *The Monastery of St Catherine Sinai*, St Catherine's Monastery Press.

Parker Kate, *A Little Local Difficulty: Lynn and the Lancastrian Usurpation*, in *Medieval East Anglia*, ed. Christopher Harper-Bill, The Boydell Press, 2005.

Patten Hope, *A Chronicle*, Walsingham, 1936.

Patten Hope, *An Account of Some Recent Discoveries at the Shrine of Our Lady of Walsingham, Norfolk*.

Pelikan Jaroslav, *Mary through the Centuries*, Yale University Press, 1996.

Percy Thomas, *Reliques of Ancient English Poetry*, London, 1839.

Pestell Tim, *Landscapes of Monastic Foundation. The Establishment of Religious Houses in East Anglia, c.650 – 1200*, Boydell Press, 2004.

Pevsner Nikolaus and Bill Wilson, *Buildings of England, Norfolk, Vol.I: Norwich and North-East*, Penguin, 1997.

Pontifical Council for Culture, *Jesus Christ, the Bearer of the Water of Life. A Christian Reflection of the 'New Age'*, Catholic Truth Society, 2003.

Pontifical Council for the Pastoral Care of Migrants and Itinerant People, *The Shrine*, Vatican City, 8 May 1999.

Pope Benedict XVI, *Beauty is a Privileged Way to Approach the Mystery of God*, General Audience, Wednesday 18 November 2009.

Pope Benedict XVI, *Meeting with the Ecclesial Movements and New Communities*, St Peter's Square, 3 June 2006.

Pope John Paul II, *The Pilgrimage in the Great Jubilee*, April 11, 1998.

Pope Paul VI, *Marialis Cultus*, 1974.

Pringle Denys, *The Churches of the Crusader Kingdom of Jerusalem Vol. II*, Cambridge University Press, 1998.

Rattue James, *The Living Stream*, Bodywell, 1995.

Rear Michael, *One Step More*, Catholic League and Church Literature Association, 1987.

Rex Richard, *The Lollards*, Palgrave, 2002.

Rex Richard, *Henry VIII and the English Reformation*, Macmillan, 1993.

Richards P., *The Red Mount Chapel, King's Lynn*, in *Walsingham: Pilgrimage and History*, R.C. National Shrine, 1999.

Richards William, *The History of Lynn, Vol. II*, Baldwin, Paternoster Row, 1812.

Riley-Smith Jonathan, *The First Crusade and the Idea of Crusading*, Philadelphia: University of Pennsylvania Press, 1991.

Riley-Smith Jonathan, *Religious warriors. Reinterpreting the Crusades*, in *The Economist*, 23 December 1995.

Rollings Peter, *Walsingham, England's Nazareth*, R.C. National Shrine Walsingham, 1998.

Rubin Miri, *Mother of God A History of the Virgin Mary*, Allen Lane, 2009.

Runciman Steven, *A History of the Crusades*, Vol. I, Penguin, 1952.

Rymer Thomas, *Foedera*, London, 1726-35.

Salih Sarah, *Two Travellers' Tales*, in Christopher Harper-Bill, ed., *Medieval East Anglia,* Woodbridge: Boydell, 2005.

Santorelli Giuseppe, *La Santa Casa di Loreto*, Loreto, 2003.

Saul Nigel, *Richard II*, Yale University Press, 1999.

Sheehy Jeremy, *Sacred Space and the Incarnation*, in *Sacred Space*, Philip North and John North (ed.), Continuum, 2007.

Smith Gavin, *Ingas and the Mid-Seventh Century Diocese*, Nomina, Vol 31, 2008.

Smith Gavin, *Recovering the lost religious place-names of England*, in At the Edge, Heart of Albion Press, September 1996, Issue 3.

Souvenir Programme of the Golden Jubilee of the Restoration, R.C. Shrine, 1984.

Spelman Henry, *History and Fate of Sacrilege*, London, 1698.

Spelman, *English Works*, London, 1727.

Spencer Brian, *Medieval Pilgrim Badges from Norfolk*, Norfolk Museums Service, 1980.

Spencer Brian, *Pilgrim Souvenirs and Secular Badges*, Boydell Press, 2010.

Sri Edward and Hahn Scott, *Queen Mother: a Biblical Theology of Mary's Queenship*, Emmaus, 2005.

Stephenson Colin, *Walsingham Way*, Darton, Longman & Todd, 1970.

Strange William, *The Shrine of Our Lady of Walsingham*, Lown and Capps of King's Lynn, 1925.

Strickland Agnes, *The Pilgrims of Walsingham or Tales of the Middle Ages: An Historical Romance*, Kessenger, 2007.

Summerscale Kate, *The Suspicions of Mr Whicher*, Bloomsbury, 2009.

Swales T.H., *Opposition to the Suppression of the Norfolk Monasteries; Expressions of Discontent; The Walsingham Conspiracy*, Norfolk Archeology, vol. 34, 1965.

Tavinor Michael, *Sacred Space and Built Environment,* in *Sacred Space*, Philip North and John North (eds.), Continuum, 2007.

The Anglican-Roman Catholic International Commission, *Mary, Grace and Hope in Christ,* Morehouse, 2005.

English Historical Documents, David Douglas (ed.), Vol. II, Eyre & Spottiswoode, 1953.

The Koran Mohammad M. (trl.), Pickthall, Star, 1930.

The Parliamentary History of England, Vol. I, Hansard, 1806.

The Ransomer, Vol. VI, January 1935.

The Tablet, 12 June 1897.

The Walsingham Pilgrim Manual, Walsingham College Trust Association, 2010.

Thomas à Kempis, *The Imitation of Christ*, Ronald Knox and Michael Oakley (transl.), Burns and Oates, 1960.

Thomas Charles, *Christianity in Roman Britain to AD 500*, Batsford, 1981.

Thurian Max, *Mary, Mother of the Lord*, Faith Press, 1963.

Tyerman Christopher, *Fighting for Christendom*, Oxford University Press, 2004.

Vatican Council II, The Conciliar and Post Conciliar Documents, Dominican Publications, 1992.

Vincent N., *The Court of Henry II*, in *Henry II*, ed. Harper-Bill C. & Vincent N., The Boydell Press, 2007,.

Kempe, Jonathan Cape, 1936.

Wace's *Roman de Rou*, (ed.) Glyn Burgess, The Boydell Press, 2004.

Warner Martin, *The Habit of Holiness*, Geoffrey Chapman, 2004.

Waterton Edmund, *Pietas Mariana Britannica: A History of English Devotion to the Most Blessed Virgin Mary, Mother of God* (1879), Kessinger Publishing, 2007.

Watts Dorothy, *Christians and Pagans in Roman Britain*, Routledge, 1991.

Webb Diana, *Pilgrimage in Medieval England*, Hambledon, 2000.

Webster Graham, *The British Celts and their Gods under Rome*, Batsford, 1986.

Whatmore L.E., *Highway to Walsingham*, The Pilgrim Bureau, 1973.

Whitelock Dorothy, *The pre-Viking age church in East Anglia, in Anglo-Saxon England, Vol I,* P. Clemoes (ed.), Cambridge University Press, 2007.

Williams Rowan, *Ponder These Things, Praying with Ikons of the Virgin*, Canterbury Press, 2002.

Yelton Michael, A*lfred Hope Patten and the Shrine of Our Lady of Walsingham*, Canterbury Press, 2006.

ACKNOWLEDGEMENTS
Photographs and Copyright

The Author and Publisher wish to thank the following for their kind permission to use pictures as illustrations in this book. Every effort has been made to acknowledge the owner of the copyright material contained herein. The Publisher would be pleased to hear from any copyright owner who has been omitted or incorrectly acknowledged.

R.C. Shrine Archives, for pictures numbered 19, 25, 29, 32, 38, 40-44 inclusive, 47, 48, 49, 65-76 inclusive, 78-82 inclusive, 90-95 inclusive, 99, 104, 106, 107, 109-119 inclusive, 122, 134-137 inclusive and for pictures on pages 80, 81, 84, 85, 95, 187, 189, 193, 195, 197, 262.

The Annunciation King's Lynn Archives, for picture on page 188.

Walsingham (Anglican) Shrine Archives, for pictures numbered 50-64 inclusive, 77, 83, 84, 124, 127 and for pictures on pages 206, 217.

Alice Moore Collection, for pictures numbered 85-87 inclusive and for picture on page 215.

Pearson Collection, for picture on page 215.

Fr Robert Fayers, for picture on page 185.

Jackson & Ryan, Architects, for picture number 126.

Tim McDonald, for picture on page 212.

Norfolk Churches Trust, for picture on page 79.

Norfolk Museums Service, for picture on page 75.

G. Santorelli, for pictures numbered 5, 6, 7, 9, 12, 13 and for pictures on pages 35, 56, 57 (Firenze, Museo del Bargello).

St Mina Monastery in Mariut, for pictures on page 46.

The Museum of the Cathedral of Astorga, for picture number 16 (photograph courtesy of Imagen Mas).

Nick Carter, for pictures on front and back cover.

© Archivo Storico Santa Casa, picture number 10.

© Museo-Pinacoteca della S. Casa, picture number 11.

© Pontificia Commissione di Archeologia Sacra, pictures numbered 4, 14, 15.

© Homer Cox, picture on page 185.

© Adrian Cummins, pictures numbered 101, 102.

© Graham Howard, pictures numbered 18, 26 (photographed by kind permission of Sir John Guinness), 27, 28, 34, 36, 37, 39, 45, 46, 88, 89, 96, 97, 98, 103, 105, 108, 120, 121, 128, 129-133 inclusive, 138-141 inclusive and pictures on pages 47, 88, 207.

© Karen Hunt, pictures numbered 30, 31.

© Antonia Moffat, picture number 8.

© Ted Monks, picture number 100.

© Peggy Powell, pictures numbered: 23, 24, 32 (photographed by kind permission of John Paxton), 33, 35.

INDEX